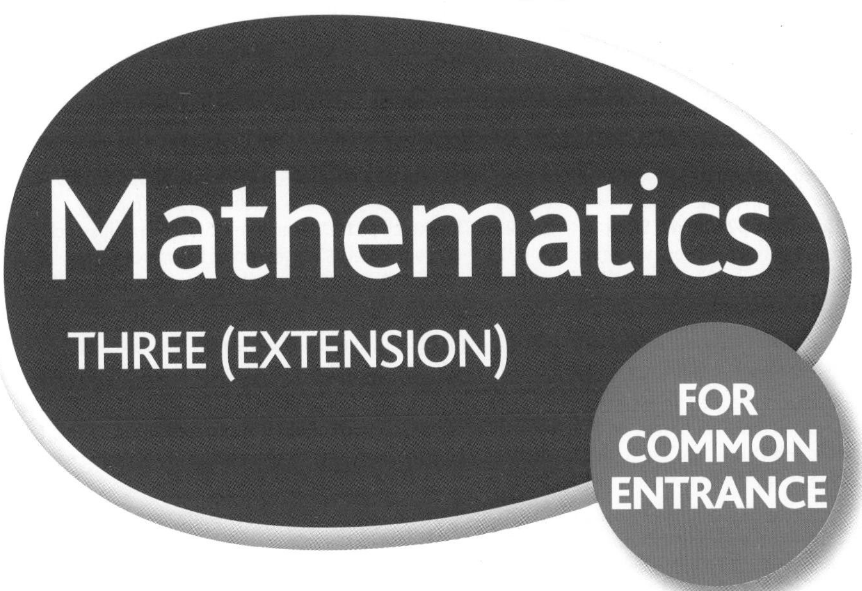

Serena Alexander

AN HACHETTE UK COMPANY

About the author

Serena Alexander has taught mathematics since 1987, originally in both maintained and independent senior schools. From 1999 she taught at St Paul's School for Boys, where she was Head of mathematics at their Preparatory School, Colet Court, before moving first to Newton Prep as Deputy Head and then to Devonshire House as Head. She is now an educational consultant, with a focus on mathematics, and an ISI reporting inspector and in addition she helps to run regular mathematics conferences for prep school teachers. She has a passion for maths and expects others to feel the same way. After a session or two with her, they normally do!

The Publishers would like to thank the following for permission to reproduce copyright material.

Photo credits **p16** © oxygenb4 – iStock via Thinkstock **p62** © satori – Fotolia.com **p85** © destina – Fotolia.com **p152** © ClaudeLux – iStock via Thinkstock **p170** © Marie Amélie bleja – iStock via Thinkstock **p210** © Hui Sieng Hii – iStock via Thinkstock **p210** © Samohin – iStock via Thinkstock **p 254** © somchaisom – iStock via Thinkstock **p271** © Photodisc/Getty Images/World Commerce & Travel 5 **p275** © Dream Cursor – Fotolia.com **p309** © Photodisc/Getty Images/World Landmarks & Travel V60 **p310** © fotoslaz – Fotolia.com

Orders: please contact Bookpoint Ltd, 130 Milton Park, Abingdon, Oxon OX14 4SB. Telephone: (44) 01235 827720. Fax: (44) 01235 400454. Email education@bookpoint.co.uk Lines are open from 9 a.m. to 5 p.m., Monday to Saturday, with a 24-hour message answering service. Visit our website at www.galorepark.co.uk for details of other revision guides for Common Entrance, examination papers and Galore Park publications.

ISBN: 978 1 4718 4683 0

First published in 2015 by

Galore Park Publishing Ltd,

An Hachette UK Company

Carmelite House

50 Victoria Embankment

London EC4Y 0DZ

www.galorepark.co.uk

Impression number 10 9 8 7 6 5 4 3 2 1

Year 2019 2018 2017 2016 2015

Cover photo © alexvv – Fotolia

Illustrations by Integra Software Services Pvt. Ltd.

Some illustrations by Graham Edwards were re-used. The publishers will be pleased to make the necessary arrangements with regard to these illustrations at the first opportunity.

Typeset in India

Printed in Italy

A catalogue record for this title is available from the British Library.

Contents

	Introduction	**viii**
Chapter 1	**Working with numbers**	**1**
	Natural numbers (also called cardinal numbers)	1
	Long multiplication and long division	2
	Problem solving	4
	Integers	5
	Working with numbers	7
	Highest common factors and lowest common multiples	10
	Order of operations	12
	Extension: Using prime factors to calculate	13
	Activity: Largest and smallest sums and differences	15
Chapter 2	**Fractions and decimals**	**16**
	Fractions	16
	Calculating with fractions	19
	Mixed addition and subtraction	21
	Calculating a fraction of an amount	22
	Multiplying fractions	23
	Dividing with fractions	24
	Problem solving	26
	Decimals	28
	Multiplying decimals	28
	Dividing with decimals	29
	Working with other metric units	32
	Units of area – metric measure	33
	Degrees of accuracy	33
	Extension: The Eye of Horus	36
	Activity: The National Elf problem	39
Chapter 3	**Using a calculator**	**40**
	The calculator	40
	Calculator problems	44
	Fractions on the calculator	46
	Estimating	46
	Extension: Using the reciprocal button	49
	Activity: Calculator puzzles and games	51

Chapter 4 **Index numbers** **53**

Indices 53
Indices and products of primes 53
Negative indices 55
Solving equations in x^2 57
Squares and square roots 57
More about roots 58
Using prime factors to find square and other roots 60
Large and small numbers 61
Standard index form 63
Standard index form and the scientific calculator 64
Extension: Calculating with roots 66
Activity: Chain letters 68

Chapter 5 **Percentages** **69**

Percentages – a review 69
Finding a percentage of an amount 69
Percentage as a decimal 71
Percentage increase and decrease 73
Percentage change 75
Finding the original amount 76
Simple interest 78
Extension: Compound interest 80
Activity: Calculator maze 84

Chapter 6 **Equations and inequalities** **85**

Solving equations 85
Using algebra to solve problems 87
Problem solving 89
Equations with fractions 91
Inexact answers 94
Solving inequalities 95
Extension: Equations with two fractions 98
Extension: Alien algebra 99
Activity: Polyhedral numbers 101

Chapter 7 **Indices in algebra** **103**

Multiplication 103
Division 104
The power 0 104
Negative index numbers 104

	Powers of powers	105
	Simplifying expressions with indices	106
	Fractions and powers	107
	Indices and brackets	107
	More about brackets	108
	Factorising	109
	Factorising and fractions	110
	Extension: Trial and improvement	111
	Extension: Fractional indices	115
	Activity: Great Uncle Ben's bequest (or heir today – gone tomorrow)	116
Chapter 8	**Sequences**	**119**
	What is a sequence?	119
	Working with sequences	119
	Finding terms	122
	Working to a rule	123
	Quadratic sequences and square numbers	124
	Problem solving	127
	Extension: Harder sequences	129
	Activity: An introduction to fractals	133
Chapter 9	**Using formulae**	**135**
	Writing a formula	135
	Substituting into formulae	137
	Area and volume formulae	139
	Calculating an unknown quantity	141
	Distance, speed and time formulae	142
	Average speed	145
	Units of formulae	146
	Extension: Rearranging formulae	148
	Activity: The cube root trick	150
Chapter 10	**Geometry**	**152**
	Bearings	152
	2D shapes	155
	Constructions	163
	Activity: Perigal's dissection	168
Chapter 11	**Pythagoras' theorem**	**170**
	Right-angle triangles	170
	Calculating the hypotenuse	171
	Using Pythagoras' theorem to solve problems	173

Finding the length of a side other than the hypotenuse 175
Problem solving 177
Isosceles triangles 179
Special triangles 180
Problem solving 182
Extension: Mixed problems 183
Activity: Pythagorean triplets 188

Chapter 12 Circles, cylinders and prisms 189
Circles 189
Fractions of circles 191
Calculating the radius and diameter 193
More circle problems 194
Calculating the volume of a prism 198
Volume of a cylinder 201
Surface area of a cylinder 202
Units of area and volume 204
Extension: More volume problems 206
Activity: Packaging the litre 210

Chapter 13 Simultaneous equations 211
What is an equation? 211
Problems in two variables 212
Solving simultaneous equations 215
Solving problems with simultaneous equations 222
Extension: Equations with more than two unknowns 224
Activity: Trigon dragon patrol 227

Chapter 14 Graphs 229
Travel graphs 229
Everyday graphs 232
From functions to graphs 234
Graphs of quadratic or non-linear functions 235
Points of intersection 237
Activity: Experiments and graphs 241

Chapter 15 Equations and brackets 242
Brackets 242
Two sets of brackets 243
Squares and differences 245

	Factorising a squared bracket	246
	The difference between two squares	247
	Solving equations by factorising	248
	Solving problems by factorising and brackets	249
	Activity: The dragon curve	252
Chapter 16	**Probability**	**254**
	Calculating probability	254
	Using theoretical probability	257
	Probability with two events	258
	Possibility space diagrams for combined events	261
	Extension: Tables and Venn diagrams	263
	Activity: Random cricket	269
Chapter 17	**Transformation geometry**	**271**
	Reflections	271
	Rotations	274
	Rotational symmetry	276
	Translations	278
	Enlargements	280
	Mixed transformations	282
	Finding a general rule for a transformation	285
	Activity: Hexaflexagons	288
Chapter 18	**Ratio and proportion**	**291**
	Ratio	291
	Proportion	294
	Area in enlargements	297
	Volume in enlargements	299
	More about area and volume	300
	Scale drawing	303
	Activity: The golden ratio	309
Chapter 19	**Looking at data**	**311**
	Investigating a set of data	312
	Grouped data	316
	Pie charts	319
	Scatter graphs	321
	Activity: Marketing the school	329
	Glossary	**330**
	Index	**336**

Introduction

This book is for pupils working towards their 13+ ISEB Common Entrance. It is intended for pupils in Year 8 who will be taking Level 3 Common Entrance or Scholarship papers. It has been written in line with the National Curriculum and the ISEB syllabus.

The book provides a sound and varied foundation on which pupils can build in the future. There is plenty of material to support this and many possibilities for extending the more able. It provides a variety of approaches, ranging from the relatively modern 'mental' to the more historical 'traditional', leaving plenty of scope to adopt the most appropriate method for each pupil. There is no prescribed teaching order and topics may be taught more than once during the year.

It may not be possible to determine which level is most suitable for each individual. For this reason, questions in each exercise are graded from Level 1 type questions through Level 2 type questions but with a majority of Level 3 questions.

At this level, algebra is developed alongside sound number work, with carefully written pencil and paper methods, geometry, probability and data handling. Problem-solving exercises are included in order to develop pupils' reasoning skills. Worked examples demonstrate methods and techniques and at the end of almost every chapter there is an extension exercise designed to stretch the most able. A final summary exercise tests understanding and retention. Teachers should use their discretion on the use of calculators. The aim is to develop good written and mental arithmetic methods.

Notes on features in this book

Words printed in **blue and bold** are keywords. All keywords are defined in the Glossary at the end of the book.

Example

Worked examples are given throughout to aid understanding of each part of a topic.

Exercise

Exercises are provided to give pupils plenty of opportunities to practise what they have learned.

Extension Exercise

Some exercises contain questions that are more challenging. These extension exercises are designed tow stretch more able pupils.

Summary Exercise

Each chapter ends with a summary exercise, containing questions on all the topics in the chapter.

Useful rules and reminders are scattered throughout the book.

Activity

The National Curriculum for Mathematics reflects the importance of spoken language in pupils' development across the whole curriculum – cognitively, socially and linguistically. Activities to develop these skills are interspersed between the chapters. These are essential for developing pupils' mathematical vocabulary and presenting a mathematical justification, argument or proof.

1 Working with numbers

You already know a great deal about numbers. You should also know that there are many different ways of working with them, particularly when they are very large or very small. The number system continues infinitely, without end, in both the positive and negative directions.

In this chapter you will look again at some basic information that will help you with later chapters.

Natural numbers (also called cardinal numbers)

Natural numbers are the numbers you use for counting: one, two, three, four, ... You can add, subtract, multiply and divide them. Although you can use a calculator to complete calculations with natural numbers, remember that you can save a great deal of time if you can do simple arithmetic in your head. Try this exercise.

Exercise 1.1

Write the numbers from 1 to 60 down your page before you start. Make a note of the time as you start and check how long it takes you to complete the exercise. For this exercise only, just write down the answers. It should take you no more than 10 minutes!

1 7×5	**6** $94 + 17$	**11** $318 + 122$	**16** $319 - 123$
2 8×9	**7** 12×8	**12** 3×15	**17** $191 + 325$
3 $36 + 123$	**8** $124 + 74$	**13** $72 \div 12$	**18** $424 \div 8$
4 $42 \div 7$	**9** $126 \div 9$	**14** $368 - 143$	**19** 8×15
5 $82 - 51$	**10** $45 - 17$	**15** 4×19	**20** $308 \div 11$
21 25×7	**27** $331 - 117$	**33** $305 - 199$	**39** 35×6
22 $302 + 99$	**28** $504 \div 3$	**34** $417 + 392$	**40** $399 + 417$
23 $125 \div 5$	**29** $680 - 156$	**35** 45×7	**41** $225 - 186$
24 $425 - 106$	**30** 19×3	**36** $720 \div 36$	**42** $225 \div 45$
25 13×3	**31** $127 + 523$	**37** $237 + 283$	**43** $225 \div 15$
26 $199 + 249$	**32** $144 \div 8$	**38** $200 - 137$	**44** 19×6

45 19 × 9

46 360 − 179

47 95 × 5

48 99 × 8

49 128 + 512

50 207 + 153

51 305 − 125

52 288 ÷ 12

53 13 × 13

54 15 × 15

55 75 × 3

56 25 × 9

57 125 × 4

58 20 × 500

59 3600 ÷ 90

60 100 000 ÷ 80

Long multiplication and long division

You should have been able to use simple mental arithmetic to answer all of the questions in that exercise. When calculations become more difficult, you may think you need to use a calculator. However, you may not have a calculator with you, or you may need to use a pencil and paper to do the calculations. You should be able to add, subtract and carry out short division and multiplication quite easily. Make sure that you can complete **long multiplication** and **long division** as easily.

Remember that for long multiplication you break the smaller number into a **multiple** of ten and a unit.

Example

Multiply: 5264 × 63

Estimate: 5000 × 60 = 300 000

The estimate tells you how many columns you need.

63 is 60 + 3

Then: 5264 × 63 = 5264 × (3 + 60)

Next to each row of the calculation, write down what you are multiplying by.

	HTh	TTh	Th		H	T	U	
			5		2	6	4	
					×	6	3	
		1	5		7_1	9_1	2	× 3
+	3	1_1	5_3		8_2	4	0	× 60
	3	3	1		6	3	2	
		1	1		1			

The carried numbers from the multiplications are in these rows.

The carried numbers from the addition are in this row.

5264 × 63 = 331 632

The method for long division is similar to that for short division but you show all the working. This is so that you can calculate the **remainders** clearly and accurately.

Examples

(i) Divide: 8921 ÷ 37

Estimate: 9000 ÷ 40 ≈ 220

		Th	H	T	U	
			2	4	1	r4
3	7	8	9	2	1	
		7	4			
		1	5	2		
		1	4	8		
				4	1	
				3	7	
				-	4	

3	7
×	2
7	4
1	

	3	7
	×	4
1	4	8
2		

8921 ÷ 37 = 241 r 4

(ii) Divide: 861 ÷ 35

Estimate: 900 ÷ 40 ≈ 22

		H	T	U •	t
			2	4 •	6
3	5	8	6	1 •	0
		7	0		
		1	6	1	
		1	4	0	
			2	1	0
			2	1	0
			-	-	-

861 ÷ 35 = 24.6

Remember that when you have remainders you can write extra zeros after the **decimal point** and carry on dividing.

Exercise 1.2

Multiply or divide, showing all your working clearly.

1	27×36	6	3648×91	11	213×69	16	1809×55
2	147×29	7	5624×72	12	$1161 \div 43$	17	$1008 \div 45$
3	389×47	8	$6293 \div 29$	13	2713×28	18	$999 \div 037$
4	$391 \div 17$	9	$7746 \div 36$	14	$13\,500 \div 36$	19	3005×17
5	$989 \div 23$	10	$9900 \div 48$	15	2145×42	20	$1155 \div 42$

Problem solving

When solving problems, you need to consider the question carefully and see if you need to add, subtract, multiply or divide. Sometimes you may need to do more than one calculation to work out the answer. Write every calculation out neatly so that you can check it through. Do remember to estimate first so you can check your answer looks sensible.

Remainders

There are different ways of dealing with remainders, depending on the problem.

1 Leave it as a remainder.

2 **Round** up to the nearest whole number.

3 Round down, ignoring the remainder.

4 Write the remainder as a **fraction**.

5 Continue dividing and writing extra zeros after the decimal point. Note that you can always reach a definite answer if the number that you are dividing by ends with a 2, 4, 5 or 8 and sometimes if it ends in 3, 6, 7 or 9

Exercise 1.3

1 There are 365 days in a year and 24 hours in a day. How many hours are there in a year?

2 How many minutes are there in a week? How many seconds are there in a week?

3 In the imperial system of weight there are 16 ounces in a pound and 14 pounds in a stone. How many ounces are there in 7 stone?

4 Julius Caesar said, with a smile:

'There are one, seven, six, oh yards in a mile.'

How many yards are there in five and a half miles?

5 A fast food shop sells on average 176 beefburgers each hour.

How many beefburgers does the shop sell in a 17-hour day?

6 There are 22 pupils in my class and we all have milk at break-time. Milk comes in cartons containing one-third of a pint. A school term lasts 12 weeks and there are five days in each week. How many pints of milk does my class drink that term?

7 Rough books come in cartons of 500. How many classes of 22 does one carton supply, assuming every pupil needs one rough book?

8 My teacher is photocopying our mathematics exam. The exam is on four sheets of paper and there are 92 pupils taking the exam.

(a) How many sheets of paper will she use?

(b) The photocopier copies 24 sheets in a minute. How long does it take my teacher to photocopy the exam for all the pupils?

9 We have sold 245 DVDs of the school play at £9.50 each.

(a) How much money have we taken?

(b) It cost £450 to film the school play and then £4.20 per DVD. How much profit or loss did we make?

10 The school chef buys 36 litres of milk at £2.40 for 4 litres, 18 dozen eggs at £1.95 per dozen and 11 kg of flour at £1.40 a kg. From that he makes a batter and then cooks 850 pancakes. What is the cost per pancake, correct to the nearest penny?

Integers

An **integer** is a whole number, so natural numbers are all integers. Integers, however, also include 0 (zero) and negative numbers such as $^-3$, $^-2$ and $^-1$

Negative integers are the set of integers (whole numbers) that are less than zero. Negative numbers can be added, subtracted, multiplied and divided in a similar fashion to natural (positive whole) numbers. Remember what happens when you are calculating with negative numbers.

For example: $4 - 4 = 0$ but $4 - (^-4) = 8$

It can help to draw a number line to see what is happening.

Examples

(i) $2 + 3$

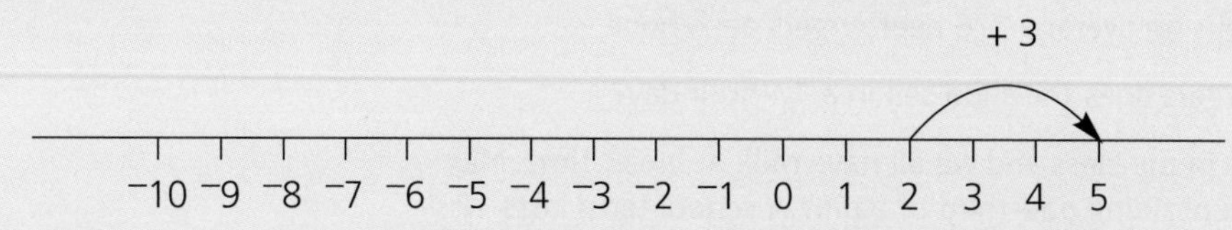

$2 + 3 = 5$

(ii) $2 + (^-3)$

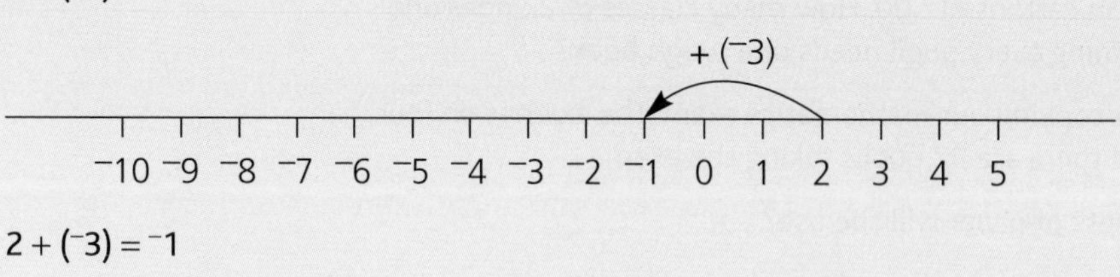

$2 + (^-3) = {^-1}$

So	$2 + 3 = 5$	but	$(^-2) + 3 = 1$	and	$2 + (^-3) = 2 - 3 = {^-1}$
Similarly	$5 - 3 = 2$	but	$3 - 5 = {^-2}$	and	$5 - (^-3) = 5 + 3 = 8$
	$2 \times 3 = 6$	but	$2 \times {^-3} = {^-6}$	and	$(^-2) \times (^-3) = 6$
	$6 \div 3 = 2$	but	$6 \div (^-3) = {^-2}$	and	$(^-6) \div (^-3) = 2$

When calculating with negative numbers you should write down the question, then your working and finally the answer.

Example

$^-3 - (^-7)$

$^-3 - (^-7) = {^-3} + 7$

$= 4$

> It is not good practice to write an operator (+, −, ×, ÷) next to a raised negative sign, so always use brackets.

Exercise 1.4

Add, subtract, multiply or divide, showing all your working clearly.

1 $^-3 - 4$

2 $5 - 8$

3 $3 + (^-6)$

4 $(^-4) \times (^-4)$

5 $3 \times (^-3)$

6 $^-8 + 5$

7 $^-13 - 9$

8 $(^-3) \times 7$

9 $12 \div (^-3)$

10 $(^-24) \div (^-8)$

11 $3 \times (^-4)$

12 $12 - (^-5)$

13 $14 - 8$

14 $^-4 - 8$

15 $^-4 - (^-8)$

16 $5 \times (^-2)$

17 $16 \div (^-4)$

18 $7 - (^-5)$

19 $^-25 \div 5$

20 $(^-5) \times (^-5)$

21 $4 - 9$

22 $7 - 3$

23 $4 \times (^-3)$

24 $12 \div (^-6)$

25 $5 + (^-6)$

26 $(^-5) + (^-2)$

27 $8 - 3$

28 $^-8 \times (^-2)$

29 $^-24 \div 8$

30 $100 \div (^-10)$

Working with numbers

Factors and multiples

Any **natural** (whole) number can be written as the **product** of other numbers.

24 can be written as 1×24, or 2×12, or 3×8 or 4×6

- 1, 2, 3, 4, 6, 8, 12 and 24 are all **factors** of 24
- 24 is a **multiple** of 1, 2, 3, 4, 6, 8, 12 and 24

If you had to write the multiples of 5 that were less than 30 you would write:

5, 10, 15, 20, 25

Prime numbers and composite numbers

A **prime number** is a number that has exactly two factors: itself and 1

The set of prime numbers starts:

2, 3, 5, 7, 11, 13, 17, 19, 23, 29 ...

A **composite number** is any positive integer greater than one that is not a prime number.

Note that the number 1 only has one factor (itself) and so does not qualify as a prime number. It is a very special number with other properties that mean that it cannot be prime.

Prime factors

A composite number can be broken down, by successive division, into factors that are prime numbers. These prime numbers are called the **prime factors** of the number.

Example

Find the prime factors of 210

2	2	1	0	
3	1	0	5	
5		3	5	
7			7	
			1	

$210 = 2 \times 3 \times 5 \times 7$

Sums and products

A **sum** is the result of an addition.

The sum of 5 and 6 is 11

A **product** is the result of a multiplication. If you are asked for the product of 5 and 6 the answer is 30

When you write 210 as: $210 = 2 \times 3 \times 5 \times 7$

you have written it as the **product of its prime factors**.

Unique factorisation property

Every number that is not zero or one can be written as a product of prime factors, but every number has a different set of prime factors. This means that every number is unique. This is known as the **unique factorisation property**.

Consider the number 1533

You can write is as the product of its prime factors: $3 \times 7 \times 73$

Then 3, 7 and 73 are the prime factors of 1533

No other number can have the same product of prime factors.

Index numbers

When the product of prime factors includes repeats of prime factors you can use **index notation** to record them.

$16 = 2 \times 2 \times 2 \times 2$

So $16 = 2^4$

4 is the **index number** that indicates there are four 2s in the product.

Exercise 1.5

1 Which of these numbers are prime numbers?

5 17 25 27 32 37 48

2 Which of these numbers are factors of 36?

1 2 3 4 5 6 7 9 10 36 72 360

3 Which of these numbers are multiples of 12?

1 2 3 4 5 6 8 12 24 36

4 (a) Which of these numbers are prime factors of 42?

1 2 3 6 7 14 21 42

(b) Which of these numbers are prime factors of 20?

1 2 4 5 10 20

5 Which of these numbers are prime factors of 17?

1 2 5 17 34

6 (a) What is the product of 12 and 7?

(b) What is the sum of 13 and 3?

(c) What is the product of 6 and 7?

7 Continue the list of prime numbers 2, 3, 5, 7, 11, 13, 17, 19, 23, 29 ... as far as 50

8 List all the factors of:

(a) 65 (b) 101 (c) 19 (d) 72

9 Write each of these numbers as a product of its prime factors.

(a) 504 (b) 136 (c) 1000 (d) 945

10 (a) List all the factors of 24 and all the factors of 42

(b) Which factors do they have in common?

(c) Which is the highest?

This is the **highest common factor (HCF)** of 24 and 42

11 Find the highest common factor of each pair of numbers.

(a) 8 and 10 (b) 20 and 30 (c) 100 and 360

12 List the first 10 multiples of 4

13 List the first 10 multiples of 6

14 List the first 10 multiples of 10

15 Look at the lists in questions 12–14. What is the lowest number that is a multiple of:

(a) 4 and 6 (b) 4 and 10 (c) 6 and 10?

These numbers are called lowest common multiples **(LCM)** of each pair of numbers.

16 Find the lowest common multiple of each pair of numbers.

(a) 8 and 10 (b) 20 and 30 (c) 100 and 360

Highest common factors and lowest common multiples

In the previous exercise highest common factors (HCF) and lowest common multiples (LCM) were quite easy to find by inspecting the various factors and multiples. For larger numbers it is not always as simple.

Consider the question: What is the highest common factor of 210 and 375?

To find out, you need to write each number as the product of its prime factors.

Example

What is the HCF of 210 and 375?

2	2	1	0
3	1	0	5
5		3	5
7			7
			1

3	3	7	5
5	1	2	5
5		2	5
5			5
			1

First you need to find all the prime factors.

$210 = 2 \times \mathbf{3} \times \mathbf{5} \times 7$

$375 = \mathbf{3} \times \mathbf{5} \times 5 \times 5$
$= 3 \times 5^3$

The common factors are 3 and 5 and so the HCF is $3 \times 5 = 15$

To find the HCF you need to work out the product of all the factors that are common to 210 and 375: 3 and 5

Suppose you had been asked to find the **lowest common multiple** of 210 and 375

For smaller numbers you could look at the first few multiples. For larger numbers you need to look at the prime factors.

The lowest common multiple is the product of all the prime factors of one number and any extra prime factors in the other(s).

Example

Find the lowest common multiple of 210 and 375

$210 = 2 \times 3 \times 5 \times 7$ $\quad$ $375 = 3 \times 5 \times 5 \times 5$

$LCM = 2 \times 3 \times 5 \times 5 \times 5 \times 7$

$= 5250$

2, 3, 5 and 7 are prime factors of 210, the extra prime factors are 5 and 5

Exercise 1.6

1 Find the HCF of the numbers in each pair.

(a) 504 and 945
(b) 136 and 504
(c) 945 and 1000
(d) 136 and 945

2 Find the HCF of 330 and 175

3 Find the HCF of 132 and 165

4 Find the HCF of 812 and 638

5 What is the largest number that divides exactly into both 1000 and 3600?

6 Peter picks 480 apples and Piper picks 600 apples. They pack their apples into identical boxes, with no apples left over. What is the largest number of apples that each box could take?

7 Find the LCM of the numbers in each pair. Use your calculator if you need to.

(a) 504 and 945
(b) 136 and 504
(c) 945 and 1000
(d) 136 and 945

8 Find the LCM of 330 and 175

9 Find the LCM of 132 and 165

10 Find the LCM of 812 and 638

11 What is the smallest number that is a multiple of both 20 and of 36?

12 (a) Ollie and Millie are counting out loud, starting at 1. Millie calls out every fourth number and Ollie every seventh number. What are the first four numbers that they both call out?

(b) Tom, Dick and Harry play the same game. Tom calls out every 20th number, Dick every 15th number and Harry every 25th number. What is the first number that they all call out?

Order of operations

When you have mixed calculations, you need to do them in the correct order. Multiplication and division must be done before addition and subtraction.

Hence $5 + 7 \times 3 = 26$ not 36   You must do the multiplication first.

Examples

(i) Work out: $5 + 7 \times 3$

$$5 + 7 \times 3 = 5 + (7 \times 3) = 5 + 21 = 26$$

(ii) Work out: $(5 + 7) \times 3$

$$(5 + 7) \times 3 = 12 \times 3 = 36$$

Can you see how the brackets make a difference to the calculation? You can use brackets to indicate that you must carry out the addition first.

Sometimes a calculation may have numbers with indices. You must do those before addition and subtraction too.

Example

Multiply: 3×5^3

$$3 \times 5^3 = 3 \times 125 = 375$$

Note that this is not $(3 \times 5)^3 = 15^3$

Think of BIDMAS to remember the rule.

Brackets
Index numbers
Divide
Multiply
Add
Subtract

Exercise 1.7

Calculate the answers.

1 $14 - 3 \times 2$

2 $(14 - 3) \times 2$

3 $\frac{92 - 8}{6 \times 7}$

4 $5 \times (28 - 4) \div 6$

5 $3 \times 4^3 - 3^6 \div 3^2$

6 $5 \times (11 - 4)^2 \div 7$

7 $5 \times 3^4 - 2^5 \div 8$

8 $\frac{3^4 - 2^4}{5}$

9 $(4 \times 3)^2 - (27 \div 9)^3$

10 $4 \times (6^2 - 18) \div 9$

Extension: Using prime factors to calculate

However good your mental arithmetic is and however quick you are with pencil and paper calculations, it is always worth checking if there is an efficient way to carry out a calculation without writing it out in full.

Consider $72^2 \div 27$

You may spot that 27 has some common factors with 72. To be sure of calculating accurately you need to write the calculation as a product of prime factors.

- $72^2 \div 27 = (2 \times 2 \times 2 \times 3 \times 3)^2 \div (3 \times 3 \times 3)$

$$= \frac{2 \times 2 \times 2 \times 3 \times \cancel{3}^1 \times 2 \times 2 \times 2 \times \cancel{3}^1 \times \cancel{3}^1}{\cancel{3}_1 \times \cancel{3}_1 \times \cancel{3}_1}$$

$$= 2 \times 2 \times 2 \times 2 \times 2 \times 2 \times 3$$

$$= 64 \times 3$$

$$= 192$$

It is often easiest to write a division as a fraction and **cancel** common factors.

You can also use prime factors to find **roots**. Under the rules of BIDMAS, roots are considered as index numbers.

Example

Calculate: $\sqrt[3]{3375} \div \sqrt{225}$

$3375 = 3 \times 3 \times 3 \times 5 \times 5 \times 5$ $\quad$ $225 = 3 \times 3 \times 5 \times 5$

$\sqrt[3]{3375} = 3 \times 5 = 15$ $\quad$ $\sqrt{225} = 3 \times 5 = 15$

$\sqrt[3]{3375} \div \sqrt{225} = 1$

You may need to combine roots and index number calculations.

Example

Calculate: $(35 \times \sqrt{225} \div \sqrt{441})^2$

$225 = 3 \times 3 \times 5 \times 5$

$\sqrt{225} = 15$

$441 = 3 \times 3 \times 7 \times 7$

$\sqrt{441} = 21$

$$(35 \times \sqrt{225} \div \sqrt{441})^2 = \left(\frac{5 \times 7 \times 3 \times 5}{3 \times 7}\right)^2$$

$$= 25^2$$

$$= 625$$

Extension Exercise 1.8

Use products of prime factors to calculate the answers to these.

1 $128 \div 16$

2 $225 \div 15$

3 $\sqrt{11025}$

4 $45^2 \div 15$

5 $\sqrt{15 \times 45 \times 27}$

6 $125^2 \div 5^3$

7 $\sqrt[3]{729} \div \sqrt{81}$

8 $490^2 \div 1225$

9 $\sqrt{45 \times 63 \times 35} \div \sqrt[3]{45 \times 75}$

10 $160^2 \div (64 \times 25)$

11 $72 \times 36^2 \div 12^3$

12 $(\sqrt{65 \times 26 \times 10} \div \sqrt{52})^2$

13 $(2160 \div 6^3)^2$

14 $\sqrt{1764} \div (\sqrt[3]{9261} \times \sqrt{256})$

15 $(98 \times 56 \div 14^3)^2$

16 $\sqrt{1225} \div \sqrt[3]{3375} \times \sqrt{144}$

17 $\sqrt[4]{40\,180} \div \sqrt[3]{343}$

18 $(\sqrt[4]{1296} \div \sqrt[3]{64})^2$

19 $\sqrt{91 \times 21 \times 39} \div \sqrt[3]{63 \times 147}$

20 $(\sqrt{2025} \div \sqrt[3]{3375})^3$

Summary Exercise 1.9

Answer questions 1–10 mentally.

1 $52 + 33$

2 $165 - 41$

3 12×8

4 $144 \div 12$

5 $334 + 159$

6 $324 - 138$

7 108×4

8 $116 \div 4$

9 148×3

10 $138 \div 6$

11 Answer these without using a calculator. Write down the question and any necessary working.

(a) $^-7 + (^-4)$

(b) $4 - (^-7)$

(c) $(^-3) \times (^-4)$

(d) $14 \div (^-2)$

(e) $^-4 + 12$

(f) $3 + (^-8)$

(g) $15 \times (^-5)$

(h) $6 - 9$

(i) $^-3 + (^-9)$

(j) $(^-18) \div (^-6)$

12 Which of these numbers are prime numbers?

1 4 5 9 13 24 31 99

13 Write down all the factors of 28

14 Which of these are multiples of 6?

1 2 3 4 6 12 15 30

15 Write down the HCF of:

(a) 16 and 24 **(b)** 252 and 714

16 Write down the LCM of:

(a) 8 and 10 **(b)** 168 and 462

Write down your working clearly for questions 17–18. Do not use a calculator.

17 On an intergalactic expedition I have packed 25 space pods weighing 12 kg each, 38 space suits weighing 28 kg each and 9 extra-terrestrial repellent missiles weighing 135 kg each. Have I packed more than the 2500 kg limit?

18 (a) The mass of one astronaut plus his kit is 84 kg. The total mass allowance on the space station is 4000 kg. If there are 23 astronauts how much mass allowance is there left?

(b) One quarter of that remaining mass allowance is for food. Each astronaut is allowed 1 kg of food per day. How many days can the astronauts survive on their food allowance?

Activity: Largest and smallest sums and differences

Take four digits: 6, 7, 8, 9

The largest number you can make with them is 9876 and the smallest is 6789

Now make two 2-digit numbers and find the difference and the sum.

For example, you can make the numbers 78 and 96

The difference is 18 and the sum 174

Can you make two 2-digit numbers that give you a smaller difference or a larger sum?

Find the smallest and largest sums and differences that you can make from two 2-digit numbers, using the digits 6, 7, 8 and 9

Now find the smallest and largest sums and differences that you can make from two 3-digit numbers, using the digits 4, 5, 6, 7, 8 and 9

Next find the smallest and largest sums and differences that you can make from two 4-digit numbers using the digits 2, 3, 4, 5, 6, 7, 8 and 9

Finally, find the smallest and largest sums and differences that you can make from two 5-digit numbers using the digits 0, 1, 2, 3, 4, 5, 6, 7, 8 and 9

Put your results in a table.

Digits	Smallest sum	Largest sum	Smallest difference	Largest difference
6, 7, 8, 9			7	
4, 5, 6, 7, 8, 9				
2, 3, 4, 5, 6, 7, 8, 9	6047			
0, 1, 2, 3, 4, 5, 6, 7, 8, 9				

What do you notice?

Try to explain your answer.

2 Fractions and decimals

Fractions have been around for centuries. It is known that the Babylonians and Egyptians used them.

This is the eye of Horus, which the Egyptians used to show some unit fractions, You will learn more about this in Exercise 2.13

Fractions

A fraction is any number that is not an integer (whole number) but includes part of a whole.

Proper fractions are fractions that are less than one, such as $\frac{1}{2}$, $\frac{7}{8}$ and $\frac{7}{33}$

Improper fractions are fractions greater than one, such as $\frac{3}{2}$, $\frac{7}{4}$ and $\frac{127}{33}$

A **mixed number** is made up of a whole number and a fraction, such as $1\frac{1}{6}$ or $3\frac{4}{7}$

Equivalent fractions are equal in value but are made up with different numbers. To find equivalent fractions you multiply or divide the **numerator** (top number) and the **denominator** (bottom number) by the same number.

- $\frac{5}{6} = \frac{5}{6} \times \frac{4}{4} = \frac{20}{24}$
- $\frac{15}{24} = \frac{15}{24} \div \frac{3}{3} = \frac{5}{8}$ You can see that 3 is a common factor of 15 and 24 and you can divide both by 3. This is called **cancelling** or **simplifying**.

A fraction is in its **lowest terms** or **simplest form** when the numerator and denominator have no common factors (except for 1).

Decimal fractions (often referred to simply as **decimals**) have place values after the **decimal point** of $\frac{1}{10}$, $\frac{1}{100}$ and $\frac{1}{1000}$

Therefore, when you write 0.5, it means $\frac{5}{10}$ which is equivalent to $\frac{1}{2}$

When you write 0.75, it means $\frac{75}{100}$ which is equivalent to $\frac{3}{4}$

When you write 0.375, it means $\frac{375}{1000}$ which is equivalent to $\frac{3}{8}$

The words **per cent** mean 'out of a hundred'. Therefore any fraction written out of 100 can also be written as a **percentage**.

When you write 0.5, it means $\frac{5}{10}$, which is equivalent to $\frac{50}{100}$ or 50%

When you write 0.25, it means $\frac{25}{100}$, which is equivalent to 25%

When you write 0.75, it means $\frac{75}{100}$, which is equivalent to 75%

You can write a fraction as a decimal by:

- finding an equivalent fraction with a denominator that is a **power of 10** (10, 100, 1000, ...)
- dividing the top number by the bottom number.

Some fractions are equivalent to **recurring decimals**.

$\frac{1}{3} = 1 \div 3 = 0.333...$

Recurring decimals are decimal numbers in which the digits after the decimal point recur in a regular pattern, such as $\left(\frac{2}{3}\right)$0.666 666 666... and $\left(\frac{9}{11}\right)$ 0.818 181 818 181...

To represent a recurring decimal, write dots over the first and last digits in the recurring pattern.

$\frac{1}{3} = 0.\dot{3}$ $\frac{1}{6} = 0.1\dot{6}$ $\frac{1}{22} = 0.0\dot{4}\dot{5}$ $\frac{1}{7} = 0.\dot{1}4285\dot{7}$

Exercise 2.1

Complete this exercise to revise these methods.

1 Replace the * in each part to make the fractions equivalent.

(a) $\frac{1}{4} = \frac{*}{8}$ (b) $\frac{12}{16} = \frac{*}{4}$ (c) $\frac{2}{5} = \frac{*}{10}$ (d) $\frac{9}{*} = \frac{3}{8}$

2 Write these improper fractions as mixed numbers.

(a) $\frac{39}{4}$ (b) $\frac{12}{5}$ (c) $\frac{28}{8}$ (d) $\frac{32}{3}$

3 Write these mixed numbers as improper fractions.

(a) $4\frac{1}{5}$ (b) $3\frac{3}{4}$ (c) $7\frac{4}{5}$ (d) $3\frac{1}{7}$

4 Write these fractions in their lowest terms.

(a) $\frac{15}{25}$ (b) $\frac{36}{54}$ (c) $\frac{14}{36}$ (d) $\frac{18}{42}$

5 Write each percentage as:

(i) a decimal

(ii) a fraction in its lowest terms.

(a) 15% (b) 24% (c) 56% (d) 125%

6 Write each decimal as:

(i) a fraction

(ii) a percentage.

(a) 0.35 (b) 1.36 (c) 0.08 (d) 0.125

7 Write each fraction as:

(i) a decimal

(ii) a percentage.

(a) $\frac{2}{5}$ (b) $\frac{14}{25}$ (c) $\frac{13}{20}$ (d) $\frac{5}{8}$

8 Write each percentage as:

(i) a decimal

(ii) a fraction in its lowest terms.

(a) $33\frac{1}{3}\%$ (c) $44\frac{4}{9}\%$

(b) $83\frac{1}{3}\%$ (d) $145\frac{5}{11}\%$

9 Write each fraction as:

(i) a decimal

(ii) a percentage.

(a) $\frac{2}{3}$ (b) $\frac{7}{9}$ (c) $\frac{1}{6}$ (d) $\frac{22}{7}$

10 Write:

(a) 12 minutes as a fraction of an hour

(b) 300 g as a fraction of a kilogram

(c) 35p as a fraction of £2.00

(d) 30 cm as a percentage of 4 metres

(e) 450 ml as a percentage of 5 litres

(f) 1.25 km as a percentage of 10 km.

Calculating with fractions

Adding and subtracting fractions

Before you can add fractions you must ensure that they have the same denominator.

When you are asked to add $\frac{3}{8}+\frac{7}{12}$ you know that you cannot directly add eighths to twelfths.

You must write both fractions as equivalent fractions. It is sensible to look for their **lowest common denominator**.

In this example the **lowest common multiple** of 8 and 12 is 24, so this is the lowest common denominator for the fractions.

When you are adding mixed numbers there is an extra stage in the calculation.

- First, add the whole numbers.
- Then add the fractions.

Example

Add: $3\frac{3}{7}+2\frac{8}{9}$

$$3\frac{3}{7}+2\frac{8}{9}=5\frac{27+56}{63} \qquad \left(\frac{3}{7}\times\frac{9}{9}=\frac{27}{63} \text{ and } \frac{8}{9}\times\frac{7}{7}=\frac{56}{63}\right)$$

$$=5\frac{83}{63}$$

$$=6\frac{20}{63}$$

The first steps in subtraction of fractions are the same as those for addition.

- First find the lowest common denominator.
- Then work out the equivalent fractions.
- Finally, do the subtraction.

When you are subtracting mixed numbers, subtract the whole numbers first then deal with the fractions.

Example

Subtract: $5\frac{4}{9}-1\frac{1}{6}$

$$5\frac{4}{9}-1\frac{1}{6}=3\frac{8-3}{18}$$
$$=3\frac{5}{18}$$

Sometimes it will not be possible to complete the subtraction in this way; this is the case when the fractional part of the second number is greater than the fractional part of the first. Then you will need to change one whole number to a fraction, with the same denominator as the fractional part.

An example will make this clear.

Example

Subtract: $5\frac{4}{9}-2\frac{5}{6}$

$$5\frac{4}{9}-2\frac{5}{6}=3\frac{8-15}{18}$$
$$=2\frac{26-15}{18}$$
$$=2\frac{11}{18}$$

You cannot calculate 8 – 15 so change one whole from the whole number 3 into 18 eighteenths: $18+8=26$, leading to $26-15=11$

Exercise 2.2

Add or subtract these fractions, giving each answer in its simplest form. If the answer is an improper fraction, write it as a mixed number.

1 $\frac{2}{3}+\frac{1}{5}$

2 $\frac{1}{8}+\frac{3}{4}$

3 $\frac{3}{8}-\frac{1}{6}$

4 $\frac{11}{12}-\frac{2}{3}$

5 $\frac{5}{9}+\frac{3}{4}$

6 $\frac{8}{15}-\frac{3}{10}$

7 $1\frac{1}{4}+3\frac{2}{3}$

8 $2\frac{2}{3}-\left({}^{-}3\frac{3}{5}\right)$

9 $4\frac{4}{5}-1\frac{3}{4}$

10 $1\frac{2}{7}+\left({}^{-}1\frac{2}{3}\right)$

11 $4\frac{3}{4}+3\frac{3}{16}$

12 $2\frac{1}{6}-\left({}^{-}1\frac{2}{15}\right)$

13 $4\frac{1}{4}-1\frac{2}{3}$

14 $3\frac{5}{6}+1\frac{7}{10}$

15 ${}^{-}1\frac{4}{5}-\left({}^{-}4\frac{3}{7}\right)$

16 $3\frac{2}{5}-2\frac{7}{10}$

17 $4\frac{7}{12}+2\frac{1}{24}+3\frac{1}{8}$

18 $1\frac{3}{7}+3\frac{2}{3}+2\frac{1}{2}$

19 $2\frac{3}{8}+1\frac{2}{3}-2\frac{1}{2}$

20 $2\frac{3}{5}+\left({}^{-}3\frac{5}{6}\right)-\left({}^{-}2\frac{7}{15}\right)$

Mixed addition and subtraction

Brackets in a calculation show you what you must do first. Always write down your working carefully, just as in these examples.

Examples

Complete these calculations. Give the answers in their simplest form.

(i) $\frac{3}{4}-\left(\frac{1}{5}+\frac{1}{6}\right)$

$$\frac{3}{4}-\left(\frac{1}{5}+\frac{1}{6}\right)=\frac{3}{4}-\left(\frac{6+5}{30}\right)$$
$$=\frac{3}{4}-\frac{11}{30}$$
$$=\frac{45-22}{60}$$
$$=\frac{23}{60}$$

(ii) $1\frac{2}{3}+\left(3\frac{2}{5}-1\frac{1}{4}\right)$

$$1\frac{2}{3}+\left(3\frac{2}{5}-1\frac{1}{4}\right)=1\frac{2}{3}+\left(2\frac{8-5}{20}\right)$$
$$=1\frac{2}{3}+2\frac{3}{20}$$
$$=3\frac{40+9}{60}$$
$$=3\frac{49}{60}$$

Exercise 2.3

Complete these calculations. Give the answers in their simplest form.

1 $\frac{2}{3}+\frac{1}{4}-\frac{2}{5}$

2 $\frac{2}{5}+\left(\frac{1}{3}-\frac{2}{9}\right)$

3 $\frac{3}{4}-\frac{1}{5}+\frac{1}{2}$

4 $\frac{3}{4}-\left(\frac{1}{5}+\frac{1}{3}\right)$

5 $\frac{2}{3}+\frac{3}{4}-\frac{7}{10}$

6 $\frac{3}{7}+\left(\frac{2}{3}-\frac{1}{4}\right)$

7 $\left(\frac{4}{5}-\frac{1}{3}\right)+\frac{3}{4}$

8 $\frac{9}{10}-\left(\frac{3}{5}+\frac{1}{4}\right)$

9 $\left(\frac{2}{5}+\frac{1}{4}\right)-\left(\frac{2}{3}-\frac{1}{5}\right)$

10 $1\frac{4}{5}-\left(\frac{2}{3}+\frac{1}{4}\right)$

11 $1\frac{4}{5}-\frac{2}{3}+\frac{1}{4}$

12 $2\frac{1}{5}-1\frac{7}{8}+\frac{3}{10}$

13 $3\frac{1}{5}-\left(1\frac{7}{8}+1\frac{3}{10}\right)$

14 $2\frac{1}{5}+\left(1\frac{7}{8}-\frac{3}{10}\right)$

15 $4\frac{1}{6}+7\frac{3}{8}-1\frac{19}{24}$

16 $1\frac{1}{4}+3\frac{2}{5}-1\frac{7}{10}$

17 $3\frac{1}{5}-\left(2\frac{2}{3}-1\frac{1}{4}\right)$

18 $4\frac{7}{10}-\left(2\frac{2}{5}+1\frac{3}{4}\right)$

Calculating a fraction of an amount

You probably use fractions without realising that you are doing so.

Quarter of an hour is 15 minutes. Just divide 60 minutes by 4

Half a metre is 50 cm. Just divide 100 cm by 2

Three-quarters of an hour is 45 minutes. This is a bit more complicated because you must divide 60 minutes by 4, and then multiply the result by 3

You can write 'of' as × and then cancel before multiplying.

Examples

(i) Work out $\frac{1}{5}$ of 25

$\frac{1}{5}$ of $25 = \frac{1}{5} \times 25$

$= 25 \div 5$

$= 5$

(ii) Calculate $\frac{3}{4}$ of 1 kg, giving the answer in grams.

$\frac{3}{4}$ of $1\text{ kg} = \frac{3}{\cancel{4}_1} \times \cancel{1000}^{250}$

$= 3 \times 250$

$= 750\text{ g}$

Exercise 2.4

Calculate these amounts.

1 $\frac{1}{4}$ of 20

2 $\frac{1}{7}$ of 42

3 $\frac{1}{8}$ of 96

4 $\frac{2}{3}$ of 45

5 $\frac{3}{4}$ of 72

6 $\frac{5}{8}$ of 104

7 $\frac{5}{6}$ of 138

8 $\frac{4}{5}$ of 72

9 $\frac{15}{26}$ of 130

10 $\frac{11}{14}$ of 126

11 $\frac{11}{20}$ of 110 km

12 $\frac{4}{9}$ of 306 m

13 $\frac{7}{20}$ of 230 miles

14 $\frac{2}{5}$ of 3 m, giving the answer in centimetres

15 $\frac{2}{3}$ of 2 hours, giving the answer in minutes

16 $\frac{3}{4}$ of 3 kg, giving the answer in grams

17 $\frac{8}{7}$ of 4 km, giving the answer in kilometres and metres

18 $\frac{5}{6}$ of 3 hours, giving the answer in hours and minutes

19 $\frac{4}{5}$ of 6 m, giving the answer in millimetres

20 $\frac{5}{12}$ of a minute, giving the answer in seconds

Multiplying fractions

So far you have been multiplying whole numbers by fractions. You use the same principle to multiply a fraction by a fraction.

Example

Multiply: $\frac{7}{15} \times \frac{9}{14}$

$\frac{7}{15} \times \frac{9}{14} = \frac{{}^{1}\cancel{7}}{{}_{5}\cancel{15}} \times \frac{\cancel{9}^{3}}{\cancel{14}_{2}}$

$= \frac{3}{10}$

7 and 14 can both be divided by the common factor 7, then 9 and 15 can both be divided by the common factor 3

If you divide by the factors before the multiplication, this leads to easier calculations.

When the multiplication involves mixed numbers, you simply change the mixed numbers into improper fractions, then you can simplify the calculation and multiply as before.

Example

Multiply: $2\frac{2}{3} \times 2\frac{1}{10}$

$2\frac{2}{3} \times 2\frac{1}{10} = \frac{\cancel{8}^{4}}{\cancel{3}_{1}} \times \frac{\cancel{21}^{7}}{\cancel{10}_{5}}$ Divide by common factors 2 and 3

$= \frac{28}{5}$

$= 5\frac{3}{5}$

You can use the same principle to multiply three or more fractions at the same time.

Example

Multiply: $\frac{4}{5} \times \frac{10}{21} \times \frac{7}{8}$

$\frac{4}{5} \times \frac{10}{21} \times \frac{7}{8} = \frac{\cancel{4}^{1}}{\cancel{5}_{1}} \times \frac{\cancel{10}^{2}}{\cancel{21}_{3}} \times \frac{\cancel{7}^{1}}{\cancel{8}_{2}}$

$= \frac{1 \times \cancel{2}^{1} \times 1}{1 \times 3 \times \cancel{2}_{1}}$

$= \frac{1}{3}$

Dividing with fractions

You know that division is the **inverse** of multiplication.

When you work out $4 \times \frac{1}{2}$ you get the answer 2 because 4 halves are the same as 2 wholes.

This calculation could also be: $4 \div 2 = 2$

or $\frac{4}{2} = 2$

or $\frac{1}{2}$ of 4 is 2

You can see that $\div 2$ is the same as $\times \frac{1}{2}$

Think how you would answer, if you were asked: 'How many halves in 4 wholes?'

You could write $4 \div \frac{1}{2} = 8$

because each whole comprises two halves so the total number of halves is eight.

Just as $\div 2$ is the same as $\times \frac{1}{2}$, so $\div \frac{1}{2}$ is the same as $\times 2$

This works for all fractions, so $\div \frac{3}{4}$ is the same as $\times \frac{4}{3}$

The result of turning the fraction upside down gives the **reciprocal**.

The rule works for mixed numbers as well. Just as we did with multiplication we must turn mixed numbers into improper fractions first.

Examples

(i) $4 \div \frac{4}{5} = \frac{\cancel{4}^1}{1} \times \frac{5}{\cancel{4}_1}$

$= 5$

(ii) $\frac{2}{3} \div \frac{4}{5} = \frac{\cancel{2}^1}{3} \times \frac{5}{\cancel{4}_2}$

$= \frac{5}{6}$

(iii) $2\frac{2}{3} \div 1\frac{1}{6} = \frac{8}{3} \div \frac{7}{6}$

$= \frac{8}{\cancel{3}} \times \frac{\cancel{6}^2}{7}$

$= \frac{16}{7}$

$= 2\frac{2}{7}$

If your answer is an improper fraction, you should turn it into a mixed number.

Exercise 2.5

Multiply or divide. Remember to give your answers in their lowest terms.

1 $\frac{2}{3} \times \frac{6}{7}$

2 $\frac{3}{5} \times \frac{10}{21}$

3 $\frac{2}{3} \div \frac{3}{5}$

4 $\frac{7}{8} \div \frac{3}{10}$

5 $\frac{5}{9} \times \frac{3}{10}$

6 $\frac{3}{8} \times \frac{16}{27}$

7 $\frac{11}{12} \div \frac{33}{48}$

8 $\frac{5}{14} \div \frac{10}{21}$

9 $\frac{5}{21} \times \frac{7}{15}$

10 $\frac{5}{8} \div \frac{15}{64}$

11 $1\frac{1}{4} \times \frac{2}{5}$

12 $3\frac{2}{3} \div 4$

13 $\frac{2}{3} \times 1\frac{1}{5}$

14 $5\frac{3}{4} \div 3$

15 $3\frac{1}{4} \div \frac{1}{3}$

16 $\left(^{-}3\frac{3}{4}\right) \times \left(2\frac{1}{6}\right)$

17 $4\frac{2}{7} \times \left(^{-}2\frac{1}{10}\right)$

18 $5\frac{3}{4} \div \left(^{-}4\frac{7}{8}\right)$

19 $1\frac{1}{4} \times 2\frac{2}{5}$

20 $\left(^{-}1\frac{3}{5}\right) \div \left(^{-}2\frac{3}{4}\right)$

21 $\frac{2}{5} \times \frac{10}{21} \times \frac{14}{15}$

22 $\frac{3}{8} \times \frac{16}{75} \times \frac{3}{4}$

23 $\frac{7}{20} \times \frac{11}{21} \times \frac{22}{25} \times \frac{5}{11}$

24 $\frac{3}{16} \times \frac{4}{5} \times \frac{7}{9} \times \frac{10}{21}$

25 $4\frac{2}{3} \times 3\frac{1}{7} \times 1\frac{1}{11}$

26 $3\frac{1}{3} \times 3\frac{1}{5} \times 1\frac{1}{8}$

27 $1\frac{1}{2} \times 2\frac{1}{6} \times \frac{2}{3} \times 5\frac{1}{7} \times \frac{7}{8}$

28 $1\frac{1}{2} \times 1\frac{1}{3} \times 1\frac{1}{4} \times 1\frac{1}{5} \times 1\frac{1}{6} \times 1\frac{1}{7}$

29 $\frac{1}{2} \times 1\frac{2}{3} \times 2\frac{3}{4} \times 3\frac{4}{5} \times 4\frac{5}{6}$

30 $1\frac{1}{2} \times 2\frac{2}{3} \times 3\frac{3}{4} \times 4\frac{4}{5} \times 5\frac{2}{5}$

Exercise 2.6

Remember the BIDMAS rule (Brackets, Indices, Divide, Multiply, Add, Subtract) to calculate the answers. Remember to give your answers in their lowest terms.

1 $1\frac{1}{5} \times 2\frac{5}{6} - \frac{8}{15}$

2 $\left(\frac{2}{3} - \frac{4}{7}\right) \div \frac{2}{15}$

3 $3\frac{3}{4} - \frac{13}{18} \div \frac{2}{9}$

4 $\left(\frac{3}{4} + \frac{3}{7}\right) \div \frac{5}{18}$

5 $\left(3\frac{1}{3} - 1\frac{4}{9}\right) \div \frac{8}{9}$

6 $\frac{3}{14} \div \left(1\frac{4}{7} - \frac{7}{10}\right)$

7 $\dfrac{3\frac{3}{5}}{1\frac{2}{7}} - \dfrac{2\frac{1}{4}}{1\frac{1}{5}}$

8 $1 - \frac{1}{2}\left(1 - \frac{1}{3}\left(1 - \frac{1}{4}\right)\right)$

9 $9\left(1 - \frac{1}{2}\left(2 - \frac{2}{3}\left(3 + \frac{1}{4}\right)\right)\right)$

10 $\dfrac{1\frac{3}{5} + 2\frac{5}{7}}{3\frac{2}{7} - 1\frac{7}{10}}$

Problem solving

Always look carefully at how the question is worded. Think whether you need to add, subtract, multiply or divide. If you need to use more than one operation, remember BIDMAS and take care with the order. Use the equals sign correctly.

Examples

(i) I have $3\frac{7}{8}$ m of string, I cut off $\frac{1}{3}$ m. What length do I have left?

$$3\frac{7}{8} - \frac{1}{3} = 3\frac{21-8}{24}$$
$$= 3\frac{13}{24}\text{ m}$$

(ii) I have $3\frac{7}{8}$ m of string, I cut off $\frac{1}{3}$ of it. What length do I have left?

$$\frac{2}{3} \text{ of } 3\frac{7}{8} = \frac{2}{3} \times \frac{31}{8}$$
$$= \frac{31}{12}$$
$$= 2\frac{7}{12}\text{ m}$$

Exercise 2.7

1 I have $6\frac{5}{6}$ m of string, I cut off $\frac{3}{4}$ m. What length do I have left?

2 I have $5\frac{1}{6}$ m of string, I cut off $\frac{1}{8}$ of it. What length do I have left?

3 I have $3\frac{3}{4}$ m of string. I divide it into five pieces of equal lengths. How long is each piece?

4 I have to make $2\frac{1}{4}$ kg of muesli. I start with $1\frac{1}{6}$ kg of oats, add $\frac{7}{8}$ kg of wheat flakes and make the rest up from my special dried fruit and nut mix. How much of my special dried fruit and nut mix do I need?

5 For my homework I had to multiply a number by $2\frac{1}{4}$, then subtract $1\frac{5}{6}$ from the result. I know that I then had the answer $\frac{7}{12}$ but have forgotten the original number. What was my original number?

6 The **area** of a rectangular field is $11\frac{1}{5}$ km^2. If one side is of length $5\frac{1}{3}$ km, how long is the other?

7 $\frac{3}{8}$ of the class are boys and $\frac{1}{3}$ of the girls wear glasses. What fraction of the class are girls that do not wear glasses? What is the smallest number of pupils in the class? (Check!)

8 Look at this sign post.

(a) How much further from the signpost is Bigtown than Smallville?

(b) How far is it from Bogton to Midham?

(c) I start at the signpost and cycle to Bogton. When I get there, I realise I should be in Bigtown. How far have I ridden, in total, when I reach Bigtown?

Decimals

Before the metric system was introduced to Britain, many calculations were carried out in terms of fractions, as were the problems in the last exercise. This was particularly true with money as the currency included halfpennies ($\frac{1}{2}$ of a penny), farthings ($\frac{1}{4}$ of a penny) and, at one time, half farthings ($\frac{1}{8}$ of a penny). Nowadays, money is based on the decimal system. If you are going to be able to manage your own money successfully then you need to be able to calculate with decimals without a calculator.

Multiplying decimals

When you multiply an amount by a number greater than one, the result will be larger than the original amount.

If you multiply an amount by a number that is less than one, the result will be smaller than the original amount.

From your work on fractions, you know that when multiplying by tenths:

- if you multiply tenths by tenths, your answer will be in hundredths
- if you multiply hundredths by tenths, your answer will be in thousandths…

Thinking about this another way, look at the number of numerals (or digits) after the decimal point.

$0.4 \times 0.3 = 0.12$

Altogether, there are two digits after the decimal points in the question, so there must be two digits after the decimal point in the answer.

However, you need to be careful!

$0.4 \times 0.5 = 0.20$

When you have written out the answer in full, you can leave off the final zero and write the answer as 0.2, but always leave in zeros at the end until you have placed the decimal point correctly.

Examples

(i) Multiply: 0.25×5

$0.25 \times 5 = 1.25$

(ii) Multiply: 0.35×0.3

$0.35 \times 0.3 = 0.105$

(iii) Multiply: 1.5×1.2

$1.5 \times 1.2 = 1.80 = 1.8$

Dividing with decimals

Dividing decimals by whole numbers

The method for dividing a decimal by a number follows the same principles as for division of whole numbers.

This is a straightforward division:

$14 \div 2 = 7$

and this is a division with a decimal:

$1.4 \div 2 = 0.7$

Sometimes you have to write extra zeros at the end of the number being divided, so that you can keep dividing until you have a final answer.

Example

Divide: $0.2 \div 4$

$0.2 \div 4 = 0.20 \div 4$

$= 0.05$

Dividing by decimals

Dividing by a decimal needs more thought.

What is $4 \div 0.5$?

You can work this out simply because you know that $40 \div 5$ is 8 and therefore $4 \div 0.5$ must be 8

It is always a good idea to check by multiplying.

Examples

(i) $6 \div 0.2$

as $60 \div 2 = 30$

then $6 \div 0.2 = 30$

Check: $0.2 \times 30 = 6$

(ii) $20 \div 0.5$

as $200 \div 5 = 40$

then $20 \div 0.5 = 40$

Check: $0.5 \times 40 = 20$

For more complicated questions, such as 40 ÷ 0.005, it can be difficult to work out exactly where the decimal point goes in the answer.

Is it 0.08, 0.8, 8, 80, 800, 8000 or 80 000?

You can try to make it simple by first eliminating the decimal point. Here is an example to show you what to do.

Example

$40 \div 0.005$

$$40 \div 0.005 = \frac{40}{0.005}$$

$$= \frac{40}{0.005} \times \frac{1000}{1000}$$

$$= \frac{40\,000}{5}$$

$$= 8000$$

Eliminate the decimal point by multiplying 0.005 by 1000 to give 5 and, at the same time, multiply the 40 by 1000 to get 40 000

That is much easier!

Exercise 2.8

Calculate the answers to these. If you can do them in your head write the question, then =, then the answer. If you need to put the calculation in a frame, show all your working carefully.

1 0.4×0.6

2 $18 \div 0.3$

3 0.02×0.006

4 $^{-}3.6 \div 0.12$

5 $0.5 \times (^{-}0.2)$

6 $3.2 \div 0.8$

7 $^{-}0.26 \times 0.3$

8 0.52×3

9 $^{-}180 \div (^{-}0.06)$

10 $240 \div 0.008$

11 $1.4 \times (^{-}1.2)$

12 2.7×0.14

13 $^{-}2.04 \div 0.6$

14 0.5×0.4

15 $(^{-}320) \div (^{-}0.5)$

16 4.8×5

17 $280 \div 0.007$

18 $0.0603 \div (^{-}0.09)$

19 $(^{-}0.005) \times 0.4$

20 $0.0036 \div 1.8$

Now that you have practised the methods, here are some money problems.

Exercise 2.9

1 I earn £4.50 a week by washing Dad's car. What do I earn in 12 weeks?

2 Five of us share £19 equally. How much money does each of us get?

3 I buy six small cartons of juice at 75p each and three hot dogs costing £1.24 each. How much do I spend in total?

4 I save £1.25p each week. What do I save in a year? (Remember that there are 52 weeks in a year.)

5 My mother bought six bargain packs of lamb chops at £2.35 each. What change did she have from a £20 note?

6 I had £1.64 change after using a £5 note to pay for eight identical pencils. How much did each pencil cost?

7 What is the total cost of 0.3 kg of tomatoes at £2.40 per kilogram and 0.6 kg of potatoes at £1.25 per kilogram?

8 How many cans of limeade costing 85p each can I buy with a £10 note? If I buy as many as possible how much change will I get?

9 My father puts 31 litres of petrol in the car's tank. The petrol costs £1.10 per litre. How much change does he have from a £50 note?

10 At the school fete my class sold 15 large cakes at £8.50 each and 56 cupcakes at 70p each. How much money did we make, in total?

11 We bought a pack of 24 cans of cola for £15 and sold them at 90p each. How much profit did we make?

12 There was a broken window in the classroom. No one owned up to breaking it, so the whole class had to share the cost of a replacement window equally. There were 24 of us in the class and the replacement window cost £69.60. How much did each of us pay?

13 We all went to an amusement park. The total entry cost for five of us came to £84. Later on, four of us, including me, had ice creams costing £3.24 in total. Three more friends joined us for lunch and we spent £42 in total. What was my share of the cost of the day out?

14 I started with £20, bought four drinks costing £1.20 each and then three tickets for the cinema. I had 80p change. What was the price of each cinema ticket?

Working with other metric units

You know that the metric system is a decimal system.

- Length is measured in **metres** (m)
  10 millimetres (mm) = 1 centimetre (cm)
  100 centimetres (cm) = 1 metre (m)
  1000 millimetres (mm) = 1 metre (m)
  1000 metres (m) = 1 kilometre (km)
- Mass is measured in **grams** (g)
  1000 milligrams (mg) = 1 gram (g)
  1000 grams (g) = 1 kilogram (kg)
  1000 kilograms (kg) = 1 tonne (t)
- Capacity is measured in **litres** (l)
  1000 cubic centimetres (cm^3) = 1 litre (l)
  1000 millilitres (ml) = 1 litre (l)
  100 centilitres (cl) = 1 litre (l)

Exercise 2.10

1 I pour the contents of four jugs equally into 100 glasses. Each jug contains 5 litres of water. How many centilitres of water are there in each glass?

2 How many boys, each weighing 45 kg, does it take to balance an elephant weighing 3.6 tonnes?

3 There are approximately 400 peanuts in a kilogram. How many peanuts does it take to balance a car weighing 1.5 tonnes?

4 Which is further, four laps of 3.5 km or 20 laps of 700 m?

5 I decide to pile some objects on top of each other. I first put a box of height 0.5 m on the floor. On top of this I lay a book of thickness 3.7 cm, and on top of the book I place a magazine, of thickness 9 mm. How high is the top of the magazine from the floor, in centimetres?

6 What is better value, 500 ml of shampoo for £2.25 or 120 ml of shampoo for 60p?

7 My car travels 46 kilometres on 1 litre of fuel. How far will I be able to travel after I spend £30 filling it up with fuel costing £1.20 per litre?

8 A group of 40 of us are going on a trip. I reckon that we each need to have 175 millilitres of water during the trip. Water comes in 2.5 litre bottles. How many bottles must I buy?

9 If a female elephant stands 2.4 m high, how much taller is she than a mouse, 18 mm high? Give your answer in millimetres.

10 The guidelines for keeping goldfish say that you need about 1.6 litres of water to every centimetre length of fish. If you used the same rule for any fish, and decided to keep a blue shark of length 4 metres, how many litres of water would you need in its tank?

Units of area – metric measure

If you calculated the area of a **rectangle** 0.4 m by 0.3 m you would find that it was 0.12 m^2.

For some of the questions in the next exercise, you will need to use the **formula** for the area of a triangle.

Area of a triangle $= \frac{bh}{2}$

Remember to check the units of measurement. Before you start to work out the area of any shape, you must make sure the units of all the dimensions are the same. If you are asked to write the answer in units that are different from those you are given, it is often much easier to change the units first.

Exercise 2.11

1 The area of a rectangle 0.2 m by 5 m is 1 square metre. Find five other rectangles that have an area of exactly 1 square metre.

2 Write down the measurements of five rectangles each with an area of 2 m^2.

3 The area of a rectangle is 4 m^2 and the length of one of its sides is 0.5 m. What is the length of the other side?

4 A rectangle with an area of 4 cm^2 has one side of 20 cm. What is the length of the other side?

5 A square has an area of 0.09 m^2. What are the lengths of its sides?

6 A triangle has a base of 40 cm and a height of 1.2 m. What is the area of this triangle, in square metres?

7 Find the height, in centimetres, of a triangle with an area of 14 cm^2 and a base of 7 cm.

8 Find the base, in centimetres, of a triangle with an area of 12 cm^2 and a height of 4.5 cm.

9 Find the base, in centimetres, of a triangle with an area of 2 m^2 and a height of 40 cm.

10 Find the height, in centimetres, of a triangle with an area of 2.4 m^2 and a base of 250 cm.

Degrees of accuracy

When you have rounded an answer to a problem, you must always say how accurate your answer is.

To do this, you can use either **significant figures** or **decimal places**. In some cases, it may be sensible to give the answer to the nearest whole number or to the nearest 100, 1000, …

Decimal places

The first decimal place in a decimal number is the first place after the decimal point.

The second decimal place is the second place after the decimal point, and so on.

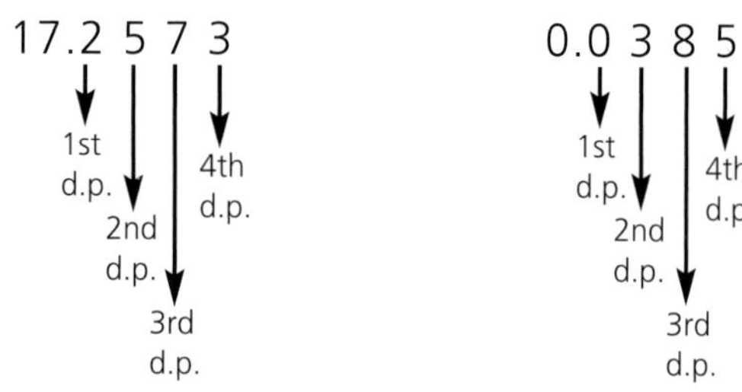

Significant figures

The first significant figure is the first non-zero digit in the number.

The second significant figure is the next digit, whatever its value, the third is the next digit, and so on.

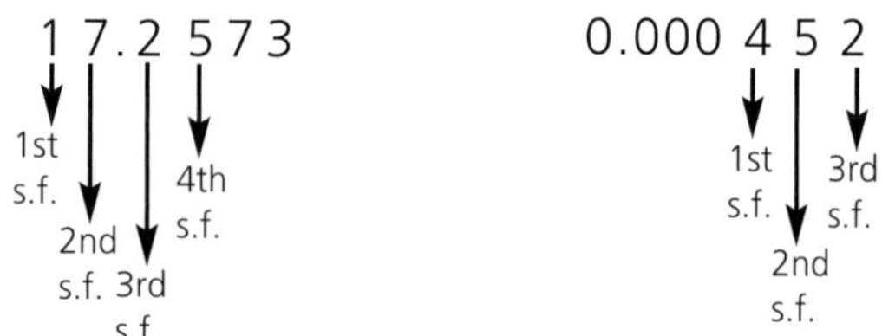

When rounding to a number of decimal places or significant figures, first consider the digit in the decimal place to which you are rounding. If the value of the digit **to the right** of this digit is 5 or more, then round up. If it is 4 or less, it stays the same.

Examples

(i) 17.2573 = 17.3 (to 1 d.p.) 17.2573 = 20 (to 1 s.f.)

(ii) 17.2573 = 17.26 (to 2 d.p.) 17.2573 = 17 (to 2 s.f.)

(iii) 17.2573 = 17.257 (to 3 d.p.) 17.2573 = 17.3 (to 3 s.f.)

17.2573 = 17.26 (to 4 s.f.)

(iv) 0.0385 = 0 (to 1 d.p.) 0.0385 = 0.04 (to 1 s.f.)

(v) 0.0385 = 0.04 (to 2 d.p.) 0.0385 = 0.039 (to 2 s.f.)

(vi) 0.0385 = 0.039 (to 3 d.p.) 0.0385 = 0.0385 (to 3 s.f.)

Exercise 2.12

Write each number correct to the number of decimal places or significant figures specified.

1 Write 516.1528 correct to:

(a) 1 s.f. (b) 1 d.p. (c) 3 s.f. (d) 3 d.p.

2 Write 0.13 652 correct to:

(a) 2 s.f. (b) 2 d.p. (c) 4 s.f. (d) 4 d.p.

3 Write 9.3568 correct to:

(a) 1 s.f. (b) 1 d.p. (c) 3 s.f. (d) 3 d.p.

4 Write 0.083 275 correct to:

(a) 1 s.f. (b) 1 d.p. (c) 4 s.f. (d) 4 d.p.

5 Write 1.9999 correct to:

(a) 1 s.f. (b) 1 d.p. (c) 3 s.f. (d) 3 d.p.

6 Write 10.909 09 correct to:

(a) 2 s.f. (b) 1 d.p. (c) 4 s.f. (d) 3 d.p.

Use your calculator to work out the solution to each of your answers. Give each answer to a sensible degree of accuracy and state what that is.

7 A length of ribbon 2 metres long is cut into nine equal pieces. How long is each piece of ribbon?

8 A class of 25 is divided into three groups, of about the same size, for a class outing. How many pupils are there in each group?

9 I have a jug containing 2.4 litres of squash. It needs to be shared among 18 boys. How much does each boy get?

10 A commercial traveller drives about 400 miles each day. How many days will it take him to travel round his distribution network of 3500 miles?

11 A delivery of 10 000 kg of builder's sand is divided among 12 houses. How much sand is delivered to each house?

12 If there are 39.375 inches to a metre, and 12 inches in a foot, how many metres are there in 10 feet?

13 When I leave the top off a bottle of cleaning fluid, about 8% evaporates in 1 hour. If I start with 240 ml, how much is left 1 hour later?

14 The population of the country of Beramania has increased by 7% over the last decade. If the population was 1.5 million 10 years ago, what is it now?

15 The local electrical shop is advertising 15% off the price of everything in its sale. If an MP3 player cost £79 before the sale, what will it cost in the sale?

Extension: The Eye of Horus

The Egyptians had a particularly interesting way of writing some fractions, based on the following myth.

Horus was the son of two of the main gods in Egyptian mythology, Isis (the nature goddess) and Osiris (the god of the underworld). He was considered the god of the sky, of light and of goodness. Horus had an evil uncle (Seth) who murdered his father, Osiris. Horus battled with Seth to avenge his father's murder. During the fight, Seth plucked out Horus' left eye and tore it apart. Thoth (god of wisdom and magic) found the eye, pieced it together – as if it were just a cracked grain of barley – and added some magic. He returned the eye to Horus, who in turn gave it to his murdered father Osiris, thereby bringing him back to life. Thereafter, Horus defeated Seth.

Each part of the eye became a hieroglyphic sign for a fraction used in measuring out bushels of grain.

⊲ for 1/2 ○ for 1/4 ⁀ for 1/8 ⊳– for 1/16 ↘ for 1/32 (for 1/64

When the fraction symbols are put together, the restored eye looks like this.

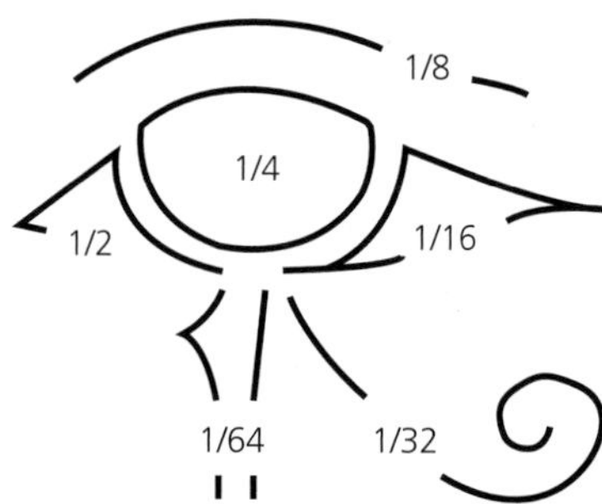

Note that if you add up the fractions, your answer is not quite 1. The missing fraction was the bit of magic needed for a dead eye to shine again with life!

Extension Exercise 2.13

1 Add the six fractions.

2 What fraction is the bit of magic needed to make the eye whole again?

3 Evaluate the following.

(a) $\left(\frac{1}{2}\right)^2$ (b) $\left(\frac{1}{2}\right)^3$ (c) $\left(\frac{1}{2}\right)^4$ (d) $\left(\frac{1}{2}\right)^5$

4 Evaluate the following.

(a) $\left(\frac{1}{4}\right)^2$ (b) $\sqrt{\left(\frac{1}{64}\right)}$ (c) $\left(\frac{1}{8}\right)^2$ (d) $\sqrt[3]{\left(\frac{1}{64}\right)}$

5 Use the six fractions from the Eye of Horus to write as many fraction **equations** as you can. As well as the basic operators +, −, × and ÷ you can use index numbers and roots, but no other numbers.

$\frac{1}{4} + \frac{1}{4} = \frac{1}{2}$ is allowed but $2 \times \frac{1}{4} = \frac{1}{2}$ = is not.

The Egyptians used to sum unit fractions to get non-unit fractions. So, to get $\frac{3}{8}$ they would add $\frac{1}{4}$ and $\frac{1}{8}$

6 Make fraction sums for these numbers, by adding the minimum possible number of the six Eye of Horus fractions.

(a) $\frac{5}{8}$ (b) $\frac{9}{16}$ (c) $\frac{21}{32}$ (d) $\frac{25}{64}$

Consider this calculation.

$$\left(\frac{1}{2} + \frac{1}{4}\right) \div \left(\frac{1}{2} + \frac{1}{2} + \frac{1}{8}\right) = \frac{3}{4} \div \frac{9}{8}$$

$$= \frac{{}^{1}\cancel{3}}{{}_{1}\cancel{4}} \times \frac{\cancel{8}^{2}}{\cancel{9}_{3}}$$

$$= \frac{2}{3}$$

This time the Eye of Horus fractions have been combined to make a completely different fraction. The denominator is not a power of 2.

You can do this only by combining two calculations with a division.

7 Using a similar method combine some of the Eye of Horus fractions to make these fractions.

(a) $\frac{1}{3}$ (b) $\frac{3}{5}$ (c) $\frac{7}{9}$ (d) $\frac{11}{21}$

8 Now try to explain a general rule about how you can use the Eye of Horus fractions to make any fraction of the form $\frac{a}{b}$ where neither a nor b is greater than 63

Remember that the Egyptians used tables to help with their fraction calculations. Such a table might help you with your explanation.

Summary Exercise 2.14

1 (a) $3\frac{3}{8} - 1\frac{1}{6}$

(b) $2\frac{3}{15} + 3\frac{9}{10}$

(c) $4\frac{4}{9} \times 3\frac{3}{8}$

(d) $5\frac{1}{4} \div 4\frac{3}{8}$

2 (a) 0.3×0.4 (b) 0.5×0.06 (c) 0.05×0.4 (d) $2.4 \div 0.04$

3 $\frac{1}{10}$ of the ties sold in the school shop are for sports colours, $\frac{7}{8}$ of the rest are plain. The remainder are prefects' ties. What fraction of the total amount are prefects' ties?

4 I buy four goldfish, each 2.2 cm long. If I need 1.6 litres of water for each centimetre of fish, how many litres of water should their tank hold?

5 If the area of a rectangle is $5\frac{1}{5}$ hectares and the length of one side is $2\frac{1}{4}$ km, what is the length of the other side? (A hectare is 10 000 m^2)

6 (a) What is the area, in square metres, of a triangle with a base of 40 cm and a height of 1.1 m?

(b) What is the base, in centimetres, of a triangle, with an area of 1 m^2 and a height of 25 cm?

7 Give these numbers correct to: (i) 2 d.p. (ii) 3 d.p.

(a) 4.2549 (b) 12.045 83 (c) 4.009 99

8 Give these numbers correct to: (i) 2 s.f. (ii) 3 s.f.

(a) 143 342 (b) 0.045 673 (c) 49 999

9 My grandmother is making her special dried fruit and nuts mix. She has adapted the recipe from her grandmother, so the recipe looks a bit unusual.

Mix:

$1\frac{3}{8}$ kg raisins

425 g flaked almonds

$\frac{5}{8}$ kg sultanas

550 g candies peel

$\frac{2}{5}$ kg hazelnuts, lightly crushed

(a) What is the mass of the total mix, in kilograms?

(b) My grandmother gives $\frac{2}{5}$ of the mix to my uncle, $\frac{1}{3}$ of the mix to my aunt and the rest to me. What is my share, in kilograms?

Activity: The National Elf problem

You might not know this but there is a national shortage of elves. The National Elf inspector has a real problem. His recruitment drive is not bringing them in. Why can he not recruit more elves?

The National Elf inspector decided to go on an elf drive and find out how many elves there actually are.

Here is the result of his first survey of a typical elf residential area.

He found that elves are peculiar characters. They like living near one or two other elves but not too close to very many. When the elf community find a rectangle of land, they divide it into a grid of 100 metre squares. They then lay an elf communication line in a **diagonal** from the top left to the bottom right of the rectangle. One elf then lives in every square crossed by the communication line.

Here is a small elf gathering.

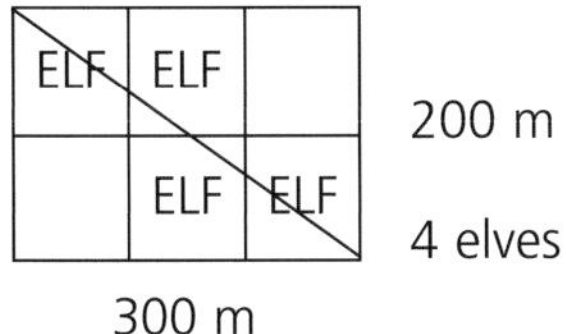

200 m

4 elves

Write down how many elves live in a rectangle:

(a) 200 m by 200 m

(b) 300 m by 400 m

Now investigate the problem further and find how many elves live in a rectangle:

(c) 800 m by 900 m

(d) $100x$ metres by $100y$ metres.

Government Elf Warning: This does not have a straightforward answer!

3 Using a calculator

From now on you will need to use a **scientific calculator.** If you do not have one already, you should ask your mathematics teacher to help you decide which is best for you. If that is not possible, go to a shop with a large selection of calculators and ask the advice of the assistant. Make sure that you stress that you want a scientific calculator suitable for GCSE examinations, not for A levels. Some calculators do so much that they are expensive and complicated to use. Your calculator needs to have **bracket functions**, **fraction buttons**, **trigonometric** and **index functions.**

Keep your calculator manual in your maths file!

The calculator

Modern calculators are changing all the time, so you cannot expect your teacher to know exactly how each calculator works and where all the necessary buttons are. You will need to refer to the **manual** when you are exploring some new areas of mathematics.

This next exercise is to help you to get to know your calculator. If you are stuck consult the manual and then, if you are still stuck, ask your teacher.

Exercise 3.1

1 Turn your calculator ON. Now turn it OFF, now turn it ON again.

2 Calculate $45 + 16$. Write down the answer.

3 Calculate $34\,537 - 12\,529$. Write down the answer.

4 Calculate $4 \div 99$. Write down the answer.

5 Calculate $45\,234 \times 416$. Write down the answer.

You have now used the four basic functions with simple calculations. Now you need to know more about your calculator.

Your calculator will probably look something like this.

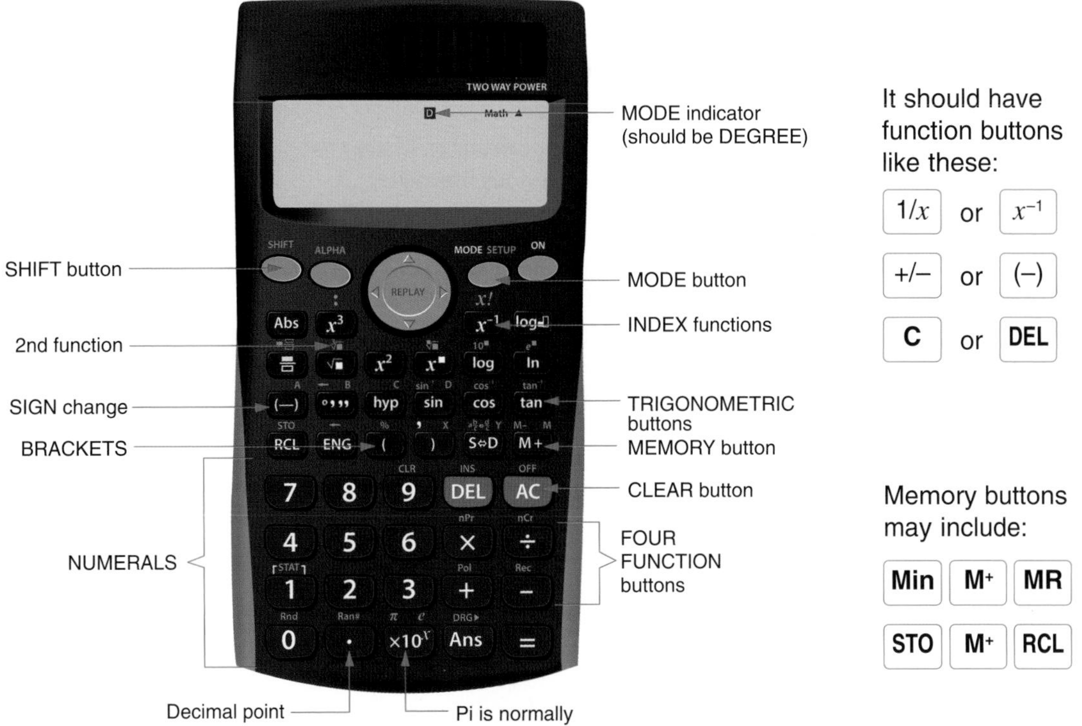

The mode

The only mode you need to know about is **normal** or **computational**. You will need to refer to your manual. Press the mode button and choose 'comp'. If you ever get peculiar answers to your calculations, then you are probably in the wrong mode!

Negative numbers

How can you use your calculator to calculate with negative numbers?

On your calculator you should find a button like this ± or (–). The 'change sign' button ± changes the sign of the number just entered.

The 'negative' button (–) is pressed before a number is entered, to make it negative. These must not be confused with the – button which is used **only** for the subtraction operation.

Exercise 3.2

1 Calculate $^{-}45 + 16$

What is your answer? Compare this to your answer to question 2 in the previous set of questions.

2 Go back and rework Exercise 1.4 but, this time, use your calculator. Check that your answers agree with the answers you had in the previous exercise.

Brackets

A scientific calculator has an in-built bracket function. It will always multiply and divide before it adds and subtracts, just as you do when you follow BIDMAS. If you do the calculation $4 + 5 \times 7$ you will see that your calculator gives you 39 as it has calculated 5×7 and then added 4

To make the calculator work in the **order of operations** as written, you will need to use the brackets buttons, (and), to key in the calculation.

Example

Use your calculator to work out $(4 + 5) \times 7$

Press the (button, which is the 'open brackets' button, before entering $4 + 5$

Then press the 'close brackets' button,), before entering $\times 7$

Answer 63. See how this differs from the answer you get when you follow. BIDMAS.

Exercise 3.3

1 Use your calculator to work these out.

(a) $(3 + 6) \times 5$

(b) $9 \times (2 + 4)$

(c) $(5 + 6) + (3 \times 5)$

(d) $(5 - 7) \times 5$

(e) $20 \div (6 + 4)$

(f) $(20 \div 5) \div (5 \times 4)$

With more complicated calculations you may need to nest brackets within brackets.

For example to calculate $2 \times (3 \times (4 + 7) + 5)$ you would need this sequence of keys:

to get the answer 76

2 Use your calculator to work these out.

(a) $4 \times (5 \times (3 \times 6) + 5)$

(b) $9 \times (2 + (24 \div 4) + 1)$

(c) $2 \times ((5 + 6) + (3 \times 5))$

(d) $20 \div ((15 \div 5) + 2)$

Fractions on the calculator

You can use brackets on the calculator when you are working with fractions.

For example suppose you have the calculation: $\frac{25}{7} - \frac{13}{5}$

Using brackets, you can write this calculation as $(25 \div 7) - (13 \div 5)$

The calculator will give the answer as a decimal:

0.9714285714 or recurring decimal $0.9\dot{7}14\,28\dot{5}$

You can convert this to a fraction using the S⟷D key to get $\frac{34}{35}$

Exercise 3.4

Use your calculator to work these out.

1 $\frac{98}{12} + \frac{98}{6}$

2 $\frac{481 \times 5}{260 \times 37}$

3 $\frac{458 - 251}{23 \times 45}$

4 $\frac{37}{54} - \frac{15}{81}$

Simple index functions

Find these buttons on your calculator.

- x^2 for squares
- $x^{\blacksquare}$ for other powers
- $\sqrt{\square}$ for square roots
- $\sqrt[\square]{\square}$ for other roots
- $\frac{1}{x}$ or x^{-1} for the reciprocal

Remember that the **reciprocal** of a fraction is the fraction turned upside down. This is the method you use when dividing by a fraction. Any number (except 0) has a reciprocal. If it is a whole number, you just write it as the denominator of a fraction with numerator 1

Exercise 3.5

1 Find the value of each power.

(a) 3^2

(b) 7^3

(c) 9^4

(d) 3^5

2 Calculate each square root.

(a) $\sqrt{784}$

(b) $\sqrt[3]{1728}$

(c) $\sqrt[4]{625}$

(d) $\sqrt[5]{16807}$

3 Use the reciprocal button to calculate $\frac{1}{8}$. Now push the reciprocal button and the equals button again, then again and again. What do you notice? Try this with some other numbers.

Using the independent memory

Your calculator can store values in its memory but you may need to consult your calculator manual to find out how to do this. Commonly you would use M+ to add a result into the memory and RCL for recall.

The memory is useful if, for example, you want to add up the answers to a number of calculations.

Example

Calculate the sum of $35 + 97$, $45 - 13$ and 66×2

On your calculator enter 3 5 + 9 7 = M+

Then 4 5 − 1 3 = M+

Then 6 6 × 2 = M+

To find the answer, enter RCL M+ and you will have 296

The calculator will not give you a wrong answer but if you enter the wrong key sequence then you will not solve the problem correctly. Always start by making an estimate, so that you can check.

Remember to clear the memory before you do another calculation. You may have a MC button but you may need to do this by storing 0 on the memory, noting that STO (or store) may be a second function.

0 STO M+

Calculators can store several **variables**, usually known as A, B and C or x, y and z (or both).

Try entering 3 + 4 SHIFT STO A (or x, depending on your calculator.)

Then when you enter RCL A you should get 7

You can then calculate with 7; for example, 5 × RCL A = which should give you 35

It is helpful to use the memory or a variable when you have a complex string of calculations, as in the next exercise. However, if you are not sure then it is better to write each stage of your calculation down.

Calculator problems

For some questions you will need to do the calculation in stages. Even when you are using a calculator it is important that you write down the calculation that you are doing at each stage.

Exercise 3.6

1 Write out your 17 times table. To do this store 17 as a variable and then multiply the variable by 2, 3, 4, ...

2 It is possible to make the number 66 by adding four consecutive numbers. What are they?

3 It is possible to make the number 1716 by multiplying three consecutive numbers. What are they?

4 Without doing the calculations, what size of answer would you expect for each calculation? Choose A, B or C.

(a) 98×48

A: About 5000 B: about 300 C: between 10 000 and 12 000

(b) $72\,954 \div 24$

A: About 4000 B: about 3000 B: between 2000 and 4000

(c) $11\,532 - 7312 + 534 - 1826$

A: About 2000 B: about 4000 C: between 1000 and 2000

Now work them out exactly and see which estimates were best.

5 It is easy to press a wrong button on your calculator. You need to check that the answer is about the right size and starts or ends in the correct digit. State how you know that the answer must be wrong in each of these four calculations.

(a) $321 \times 3 = 1926$

(b) $1234 - 692 = 1926$

(c) $80\,892 \div 24 = 1926$

(d) $241 \times 9 = 1926$

6 The most common mistake is to press an adjacent key (for example 4 instead of 1) or to switch round two digits (for example keying 21 instead of 12). Find which mistake was made in each of the four calculations above.

7 Using the memory efficiently can save you a lot of time. Investigate this number pattern. It uses the same calculation in every line. If you store the answer to that calculation in the calculator's memory and then recall it, you will save time.

$137 \times 1 \times 73 =$

$137 \times 2 \times 73 =$

$137 \times 3 \times 73 =$

$137 \times 4 \times 73 =$

How far could you continue the pattern until the pattern in the result changes?

8 Here is a similar pattern for you to investigate.

$143 \times 1 \times 7 =$

$143 \times 2 \times 7 =$

$143 \times 3 \times 7 =$

$143 \times 4 \times 7 =$

How far could you continue this pattern until the pattern in the result changes?

9 Consider this calculation: $\frac{515 + 139}{342 - 124}$

There are two ways of approaching this on your calculator.

(a) Use the memory function.

Complete the subtraction in the denominator (bottom), then store the answer in the memory. Complete the addition in the numerator (top) and then divide by the number in the memory.

(b) Use the brackets function.

Calculate (515 + 139) ÷ (342 − 124)

Did you get the same answer both times?

10 Famous chessboard problem

A philosopher helped his ruler in a time of great difficulty and was offered anything he wanted as a reward. The philosopher said he simply wanted one grain of rice on the first square of a chessboard, two grains on the second, four on the third, eight on the fourth and so on, doubling each time. The ruler laughed and was pleased that he did not have to pay out lots of money. Use the constant function (×2) to work out how many grains of rice there were on the 20th square, and why the ruler soon stopped laughing!

Fractions on the calculator

Look for the fraction button on your calculator.

It usually looks like this: [$\frac{\square}{\square}$]

To enter a mixed number, for example $1\frac{2}{5}$, you press the keys in this sequence.

[1] [$\frac{\square}{\square}$] [2] [$\frac{\square}{\square}$] [5] [=]

The display may read 1⌟2⌟5 or 7⌟5 or $1\frac{2}{5}$

Decide how you would prefer it to look and refer to your calculator manual to set up the best display for you. There is usually a second function that is a toggle switch to convert improper fractions to mixed numbers and vice versa. It may look like $a\frac{b}{c} \leftrightarrow \frac{d}{c}$

Now add $2\frac{1}{3}$ by entering [+] [2] [$\frac{\square}{\square}$] [1] [$\frac{\square}{\square}$] [3] [=] and you should get the answer $3\frac{11}{15}$

Exercise 3.7

Use your calculator to work out the answers to the first five questions in each of Exercises 2.2 to 2.8

Estimating

When you use your calculator you may have discovered that it is very easy to miss out a zero or the decimal point. Before you do any calculation, it is good practice to estimate the expected answer. Then, when you complete your calculation on the calculator, you should be able to spot most errors immediately.

The easiest way to estimate is firstly to write each number to one significant figure and then to work out the answer.

Examples

(i) Calculate: 0.48×3212

Estimate: $0.48 \times 3212 \approx 0.5 \times 3000$

≈ 1500

Using the calculator: $0.48 \times 3212 = 1541.76...$

$= 1540$ (to 3 s.f.)

(ii) Calculate: $\dfrac{34.12}{621 \times 0.048}$

Estimate: $\dfrac{34.12}{621 \times 0.048} \approx \dfrac{30}{600 \times 0.05}$

$\approx \dfrac{30}{30}$

≈ 1

Using the calculator: $\dfrac{34.12}{621 \times 0.048} = 1.1446...$

$= 1.14$ (to 3 s.f.)

In the second example above, it is important to press the calculator keys in the correct sequence. This is how it should be done.

The calculator will only give the correct answer if you enter the correct calculation.

Exercise 3.8

Estimate the answer to each question. Show all your working clearly. Then use your calculator to work out the accurate answer. Give your answers correct to 3 significant figures.

1 925×0.0052

2 $348 \div 0.056$

3 0.053×0.9873

4 $0.836 \div 38$

5 $\dfrac{291}{0.721 \times 0.683}$

6 $\dfrac{38.3 \times 5.42}{0.0572}$

7 $\dfrac{3.450 \times 24.98}{0.721 \times 382}$

8 $\dfrac{9.34}{0.251} + \dfrac{361}{0.732}$

9 $\dfrac{0.0053}{0.921} + \dfrac{16.8}{59132}$

10 $\dfrac{34.12 \times 0.671}{0.045} + \dfrac{0.0124}{0.681 \times 37.3}$

11 $\dfrac{21.7 \times 3.8}{0.47 \times 0.51} - \dfrac{0.69 \times 312}{0.71 \times 381}$

12 $\dfrac{0.31 \times 481}{38} \div \dfrac{491}{0.68 \times 415}$

Exercise 3.9: Star challenge

Use your calculator to solve this puzzle. If you have answered the questions correctly, the answer will look like letters. (5 is S, 1 is I, 8 is B)

Start at Earth. Calculate the answer to the calculation at each star station. That will tell you which star station to go to next. One of the answers does not tell you where to go next – that is because it is your final stop.

$80\{30^2 + 3 \times (106 - 69)\}$

$4 \times \{9 \times (119 + 14) + 100\}$

$\dfrac{135 \times 101}{3 \times 9}$

$\dfrac{50\,(26^2 - 13)}{13 \times 17}$

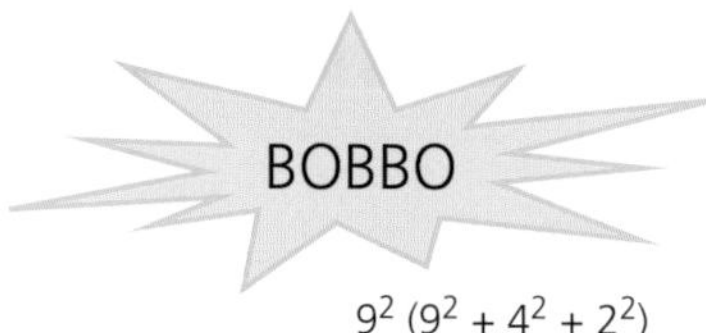

$9^2\,(9^2 + 4^2 + 2^2)$

$(29 + 16) \times (81 + 98)$

EARTH

$5 \times (26 + 42) + 25 \times (29 + 18)$

$\dfrac{100^2 + 3 \times 30^2}{\sqrt{625}}$

Copy and complete this sentence.

The journey should be EARTH TO … to … to … to … to … to … and finally to … , where the message is … .

Extension: Using the reciprocal button

Look again at the reciprocal button and see how it can help you solve problems.

Consider the calculation $\frac{1}{3^2 + 4^2}$

Work this out, using either the memory or the brackets function on your calculator.

Now try just working out the bottom line. You should get the result 25

Now press the reciprocal button  . Your answer should be the same as before.

Your working for the above should look like:

either $\frac{1}{3^2+4^2} = 1 \div 25 = 0.04$ or $\frac{1}{3^2+4^2} = \frac{1}{25} = 0.04$

As your calculations become more complicated it is a good idea to write down each stage as you go through it. Record any results your calculator gives you, in case you need to use them again.

Extension Exercise 3.10

1 Use the reciprocal button on your calculator to work out the answers to these.

(a) $\frac{1}{5 \div 25}$

(b) $\frac{5^2}{3^2+4^2}$

(c) $\frac{1}{3^2+4^2}$

2 Calculate $1 \div \frac{1}{4}$ or $\frac{1}{\frac{1}{4}}$. Try this for other numbers.

3 What is special about the reciprocals of multiples of 11?

4 The ancient Egyptians found reciprocals very useful because they could write only **unit** fractions such as $\frac{1}{5}$ and not multiple fractions such as $\frac{3}{5}$

$\frac{3}{5}$ had to be written as the sum of **unit** fractions.

Can you find which three **different** unit fractions add up to $\frac{3}{5}$?

5 Look at this reciprocal series: $1, \frac{1}{1+1}, \frac{1}{1+\frac{1}{1+1}}, \frac{1}{1+\frac{1}{1+\frac{1}{1+1}}}, \ldots$

Work out the value of each fraction. Try continuing the series. Write down your answer each time. If you were to continue the series forever what do you think the final answer would be?

6 **(a)** I am filling a tank by using a hosepipe that will fill the whole tank in 10 minutes. What fraction of the tank will be full after I have run the water for one minute?

(b) If I use a different hosepipe to fill the tank – one that would fill the tank in 5 minutes – how full will the tank be after one minute?

(c) If I turn on both hosepipes, how full will the tank will be after:

(i) one minute

(ii) two minutes?

(d) How long does it take to fill the tank (from empty), using both hosepipes?

7 I am filling a tank with two pipes. If the first hosepipe fills the tank in x minutes and the second fills it in y minutes, write an expression in x and y to give the time it takes to fill the tank, if I start both hosepipes together.

8 An intergalactic traveller is trapped in an ancient water torture tank. The evil alien switches on two taps. One would fill the tank on its own in 9 minutes, and the other would fill the tank on its own in 6 minutes. It takes the intergalactic traveller 3 minutes and 30 seconds to inflate his oxygen-making mask. How many seconds are left before the tank is full?

Summary Exercise 3.11

Use you calculator to answer the questions.

1 $51.6 \times 11.5 - 309.99$

2 $309.97 - 51.3 \times 5.42$

3 $319 \div 5.8 + 425 \div 8.6$

4 **(a)** $\frac{3}{13} + \frac{14}{15}$ **(b)** $2\frac{5}{7} - 1\frac{4}{9}$ **(c)** $3\frac{7}{11} \times 1\frac{5}{14}$ **(d)** $6\frac{5}{17} \div 2\frac{10}{11}$

5 **(a)** $12\frac{2}{5} - 3\frac{1}{5} \times 3\frac{3}{4}$ **(b)** $\dfrac{7\frac{31}{32} + \frac{7}{8}}{7\frac{1}{2} - 5\frac{7}{8}}$

6 **(a)** Evaluate: $\left(1 - \frac{1}{50}\right)\left(1 - \frac{1}{49}\right)\left(1 - \frac{1}{48}\right)$

(b) What happens if you extend the multiplication pattern in part **(a)** as far as $\left(1 - \frac{1}{2}\right)$?

7 **(a)** Estimate your answers to these, showing all your working clearly. Give your answers correct to one significant figure.

(i) $\dfrac{34.8 + 51.2}{0.49 \times 39.9}$ **(ii)** $\dfrac{312.3 \times 0.789}{41.3 \times 0.052}$

(b) Now work out the answers to **(i)** and **(ii)** exactly. Give the full values shown on your calculator.

8 Use your calculator to find the answers to these. If you turn your calculator upside down and ignore the decimal point, then each answer will make a word.

(a) $\dfrac{5^2(6631 - 5084)}{\sqrt[8]{390625}}$

(b) $\dfrac{1}{9}\left(5 - \dfrac{23}{1000}\right)$

(c) $56[(10 \times 23^2) + (13 \times 31)]$

(d) $\dfrac{10^7}{5^2 \times 2^3} + \dfrac{380^2 + 24^2 + 2^3}{7 \times 2^2}$

9 Write a question of your own that will result in a word when the calculator is turned upside down.

Work out what you want the answer to be, then work out the question.

Activity: Calculator puzzles and games

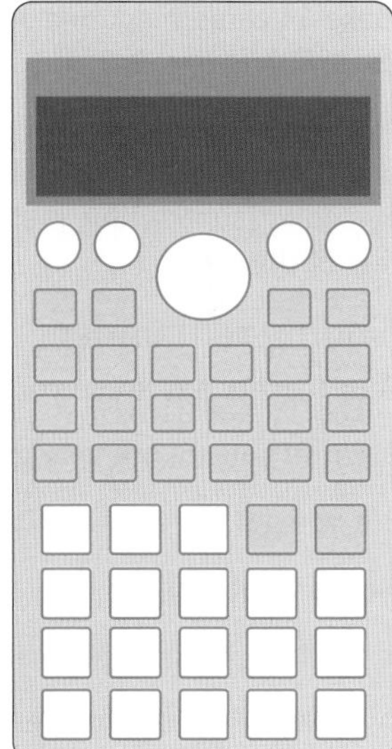

First draw a copy of your calculator in your exercise book (or copy this one). Label all the function buttons that you have used in this chapter. With a different colour label all the second function buttons that you have used. On the display, note the code that tells you what mode you are in.

Guess the number

Ask a friend to think of a number between ten and ninety-nine. Ask them to write it down. Then, using a calculator, tell them to:

Double it: 

Add 6: + 6 =

Divide by 2: ÷ 2 =

Add 2: + 2 =

Multiply by 8: 

Subtract 40: 

Now ask them the result. On your calculator enter the result and then just divide by 8 You will have the original number! Can you work out why?

Down to zero

Press the random number button on your calculator (usually a second function marked Ran#). If this gives a three figure decimal then multiply by 1000 to make a three digit integer.

The game is to see how many stages it takes you to reach zero. At each stage you can subtract or divide by a **single** digit number. The result at each stage must be a whole number.

Try a race with a friend. You will have to record every stage of your calculation!

Countdown

Make 14 cards. Mark one of the following numbers on each card: 100, 75, 50, 25, 10, 9, 8, 7, 6, 5, 4, 3, 2, 1

Pick six of them at random. Then use the calculator to give you a three figure random number. Can you make that number from your six numbers on the cards by adding, subtracting, multiplying or dividing as necessary? Can you beat the rest of the class?

Finding remainders

Your teacher has asked you what the remainder is when you divide 1760 by 19

Because you are not very good at long division you secretly use your calculator.

But you get the answer 92.631 579 which is not much help.

Here's what you do:

- subtract the integer answer − 9 2 =
- multiply the decimal remainder by the divisor × 1 9 =
- you get the remainder! 12

Try this for some other long division questions.

Index numbers

Indices

In Chapter 1, you saw that you can write the prime factors of 375 as $375 = 3 \times 5 \times 5 \times 5 = 3 \times 5^3$

The small, raised 3 is the **index number** and tells you how many times 5 appears when the number (in this case 375) is written as the product of its prime factors.

Indices and products of primes

Index numbers do not appear only in products of prime factors. Here are some more examples of index numbers.

$5 \times 5 \times 5 \times 5 \times 5 = 5^5 = 3125$ You read 5^5 as 'five to the **power** 5'

$5 \times 5 \times 5 \times 5 = 5^4 = 625$ You read 5^4 as 'five to the power 4'

$5 \times 5 \times 5 = 5^3 = 125$ You read 5^3 as 'five cubed'.

$5 \times 5 = 5^2 = 25$ You read 5^2 as 'five squared'.

$5 = 5^1$ or $5 = 5$

In the number 5^3 the small 3 is the index and the 5 is the base.

What happens when you multiply and divide numbers with indices?

$5^3 \times 5^2 = (5 \times 5 \times 5) \times (5 \times 5)$

$= 5^5$ Notice that $3 + 2 = 5$

When you **multiply** powers of the same base number, you **add** the indices.

$5^4 \div 5^2 = 5 \times 5 \times 5 \times 5 \div 5 \times 5$

$= 5^2$ Notice that $4 - 2 = 2$

When you **divide** powers of the same base number, you **subtract** the indices.

As a general rule:

If you multiply numbers written in index form, the index of the result, on the right-hand side, is the sum of the indices of the numbers being multiplied, on the left-hand side.

$3^4 \times 3^2 = 3^{4+2} = 3^6$

If you divide one number written in index form by another, the index of the result is the index of the first number on the left-hand side minus the index of the second.

$2^6 \div 2^2 = 2^{6-2} = 2^4$

Example

Simplify these numbers. If possible, leave the answer in index form.

(i) $2^4 \times 2^6$ (ii) $6^7 \div 6^2$ (iii) $3^3 \times 3$

(i) $2^4 \times 2^6 = 2^{10}$ as $4 + 6 = 10$

(ii) $6^7 \div 6^2 = 6^5$ as $7 - 2 = 5$

(iii) $3^3 \times 3 = 3^4$ as 3 is 3^1 therefore $3 + 1 = 4$

These rules are true only when considering powers of the same number. They do not apply if the base numbers are different.

$5^3 \times 2^3$ does not equal either 5^6 or 2^6 but it does equal 10^3

$5^3 + 5^3$ does not equal 5^6 but equals 2×5^3

2×5^3 does not equal 10^3 2×5^3 cannot be simplified in index form.

Exercise 4.1

Simplify these numbers. Leave your answers in index form.

1 (a) $3^3 \times 3^2$ (c) $6^7 \times 6^4$ (e) $4^3 \times 4^3 \times 4^3$

(b) $7^2 \times 7^5$ (d) $3^2 \times 3^2 \times 3$ (f) $7^3 \times 7 \times 7$

2 (a) $2^5 \div 2^2$ (c) $4^7 \div 4^3$ (e) $5^8 \div 5^7$

(b) $7^5 \div 7$ (d) $3^5 \div 3^2$ (f) $7^3 \div 7$

3 (a) $4^3 \times 4^3 \div 4^2$ (c) $5^7 \times 5^2 \div 5^4$ (e) $4 \times 4^3 \div 4^4$

(b) $7^2 \times 7^4 \div 7^5$ (d) $3^2 \times 3^2 \div 3$ (f) $7^3 \times 7^2 \div 7$

4 (a) $3^8 \times 3^3 \div 3$ (c) $7^3 \times 7^2 \div 7^4$ (e) $2^2 \times 2^3 \div 2^5$

(b) $5 \times 5^3 \div 5^2$ (d) $3 \times 3 \div 3^2$ (f) $7 \times 7^4 \div 7^5$

5 Simplify these numbers. If possible, leave the answers in index form.

(a) $3^3 \times 3^3$
(b) $8^5 \div 8^2$
(c) $6^7 \times 5^6$
(d) $7^2 \div 2^2$
(e) $6^7 \div 5^2$
(f) $4^3 \times 4$
(g) $2^2 \times 2^3 \times 2^2$
(h) $3^2 \times 5^3 \times 2^2$
(i) $7^3 \times 7^3 \times 3^2$
(j) $3^2 \times 3^3 \div 3^2$
(k) $6^7 \times 5^5 \div 6^2$
(l) $5^5 \times 5^5 \div 5^3$
(m) $4^8 \times 3^3 \times 5^2$
(n) $6^7 \times 6^5 \div 6^2$
(o) $2^4 \times 3^4 \div 6^2$

6 Simplify these numbers. If possible, leave the answers in index form.

(a) $2^3 + 3^3$
(b) $7^2 \div 7^2$
(c) 3×4^2
(d) 5×5^2
(e) $4^5 + 4^5 + 4^5$
(f) 3×7^3

Negative indices

What happens when you divide 5^3 by 5^6?

You can look at this in two ways.

$5^3 \div 5^6 = 5^{3-6}$ or $5^3 \div 5^6 = \frac{5^3}{5^6}$

$= 5^{-3}$ $\qquad = \frac{\cancel{5}^1 \times \cancel{5}^1 \times \cancel{5}^1}{\cancel{5}^1 \times \cancel{5}^1 \times \cancel{5}^1 \times 5 \times 5 \times 5}$

$= \frac{1}{5^3}$

Therefore you can see that $5^{-3} = \frac{1}{5^3}$

Here is another interesting example.

$5^3 \div 5^3 = 5^{3-3} = 5^0$

But $5^3 \div 5^3 = 1$

It follows therefore that $5^0 = 1$

Any positive number raised to the power 0 is 1

The table of powers of 5 going through zero into negative indices can be written like this.

$5^2 = 5 \times 5 = 25$ $\qquad 5^{-1} = \frac{1}{5}$

$5^1 = 5$ $\qquad 5^{-2} = \frac{1}{25}$

$5^0 = 1$ $\qquad 5^{-3} = \frac{1}{125}$ and so on.

Exercise 4.2

Complete this exercise. Use a calculator if you need to.

1 Write these in index form.

(a) $\frac{1}{2\times2\times2}$ (d) $\frac{1}{8\times8}$

(b) $\frac{1}{9\times9}$ (e) $\frac{1}{2\times2\times2\times2\times2}$

(c) $\frac{1}{3\times3\times3}$ (f) $\frac{1}{4\times4\times4}$

2 Write your answers to Q1 as fractions.

3 Write these in index form.

(a) $\frac{1}{9}$ (c) $\frac{1}{49}$ (e) $\frac{1}{128}$ (g) $\frac{1}{216}$

(b) $\frac{1}{16}$ (d) $\frac{1}{144}$ (f) $\frac{1}{27}$ (h) $\frac{1}{625}$

4 Simplify these, leaving your answers in index form.

(a) $3^3 \div 3^6$ (c) $6 \div 6^4$ (e) $4^3 \div 4^7$

(b) $7^3 \div 7^5$ (d) $3^2 \div 3^2$ (f) $7 \div 7^5$

5 Simplify these, leaving your answers in index form.

(a) $2^5 \times 2^{-2}$ (c) $4^{-7} \times 4^3$ (e) $5^{-8} \times 5^7$

(b) $7^5 \times 7^{-1}$ (d) $3^5 \times 3^{-2}$ (f) $7^{-3} \times 7$

6 Simplify these, leaving your answers in index form.

(a) $3^3 \times 3^{-3}$ (c) $6^3 \times 6^{-5}$ (e) $4^2 \times 4^{-3}$

(b) $4^2 \div 4^{-2}$ (d) $3^2 \div 3^{-5}$ (f) $7^3 \div 7^{-7}$

7 Simplify these, leaving your answers in index form.

(a) $4^3 \times 4^3 \times 4^{-2}$ (d) $3^2 \times 3^2 \times 3^{-3}$

(b) $7^2 \times 7^4 \times 7^{-9}$ (e) $2^3 \times 2^3 \times 2^{-2}$

(c) $5^7 \times 5^2 \times 5^{-4}$ (f) $7^3 \times 7^2 \times 7^{-5}$

8 Simplify these, leaving your answers in index form.

(a) $4^3 \times 4^4 \div 4^{-2}$ (d) $3^4 \div 3^2 \times 3^{-3}$

(b) $7^3 \times 7^4 \div 7^{-2}$ (e) $2^3 \times 2^4 \div 2^{-5}$

(c) $5^3 \div 5^2 \times 5^{-1}$ (f) $7^3 \times 7^2 \div 7^{-5}$

Solving equations in x^2

You know that $3 \times 3 = 9$ and also that $^-3 \times {}^-3 = 9$

This means that any positive number has two square roots, one positive and one negative.

So equations such as $x^2 = 9$ have two solutions.

Example

Solve the equation: $x^2 = 9$

$x^2 = 9$

$x = 3$ or $^-3$

$x = {}^\pm 3$

The symbol ± means positive or negative.

Exercise 4.3

Solve these equations.

1 $x^2 = 1$	**5** $y^2 = 4$	**9** $b^2 = 0.16$
2 $a^2 = 100$	**6** $a^2 = 64$	**10** $y^2 = 400$
3 $b^2 = 49$	**7** $x^2 = 0.09$	**11** $x^2 = 0.0001$
4 $c^2 = 81$	**8** $a^2 = 1600$	**12** $s^2 = 0.25$

Squares and square roots

As x^2 is the square of x and of ^-x then x and ^-x are the **square roots** of x^2

1 is the square of 1 and of $^-1$	1 and $^-1$ are the square roots of 1
4 is the square of 2 and of $^-2$	2 and $^-2$ are the square roots of 4
9 is the square of 3 and of $^-3$	3 and $^-3$ are the square roots of 9
16 is the square of 4 and of $^-4$	4 and $^-4$ are the square roots of 16

For the time being, you rarely need to use the negative square root. For the rest of this chapter you will consider only positive square roots.

The positive square root of 4 is written as:

$\sqrt{4} = 2$

The sign for 'square root' is unusual, there are no other mathematical symbols quite like it. Where does it come from? One story is that it represents the root of a tree! You could try using the internet to find out more.

Exercise 4.4

Write down these squares and square roots.

For Q1–10 give your answer as a whole number or an exact decimal.

1 $\sqrt{16}$

2 $\sqrt{25}$

3 $\sqrt{10\,000}$

4 0.4^2

5 1.2^2

6 $\sqrt{0.25}$

7 0.1^2

8 0.01^2

9 $\sqrt{0.0036}$

10 $\sqrt{1.21}$

For Q11–20, give your answer as: **(a)** a fraction **(b)** a decimal.

11 $\sqrt{0.01}$

12 $\left(\frac{1}{10}\right)^2$

13 $\sqrt{\frac{1}{9}}$

14 $\left(\frac{1}{2}\right)^2$

15 $\left(\frac{2}{3}\right)^2$

16 $\sqrt{\frac{4}{25}}$

17 $\sqrt{\frac{4^2}{2^2}}$

18 $\left(\frac{\sqrt{16}}{\sqrt{36}}\right)^2$

19 $\sqrt{\frac{1.6^2}{2^2}}$

20 $\left(\frac{\sqrt{0.04}}{0.2}\right)^2$

More about roots

In the last exercise, the square roots were all either whole numbers or exact decimals. This is because you were finding the square roots of **perfect squares**.

You can use a calculator to find the square root of a number that is not a perfect square.

$\sqrt{2} = 1.414\,213\,5\ldots$

$\sqrt{3} = 1.732\,050\,8\ldots$

$\sqrt{5} = 2.236\,067\,9\ldots$

You can see that these numbers are not exact. The calculator display will give you an answer with several decimal places, but these will carry on and on. The three dots indicate this; however, you would usually write them to a fixed number of decimal places or significant figures. These roots, $\sqrt{2}$, $\sqrt{3}$, $\sqrt{5}$, are called **surds**.

Example

(i) Find $\sqrt{10}$, giving your answer correct to 2 decimal places.

$\sqrt{10} = 3.162\,277\,6...$

$= 3.16$ (to 2 d.p.)

(ii) Find $\sqrt{45}$, giving your answer correct to 3 significant figures.

$\sqrt{45} = 6.708\,203\,9...$

$= 6.71$ (to 3 s.f.)

Always write down the numbers with more decimal places or significant figures than you need, followed by three dots.

You can also use your calculator to find cube and other roots. The **cube root** of a number is the number that, when cubed, gives that number.

To cube a number, you multiply that number together three times.

$\sqrt[3]{8} = 2$ as $2 \times 2 \times 2 = 2^3 = 8$

The fourth root of a number is the number that, when raised to the power 4, gives that number.

To raise a number to the power 4, you multiply that number together four times.

$\sqrt[4]{625} = 5$ as $5 \times 5 \times 5 \times 5 = 5^4 = 625$

Most numbers do not have an exact cube or other root.

Examples

(i) Find $\sqrt[3]{100}$, giving your answer correct to 2 decimal places.

$\sqrt[3]{100} = 4.641\,588...$

$= 4.64$ (to 2 d.p.)

(ii) Find $\sqrt[5]{200}$, giving your answer correct to 3 significant figures.

$\sqrt[5]{200} = 2.885\,39...$

$= 2.89$ (to 3 s.f.)

Exercise 4.5

1 Use your calculator to find these square roots. Give your answers correct to 1 decimal point.

(a) $\sqrt{2}$ (b) $\sqrt{7}$ (c) $\sqrt{20}$ (d) $\sqrt{99}$

2 Use your calculator to find these square roots. Give your answers correct to 3 significant figures.

(a) $\sqrt{48}$ (b) $\sqrt{120}$ (c) $\sqrt{250}$ (d) $\sqrt{9999}$

3 **(a)** Use you calculator to find these squares. Do not round your answers.

(i) 1.4^2 **(ii)** 1.41^2 **(iii)** 1.414^2

(b) Calculate $\sqrt{2}$, giving your answer to 3 decimal places.

(c) Explain what is wrong with the statement $\sqrt{2} = 1.41$

4 Use your calculator to find these roots. Give your answers correct to 2 decimal places.

(a) $\sqrt[3]{20}$ **(b)** $\sqrt[4]{100}$ **(c)** $\sqrt[5]{500}$ **(d)** $\sqrt[3]{999}$

5 Use your calculator to find these roots. Give your answers correct to 3 significant figures.

(a) $\sqrt[4]{49}$ **(b)** $\sqrt[3]{63}$ **(c)** $\sqrt[5]{7235}$ **(d)** $\sqrt[3]{419}$

Using prime factors to find square and other roots

What do you know about the number 36?

Written as the product of its prime factors:

$36 = 2 \times 2 \times 3 \times 3$

$= 2^2 \times 3^2$

As both the index numbers are even, you can see that 36 must be a **square number**. You can rearrange the factors like this.

$36 = (2 \times 3)^2$

Therefore: $\sqrt{36} = 2 \times 3 = 6$

You can use the same idea with larger numbers.

Example

By writing 1296 as the product of its prime factors, find the value of $\sqrt{1296}$

$1296 = 2 \times 2 \times 2 \times 2 \times 3 \times 3 \times 3 \times 3$

$= 2^4 \times 3^4$

$= (2^2 \times 3^2)^2$

$\sqrt{1296} = 2^2 \times 3^2$

$= 4 \times 9$

$= 36$

You can use the same method to work out the fourth root of 1296

Example

By writing 1296 as the product of its prime factors, find the value of $\sqrt[4]{1296}$

$$1296 = 2 \times 2 \times 2 \times 2 \times 3 \times 3 \times 3 \times 3$$
$$= 2^4 \times 3^4$$
$$= (2 \times 3)^4$$
$$\sqrt[4]{1296} = 2 \times 3$$
$$= 6$$

Exercise 4.6

1 Write each number as the product of its prime factors and thus calculate its square root.

(a) 2025 (b) 1089 (c) 3136 (d) 1521 (e) 1225 (f) 7056

2 Write each number as the product of its prime factors and thus calculate its cube root.

(a) 64 (b) 125 (c) 216 (d) 3375 (e) 1728 (f) 13 824

3 Calculate these roots.

(a) $\sqrt[4]{81}$ (b) $\sqrt[6]{729}$ (c) $\sqrt[4]{625}$ (d) $\sqrt[8]{256}$ (e) $\sqrt[5]{7776}$ (f) $\sqrt[5]{248832}$

Large and small numbers

Most problems that you have to solve have quite ordinary numbers, but, as scientists explore the world of science, geography and astronomy, they often come across very large numbers and very small numbers.

Consider these facts about the Universe.

A **light year** is a unit of distance in astronomy. It is the distance travelled by light in one year. Light moves at a **velocity** of about 300 000 000 metres (m) each second. In one year, it can travel about 10 trillion kilometres. More precisely, light will travel about 9 461 000 000 000 kilometres in a year.

The distance from Earth to the nearest large galaxy, called *Andromeda*, is 21 quintillion kilometres, which is 21 000 000 000 000 000 000 km.

A **parsec** is equal to 3.3 light years. Using the light year, you can say that:

- the Crab supernova remnant is about 4000 light years away from Earth
- the Milky Way galaxy is about 150 000 light years across
- Andromeda is about 2.3 million light years away.

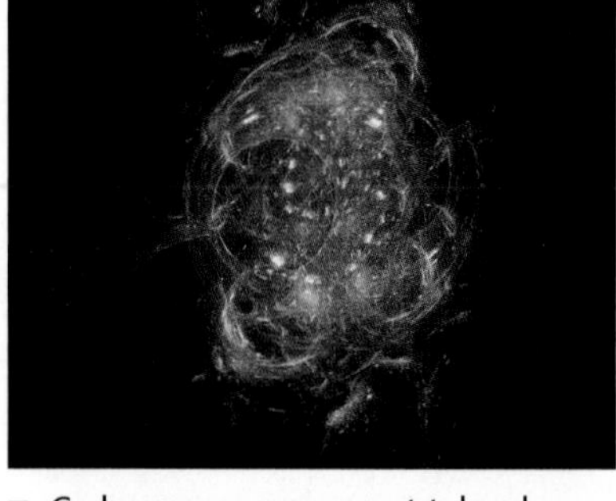

■ Crab supernova remnant taken by the Hubble telescope

At the other end of the scale:

- the breadth of a typical human cell is 10^{-5} metres (10 microns)
- light travels almost 30 cm in one nanosecond, which is one billionth (10^{-9}) of a second
- 100 nanoseconds is the exposure time of the fastest stroboscopic camera.

Now look at your calculator. You will see that the display can only show 8 or 10 digits, so calculating with these very large and very small numbers is extremely difficult. The solution is to write them in a short way, so that you can use a calculator.

Writing these numbers in a short way not only makes calculations easier but also makes it much easier to compare their relative sizes. It also takes less time to write them.

You can use a short form of these numbers, based on the fact that, in the decimal number system, you can write the powers of ten with indices.

Examples

Write these numbers as powers of 10

(i) 100 000 (ii) 0.000 01

(i) $100\,000 = 10^5$ (ii) $0.000\,01 = 10^{-5}$

The number of zeros in the original number indicates the size of the index number.

Standard index form

In **standard index form**, you write a number as the product of a number between one and ten and a power of ten.

Example

Write each number as a single figure multiplied by a power of ten.

(i) 5000 (ii) 0.006

(i) $5000 = 5 \times 1000$
$= 5 \times 10^3$

(ii) $0.006 = 6 \times 0.001$
$= 6 \times 10^{-3}$

Most numbers have more than one non-zero digit and they may include decimal fractions.

Example

Write these numbers in standard index form.

(i) 5850 (ii) 0.0063

(i) $5850 = 5.85 \times 1000$
$= 5.85 \times 10^3$

(ii) $0.0063 = 6.3 \times 0.001$
$= 6.3 \times 10^{-3}$

Look at the place value of the first significant figure. That will help you to write the correct power of ten.

Exercise 4.7

1 Write each of these numbers as a power of ten.

(a) 10 000
(b) 1000
(c) 0.001
(d) 0.000 001
(e) 10 000 000 000
(f) 0. 000 000 01

2 Write each of these numbers as a single-digit multiplied by a power of ten.

(a) 30 000
(b) 0.000 04
(c) 0.09
(d) 0.0006
(e) 0.000 000 07
(f) 80 000 000

3 Write each of these numbers out in full. Remember to put the spaces in the correct position after each group of three digits.

(a) 2×10^2
(b) 6×10^{-5}
(c) 7×10^8
(d) 2.8×10^3
(e) 4.9×10^2
(f) 3.65×10^{-7}

4 Write each of these numbers in standard index form.

(a) 3900
(b) 809 000 000 000
(c) 20 050 000
(d) 607 500
(e) 39 000
(f) 9 080 000

5 Write each of these numbers in standard index form.

(a) 0.005
(b) 0.006 84
(c) 0.000 032
(d) 0.000 000 809
(e) 0.54
(f) 0.000 019 09

Standard index form and the scientific calculator

Try this multiplication on your scientific calculator.

450 000 × 250 000

The display may look something like this.

1.125 × 10^11

This is the calculator's way of displaying 1.125×10^{11}

Now do the division 0.000 004 ÷ 500 000

The display may look something like this.

8 × 10^-12

If you do not understand the display, refer to the manual that came with the calculator.

Example

How many millimetres are there in 250 000 km?

250 000 km = 250 000 × 1000 × 1000 mm

$= 2.5 \times 10^{11}$ mm

= 250 000 000 000 mm

Exercise 4.8

Use you calculator to answer these next questions. Take care to read the display correctly and give your answers in standard index form and then write them out in full.

1 The **circumference** of the Earth is 40 000 km. What is this in millimetres?

2 How many seconds are there in a century?

3 The average annual wage in the UK is £27 000. If the health service employs 1.6 million people, estimate the amount that they must pay out in wages every year. Assume every employee receives the average wage.

4 Each of the 2.4 million employees has four weeks holiday (20 working days). How many working days is that in total?

5 'Micro' is the prefix for one millionth. For example, one microsecond is one millionth of a second. Write 9 microseconds in minutes.

6 'Mega' is the prefix for 1 million. For example, one megabuck is one million dollars. The current rate of exchange is 1.75 American dollars to one pound sterling. Write 5.5 megabucks in pounds.

7 The circumference of the Earth is 40 000 km. The **diameter** of a 10p coin is 24 mm. How many 10p coins would you need to lay, with no gaps, to cover the length of the equator? What would this be worth?

8 The biggest dinosaur was *Ultrasaurus*. The name *Ultrasaurus* means the largest lizard. One *Ultrasaurus* found in Colorado would have been more than 30 metres long, standing 18 metres high and weighing 136 tonnes. What are these measurements in millimetres and in milligrams?

9 *Ornithominus* was probably the fastest dinosaur. It could run at 80 km/h. What is this speed, in millimetres per second?

10 The maximum speed of a F35 Lightening Fighter aircraft is 1930 km/h. What is this speed, in millimetres per second?

11 Radio frequency is measured in hertz, or more usually kilohertz (1000 Hz) or megahertz (10^6 million hertz). In order to find the wavelength of the frequency, you divide 300 000 by the frequency. If the frequency of a radio station is 200 kHz, what is its wavelength?

12 A kilobyte of computer memory is different from a normal 'kilo' unit. It is not one thousand bytes but 2^{10} bytes. A megabyte is 2^{10} kilobytes. The bit is the smallest particle of memory storage and there are eight bits in a byte. How many bits are there in 4 megabytes?

13 **(a)** Very large distances are measured in light years. You know that light travels at 300 000 km/s and that the distance it travels in a year is called a light year. From this information, show that one light year is equal to 9.5×10^{12} kilometres.

(b) The nearest star (apart from the Sun) is Proxima Centauri, which is 4.3 light years away. How far is this, in kilometres?

14 A newer unit of astronomical measurement is the parsec. One parsec is roughly 3.25 light years. How many kilometres is a parsec?

15 An aeon is 10^9 years. The Sun was formed 4.5 aeons ago. How many years ago is that?

Extension: Calculating with roots

You know how to find the square root of a square number, such as 1, 4, 9, 16...

Use your calculator to work out $\sqrt{3}$

There is no integer answer, and the number that is shown on your calculator, 1.732... is only an approximation of $\sqrt{3}$

The same is true for any other number that is not a perfect square number.

Therefore, you write the exact value of the square root of 3 as $\sqrt{3}$ This is an example of a **surd.**

Now consider the calculation $\sqrt{3} \times \sqrt{3}$

Because the numbers in the calculation are expressed as square roots you can simply multiply.

$\sqrt{3} \times \sqrt{3} = \sqrt{9} = 3$

This can be useful for other, more complicated calculations, such as

$\sqrt{3} \times \sqrt{12} = \sqrt{36} = 6$

Extension Exercise 4.9

Work out these products of square roots. Some will give integer answers, some will not. If necessary, leave the answer in **surd** form.

1 $\sqrt{3} \times \sqrt{48}$

2 $\sqrt{8} \times \sqrt{32}$

3 $\sqrt{3} \times \sqrt{7}$

4 $\sqrt{3} \times \sqrt{2} \times \sqrt{6}$

5 $\sqrt{2} \times \sqrt{2} \times \sqrt{2}$

6 $\sqrt{5} \times \sqrt{25}$

7 $\sqrt{12} \times \sqrt{27}$

8 $\sqrt{7} \times \sqrt{8}$

9 $\sqrt{3} \times \sqrt{18}$

10 $\sqrt{8} \times \sqrt{18}$

You should have found four numbers that you had to leave in surd form.

$\sqrt{8}$ $\sqrt{125}$ $\sqrt{48}$ $\sqrt{54}$

Although these are not integer square roots they are multiples of square numbers.

$\sqrt{8} = \sqrt{4 \times 2}$ You know that $4 \times 2 = 8$

$= \sqrt{4} \times 2$ The square root of 4 is 2

$= 2\sqrt{2}$ The 2 outside the square root replaces the 4 inside the square root.

$\sqrt{125} = \sqrt{25 \times 5} = 5\sqrt{5}$

Use this method to simplify these roots.

11 $\sqrt{27}$

12 $\sqrt{162}$

13 $\sqrt{72}$

14 $\sqrt{2} \times \sqrt{3} \times \sqrt{10}$

15 $\sqrt{2} \times \sqrt{4} \times \sqrt{8}$

16 $\sqrt{3} \times \sqrt{5} \times \sqrt{15}$

17 $\sqrt{8} \times \sqrt{24}$

18 $\sqrt{12} \times \sqrt{15}$

19 $\sqrt{2} \times \sqrt{18} \times \sqrt{4}$

20 $\sqrt{3} \times \sqrt{12} \times \sqrt{15}$

Summary Exercise 4.10

1 Write these in index form.

(a) $3 \times 3 \times 3$

(b) $2 \times 2 \times 2 \times 2 \times 2 \times 2$

(c) $4 \times 4 \times 4 \times 4 \times 4$

(d) $7 \times 7 \times 7$

2 Now write down the answers to question 1

3 Write these numbers in index form.

(a) 8 (b) 125 (c) 128 (d) 81

4 Write these numbers as fractions.

(a) 2^{-2} (b) 3^{-5} (c) 7^{-3}

5 Simplify these, if possible, leaving your answers in index form.

(a) $3^2 \times 3^4$

(b) $7^5 \div 7^2$

(c) $3^2 \div 3^5$

(d) $3^3 + 3^3$

(e) $5^2 \div 3^3$

(f) $3^3 \times 5^2$

6 Simplify these, leaving your answers in index form.

(a) $4^2 \times 4^{-3}$

(b) $3^{-2} \div 3^{-3}$

(c) $4^{-2} \times 4^{-2}$

(d) $2^7 \times 2^{-5}$

(e) $5^{-2} \div 5^2$

(f) $7^2 \times 7^{-2}$

7 Solve these equations.

(a) $x^2 = 16$ (b) $a^2 = 100$ (c) $b^2 = \frac{1}{\sqrt{4}}$

8 Work out these squares and square roots.

(a) $\sqrt{16}$ (b) 1.1^2 (c) 0.3^2 (d) $\sqrt{0.04}$

9 Find the value of each standard index form number.

(a) 7×10^4

(b) 2.75×10^6

(c) 1.5×10^{-4}

(d) 9.702×10^{-3}

10 Write these numbers in standard index form.

(a) 47 000

(b) 0.0081

(c) 506 000 000

(d) 0.000 402

11 Calculate the number of milligrams in 6.2 tonnes and give your answer in standard index form.

12 Evaluate each expression.

(a) $\sqrt{5} \times \sqrt{5}$

(b) $\left(\sqrt{3}\right)^2$

(c) $\sqrt{3} \times \sqrt{48}$

(d) $\sqrt{5} \times \sqrt{28} \times \sqrt{35}$

Activity: Chain letters

Someone in your family may have received a letter or email reading something like this.

TO | Attach
CC | Send
Subject | Cancel

'How do you like receiving letters? Most of us do, and this letter is to guarantee that you receive hundreds of letters. All you have to do is to send a letter to the person at the top of the list below. Then copy out this letter 5 times, take off the top person from the list and add your name at the bottom. Then send the five copies to five of your best friends.'

1 John Smith
2 Sara Ing
3 Pete Black
4 Imran Patel
5 Claire Jones

PS Don't break the chain and don't tell the post office.

How true is the claim that you will receive hundreds of letters? This letter takes five stages to move you up to the top of the list.

Therefore your five friends will send letters to five friends who will send letters to five friends who will send letters to five friends who will send letters to five friends who will all send me a letter.

1 How many letters would I receive if everyone followed the instructions? (Not 25!)

2 How many letters should I receive if there were six people on the list and I had sent letters to six friends?

3 How many letters would I receive if there were five people on the list but everybody in the chain sent out 10 copies to friends?

4 Investigate this for different numbers of people on the list and different numbers of copies. Can you find a rule linking the theoretical number of letters that you receive and the number of copies that you send out?

5 One of the most famous chain letter scams asked you to send £10 to the person at the top of the list and then 'sell' your letters for £1 each to ten other people. This time there was a list of 10 people before you were sent the £10s. How many people should have been in the chain by then? How does this compare to the population of Britain?

A great many people lost their £10 because everybody else had heard of it first – and most people broke the chain!

You will not be surprised to learn that these chain letters are now illegal.

5 Percentages

In *Mathematics for Common Entrance Books One* and *Two* you saw that percentages are a useful way of comparing values. In Chapter 2 of this book, you revised converting fractions and decimals to percentages.

Percentages – a review

You should know how to form a percentage and to find a percentage of an amount. Here are some examples to remind you.

Forming a percentage

Example

My maths result was 24 out of 40. What is this as a percentage?

$$\text{Percentage} = \frac{\overset{6}{\cancel{24}}}{{}_{1}\cancel{40}} \times 10\cancel{0}$$

$$= 60\%$$

Finding a percentage of an amount

If you remember that a percentage is a type of fraction, finding a percentage of an amount is quite straightforward.

Example

In a sale, the price of everything is reduced by 20%

What is the sale price of a MP3 player previously priced at £88?

$$\text{Discount} = \frac{2\cancel{0}}{10\cancel{0}} \times 88$$

$$= \frac{176}{10}$$

$$= £17.60$$

Sale price = £88.00 – £17.60

= £70.40

The question did not ask for the discount but for the sale price so there is one more calculation to do.

The next exercise will help you to revise these concepts. When you write percentages as fractions you may be able to cancel the numbers so you should not need a calculator. You could use a calculator to check your answers, to verify your arithmetic.

Exercise 5.1

1 Write each fraction as: (i) a percentages (ii) a decimal.

(a) $\frac{1}{5}$ (b) $\frac{3}{10}$ (c) $\frac{5}{8}$ (d) $\frac{4}{25}$

2 Write each percentage as: (i) a decimal (ii) a fraction.

(a) 14% (b) 65% (c) 33% (d) 44%

3 Each of these percentages contains a fraction, but you should recognise their fraction equivalents.

Write each one as: (i) a fraction (ii) a decimal.

(a) $12\frac{1}{2}\%$ (b) $66\frac{2}{3}\%$ (c) $16\frac{2}{3}\%$ (d) $37\frac{1}{2}\%$

4 These are recurring decimals.

Write each one as: (i) a fraction (ii) a percentage.

(a) $0.\dot{3}$ (b) $0.8\dot{3}$ (c) $0.\dot{2}$

5 88% of my class had a BCG inoculation. What percentage did not?

6 It is said that 64% of people fail their driving test first time. What is the percentage pass rate?

7 What is 10% of £35?

8 What is 60% of 3 m?

9 What is 25% of two hours?

10 What is 35% of £5?

11 What is 63% of 500 km?

12 In my class of 25, 11 of us had flu. What percentage of the class had flu?

13 The cost of cat food has risen 5%. If the original price was 40p per can, what is it now?

14 In the sale, prices are marked down by 12%. What is the sale price of:

(a) a pair of trainers normally costing £25

(b) a jacket normally costing £35

(c) a CD player normally costing £40?

15 We picked 65 apples but 26 of them had maggots in them. What percentage of apples did not contain maggots?

16 I have negotiated a rise of 15% in my pocket money. If it used to be £5 per week, what is it now?

17 Extra-long jeans cost 5% more than standard-length ones. If standard jeans cost £25, how much are extra-long jeans?

18 I cooked 144 mince pies for the Christmas Fayre, but 48 of them burned. What percentage of them did not burn?

19 The service charge at our local café is 15%. How much service was added to our food bill of £25?

20 Our computer suppliers offer a 10% discount on orders over £100. Boxes of 10 DVDs usually cost £19. How many boxes must we buy before we qualify for the discount and how much will we save?

Percentage as a decimal

In the first exercise you used the fraction method to answer the questions without using a calculator. The numbers could be cancelled quite easily to make the arithmetic more straightforward. Normally, you will need to use a calculator as you will be working with more complicated numbers. When you are using a calculator, it is more efficient to convert the percentages to decimals.

Example

In a sale, prices are reduced by $12\frac{1}{2}\%$

Work out the discount on a computer normally costing £599

Discount = $12\frac{1}{2}\%$ of £599 $12\frac{1}{2}\% = 0.125$

= 0.125 × £599   Write down the calculation.

= £74.875   Write the full calculator display.

= £74.88 (to 2 d.p.)   Round to the nearest penny.

Note how the answer is structured. It is important that you write your calculations clearly. Always write out the full answer given on the calculator display before rounding it, in case you need to use it in a subsequent calculation.

If you concentrate on developing good habits you will not have to unlearn bad ones!

You can use the same method as before when you use a calculator to work out a percentage.

Example

I opened my building society account with £120 and a year later, after interest was added, I had £123.30 in the account.

What rate of interest was applied?

Interest earned = 123.30 − 120 = £3.30 — Calculate the difference between the two amounts.

Interest rate $= \frac{3.3}{120} \times 100$ — Divide the interest earned by the original amount.

$= 2.75\%$

Exercise 5.2

Use a calculator for this exercise. Write down all the stages in the working carefully.

1 VAT is currently 20%. Write down the value of the VAT that must be added to the basic cost of each article.

(a) Teddy bear £12

(b) Tablet £395

(c) Tennis racquet £49

(d) Bicycle £250

(e) Baseball cap £9.50

(f) Football £25

2 Find the selling price of each article in question 1

3 In a sale, all prices are reduced by 15%. What discount would be given on each of these articles?

(a) T-shirt £15

(b) Pencil case £4

(c) Wrist watch £35

(d) Alarm clock £12

(e) Sound system £150

(f) Kettle £25

4 What is the sale price of each of the articles in question 3?

5 My grandfather opened a building society account for me and deposited £80 as a starting balance.

The interest rate was 3%. How much interest did I earn in one year?

6 A computer was marked at £699, but we bought it in the sale for £560. By what percentage was the price of the computer reduced?

7 Tennis balls are normally sold at 99p each. In the sale there are two bargain packs. I can buy either four balls for £3.60 or six balls for £5.50

Which pack gives the larger percentage discount?

8 Theatre tickets are normally £12, but if a party of 10 or more people book as a group they save 15%. How many tickets do they have to buy to save the normal price of two tickets?

Percentage increase and decrease

You have been learning about amounts rising or falling by a **percentage increase** or **percentage decrease.** It can be quite difficult to work out, from the words used, whether some changes result in a rise or fall. These are the terms that you are most likely to meet.

Decrease	**Increase**
Discount	Premium
Sale price	Surcharge
Income tax	Value added tax (VAT)
Devaluation	Service charge/Tip
No-claims bonus	Commission
Loss	Profit

Percentage problems are often set in the context of money. Some decreases, such as discounts, sale prices and no-claims bonuses, are welcome, as they save you money. Others, such as income tax and service charges, are not so good because they leave you with less money, or you need to spend more.

Most increases cost you money. If you are **buying** services, then commission, VAT and service charges are all added to the bill, thereby increasing the cost. However, if you are **selling** services then such percentages can make up your earnings. Some workers, such as estate agents, rely entirely on percentage commissions for their income.

Calculating percentage increase and decrease

Previously, you calculated VAT as a percentage of the original price and then added it to the original price to find the selling price.

You can do this in one calculation. Consider the original price as being 100% of itself, you then add VAT as 20% of the original price. That gives you 120%.

Original price + VAT = new price

$$100\% + 20\% = 120\% \text{ or } 1.2$$

The number 1.2 is the **multiplying factor** or **multiplier.** If you take the prices in question 1 of the last exercise and multiply them all by 1.2 you should get the prices you worked out in question 2

A sale price involves a percentage decrease and so the percentage calculation looks like this.

Original price − discount = new price

$$100\% - 15\% = 85\% \text{ or } 0.85$$

The number 0.85 is the **multiplying factor.** If you multiply all the prices in question 3 of the last exercise by 0.85 you should get the prices in question 4

Examples

(i) A service charge of 12% is added to my bill of £52.50 in a restaurant. What is the total amount of my bill?

$100\% + 12\% = 112\%$

Total amount $= 1.12 \times 52.50$

$= £58.80$

(ii) The value of my car has fallen by 12% over the last year. If it was worth £5000 last year, what is its current value?

$100\% - 12\% = 88\%$

New value $= 0.88 \times 5000$

$= £4400$

Exercise 5.3

1 Multiply all the prices in question 1 of the previous exercise by 1.2 and check that you get your answers for question 2

2 Multiply all the prices in question 3 of the previous exercise by 0.85 and check that you get your answers for question 4

3 Write down the multiplying factor for each percentage change.

(a) an increase of 4%

(b) a surcharge of 5%

(c) a discount of 8%

(d) income tax at 20%

(e) a saving of 18%

(f) a no claims bonus of 15%

(g) commission at 8%

(h) a service charge of $12\frac{1}{2}\%$

(i) a premium of 10%

(j) a devaluation of 16%

(k) a decrease of 32%

(l) supertax at 40%

4 Trainers are normally sold at £49 per pair. In the sale the price is reduced by 12%. What is the sale price of the trainers?

5 A service charge of 12% is added to my bill. If the bill was £25 before the service charge was added, what is the total amount (including the service charge) I have to pay?

6 My local pizza take-away is offering 10% off all orders over £15 this week. If I order two pizzas at £8.25 each, what will I have to pay?

7 We are trying to sell our house for £450 000. The estate agent's commission will be 2%. How much money would we receive from the sale?

8 A new car is said to devalue by 15% in its first year and 10% in its second year. If my mother bought a new car costing £8500 two years ago, what was its value at the end of one year? What was its value at the end of two years?

9 A length of bungy jumping elastic is said to stretch up to 22% of its original length. If its original length is 20 m, what is its maximum stretched length?

10 Water increases in volume by 4% when it freezes and becomes ice. What is the frozen volume of 4 litres of water? Give your answer in cubic centimetres. (1 litre = 1000 cm^3)

Percentage change

A percentage is a useful way of recording change because it does not look at the actual values themselves but at the proportion by which the amount has changed.

The percentage change can be identified from the **multiplying factor**.

1.20 means a percentage increase of 20% $(1 + 0.2 = 1.20)$

0.72 means a percentage decrease of 28% $(1 - 0.28 = 0.72)$

You have been finding new values by using the calculation:

new amount = original amount × multiplying factor

This can be rearranged to give:

$$\text{multiplying factor} = \frac{\text{new amount}}{\text{original amount}}$$

Example

A car dealer buys a car for £1250

He spends £200 on repairs and then sells the car for £2755

What is his percentage profit?

$$\text{Multiplying factor} = \frac{\text{new amount}}{\text{original amount}}$$

$$= \frac{2755}{1250 + 200}$$

$= 1.90$ is 190%

The dealer made a 90% profit.

Exercise 5.4

In each question, write down the original value and the new value and decide whether there has been an increase or a decrease.

1. The price of a shirt was £25 before the sale and £22 in the sale.
2. The bill was £52.50 and after VAT and service were added it was £67.86
3. I bought a car for £4500 and sold it for £3825
4. There were 416 pupils in the school last year. This year there are 395
5. The account was £300; with commission and tax we paid £423
6. I earn £28 000 per year. I take home £1750 per month.
7. A wholesaler buys 100 DVDs for £50 and then she sells them in bundles of five DVDs for £8
8. We paid insurance premiums of £220 last year. We pay premiums of £190 this year.
9. The tickets cost £15 each. We paid £240 for tickets for a group of 20 of us.
10. Now work out the percentage change in each of questions 1–9

Finding the original amount

Many of the prices that you see include tax. During the sales, prices are reduced. In both cases, it is useful to be able to find the original cost of the item.

Prices you see in most shops already have VAT added and during the sales you see the sale price. If you are running your own business it is important to know how much money you will need to give to the government (the VAT element of a price) and how much money you will actually get for the goods you sell.

Look again at the calculation:

new value = original value × multiplying factor

Once again, this can be rearranged to give:

$$\text{original amount} = \frac{\text{new amount}}{\text{multiplying factor}}$$

When you know the value after a percentage increase or decrease, you can find the original value by substituting into this formula.

Example

VAT at 20% has been added to the price of an article, which is now offered at £23.40. Find the original price.

new value = original value × multiplying factor

£23.40 = original value × 1.2

original value = 23.40 ÷ 1.2

= £19.50

Exercise 5.5

Work out the original amount in each question. Give your answers correct to 2 d.p. if they are not whole numbers.

1 A second-hand car dealer makes a 20% profit when he sells a car for £5640. How much did he pay for the car?

2 The price of a sound system being sold for £144 includes VAT at 20%. What is the price without VAT?

3 The value of our house has dropped 8% in the last year. It is now worth £552 000. What was it worth last year?

4 Our local MP won 42% fewer votes in this election than in the previous election. He won 14 500 votes this time. How many did he win the time before?

5 A sports shop is selling off last year's rugby shirts to make room for this year's new stock.

By selling each shirt for £28.70 the shop is giving an 18% discount. What was the original selling price of these shirts?

6 The volume of water increases by 4% when it freezes and becomes ice. What volume of water in litres is equivalent to a block of ice 10 cm × 10 cm × 25 cm?

7 My height has increased by 5% this year and I am now 1.60 m tall. What was my height last year?

8 The number of pupils boarding at my school has dropped by 8% in the last five years. There are 142 pupils boarding now. How many were boarding five years ago?

9 A wholesaler buys potatoes in 25 kg bags and sells the potatoes to the public in bags of 10 kg to make 25% profit. If he sells the 10 kg bags at £3.60 each, what did he pay for the 25 kg bags?

10 A car is said to devalue 15% in its first year and then 10% in its second. If our two-year-old car is worth £6120 now what was it worth last year? What did we pay for it when it was new?

In the last exercise you were asked to find the original amount. The next exercise has mixed questions.

Exercise 5.6

Decide whether you need to find the original amount or the new amount. Write your answers correct to 2 d.p. if they are not whole numbers.

1 I pay a £300 premium for my car insurance after a no claims bonus of 20% What is my premium without the no claims bonus?

2 An art dealer paid £4000 for a painting and sold it at a 15% loss. What was the selling price?

3 Tax at 25% is paid on a company's profits of £90 000

How much tax do they pay?

4 My accountant charges me 45% of the amount that he saves my company over the year. If I paid him £675 this year how much has he saved my company?

5 The bill including service at 15% came to £48.30

What would the bill have been without the service added?

6 The number of Labour councillors in our local council rose by 5% at the last local election. Previously, there were 60 Labour councillors. How many are there now?

7 The library charges have risen by 11%. The charge is now 12p per book per day. What was the charge before the rise?

8 In hot weather the volume of air can expand by up to 10%. If I need a maximum of 16 litres of air in my tyres when they are hot, how many cubic centimetres of cold air should I put in?

Simple interest

When you put money into a bank or building society, you are rewarded by receiving **interest**. However, if you borrow money from a bank or building society interest is charged and you pay back more than you borrowed. The interest that you are charged for borrowing money is calculated at a higher **rate** than the interest you are allowed on savings.

Examples

(i) I put £150 into my savings account and I receive 3% interest at the end of the year. How much money did I have in my account at the end of the year?

Original amount = £150 Interest = 3% Multiplying factor = 1.03

Amount in account = 103% of £150

$= 1.03 \times 150$

$= £154.50$

(ii) I pay £205 for clothes and I use my credit card. I find I have to pay £229.60. What rate of interest have I been charged?

Original amount = £205 New amount = £229.60 Increase = £24.60

$$\text{Interest rate} = \frac{\text{increase}}{\text{original amount}} \times 100\%$$

$$= \frac{229.6 - 205}{205} \times 100\%$$

$$= \frac{24.6}{205} \times 100\%$$

$$= 12\%$$

I have been charged 12% interest.

(iii) I borrowed a sum of money for a year at 7% interest. I had to pay back a total of £481.50. How much money did I borrow?

New amount = £481.50 Interest = 7% Multiplying factor = 1.07

$$\text{Original amount} = \frac{\text{new amount}}{\text{muliplying factor}}$$

$$= \frac{481.5}{1.07}$$

$$= £450$$

Exercise 5.7

In this exercise, take care to identify what exactly you need to calculate: the new amount, the interest rate or the original amount.

1 I pay £99 for games equipment on my credit card. I find I have to pay back a total of £113.85. What rate of interest have I been charged?

2 My uncle put £250 into my savings account. I receive 2.5% interest at the end of the year. How much money did I have in my account at the end of the year?

3 My brother checked his bank account and found that he had been charged 5% interest on a bank loan and he now has to pay back £630. How much money did he borrow?

4 An investment of £50 000 is left for a year in an account that pays 3.5% interest. How much will the investment earn in the year?

5 A couple want to borrow some money to buy a house. Their building society will charge them 4.2% interest. If they have to pay back £312 600 in total, how much are they borrowing?

6 A loan company lent a customer £1250. At the end of the year the customer had to repay a total of £1500, to include the interest. What interest rate was he charged?

7 My building society paid 2.75% interest in 2014 and 2.85% interest in 2015. If I had £422.71 in my account in January 2016. How much did I have in my account in January 2015? How much did I have in January 2014?

8 **(a)** I found out that my great-aunt put £100 into a building society account for me when I was born. Everyone then forgot about it. The money has been earning 3% interest per year. How much money do I have in my account on my thirteenth birthday?

(b) However, I discovered that because I am under 18 and not earning a salary, I am entitled to extra interest of 1% per annum. What is the amount that I now receive on my thirteenth birthday?

Extension: Compound interest

Look again at question 8 in the last exercise. Look at the situation in more detail.

If I invest £100 for a year at 3% at the end of the year I will have £100 $\times$ 1.03 in my account.

If I keep that amount in my account for another year at the same interest rate I will have ((£100 $\times$ 1.03) $\times$ 1.03) in my account.

This amount can be written as £100 $\times$ 1.03^2

If I keep this amount in my account for a third year, at the same interest rate, I will then have (100 $\times$ 1.03^2) $\times$ 1.03) in the account.

This amount can be written as £100 $\times$ 1.03^3

If this then continues for 13 years then the amount in the account will total:

£100 $\times$ 1.03^{13}

You can use a calculator to work this out.

Find the power button on your calculator, it may look like this $x^{\blacksquare}$.

It may be slightly different and it may be a second function.

You work out 1.03^{13} by entering 1.03 then pressing the $x^{\blacksquare}$ button, then entering 13 and finally = to get the answer.

If this does not work, ask your teacher for help or refer to the calculator manual.

You should get the answer 1.468 533 713...

Then multiply by 100 to get the final amount £146.85 (to 2 d.p.).

You could do the whole calculation in one sequence, by entering 100 then [×] and then open brackets [(], followed by 1.03 then the [$x^{■}$] button and 13, then close the brackets [)]. Finally, press [=] and you should get the answer 146.853 371 3...

In question 8(b) the interest rate has increased by 1% and is now 4%. So you repeat the calculation, using 1.04 instead of 1.03. This time your answer should be 166.507 350 7...

Warning: A common mistake is to increase the first answer 146.853 371 3... by 1% but, as you should be able to see, this does not give the correct answer. It is always important to work out percentage problems from first principles.

The interest gained over several years, by adding it to the amount invested, is called **compound interest.** If C is the capital invested, at x% for n years then the formula for the amount received at the end of that period is:

$$\text{new amount} = C\times\left(1+\frac{x}{100}\right)^n$$

Example

If £150 is invested for 10 years at 5%, how much is in the bank after 10 years?

$$\text{new amount} = C\times\left(1+\frac{x}{100}\right)^n$$

$$= 150 \times 1.05^{10}$$

$$= £244.334\,19$$

$$= £244.33 \text{ (to 2 d.p.)}$$

Extension Exercise 5.8

1 Great-aunt Flo invested £500 on the birth of baby Renata. The interest rate was fixed at 3.5%.

Calculate how much will be in the bank when Renata is:

(a) five years old
(b) ten years old
(c) 18 years old
(d) 21 years old.

2 Banks pay higher interest for larger deposits. Suppose I invest £6000 in a bank at a fixed interest rate of 4%. Calculate the amount that will be in the bank after:

(a) one year
(b) three years
(c) five years.

3 The value of a car falls by 12% each year. A car cost £12 000 when it was new.

(a) Write down what it will be worth when it is:

(i) two years old

(ii) five years old

(iii) ten years old.

(b) What does the car actually lose in value in its first year?

(c) What does the car actually lose in value in its tenth year?

4 I receive an annual salary of £20 000 when I start a new job.

(a) If my pay increases at a steady rate of 5% per annum, what should I be earning in 5 years' time?

(b) How many years will it take for my salary to double to £40 000 per annum?

(c) If I am 30 years old now and my salary continues to increase at the same rate, will I ever receive £60 000 before I retire at 65 years old?

(d) What salary will I be receiving before I retire?

5 (a) The population of China was expanding at 10% per annum. How many years did it take for the population to double?

(b) After strict population controls the population of China started to fall by 2% per annum. How many years will it take to halve the size of the population?

6 Assuming an average inflation rate of 5%, write down the probable cost in ten year's time of:

(a) a family car (now £6500)

(b) a television (now £350)

(c) a kilogram of best rump steak (now £10)

Assuming the same rate of inflation, what would the cost of these items have been ten years ago?

7 (a) Draw the graph of $y = 1.05^x$, taking values of x from 0 to 10

(b) With an average interest rate of 5%, use your graph to find how many years it will be for a price to rise by:

(i) a quarter (ii) a half (iii) a third.

(c) Will the answer depend on the original price of the goods? Explain your answer.

Summary Exercise 5.9

1 I scored 63 marks out of 80 for my mathematics test. What is this as a percentage?

2 Last year I spent 1 hour and 30 minutes on my homework each night. This year I have to spend 25% longer. How much time do I now spend on homework?

3 We collected 12% fewer apples from our garden this year. Last year we collected 308 kg. How many apples did we collect this year?

4 Fred estimated that there were 500 words in his English essay. He then counted and found there were 524 words. What was the percentage error of his estimate?

5 In a sale, prices of all items are reduced by 25%.

(a) If the price of a leather jacket was normally £175, what would the sale price be?

(b) The price of a jumper in the sale was £11.80. What was its original price?

6 (a) The value of the Boshida laptop has dropped by 25%. The old price was £630. What is the new price?

(b) When the Boshida laptop first came out VAT was 17.5%. It is now 20%. If the price before VAT was £500, what difference did the change in VAT make to the price?

(c) The new model Boshida laptop version 2 is sold for £999.99.

How much of this is VAT at 20%. Give your answer to the nearest penny.

7 My monthly allowance has risen by 40%. If it is now £28 per month, what was it before?

8 The value of my house has dropped by 12% in the last year. I am told that it is worth £340 800 now. What was my house worth a year ago?

9 My journey to work at my usual speed takes 20 minutes. How long will my journey take if I increase my speed by 25%?

10 I had £2000 in the bank at the start of last year. Last year the interest rate was 4% and this year it has dropped to 3.5%. How much money will I have in the bank at the end of this year?

Activity: Calculator maze

Look at this calculator maze.

You have £100 at the start. As you take each path you either lose or win the percentage shown. The amount is added to your initial amount.

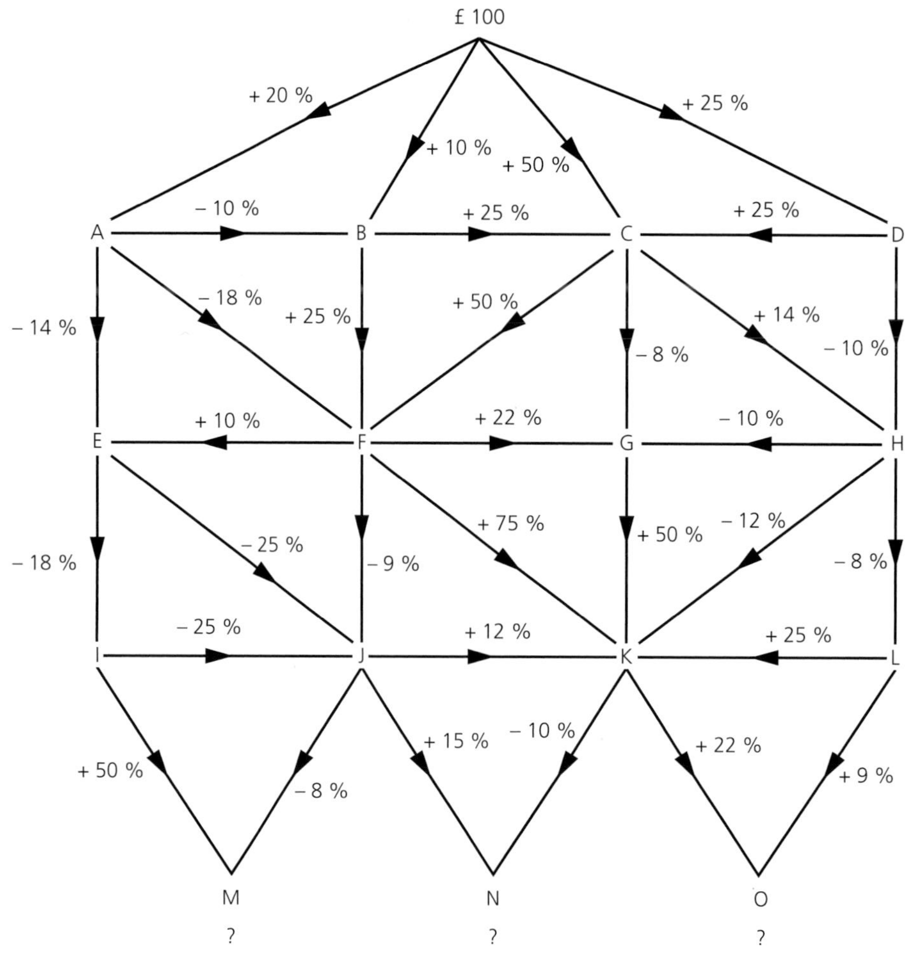

(a) Find the path that will give you the highest final amount.

(i) Write down the path.

(ii) Write down your final amount.

(b) Find the path that will give you the closest value to £500

(i) Write down the path.

(ii) Write down your final amount.

6 Equations and inequalities

Solving equations

In this chapter you are going to solve some equations of increasing difficulty before moving on to solving inequalities. First, note two important points when you are solving equations.

- Keep the equation balanced; whatever you do to one side you must do to the other.
- Show what you are doing to both sides clearly in brackets.

Examples

(i) Solve the equation: $a - 5 = 3$

(+ 5) $a - 5 = 3$ (+ 5)

$a = 8$

Check: $8 - 5 = 3$

(ii) Solve the equation: $\frac{x}{3} = 2$

(× 3) $\frac{x}{3} = 2$ (× 3)

$x = 6$

Check: $6 \div 3 = 2$

Sometimes it will take two or more stages to solve the equation.

Remember that your answer may be negative or a fraction.

Examples

(i) Solve the equation: $\frac{x}{3} + 5 = 2$

(– 5) $\frac{x}{3} + 5 = 2$ (– 5)

(× 3) $\frac{x}{3} = {}^{-}3$ (× 3)

$x = {}^{-}9$

Check: ${}^{-}9 \div 3 + 5 = 2$

(ii) Solve the equation: $4b - 5 = 6$

(+ 5) $4b - 5 = 6$ (+ 5)

(÷ 4) $4b = 11$ (÷ 4)

$b = \frac{11}{4}$

$b = 2\frac{3}{4}$

Check: $4 \times 2\frac{3}{4} - 5 = 6$

Remember that the summary of actions applies to both sides of the equation every time. When you are confident with this, you can just write it down the right-hand side.

It may take three or even more stages to solve some equations. Always try to keep the x-term positive and if there are brackets, then multiply them out first.

Remember to do the mental check to make sure your answer is correct.

Examples

(i) Solve the equation: $4 - 5z = 7 - z$

$4 - 5z = 7 - z$ (+ 5z)

$4 = 7 + 4z$ (– 7)

${}^{-}3 = 4z$ (÷ 4)

$\frac{{}^{-}3}{4} = z$

$z = \frac{{}^{-}3}{4}$

Check: $4 - \frac{{}^{-}15}{4} = 7\frac{3}{4}$; $7 - \frac{{}^{-}3}{4} = 7\frac{3}{4}$

(ii) Solve the equation: $4 - (5 - 2x) = 3(5 + 2x) - x$

$4 - (5 - 2x) = 3(5 + 2x) - x$ (B) B stands for multiply out brackets

$4 - 5 + 2x = 15 + 6x - x$ (S) S stands for simplify

${}^{-}1 + 2x = 15 + 5x$ (– 2x)

${}^{-}1 = 15 + 3x$ (– 15)

${}^{-}16 = 3x$ (÷ 3)

$\frac{{}^{-}16}{3} = x$

$x = {}^{-}5\frac{1}{3}$

Check: $4 - (5 - 2 \times ({}^{-}5\frac{1}{3})) = 4 - (5 + 10\frac{2}{3}) = {}^{-}11\frac{2}{3}$

$3(5 + 2 \times ({}^{-}5\frac{1}{3})) - ({}^{-}5\frac{1}{3}) = 3(5 - 10\frac{2}{3}) + 5\frac{1}{3} = 15 - 32 + 5\frac{1}{3} = {}^{-}11\frac{2}{3}$

Exercise 6.1

Here is a warm up exercise. The number of stages involved in solving the equations increases, as in the examples above.

1 $3 + a = 11$

2 $2 = b - 5$

3 $9c = 15$

4 $\frac{x}{4} = 8$

5 $5y + 1 = 7$

6 $9 + \frac{x}{4} = 3$

7 $7 = 2z - 8$

8 $11 = 7 - s$

9 $5x + 4 = 2x + 7$

10 $3 - 2y = 9 + y$

11 $2x + 4 = 6 - x$

12 $5 - 7a = 10 - 2a$

13 $3(c + 4) = 2(c - 1)$

14 $5x + (4 - x) = 3(x - 1)$

15 $3 - (y + 4) = 4y - 1$

16 $5a - 3(3 - 2a) = 2(a + 1)$

17 $\frac{1}{3}(z - 5) = 3$

18 $8 = \frac{3x - 5}{2}$

19 $\frac{3}{5}(y - 2) = 4$

20 $\frac{5x}{4} - 4 = 2x$

Using algebra to solve problems

By now, you should be quite proficient in solving equations in various forms. The ability to solve equations is a very useful skill. You will often have to solve problems that involve an unknown quantity. The most efficient way to do this is to represent the unknown quantity by a letter such as x and then form an equation and solve it.

Make sure that you define your unknown (x) carefully at the beginning of your solution. When you have your answer, check it by putting the value you have found back into the original problem. Remember always to answer the question and to express the answers in the correct units if appropriate.

Questions often involve ages. Look carefully at the next example and see how the solution is constructed.

First, write the two ages in terms of x

Second, write the ages in ten years' time in terms of x

Finally, write down the equation and solve it.

It can be helpful to write down a few simple expressions, relating to the information you are given, before writing the equation.

Example

My mother's age is three times my age. In ten years' time my age will be half my mother's age. How old am I?

Let my age now be x years.

Now if my age is x my mother's age is $3x$

In ten years' time my age will be $x + 10$, my mother's age will be $3x + 10$

$$3x + 10 = 2(x + 10) \quad \text{(B)}$$

$$3x + 10 = 2x + 20 \quad (-\,2x)$$

$$x + 10 = 20 \quad (-\,10)$$

$$x = 10$$

I am ten years old.

Exercise 6.2

1 My age is a. Write an expression in a for the age of:

- (a) my brother, who is ten years younger than I am
- (b) my sister, who is four years older than I am
- (c) myself, five years ago
- (d) myself, in nine years' time
- (e) my brother in nine years' time
- (f) my sister five years ago.

2 My brother is ten years younger than I am. In nine years' time I will be twice as old as my brother. Using two of your answers above, form an equation in x and solve it to find my age now.

3 My age is x. Write an expression in x for:

- (a) my father's age, given that my father is four times my age
- (b) my age in six years' time
- (c) my father's age in six years' time.

4 My father is four times my age. In six years time my father will be three times as old as I am. Using two of your answers from above, form an equation and solve it to find my father's age.

5 My sister is 2 years older than I am. My father is four times as old as my sister. Given that I am y years old, find in terms of y:

- (a) my sister's age
- (b) my father's age.

My father is five times as old as I am.

- (c) Form an equation in y and solve it to find my age.

6 My mother is three times as old as I am and my father is four times as old as I am.

(a) Given that I am x years old find, in terms of x:

(i) my mother's age

(ii) my father's age.

(b) My father is 9 years older than my mother. Form an equation in x and solve it to find my age.

7 My brother is four years younger than I am. Four years ago I was twice his age.

(a) Given that my age now is a years find, in terms of a:

(i) my brother's age now

(ii) my age 4 years ago

(iii) my brother's age 4 years ago.

(b) Form an equation in a and solve it to find my brother's age now.

8 In 12 years' time I will be twice as old as I am now. How old am I now?

9 Eight years ago I was half as old as I am now. How old am I now?

10 In 24 years' time I will be three times as old as I am now. How old am I now?

Problem solving

The questions in the next exercise do not involve ages but you can use the same method as before to answer them.

Exercise 6.3

1 A farmer goes to market and buys some chickens. The following week he goes to market again and buys more chickens. This time he buys four more than he bought in the previous week. He also buys lots of ducklings; in fact, he bought twice as many ducklings as chickens that week.

(a) Let the number of chickens that he bought the first week be c. Work out, in terms of c:

(i) the number of chickens he bought the second week

(ii) the number of ducklings he bought the second week.

(b) The total number of chickens and ducklings he bought the second week is four times the total number of chickens he bought the first week. Form an equation in c and solve it.

(c) How many ducklings did he buy?

2 In a bag of marbles there are four times as many red marbles as yellow marbles, and three times as many green marbles as red marbles.

(a) Let the number of yellow marbles be y. Work out, in terms of y:

(i) the number of red marbles in the bag

(ii) the number of green marbles in the bag.

(b) Given that there are 34 marbles in the bag, form an equation in y and solve it to find the number of yellow marbles in the bag.

3 My brother, my sister and I were picking strawberries. I picked 3 kg more than my sister, but my brother picked twice as many as I did.

(a) Let the number of kilograms that I picked be x. Work out, in terms of x:

(i) the number of kilograms my sister picked

(ii) the number of kilograms my brother picked.

(b) Given that we picked 21 kg altogether, form an equation in x and solve it to find how many kilograms of strawberries my sister picked.

4 A company makes Widgets and Fidgits. They make 4p more profit on Widgets than they do on Fidgits.

(a) The profit on a Fidgit is f pence. Work out, in terms of f:

(i) the profit on one Widget

(ii) the profit on 100 Fidgits

(iii) the profit on 200 Widgets.

(b) For every batch of 100 Fidgits and 200 Widgets the company makes £23 in total. Form an equation in f and solve it to find the profit on each Widget and each Fidgit.

5 I have dripped juice over my maths prep and cannot read the questions clearly. They now look like this.

(a) A plant was cm high. It has grown 10%. What is its new height?

(b) My pocket money was p and has risen by 20%. What is it now?

(c) After a 10% rise I now earn £ for my paper round. What did I earn before?

(d) My puppy eats more and more each week. This week he ate kg of 'Doggyo' which is 25% more than last week. How much did he eat last week?

I called my friend Freda for help. Freda says the answers are:

(a) 35.2 cm (b) £6 (c) £15 (d) 4 kg.

It was helpful to have the answers but my teacher expects me to show all my working. Write down how you could replace each by x and work out the exact question.

For each of the next questions, form an equation in x and solve it to find the answer to the question.

6 This year, there are five more boys in the school than there are girls. Altogether there are 195 pupils in the school. How many are girls?

7 In any one day I spend a third of it asleep, I spend four times as much time at school as I spend on my homework, one hour watching television and three hours doing everything else. How much time do I spend on my homework?

8 My class want to raise £250 for charity. We are going to do this by washing cars. The cost of materials is £15 for all the cloths and brushes, then 75p per car for shampoo. The headmaster says we can only charge £5 per car. How many cars do we have to wash to raise £250?

9 In science we are using a balance to weigh chemicals. Given that 5 mg and three measures of chemical A have the same mass as 2 mg and eight measures of chemical A, what is the mass of one measure of chemical A?

10 The average height of the 18 boys in my class is 10 cm more than the average height of the 20 boys in the class below. The total of all the heights of the 18 boys in my class is 100 cm less than the total height of the 20 boys in the class below. What is the average height of my class?

Equations with fractions

You are familiar with the rule 'multiply out brackets first' when solving equations, but what happens when the term in brackets is multiplied by a fraction.

For example, how could you work out $\frac{1}{3}(2x + 1) = 5$?

You could multiply each term inside the brackets by the fraction but that would give:

$$\frac{2x}{3} + \frac{1}{3} = 5$$

which is not a very inviting calculation.

It is much better to **multiply both sides** of the equation by the denominator of the fraction first ($\times$ 3), giving:

$$2x + 1 = 15$$

This is a much simpler equation to solve.

Example

Solve the equation: $\frac{1}{3}(2x + 1) = 5$

$$\frac{1}{3}(2x + 1) = 5 \quad (\times 3)$$

$$2x + 1 = 15 \quad (-1)$$

$$2x = 14 \quad (\div 2)$$

$$x = 7$$

Exercise 6.4

Solve these equations, which all involve fractions. Remember to multiply both sides of the equation by the denominator first.

1 $\frac{x}{3} = 4$

2 $\frac{1}{4}x = 3$

3 $\frac{2x}{5} = 4$

4 $\frac{3}{4}x = 6$

5 $\frac{(x+2)}{3} = 4$

6 $\frac{(2x-3)}{5} = 2$

7 $\frac{1}{5}(4-3x) = 4$

8 $\frac{(3-4x)}{2} = x$

9 $\frac{1}{4}(2-x) = x$

10 $\frac{2(2x-1)}{3} = x$

Multiple terms

Towards the end of the last exercise, some of the equations had the unknown in more than one term. These occurred on both sides of the equals sign. You need to be able to solve equations in which this happens.

Example

Solve the equation: $\frac{x}{4} + 3 = 2x$

It is still correct to follow the general rule, multiply both sides by the denominator, but be careful to multiply **every term** on each side of the equals sign by the denominator.

$$\frac{x}{4} + 3 = 2x \quad (\times 4)$$

$$\frac{\cancel{4} \times x}{\cancel{4}} + 4 \times 3 = 4 \times 2x \quad \text{(cancel)}$$

$$x + 12 = 8x \quad (-x)$$

$$12 = 7x \quad (\div 7)$$

$$\frac{12}{7} = x$$

$$x = 1\frac{5}{7}$$

Sometimes you may need to add brackets before you multiply.

Example

Solve the equation: $\frac{2}{3}(x + 4) = 3x - 4$

$$\frac{2}{3}(x + 4) = 3x - 4 \quad (\times 3)$$
$$2(x + 4) = 3(3x - 4) \quad (B)$$
$$2x + 8 = 9x - 12 \quad (-2x)$$
$$8 = 7x - 12 \quad (+12)$$
$$20 = 7x \quad (\div 7)$$
$$\frac{20}{7} = x$$
$$x = 2\frac{6}{7}$$

Exercise 6.5

Solve these equations

1 $\frac{x}{3} + 1 = 4$

2 $\frac{x}{5} - 3 = 1$

3 $\frac{x}{2} + 3 = x$

4 $\frac{x}{7} - 3 = x$

5 $4 + \frac{x}{2} = 3$

6 $4 - \frac{x}{5} = x$

7 $\frac{x}{3} = 14 + x$

8 $\frac{1}{3}x = 4 - 2x$

9 $\frac{2x}{3} + 3 = 2$

10 $4 - \frac{3x}{5} = 2x$

11 $\frac{2x}{5} = x + 2$

12 $\frac{3}{4} = 3x - 5$

13 $\frac{1}{3}(x + 3) = x + 2$

14 $\frac{3}{5}(2x + 3) = 2 - 3x$

15 $2x + 1 = \frac{2x}{7} - 2$

16 $\frac{2(3 + 2x)}{5} = 3x - 2$

Inexact answers

Many problems in mathematics have just one exact answer, such as $4 \times 7 = 28$

Other problems have a range of possible answers.

For example: 'It takes me between 10 and 15 minutes to get to school.'

I could write this as:

$10 \leqslant$ time to get to school $\leqslant 15$

Remember that:

- $>$ means 'is greater than'
- $<$ means ' is less than'
- $\geqslant$ means 'is greater than or equal to'
- $\leqslant$ means 'is less than or equal to'.

Consider this **inequality**:

$2 < x < 5$

This is mathematical shorthand for: x is greater than 2 but less than 5

You can show this on the number line.

The integer values of x that satisfy this inequality are 3 and 4

Consider this pair of inequalities:

$x < {}^{-}1 \qquad x \geqslant 4$

These mean that x is less than ${}^{-}1$, or x is greater than or equal to 4

This can be shown on the number line; note that a hollow circle represents $<$ or $>$ and a solid circle represents $\leqslant$ or $\geqslant$
In this case the hollow circle represents $<$

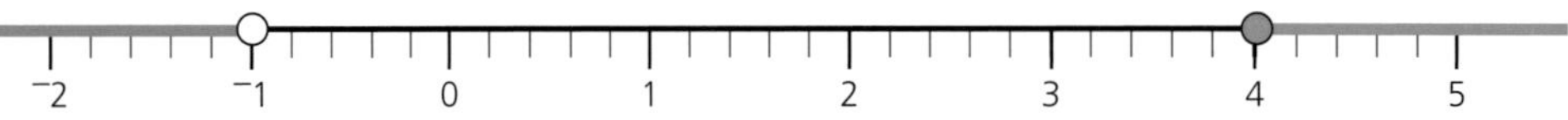

Note that there are **no values** of x that satisfy this pair of inequalities simultaneously.

Example

Show the inequality $4 \leqslant x < 7$ on a number line and list all the integer solutions.

$x = 4, 5$ or 6

Exercise 6.6

Give all the possible integer values of x that satisfy each inequality.

Show the range on a number line.

1 $3 \leqslant x < 6$

2 $1 \leqslant x \leqslant 4$

3 $5 < x \leqslant 8$

4 $0 < x < 5$

5 $^-2 \leqslant x < 3$

6 $^-5 > x \geqslant {}^-7$

7 $3 \geqslant x > {}^-1$

8 $2 \geqslant x > {}^-2$

9 $x \geqslant 4$ or $x < 8$

10 $x < 10$ or $x \geqslant 5$

Solving inequalities

An **inequality** is written like an equation, but uses an inequality ($<$, $>$, $\leqslant$ or $\geqslant$) sign instead of an equals ($=$) sign. To solve an inequality, you follow the same steps that you use when solving equations.

Examples

(i) Solve the inequality: $4a > 24$

$4a > 24$ (÷ 4)

$a > 6$

(ii) Solve the inequality: $b - 4 > 6$

$b - 4 > 6$ (+ 4)

$b > 10$

Exercise 6.7

Solve each inequality.

1 $3x < 6$

2 $5y \geqslant 15$

3 $7z \geqslant 21$

4 $14 < \frac{x}{2}$

5 $21 \geqslant 3a$

6 $b + 4 < 6$

7 $4 + c < 5$

8 $3s + 7 > 9$

9 $3 + 2t \geqslant 5$

10 $7 < v - 4$

11 $\frac{x}{3} - 2 \leqslant 7$

12 $3 + \frac{x}{4} > 3$

13 $14 \geqslant 6 + \frac{x}{3}$

14 $5 \leqslant \frac{x}{5} + 3$

Inequalities with negatives

You solved the inequalities in the previous exercise by adding or subtracting positive integers on both sides, or by multiplying or dividing both sides by positive integers.

Now consider the inequality: $4 > 1$

What happens when you apply a negative number, such as $^{-}2$?

- $4 > 1$ Add $^{-}2$ to both sides. $4 + (^{-}2) > 1 + (^{-}2) \rightarrow 2 > {}^{-}1$ ✓
- $4 > 1$ Subtract $^{-}2$ from both sides. $4 - (^{-}2) > 1 - (^{-}2) \rightarrow 6 > 3$ ✓
- $4 > 1$ Multiply both sides by $^{-}2$ $4 \times (^{-}2) > 1 \times (^{-}2) \rightarrow {}^{-}8 > {}^{-}2$ ✗
- $4 > 1$ Divide both sides by $^{-}2$ $4 \div (^{-}2) > 1 \div (^{-}2) \rightarrow {}^{-}2 > {}^{-}\frac{1}{2}$ ✗

This time the resulting inequalities are **not** all true.

$^{-}8$ is **not greater** than $^{-}2$ but less and $^{-}2$ is **not greater** than $^{-}\frac{1}{2}$ but less.

Multiplying or dividing an inequality by a negative constant **reverses** the inequality:

If $^{-}x > 4$ then $x < {}^{-}4$

You know that it is sensible to keep the x-term positive when solving equations. This is particularly true when solving inequalities, as it avoids complications.

Examples

(i) Solve the inequality: $7 - 2x > 6$

$$7 - 2x > 6 \quad (+\,2x)$$
$$7 > 6 + 2x \quad (-\,6)$$
$$1 > 2x \quad (\div\,2)$$
$$\frac{1}{2} > x$$
$$x < \frac{1}{2}$$

(ii) Solve the inequality: $3 - \frac{x}{4} \leqslant 4$

$$3 - \frac{x}{4} \leqslant 4 \quad (\times\,4)$$
$$12 - x \leqslant 16 \quad (+\,x)$$
$$12 \leqslant 16 + x \quad (-\,16)$$
$${}^{-}4 \leqslant x$$
$$x \geqslant {}^{-}4$$

Exercise 6.8

Solve each inequality.

1 $3 + 2x < 4$

2 $5 > 3 - 4x$

3 $3 - 2x \leqslant 7 + 3x$

4 $3 + 4x > 7x - 5$

5 $16 \geqslant 4 - \frac{x}{3}$

6 $4 + \frac{3x}{4} > 9$

7 $7 - 3 \leqslant 5x - 1$

8 $\frac{x}{4} - 1 > 6$

9 $8 - \frac{x}{3} \geqslant 5$

10 $5 < 6 - \frac{x}{2}$

11 $x + 5 \leqslant 2$

12 $7 - \frac{3x}{5} < 3$

13 $4 + 2x < 9 - 2x$

14 $3 + 4(x - 3) > x$

15 $5 - 2(x + 5) \leqslant 3x$

16 $3(x - 4) > 5(4 - 2x)$

17 You are told that $x > {}^{-}5$

(a) What is the smallest perfect square that x could be?

(b) What is the smallest prime number that x could be?

18 Consider the inequality $10 \leqslant x < 26$. Give the value of x if x is:

(a) odd and square

(b) even and a triangular number

(c) a factor of 90 and a multiple of 9

(d) prime and a factor of 299

19 (a) Solve this inequality: $9 - 3x > 2 - x$

(b) Give two prime numbers that satisfy the inequality.

20 (a) Solve this inequality $2(3x + 2) < 4 - 3(2 - x)$

(b) Write down any numbers from the box that satisfy the inequality.

$^{-}3$	$^{-}2$	2	4

Extension: Equations with two fractions

You know how to solve equations that include one fraction and thus only one denominator. What happens when an equation has two fractions?

If there is only one x-term in the fraction then you do not need to multiply out both fractions, just the fraction on the same side as the x-term.

Example

Solve the equation: $\frac{3x}{4} = \frac{2}{5}$

$$\frac{3x}{4} = \frac{2}{5} \qquad (\times 4)$$

$$\frac{4 \times 3x}{4} = \frac{2 \times 4}{5} \qquad \text{(Simplify)}$$

$$3x = \frac{8}{5} \qquad (\div 3)$$

$$x = \frac{8}{15}$$

When the terms in one or both fractions are not simply multiples of x, you need to multiply **every term** by both denominators. You may need to add brackets.

Example

Solve the equation: $\frac{4}{x+2} = \frac{3}{5-x}$

$$\frac{4}{x+2} = \frac{3}{5-x} \qquad (\times (x+2)(5-x))$$

$$\frac{4 \times (5-x)\cancel{(x+2)}}{\cancel{x+2}} = \frac{3 \times \cancel{(5-x)}(x+2)}{\cancel{5-x}} \qquad \text{(Cancel) and (B)}$$

$$20 - 4x = 3x + 6 \qquad (+4x)$$

$$20 = 7x + 6 \qquad (-6)$$

$$14 = 7x \qquad (\div 7)$$

$$2 = x$$

$$x = 2$$

Extension Exercise 6.9

Solve these equations.

1 $\frac{2x}{3} = \frac{1}{4}$

2 $\frac{3x}{4} = \frac{2}{5}$

3 $\frac{3}{7}x = \frac{2}{5}$

4 $\frac{2}{3} = \frac{3x}{5}$

5 $\frac{3}{4} = \frac{4x}{9}$

6 $\frac{x}{3} = \frac{5}{6}$

7 $\frac{x}{4} + 2 = \frac{x}{3}$

8 $\frac{2x}{3} - 7 = \frac{x}{5}$

9 $\frac{3x}{4} - 2 = \frac{2}{3}$

10 $\frac{5}{x+3} = \frac{2}{1-x}$

11 $\frac{2x-3}{5} = \frac{x}{2}$

12 $\frac{x}{4} + 2 = \frac{1}{3}$

13 $\frac{x}{x+3} = \frac{3}{5}$

14 $\frac{3x}{5} = \frac{1}{3} - 4x$

Extension: Alien algebra

Out in the galaxy there is an alien race that uses symbols in a different way from us. See if you can solve these alien problems.

Extension Exercise 6.10

1 The symbol ▲ between two numbers means 'greater than half of'. Then:

5 ▲ 8 is true, because 5 is more than 4, half of 8

5 ▲ 10 is not true, because 5 is equal to 5, half of 10

5 ▲ 12 is not true, because 5 is less than 6, half of 12

(a) State which of these statements are true. Explain each of your answers briefly.

(i) 2 ▲ 3

(ii) 2 ▲ 4

(iii) 19 ▲ 10

(iv) 3 ▲ 7

(v) 101 ▲ 200

(vi) 3 ▲ 3^2

(b) Now state which of these statements are always true. Explain each answer with a brief statement.

(i) x ▲ $x + 1$

(ii) x ▲ $2x$

(iii) x ▲ $2x + 1$

(iv) x ▲ $2x - 1$

(v) x ▲ $2(x + 1)$

(vi) x ▲ x^2

(c) In part **(b)** some statements were not always true but could sometimes be true. Give the range of values for x that would make those statements true.

2 The symbol ★ between two numbers means 'less than one more than half of'. Then:

4 ★ 8 is true, because 4 is less than 1 more than half of 8, $(8 \div 2 + 1 = 5)$

4 ★ 6 is not true, because 4 is equal to 1 more than half of 6 $(6 \div 2 + 1 = 4)$

4 ★ 4 is not true, because 4 is more than 1 more than half of 4 $(4 \div 2 + 1 = 3)$

(a) State which of these statements are true. Explain each answer with a brief statement.

(i) 4 ★ 7 **(iii)** 7 ★ 11 **(v)** 101 ★ 200

(ii) 3 ★ 5 **(iv)** 50 ★ 51 **(vi)** 5 ★ 5^2

(b) Now state which statements are always true. Explain each answer with a brief statement.

(i) x ★ $x + 1$ **(iii)** x ★ $2x + 1$ **(v)** x ★ $2(x + 1)$

(ii) x ★ $2x$ **(iv)** x ★ $2x - 1$ **(vi)** x ★ x^2

(c) In part **(b)** some statements were not always true but could sometimes be true. Give the range of values of x that would make those statements true.

Summary Exercise 6.11

1 Solve these equations.

(a) $3a + 2 = 5$ **(d)** $4x + 1 = 4 - 2x$

(b) $6 - 2b = 3$ **(e)** $3y - 1 = y + 9$

(c) $3(2c - 1) = 7$ **(f)** $\frac{1}{3}(2 - 3z) = 4$

2 My sister is three times as old as I am. Four years ago my sister was four times as old as I was. If my age now is a years, find, in terms of a:

(a) my sister's age now

(b) my age 4 years ago

(c) my sister's age four years ago.

(d) Now form an equation in a and solve it to find my sister's age now.

3 For the same amount of money I can buy either five sticks of liquorice and eight penny sweets or four sticks of liquorice and 12 penny sweets.

(a) Let the cost of a stick of liquorice be x pence. What is the cost, in terms of x, of five sticks of liquorice and eight penny sweets?

(b) What is the cost, in terms of x, of four sticks of liquorice and 12 penny sweets?

(c) Write an equation in x and solve it to find the cost of a stick of liquorice.

4 Solve these equations.

(a) $\frac{x}{3} + 5 = 2$

(b) $4 - \frac{2x}{3} = 1$

(c) $\frac{x}{4} = \frac{2}{3}$

(d) $\frac{1}{3}(2x + 4) = 3$

(e) $\frac{2x}{5} + 4 = x$

(f) $\frac{3}{4} = 3 - \frac{2x}{5}$

5 Find all the integer values of x that fit these inequalities. In each case show the range on a number line.

(a) $1 \leqslant x < 5$

(b) $^{-}3 < x \leqslant 1$

6 Solve each inequality and give three values of x that satisfy it.

(a) $2x - 7 < 1$

(b) $\frac{x}{5} \geqslant 3 - x$

(c) $3(2 - 3x) \geqslant 2 - (3x + 1)$

Activity: Polyhedral numbers

A **tetrahedron** is a triangular-based pyramid. A regular tetrahedron has a net of four equilateral triangles.

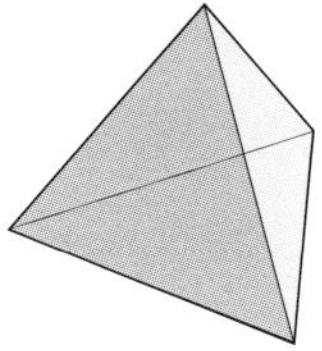

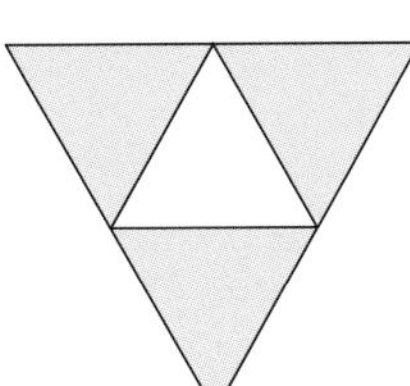

Tetrahedral numbers are made up from forming tetrahedrons from triangles:

1

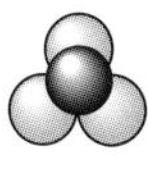

4

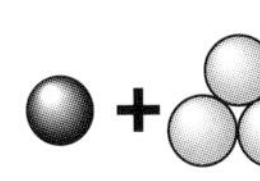

1+ 3 = 4

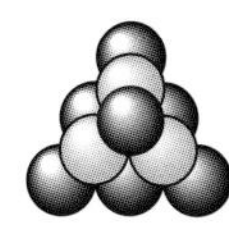

10

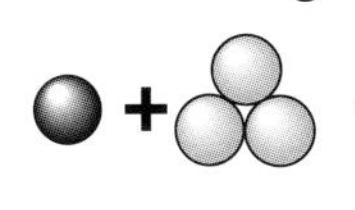

1 + 3 + 6 = 10

1 What are the set of numbers being added together called?

2 Copy this table and extend it by another three rows.

n		Tetrahedral number
1	1	1
2	1 + 3	4
3	1 + 3 + 6	10
4	1 + 3 + 6 + 10	
5	1 +	
6		
7		
8		

3 **(a)** What is the 10th tetrahedral number?

(b) What is the 100th tetrahedral number?

4 By considering the formula for the nth triangular number, or otherwise, find a formula for the nth tetrahedral number.

The next set of polyhedral numbers are those formed by square-based pyramids. The first such number will be 1, the second $1 + 4 = 5$, the third $1 + 4 + 9 = 14, \ldots$

The next set of polyhedral numbers will be those formed by the sum of the pentagonal numbers.

5 Investigate sets of polyhedral numbers and see what rules you can find. You might find it interesting to include Pascal's triangle as part of your investigation.

For example, Pascal's triangle

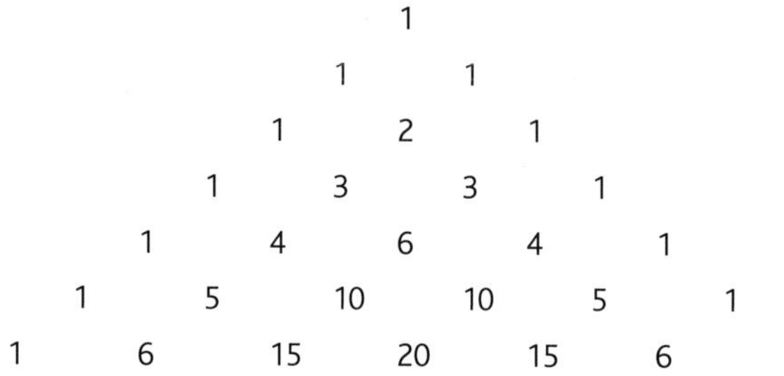

7 Indices in algebra

You have already learned about numbers with numerical indices. In this chapter you will look at using algebra with indices.

First, remember what you learned about indices and then see how you can apply the same rules to algebra.

Multiplication

Look at this expression: $2^3 \times 2^2$

You can simplify this as:

$$2^3 \times 2^2 = (2 \times 2 \times 2) \times (2 \times 2)$$
$$= 2^5$$
$$= 32$$

Similarly: $x^3 \times x^2 = (x \times x \times x) \times (x \times x)$

$$= x^5$$

Therefore the general rule is: $x^a \times x^b = x^{a+b}$

The rule is to add the index numbers even if there are more than two terms.

Exercise 7.1

Simplify these, leaving your answers in index form.

1 $x^2 \times x^5$

2 $b^3 \times b^3$

3 $a^4 \times a^3$

4 $2^3 \times 2^2 \times 2^4$

5 $2^a \times 2^b$

6 $3^2 \times 3^3$

7 $a^3 \times a^2 \times a^4$

8 $3^a \times 3^b$

9 $x^2 \times x^2 \times x^2$

10 $3^2 \times 3^2 \times 3^2$

11 $x^2 \times x^3 \times x$

12 $b^2 \times b^4 \times b$

13 $a \times a^5 \times a^2$

14 $2^x \times 2^y \times 2$

15 $a^x \times a^y$

16 $2^a \times 3^b$

17 $a \times a^y \times a^y \times a$

18 $x^a \times y^a$

19 $x \times x^x \times x^y$

20 $a^y \times b^y \times b^y$

Division

Look at these divisions.

$16 \div 4 = 4 \qquad 81 \div 3 = 27$

They can be written as:

$2^4 \div 2^2 = 2^2 \qquad 3^4 \div 3^1 = 3^3$

From these examples, it follows that the general rule is:

$x^a \div x^b = x^{a-b}$

The rule is to subtract the indices, even if the resulting index is 0

Exercise 7.2

Simpify these, giving your answers in index form.

1 $a^6 \div a^5$

2 $b^7 \div b^3$

3 $x^6 \div x^3$

4 $2^6 \div 2^3$

5 $3^x \div 3^y$

6 $a^5 \div a^4$

7 $x^5 \div x$

8 $5^3 \div 5^3$

9 $x^7 \div x^2$

10 $a^x \div a^x$

11 $4y^5 \div y$

12 $x^x \div x$

13 $4x^a \div 2x^3$

14 $3a^b \div 6a^c$

The power 0

Look again at the division $5^3 \div 5^3$

Using the above rule gives: $5^3 \div 5^3 = 5^0$

You know that if you divide a number by itself the answer is always 1

Thus: $5^0 = 1$

In general terms:

$$\begin{aligned} x^a \div x^a &= x^{a-a} \\ &= x^0 \\ &= 1 \end{aligned}$$

Negative index numbers

Remember that index numbers can be negative.

$10^{-2} = \frac{1}{10^2} = \frac{1}{100}$

Similarly $x^{-3} = \frac{1}{x^3}$

Exercise 7.3

Simplify these, giving your answers in index form.

1 $2^4 \div 2^7$
2 $a^3 \div a^6$
3 $x^2 \div x^5$
4 $x^7 \div x^7$
5 $7^a \div 7^b$
6 $x^4 \div x^5$
7 $b \div b^5$
8 $a^2 \div a^2$
9 $x^4 \div x^2$
10 $a^2 \div b^2$
11 $2x^2 \div x^3$
12 $a^3 \div 5a^6$
13 $y^6 \div 3y^3$
14 $4x^2 \div 16x^5$

Powers of powers

An expression containing an index number may itself be raised to a power.

Examples

(i) Simplify this expression: $(2^4)^2$

$(2^4)^2 = 2^4 \times 2^4$
$= (2 \times 2 \times 2 \times 2) \times (2 \times 2 \times 2 \times 2)$
$= 2^8$
$= 256$

(ii) Simplify this expression: $(x^4)^2$

$(x^4)^2 = x^4 \times x^4$
$= (x \times x \times x \times x) \times (x \times x \times x \times x)$
$= x^8$

In general terms: $(x^a)^b = x^{ab}$

You can take this a step further.

Example

Simplify: $(2^3)^2 \div (2^2)^2$

$(2^3)^2 \div (2^2)^2 = 2^6 \div 2^4$
$= 2^2$
$= 4$

In general terms $(x^a)^b \div (x^c)^d = x^{ab - cd}$

Exercise 7.4

Express these in index form.

1 $(3^4)^2$
2 $(2^3)^2$
3 $(x^3)^2$
4 $(a^3)^5$
5 $(2b^3)^2$
6 $(3a^3)^5$
7 $(4^a)^b$
8 $(x^m)^m$
9 $(3a^m)^2$
10 $(2x^m)^m$
11 $(3^2)^3 \div (3^2)^4$
12 $(4^4)^3 \div (4^2)^2$

13 $(2^2)^2 \div (2^2)^3$ 15 $(a^2)^4 \div (a^2)^2$ 17 $(2a^4)^3 \div (a^2)^3$ 19 $(3a^3)^3 \div (9a^2)^2$

14 $(x^3)^4 \div (3x^2)^3$ 16 $(x^2)^2 \div (3x^3)^3$ 18 $(4x^2)^2 \div (x^2)^2$ 20 $(3b^2)^3 \div (9b^2)^3$

Simplifying expressions with indices

You often need to simplify or combine expressions in algebra.

Examples

(i) Simplify this expression: $2x^2 \times 3x^3$

$2x^2 \times 3x^3 = 2 \times x \times x \times 3 \times x \times x \times x$

$= 6x^5$

(ii) Simplify this expression: $3ab^3 \times 4a^2$

$3ab^3 \times 4a^2 = 12a^3b^3$

Remember the different rules for adding or subtracting, and for multiplying or dividing.

You can add (or subtract) **like terms:**

$a^2b + a^2b + a^2b = 3a^2b$

$a^2b + 3a^2b + a^2b = 5a^2b$

but not **unlike terms:**

$ab + a^2b + ab^2 = ab + a^2b + ab^2$

This expression cannot be simplified.

You can multiply together **any** terms.

$a^2b \times a^2b \times a^2b = a^6b^3$

$ab \times a^2b \times ab^2 = a^4b^4$

Exercise 7.5

Simplify these expressions, if possible.

1 $a \times a^2 \times a^3$

2 $3a \times 2a^2 \times a^3$

3 $3b + b^2 + 2b^3$

4 $2b^2 + b^2 + 3b^2$

5 $2ab \times a^2b \times 3ab^2$

6 $4x^2y + x^2y + 3x^2y$

7 $4xy + x^2y - xy$

8 $4xy + x^2y - xy^2$

9 $3ac \times a^2b \times 4bc$

10 $2bc + a^2b + 4ac$

Fractions and powers

You can use the same methods to cancel or simplify a fraction in algebra as for a numerical fraction. Algebraic fractions may have common factors in the same way as ordinary fractions do.

Example

Simplify this expression: $3x^3y^2 \div 6xy$

$$3x^3y^2 \div 6xy = \frac{3x^3y^2}{6xy}$$

$$= \frac{\not{3} \times \not{x} \times x \times x \times \not{y} \times y}{\not{6}_2 \times \not{x} \times \not{y}}$$

$$= \frac{x^2y}{2}$$

3, x and y are all common factors.

Exercise 7.6

Simplify each expression if possible. Give your answers in their simplest form.

1 $\frac{3a^2b}{a}$

2 $\frac{3a^2b}{b}$

3 $\frac{6a^2b}{2b}$

4 $\frac{8xy^2}{2xy}$

5 $\frac{15xy}{3xy}$

6 $\frac{3a^2b}{5b}$

7 $\frac{3a^2b}{24b^3}$

8 $\frac{2mn}{8m^2n}$

9 $\frac{24x^2y^3}{15x^3y}$

10 $\frac{6b^5c^2}{9bc^3}$

11 $\frac{12x^3y^2}{4x^2y}$

12 $\frac{18a^3b^2}{6ab^3}$

13 $\frac{6x^2y^2}{4x^3y^2}$

14 $\frac{15a^2bc^3}{10ab^2c}$

15 $\frac{18x^3y^2z}{12x^2yz^2}$

Indices and brackets

When there is a number before a term in brackets, you know that you must multiply everything inside the brackets by that number.

Example

Simplify this expression: $2(3x + 4)$

$2(3x + 4) = 6x + 8$

When there is an x (or any other letter representing an unknown) outside the brackets, then you multiply through by x in the same way as for numbers.

Examples

(i) Simplify this expression: $x(x + 2)$

$x(x + 2) = x^2 + 2x$

(ii) Simplify this expression: $x(x^2 + 2x)$

$x(x^2 + 2x) = x^3 + 2x^2$

(iii) Simplify this expression: $x^2(x^2 + 2x)$

$x^2(x^2 + 2x) = x^4 + 2x^3$

Exercise 7.7

Multiply out the brackets.

1 $x(2x + 1)$

2 $x(3x - 1)$

3 $x(4 - 3x)$

4 $2x(x + 4)$

5 $3x(2x - 5)$

6 $x^2(x + 1)$

7 $x(x^2 + x - 1)$

8 $x^2(4 - 3x)$

9 $2x^2(3x - 2)$

10 $x^2(2x^2 + 3x + 4)$

11 $x^3(x^2 + 1)$

12 $3x^3(2x^2 - 4x + 3)$

More about brackets

When you multiply a bracket by a negative number the sign of each number or term inside the brackets will change.

Remember that multiplying by a negative changes the sign.

Example

Simplify this expression: $x(3x + 2) - 2x(x - 4)$

$$x(3x + 2) - 2x(x - 4) = 3x^2 + 2x - 2x^2 + 8x$$
$$= x^2 + 10x$$

Expressions may have more than one unknown.

Example

Simplify this expression: $2x(3x + y) - y(2x + y)$

$$2x(3x + y) - y(2x + y) = 6x^2 + 2xy - 2xy - y^2$$
$$= 6x^2 - y^2$$

Exercise 7.8

Multiply out the brackets and simplify each expression.

1 $x(2x + 1) + 2x(x - 3)$

2 $x(2x + 5) - x(x - 3)$

3 $x(3x - 1) + x(3 - x)$

4 $x(2 - x) - 2x(x + 1)$

5 $x(2x - 5) - 2x(4 - x)$

6 $3x(2x + 1) - 2x(x + 3)$

7 $2x(3x - 1) + 3x(x - 3)$

8 $2x(x - 3) - x(3x + 1)$

9 $x(3x + 4) - 2x(3 - 2x)$

10 $4x(3x - 1) - 2x(4 + 6x)$

11 $x(x + y) + y(x + y)$

12 $2x(3x + y) - 2y(x + 2y)$

13 $x(2x - y) + y(3x + 2y)$

14 $xy(2x + y) - y(3x^2 + xy)$

15 $x(3y - x) + 2x(3x + y)$

16 $xy^2(3x + 2) - x^2y(4 - 2y)$

17 $x^2(4 + 3y) - 4x(2x + 2xy)$

18 $xy(3y - 2x) - x^2(4y + y^2)$

19 $3x^3(2x - 3y + 1) - 2y(3x^3 + 4)$

20 $2x^2y(3x + 4y) - 3xy^2(2x + 3y)$

Factorising

In the last exercise you multiplied the term inside the brackets by a number or letter before the brackets.

Factorising is the reverse process. You take out a common factor from each term and write it outside the brackets.

- $6x^2 + 2y = 2(3x^2 + y)$ — 2 is the common factor.
- $6x^2 + 5xy = x(6x + 5y)$ — x is the common factor.
- $6x^2y + 3xy = 3xy(2x + 1)$ — $3xy$ is the common factor.
- $6x^2 + 5y$ — Does not factorise.

Exercise 7.9

Factorise these expressions if possible. Some of the first six questions have a number as a common factor.

1 $3x + 6$

2 $8y - 4$

3 $6 + 9x$

4 $18 - 4y$

5 $24x + 16$

6 $7x - 6$

Some of the next six questions have a letter as a common factor.

7 $x^2 + 5x$

8 $y^2 - 7y$

9 $3x + x^2$

10 $5x - y^2$

11 $x^3 + 2x$

12 $x^3 - 3x^2$

Some of the next six questions have both a number and a letter as common factors.

13 $2x^2 + 4x$

14 $6a - 9a^2$

15 $9xy + 6y^2 - 3y$

16 $9a^2 - 8b$

17 $12x^2 - 9xy + 6x$

18 $8ab - 4a^2$

Now try these. Remember that some may not factorise.

19 $3xy + 16x^2 + 4x$

20 $8a^2b + 14ab$

21 $8x^2 + 5y^2$

22 $12y^2 - 9y + 3x$

23 $12y + 8x^2y - 16y^2$

24 $3a^2 + 6b^2 - 2ab$

25 $12xy + 16x^2y - 4xy^2$

26 $14x^2 + 8xy + 3y^2$

27 $10xy + 14y^2 - 4$

28 $16x^2 - 12xy - 9$

29 $16x^2 - 14xy - 6x$

30 $20a^2b - 4ab^2 - 2b$

31 $20a^2b - 4ab^2 + 8ab$

32 $16xy^2 + 8x^2 - 2xy$

Factorising and fractions

You may be able to simplify an expression that is a fraction by factorising and then cancelling.

Example

Simplify this expression: $\frac{12m - 6m^2}{6m}$

$\frac{12m - 6m^2}{6m} = \frac{6m(2 - m)}{6m}$ 6m is a common factor.

$= 2 - m$

Exercise 7.10

Simplify each expression, if possible.

1 $\frac{2x - xy}{x}$

2 $\frac{xy - 3xy^2}{y}$

3 $\frac{3ab - 9a}{3}$

4 $\frac{5u^2v + 15uv^2}{5uv}$

5 $\frac{9x - 2y^2}{3}$

6 $\frac{6x^2 - 9xy}{3x}$

7 $\frac{4ab + b^3}{b}$

8 $\frac{7cd + 14d^2}{7c}$

9 $\frac{3p^2 - 9pq}{3p}$

10 $\frac{25mn - 10m^2}{15m}$

Extension: Trial and improvement

In previous work on solving problems, you were able to make an equation in an unknown, such as x, and then solve it.

The equations you make may not always be simple to solve.

Consider this problem.

My garden is rectangular. The length is 5 m greater than the width and the area is 130 m^2. Find the length and the width of the garden, correct to the nearest 10 cm.

Let the width of the garden be x

Then the length will be $x + 5$

An expression for the area would be $x(x + 5)$

The equation is:

$x(x + 5) = 130$

$x^2 + 5x = 130$

Because there is an x^2 in the equation, you cannot solve it in the usual way so you need a different method.

Trial and improvement methods work in the opposite way to normal equation solving. First you make an estimate of the answer, then substitute that answer into the equation, and see how accurate it is. Then you make a better estimate and try again.

You continue doing this until you have either the correct answer, or one that is very close to it. It is very important to record all your results so that you can use your earlier results to help you find the correct answer more quickly.

The best way to record your results is in a table. For the example above the table would look like this.

Width	Length	Area	Note
8	13	104	too small
9	14	126	too small
10	15	150	too big

Now you know that x lies between 9 and 10, and appears to be closer to 9. You will need to look at decimals. Start with numbers that have one decimal place.

Width	Length	Area	Note
9.1	14.1	128.31	too small
9.2	14.2	130.64	too big

You can now see that x lies between 9.1 and 9.2, and appears closer to 9.2. However, you have been asked to give an answer correct to one decimal place. You can only approximate to one decimal place from an answer written correct to two decimal places, so you need to continue the table with numbers with two decimal places.

Width	Length	Area	Note
9.15	14.15	129.4725	too small
9.16	14.16	129.7056	too small
9.17	14.17	129.9389	too small
9.18	14.18	130.1724	too big

The width is between 9.17 m and 9.18 m and so, to the nearest 10 cm, the garden is 9.2 m by 14.2 m.

However, you could have stopped at 9.15 because you know that the width is between 9.15 m and 9.20 m and so, to the nearest 10 cm, the width must be 9.2 m.

Here is a typical question and worked solution.

Example

I have a box with a square base. Its height is 5 cm greater than its width.

(i) Show that the volume of the box can be written as the expression $x^2(x + 5)$ where x is the width of the box.

(ii) Given that the volume of the box is 90 cm^3, use trial and improvement to find the value of x correct to one decimal place.

(i) If the width $= x$ cm

then the length $= x$ cm

and the height $= (x + 5)$ cm

so the volume $= x \times x \times (x + 5)$

$= x^2(x + 5)$

(ii) Draw up a table of values.

x	x^2	$(x + 5)$	Volume	Notes
3	9	8	72	too small
4	16	9	144	too big
3.5	12.25	8.5	104.125	too big
3.4	11.56	8.4	97.104	too big
3.3	10.89	8.3	90.387	too big
3.2	10.24	8.2	83.968	too small
3.25	10.562	8.25	87.140	too small

Therefore x lies between 3.25 and 3.30, and so: $x = 3.3$

and the width is 3.3 cm, correct to 1 decimal place.

Exercise 7.11

1 Solve these equations by trial and improvement, giving your answers correct to: **(i)** 1 decimal place **(ii)** 2 decimal places.

(a) $x(x-3)=25$

(b) $x^2+5x=60$

(c) $(x-3)(x+5)=100$

2 **(a)** A rectangle has a base that is 6 cm greater than its height. Given that the height is h cm, draw a sketch of the rectangle and write an expression for the length of the base.

(b) Write an expression for the area of the rectangle.

(c) The area of the rectangle is 118 cm². Copy and continue the table below and, using trial and improvement methods, find the height and the base length of the rectangle, correct to 1 decimal place.

Height	Length	Area	Note
8	14	112	too small
9	15		

3 The height of a parallelogram is 5 cm less than the length of its base.

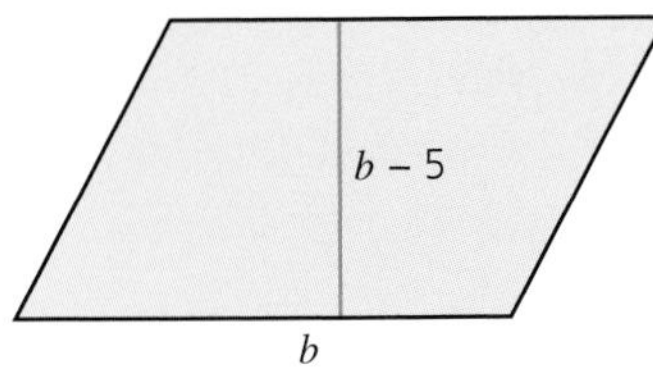

(a) Write an expression in b for the area of the parallelogram.

(b) The area of the parallelogram is 40 cm². Copy and continue the table below and, using trial and improvement methods, work out the value of b, correct to 2 decimal places.

b	$b-5$	Area	Note
10	5		

4 My bedroom is 2 m longer than it is wide. The floor area is 70 m². Use trial and improvement to work out the length and width of the room. Give your answer correct to the nearest 10 cm.

5 The height of a rectangle is 5 cm more than the length of its base. If the area of the rectangle is 23 cm² what is its height, to the nearest millimetre?

6 The area of my garden is 120 m². Its length is one and a half times the width. How long is my garden? Give your answer correct to the nearest 10 cm.

7 The height of a triangle is 3 cm more than the length of the base. The area of the triangle is 60 cm^2. Use trial and improvement to work out the base length and height of the triangle. Give your answer correct to one decimal place.

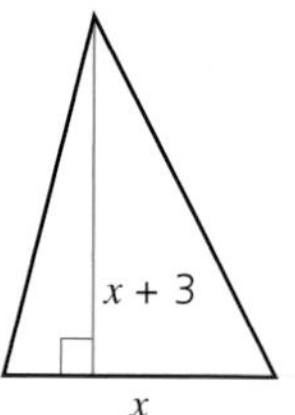

8 The height of this triangle is two-thirds the length of its base and its area is 31 m^2. Find the length of the base, correct to the nearest 10 cm.

9 A square photograph is surrounded by a border that is 4 cm wide.

(a) Taking the length of a side of the photograph to be x cm, write an expression for the length of a side of the border.

(b) Write an expression for the area of the border.

(c) Given that the area of the border is 248 cm^2, use trial and improvement methods to find the dimensions of the photograph correct to the nearest millimetre.

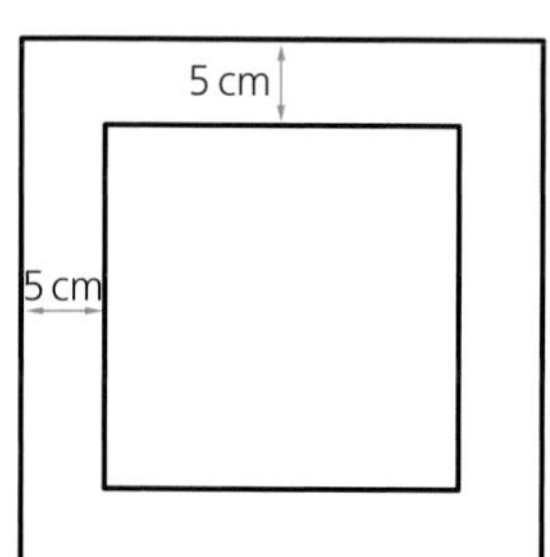

10 **(a)** Given that the formula for the area of a trapezium is:

$$\text{area} = \frac{h(a+b)}{2}$$

where a and b are the lengths of the **parallel** sides and h is the height, write an expression for the area of this trapezium.

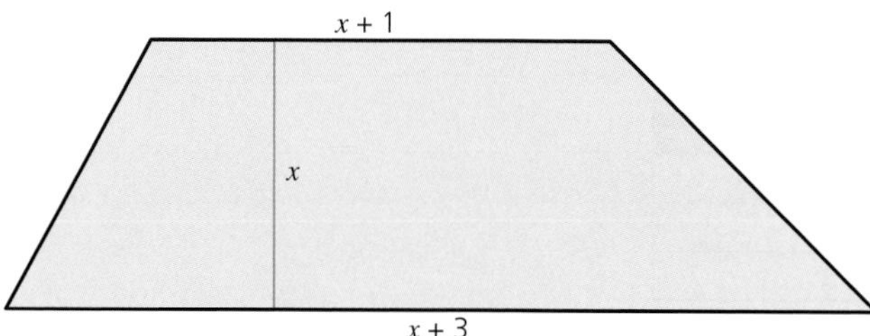

(b) The area of the trapezium is 20 cm^2. Copy and complete this table and continue it to find, by trial and improvement, the value of x, correct to 2 decimal places.

x	$x + 2$	Area	Note
3	5	15	
4			

Extension: Fractional indices

- Remember that $x^a \times x^a = x^{2a}$
- Then the square root of x^{2a} is x^a

Therefore to find the **square root**, you **halve** the index number:

- the square root of x^{4a} is x^{2a}
- the square root of x^a is $x^{\frac{a}{2}}$
- the square root of x is $x^{\frac{1}{2}}$

Extension Exercise 7.12

Evaluate each expression.

1 $9^{\frac{1}{2}}$

2 $16^{\frac{1}{4}}$

3 $25^{\frac{1}{2}}$

4 $27^{\frac{1}{3}}$

5 $16^{\frac{1}{2}}$

6 $125^{\frac{1}{3}}$

7 $8^{\frac{1}{3}}$

8 $(x^2)^{\frac{1}{2}}$

9 $(4x^2)^{\frac{1}{2}}$

10 $(9x^2)^{\frac{1}{2}}$

11 $(x^2)^{\frac{1}{2}} \times (x^3)^{\frac{1}{3}}$

12 $(4x^2)^{\frac{1}{2}} \div (2x)^2$

Summary Exercise 7.13

1 Simplify each expression, leaving your answer in index form.

(a) $a^3 \times a^2$ (b) $b^4 \times b$ (c) $c^3 \times d^2$

2 Simplify each expression, leaving your answer in index form.

(a) $a^4 \div a^2$ (b) $b^6 \div b^3$ (c) $c^4 \div c$

3 Simplify each expression, leaving your answer in index form.

(a) $a^2 \div a^4$ (b) $b^3 \div b^3$ (c) $c \div c^5$

4 Simplify each expression, if possible.

(a) $a^4 \times a^2 + a^5$ (b) $3b^3 + 2b^3 - b^3$ (c) $c^4 + c + c^2$

5 Simplify each expression, if possible.

(a) $\frac{3 \times a^2 \times b^3}{6 \times a \times b}$ (b) $\frac{15ab^2c}{3bc^2}$ (c) $\frac{18a^2b}{4b}$

6 Multiply out the brackets.

(a) $x(x + 3)$ (b) $2x(3x - 5)$ (c) $x^2(6 - x)$

7 Multiply out the brackets and simplify.

(a) $x(x+3)+x(3x-2)$

(b) $3x(2x-6)-2x(5-2x)$

8 Factorise each expression, if possible.

(a) $3x+9$

(b) $12x-7$

(c) $4xy+2y^2$

(d) $3x^2-12y$

(e) $3x^2-12x+3$

(f) $4x^2y-8y^2+6x$

(g) $12x^2y+5y^2-8y$

(h) $9x^3-6x^2y+15x^2$

9 The width of this rectangle is 7 cm less than its length. Its area is 55 cm².

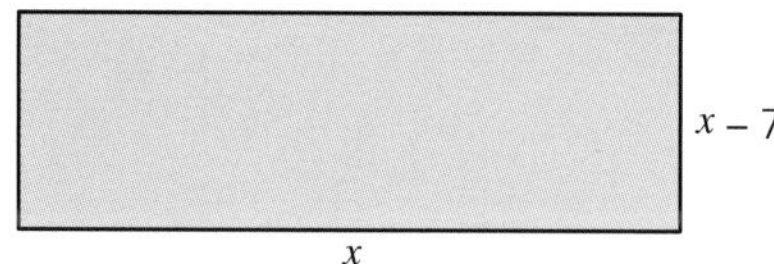

Copy and complete this table to find the length and width of the rectangle to 2 decimal places. Use trial and improvement.

x	$x-7$	Area	Note
12	5	60	too big
11			

Activity: Great Uncle Ben's bequest (or heir today – gone tomorrow)

I was very surprised to get this letter from my rich Great Uncle, Ben.

'Sumalot'
Times Square
Percentchester
Sumerset
PC7 1AB

Dear Great Nephew,

Thank you very much for the birthday card. I really liked the bright red 75 you drew on the front. I do hope you are well and behaving yourself. I was very pleased to hear from Mum and Dad that you are working hard at school. Your mathematics test result was excellent.

It made me think. I believe that you deserve some of my fortune for working so hard. I want to give you some money now and some more each year. All you have to do is choose one of these schemes.

(a) £100 now, then £90 next year, then £80 the year after and so on.
(b) £10 now, then £20 the year after, £30 the year after and so on.

(c) £10 now, one and half that amount the year after, one and a half times THAT amount the following year and so on.
(d) £1 now, £2 the year after, £4 the year after that, £8 the year after that and so on.

Of course these schemes can only operate while I am still alive.

I look forward to hearing which of these you choose and exactly why you chose it!!

Lots of love,

Great Uncle Ben

Write a reply to this letter and include the mathematical reasons for your choice.

You could use a spreadsheet program to analyse the four schemes.

Using the spreadsheet program

1 Log on to the computer. Open your spreadsheet program. Then open a **New** document and **Save** it as **Great Uncle**.

2 In cell A1 type 'year', in cell A2 type '1' and in cell A3 type the correct formula to add one to the value in cell A2. When your formula produces the value '2' in cell A2 click on the cell, keep the mouse button down and drag down 10 cells to A11. From the **Calculate** menu select **Fill down**. You should now have the numbers 1 to 10 in the year column.

3 In cell B1 type 'scheme A'. In this scheme you can see that you are given £100 in the first year, and then £10 less each year. Type '100' in cell B2, and then type the correct formula in cell B3 to deduct £10. When your formula produces '90' in cell B3, then fill down the formula to cell B11 as before. In B11 you will have '0'. Assume that Uncle Ben does not expect *you* to pay *him* £10 in year 12

4 The important part of Uncle Ben's problem is to work out the total amount that he is giving you. In cell C1 type 'total A'. Cell C2 will need the formula '= B2' but cell C3 will need the formula '= B2 + B3'

   Fill down this formula in column C

5 Cells D1 and E1 will need 'scheme B' and 'total B'. You should be able to write the correct formulae for these, you may like to fill down the D and E columns until D11 and E11 to see what happens if Uncle Ben lives for 10 years.

6 Cells F1 and G1 will need 'scheme C' and 'total C'. The formulae in the F columns are interesting as, having started with £10, you are going to multiply the contents of each preceding cell by 1.5

   Remember that 'multiply' is shown by the asterisk above 8

7 Cells H1 and I1 are for 'scheme D' and 'total D'. Again you are going to multiply the preceding cell by a number.

Saving and printing

8 **Save** your work. Highlight all cells from A1 to I11 and pull down the **Options** menu to select **Print** area, then press return for **OK**.

9 From the **View** menu select **Page** view.

10 From the **File** menu select **Page set up** and select **Landscape**.

11 From the **Format** menu select **Insert footer** and type your name and form. Now print your document.

12 Go back to the **View** menu and select **Display**. Click in the **Display formula** box and then **Print** again. Then go back to **Display** and deselect **Display formula**.

Drawing graphs

One really useful facility of the spreadsheet package is its ability to draw graphs from the data. You do not need graphs of all the columns above but only the data in columns A, C, E, G and I.

13 Deselect **Page view** from the **View** menu. In cell A15 type '= A1'. Now highlight–click–highlight and fill down the next 10 cells.

14 In cell B15 type '= C1', and fill down, in cell C15 type '= E1' and fill down, in cell D15 type '= G1' and fill down and finally in cell E15 type '= I1' and fill down. You now have a new table containing the relevant data only.

15 Highlight cells from A15 to E25. From the **Options** menu select **Make chart**. Select **Line graph**.

16 Follow the instructions on the next few screens.

17 You should now have a chart showing the information that you calculated earlier.

Printing the chart

18 Your chart should have little black squares on each corner. Click on the chart and move it to a blank area of the spreadsheet. Highlight all the cells surrounding your chart.

19 From the **Options** menu select **Print area** and press return for **OK**.

20 Now select **Print** from the **File** menu. Before pressing return for **OK**, deselect **print row headings**, **print columns headings** and **print cell grid**.

Finally...

21 Select **New** from the **File** menu. Select **Word-processing** and answer Uncle Ben's letter.

8 Sequences

What is a sequence?

A sequence is a succession of terms that are connected by a rule.

For example, 2, 4, 6, 8, 10, ... is the sequence of **even numbers**. Each term is generated by adding 2 to the term before it.

Some sequences follow numerical rules. Others, such as prime numbers, do not.

Exercise 8.1: A review

Write down the next three numbers in each sequence.

If you can find a numerical rule write it down.

1 1, 3, 5, 7, 9, ..., ..., ...

2 1, 4, 9, 16, 25, ..., ..., ...

3 3, 6, 9, 12, 15, ..., ..., ...

4 1, 3, 6, 10, 15, ..., ..., ...

5 1, 4, 7, 10, 13, ..., ..., ...

6 0, 3, 8, 15, 24, ..., ..., ...

7 1, 1, 2, 3, 5, 8, 13, ..., ..., ...

8 1, 2, 4, 7, 11, ..., ..., ...

9 2, 6, 10, 14, 18, ..., ..., ...

10 1, 6, 11, 16, 21, ..., ..., ...

Working with sequences

You probably found the missing terms in the above sequences by looking at the **difference** between two terms. The differences usually follow a pattern that can be continued. However, using this method is not so helpful when you are trying to find, for example, the 100th term in a sequence.

The sequence in question 4 above is:

1, 3, 6, 10, 15, 21, 28, 36, 45, 55, ...

This is the sequence of **triangular numbers**.

To find the 100th term you have to look at the pattern of the numbers and try to find a rule that works for all the terms in that sequence.

Before moving on, think back to the four types of sequence that you studied in *Mathematics for Common Entrance Book Two*.

1 Sequences based on a times table

Sequences based on a times table have a regular pattern of differences.

For example, in the sequence: 6, 12, 18, 24, 30, 36, ...
The difference is always 6: 6 6 6 6 6

The hundredth term would be $100 \times 6 = 600$

The nth term is $n \times 6 = 6n$

The mathematical way to describe a sequence that increases (or decreases) by the same number each time is to say that its **first differences** are the same, or **constant**.

Other sequences that have a regular pattern of differences may be compared to a times table.

For example, the sequence: 5, 11, 17, 23, 29, 35, ...
The difference is always 6: 6 6 6 6 6
Each term is 1 less than a number in the 6 times table.

The hundredth term would be $100 \times 6 - 1 = 600 - 1 = 599$

The nth term is $n \times 6 - 1 = 6n - 1$

2 Sequences based on square numbers

Sequences based on square numbers increase by consecutive odd numbers.

Expressed mathematically, the differences for sequences based on square numbers form a sequence of consecutive odd numbers.

These are the square numbers: 1, 4, 9, 16, 25, 36, ...
The sequence of differences is: 3, 5, 7, 9, 11, ...

The hundredth term would be:

$100^2 = 100 \times 100 = 10\,000$

The nth term is n^2

Other sequences with differences that are consecutive odd numbers can be compared to the sequence of square numbers.

For example, for the sequence: 3, 6, 11, 18, 27, 38, ...
The sequence of differences is: 3, 5, 7, 9, 11, ...

Comparing this sequence to the square numbers, you can see that each term is 2 more than a square number.

The hundredth term would be $100^2 + 2 = 100 \times 100 + 2 = 10\,002$

The nth term is $n^2 + 2$

3 Sequences based on triangular numbers

The sequence of differences for triangular numbers increases by one each time. This is the sequence of counting numbers.

These are the triangle numbers: 1, 3, 6, 10, 15, 21, ...
The sequence of differences is: 2, 3, 4, 5, 6, ...

The hundredth term would be $\frac{1}{2} \times 100 \times 101 = 50 \times 101$
$= 5050$

The nth term is $\frac{1}{2}n(n + 1)$

Other sequences with differences that increase by one each time can be compared to the triangular numbers.

For example, for the sequence: 4, 6, 9, 13, 18, 24, ...
The sequence of differences is: 2, 3, 4, 5, 6, ...

Comparing this sequence to the triangular numbers you can see that each term is 3 more than a triangular number.

The hundredth term would be $\frac{1}{2} \times 100 \times 101 + 3 = 50 \times 101 + 3$
$= 5053$

The nth term is $\frac{1}{2}n(n + 1) + 3$

> Sometimes the sequence of triangular numbers starts with 0:
> 0, 1, 3, 6, 10, 15, ...
>
> For this sequence the nth term is $\frac{1}{2}n(n - 1)$

4 Sequences based on adding the previous two terms

Each term in the famous Fibonacci sequence is formed by adding the previous two terms together.

This is the basic Fibonacci sequence: 1, 1, 2, 3, 5, 8, 13, 21, ...
The sequence of differences is: 0, 1, 1, 2, 3, 5, 8, ...

You see that after the first one or two terms the sequence of differences is the same as the actual sequence. This is how you can identify similar sequences.

For example, for the sequence: 1, 3, 4, 7, 11, 18, 29, ...
The sequence of differences is: 2, 1, 3, 4, 7, 11, ...

When the sequence of differences is the same as the original sequence then you have a Fibonacci-style pattern.

Exercise 8.2

1 (a) Using the information you have just been given, state whether each sequence in Exercise 8.1 was based on:

(i) a times table

(ii) the square numbers

(iii) the triangular numbers

(iv) a Fibonacci-style sequence.

(b) Write down the nth term of each of the sequences, unless it was a Fibonacci-style sequence.

2 Write down the next three terms and the nth term of each sequence.

(a) 2, 5, 8, 11, 14, ..., ..., ...

(b) 2, 5, 10, 17, 26, ..., ..., ...

(c) 2, 4, 7, 11, 16, 22, ..., ..., ...

(d) 2, 7, 12, 17, 22, 27, ..., ..., ...

3 You have been looking at increasing sequences. Now look at each of these decreasing sequences and write the next three terms and the nth term.

(a) $^{-}5$, $^{-}10$, $^{-}15$, $^{-}20$, $^{-}25$, ..., ..., ...

(b) $^{-}3$, $^{-}6$, $^{-}9$, $^{-}12$, $^{-}15$, ..., ..., ...

(c) $^{-}7$, $^{-}14$, $^{-}21$, $^{-}28$, $^{-}35$, ..., ..., ...

(d) $^{-}4$, $^{-}8$, $^{-}12$, $^{-}16$, $^{-}20$, ..., ..., ...

4 Using your answers to Q3, write the next three terms and the nth term of each of these decreasing sequences.

(a) 30, 25, 20, 15, 10, ..., ..., ...

(b) 9, 6, 3, 0, $^{-}3$, ..., ..., ...

(c) 100, 93, 86, 79, 72, ..., ..., ...

(d) 20, 16, 12, 8, 4, ..., ..., ...

5 Write the next three terms and the nth term of each of these decreasing sequences.

(a) 15, 12, 9, 6, 3, 0, ..., ..., ...

(b) 99, 88, 77, 66, 55, 44, ..., ..., ...

(c) 51, 49, 47, 45, 43, ..., ..., ...

(d) 5, 2, $^{-}1$, $^{-}4$, ..., ..., ...

Finding terms

In all of the sequences you have considered so far, you have found the next term by adding or subtracting a number, or by multiplying or dividing by a number. You have also looked at sequences based on the square numbers. Remember that sequences could also be based on **cube numbers**, numbers to the power 4, and so on.

Exercise 8.3

1 Write down the next three terms in each sequence.

(a) 1, 2, 4, 8, 16, ..., ..., ...

(b) 8, 4, 2, 1, ..., ..., ...

(c) 0.1, 0.5, 0.25, 0.125, ..., ..., ...

(d) 100, 10, 1, 0.1, ..., ..., ...

(e) 25, 5, 1, 0.2, ..., ..., ...

2 (a) Write down the next three terms in each sequence.

(i) 1, 8, 27, 64, ..., ..., ...

(ii) 1, 16, 81, 256, ..., ..., ...

(b) Deduce the nth term of each sequence.

3 Some sequences combine rules, so that you have to deduce the terms from more than one pattern. Write down the next three terms of each sequence.

(a) 1, 3, 2, 4, 3, ..., ..., ...

(b) 1, 1, 3, 2, 5, 3, ..., ..., ...

(c) 1, 2, 3, 2, 5, 2, ..., ..., ...

(d) 1, 2, 3, 4, 5, 8, 7, ..., ..., ...

4 Fill in the missing terms in each sequence.

(a) 5, 8, ..., 14, 17, ...

(b) 0, 3, ..., 15, ..., 35, ...

(c) 4, ..., 1, 0.5, ...

(d) 2, 3, 5, ..., 8, 9, ...

(e) 2, 5, ..., 12, ..., 31, ...

5 Now here are some different sequences that you might recognise. Write down the next three terms of each sequence. Note that they might not follow a rule.

(a) 2, 3, 5, 7, 11, ..., ..., ...

(b) M, T, W, T, ..., ..., ...

(c) J, F, M, A, M, J, J, ..., ..., ...

(d) O, T, T, F, F, ..., ..., ...

Working to a rule

Sometimes you are given the rule for the nth term of a sequence. From that, you can work out the terms in the sequence.

Example

The nth term of a sequence is $3n + 1$

Work out the first, second and tenth terms of the sequence.

First term $= 3 \times 1 + 1$
$= 4$

Substitute into the formula for the sequence just as you would in any other formula.

Second term $= 3 \times 2 + 1$
$= 7$

Tenth term $= 3 \times 10 + 1$
$= 31$

Exercise 8.4

1 (a) The nth term of a sequence is $5n - 2$. Work out the first, second, fifth and tenth terms of the sequence.

(b) What is the first term that is greater than 100?

2 (a) The nth term of a sequence is $6n + 3$. Work out the first, second, third and tenth terms of the sequence.

(b) What is the first term that is greater than 100?

3 (a) The nth term of a sequence is $20 - 3n$. Work out the first, second, third and tenth terms of the sequence.

(b) What is the first term that is less than 0?

4 (a) The nth term of a sequence is $n^2 + 3$ Work out the first, fifth, tenth and 20th terms of the sequence.

(b) What is the first term that is greater than 200?

5 (a) The nth term of a sequence is $2n^2$. Work out the first, second, third and fifth terms of the sequence.

(b) What is the first term that is greater than 100?

6 (a) The nth term of a sequence is $100 - 2n^2$. Write down find the first, second, fourth and tenth terms of the sequence.

(b) What is the first term that is less than 0?

7 (a) The nth term of a sequence is $n(n - 2)$. Work out the first, second, fifth and tenth terms of the sequence.

(b) What is the first term that is greater than 100?

8 (a) The nth term of a sequence is $(n - 1)(n + 2)$. Work out the first, second, fifth and tenth terms of the sequence.

(b) What is the first term that is greater than 200?

Quadratic sequences and square numbers

The rules for the sequences in questions 4 to 8 of the last exercise involve n^2. Sequences like these are called **quadratic sequences.**

Consider this pattern of numbers.

1

$1 + 3$

$1 + 3 + 5$

$1 + 3 + 5 + 7$

If you add up the numbers you will have the sequence:

1, 4, 9, 16, 25, ...

This is the sequence of square numbers, so the nth term is n^2

Sometimes it is easier to think about sequences if you have a series of drawings or patterns to look at.

Exercise 8.5

1 (a) Draw the next two patterns in this sequence.

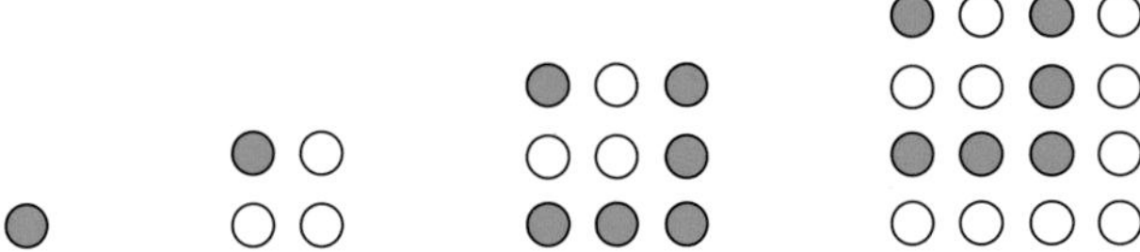

(b) Explain why the pattern of adding odd numbers gives the sequence of square numbers.

2 Look at these rectangular numbers.

In each rectangle the length is always one more than the width.

(a) Draw the next two rectangular numbers.

(b) Copy and complete this table, and hence find the rule for the nth term.

Pattern number	Dots up	Dots along	Rectangular number
1	1	2	$1 \times 2 = 2$
2	2	3	$2 \times 3 = 6$
3			
4			
5			
6			
n			

3 Here are the first four triangular numbers.

(a) Draw the next two triangular numbers.

(b) Copy and complete this table.

Pattern number	Triangular number
1	1
2	3
3	
4	
5	

(c) Compare the number of dots in the rectangular numbers with the number of dots in the triangular numbers. What do you notice?

(d) Now write the rule for the nth triangular number.

Use the results for square, rectangular and triangular numbers to find the rule for the nth term of each of these sequences.

4 A square with one corner dot missing

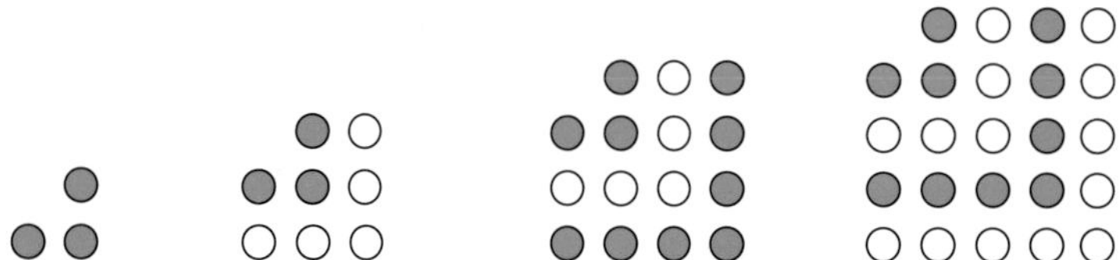

5 A rectangle in which the width is 2 units less than the length

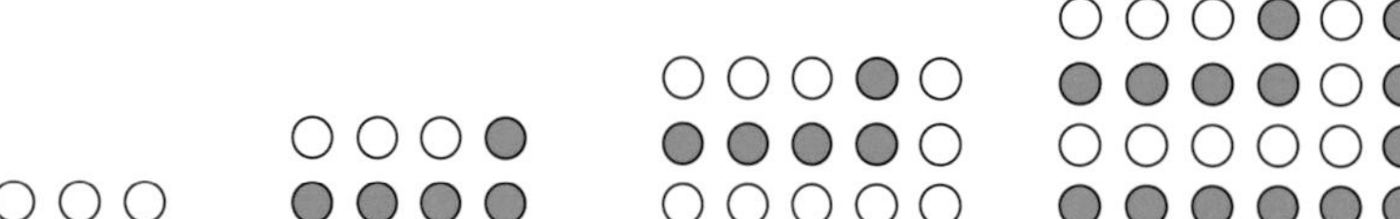

6 A truncated triangle

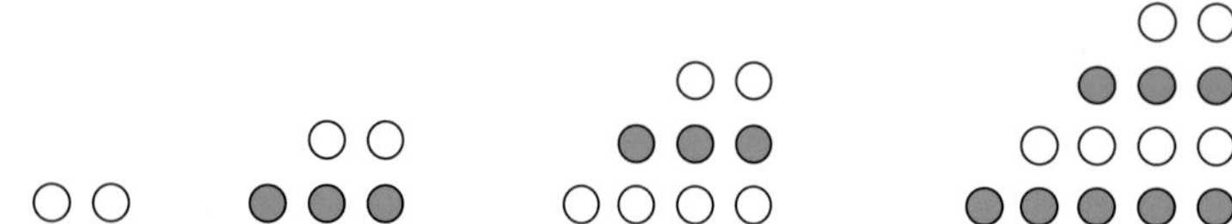

7 Two truncated squares

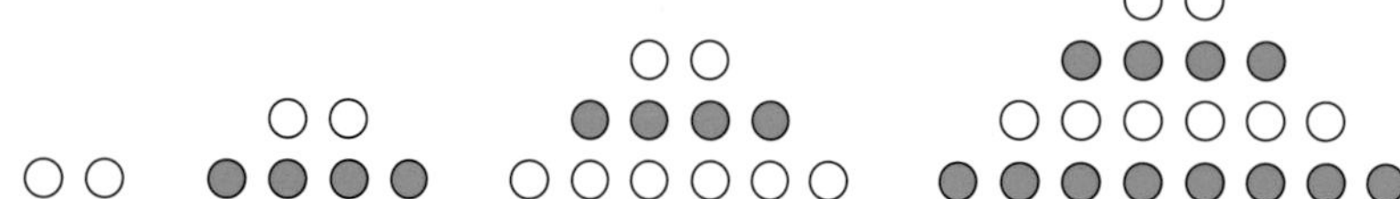

Problem solving

The patterns and sequences in the next exercise may need a little more thought.

Exercise 8.6

1 Look at this pattern.

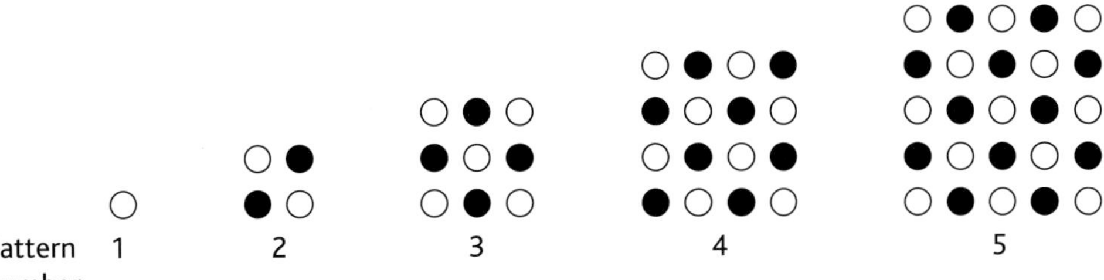

(a) Copy and complete this table.

Pattern number	White balls	Black balls	Total balls
1	1	0	1
2	2	2	4
3	5		
4	8		
5			
6			

(b) How many balls in total will there be in pattern number 10?

(c) How many black balls will there be in pattern number 10?

(d) How many white balls will there be in pattern number 10?

(e) Write down the total number of balls in the nth pattern.

(f) Write down the total numbers of black balls and white balls in the nth pattern.

2 Look at this pattern.

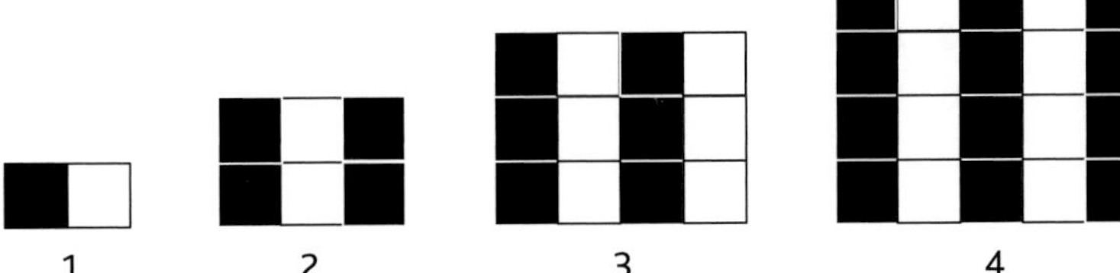

(a) Copy and complete this table.

Pattern number	Black squares	White squares	Total squares
1	1	1	2
2	4	2	6
3	6		
4			
5			
6			

(b) How many squares in total will there be in pattern number 10?

(c) How many white squares will there be in pattern number 10?

(d) How many black squares will there be in pattern number 10?

(e) Write down the total number of squares in the nth pattern.

3 Look at this pattern.

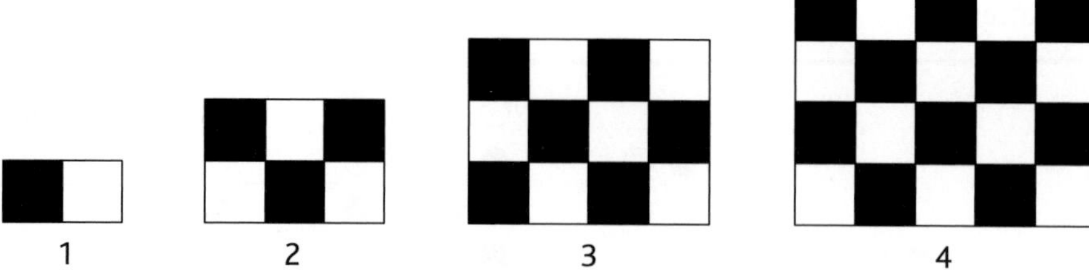

Pattern number 1 2 3 4

(a) Copy and complete this table.

Pattern number	Black squares	White squares	Total squares
1	1	1	
2	3		
3			
4			
5			
6			

(b) How many black squares will there be in pattern number 20?

(c) How many white squares will there be in pattern number 50?

(d) How many squares in total will there be in pattern number 100?

(e) Write down the total number of black squares in the nth pattern.

4 Look at this pattern.

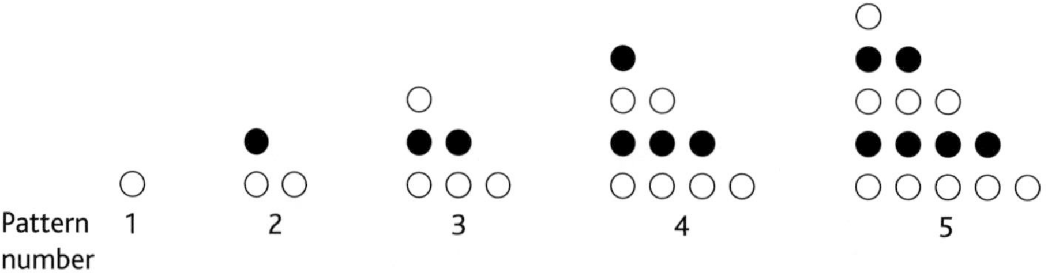

Pattern number 1 2 3 4 5

(a) Copy and complete this table.

Pattern number	White balls	Black balls	Total balls
1	1	0	1
2	2	1	3
3	4	2	
4	6		
5			
6			

(b) How many balls in total will there be in pattern number 10?

(c) How many black balls will there be in pattern number 10?

(d) How many white balls will there be in pattern number 10?

(e) Write down the total number of balls in the nth pattern.

(f) Write down the total numbers of black balls and white balls in the nth pattern.

5 Look at this pattern.

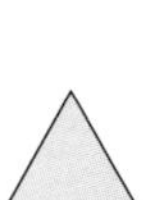

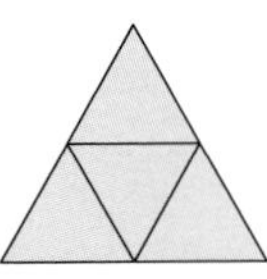

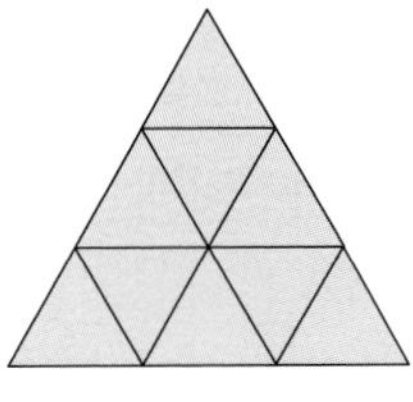

Pattern number 1 2 3

(a) Copy and complete this table.

Patternnumber	Lines	Triangles
1	3	1
2	9	4
3		
4		
5		
6		

(b) How many lines in total will there be in pattern number 10?

(c) How many triangles will there be in pattern number 10?

(d) How many lines will there be in pattern number 100?

(e) Write down the total number of lines in the nth pattern.

(f) Write down the total number of triangles in the nth pattern.

Extension: Harder sequences

The sequences you have been working with are quite straightforward. This is not true for all sequences.

When you meet a new sequence, try to find the rule.

Look for patterns in the **differences** between the terms and check if they increase by a fixed number, or if they are based on the square numbers, triangular numbers, rectangular numbers. Sometimes the terms are formed by a pattern of products, such as 1×2, 2×3, 3×4, …

Example

Find the next three terms and the rule for the nth term of this sequence.

5, 10, 17, 26, ..., ...

Start with the pattern of differences.

$10 - 5 = \mathbf{5}$ $17 - 10 = \mathbf{7}$ $26 - 17 = \mathbf{9}$

The pattern $+5, +7, +9$ is the same as that of the differences for the square numbers but starts with the second term:

4, 9, 16, 25

Continuing the sequence of differences, the next three odd numbers are 11, 13 and 15

The next three terms are 37, 50, 65

Now using what you know about the sequence, and comparing it to the sequence of square numbers, you can rewrite it as:

$2^2 + 1 = 5$, $3^2 + 1 = 10$, $4^2 + 1 = 17$

The nth term is $(n + 1)^2 + 1$

Extension Exercise 8.7

1 Write down the nth term for each sequence.

(a) 2, 4, 7, 11, ...

(b) 3, 9, 18, 30, ...

(c) 2, 6, 10, 14, ...

(d) 4, 10, 18, 28, ...

(e) 2, 7, 14, 23, ...

2 What sequence do you get if you add a square number to the pattern number $(1 + 1, 4 + 2, 9 + 3)$? What is the rule?

3 What sequence do you get if you multiply each triangular number by 8 and then add 1? What is the rule for this sequence?

4 What sequence do you get if you multiply each triangular number by 2 and subtract the pattern number? What is the rule for this sequence?

5 What sequence do you get if you multiply each triangular number by 3 and subtract the pattern number? What is the rule for this sequence?

6 What sequence do you get if you multiply each triangular number by 2 and subtract the corresponding square number? What is the rule for this sequence? Can you explain it with algebra?

Summary Exercise 8.8

1 Write down the next three terms of each sequence.

(a) 2, 7, 12, 17, …, …, … (b) 16, 4, 1, $\frac{1}{4}$, …, …, … (c) 4, 2, 0, $^{-}2$, …, …, …

2 Look at these patterns of matches.

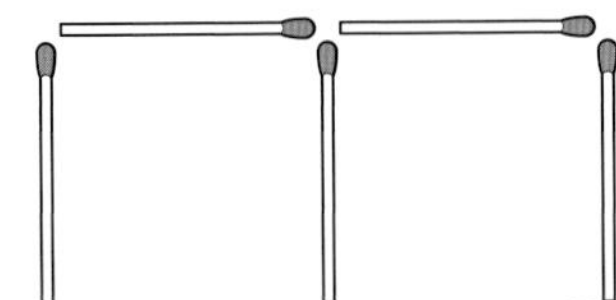
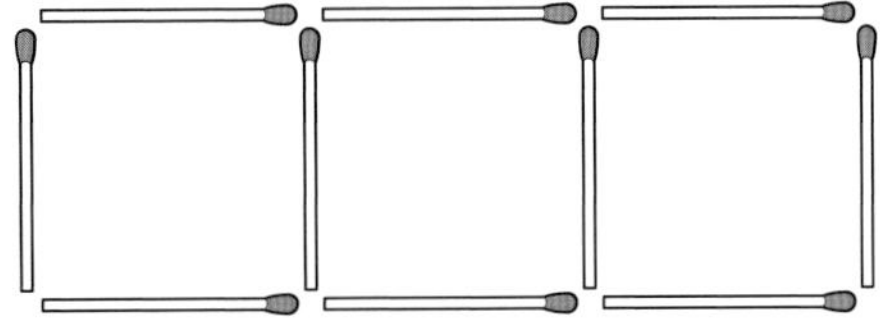

(a) How many matches will there be in the fourth pattern?

(b) How many matches will there be in the tenth pattern?

(c) What is the rule for the number of matches that will be in the nth pattern?

3 (a) Draw the next two patterns in this sequence.

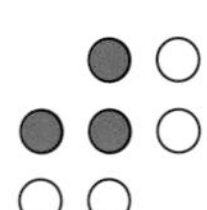
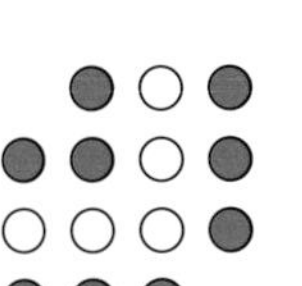
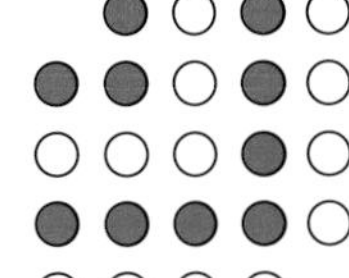

(b) Copy and complete this table.

Pattern number	White balls	Red balls	Total balls
1	0	2	2
2	4	3	7
3	5		
4			
5			
6			

(c) Add a final row to the table and work out the numbers of white balls and red balls and hence the total number of balls, in the nth row.

4 The nth term in a series is $20 - 3n$. Work out the first, fourth, sixth and tenth terms.

5 For each sequence, work out the next three terms and hence find the rule for the sequence.

(a) 4 7 10 13 16

(b) 2 7 14 23 34

(c) 5 3 1 $^{-}1$ $^{-}3$

6 This pattern of numbers is called Pascal's triangle. It includes several of the sequences that you have studied in this chapter. Try adding up each row of the triangle like this:

				1						1
			1	+	1					2
		1	+	2	+	1				4
	1	+	3	+	...	+	1			...
1	+	...	+	6	+	...	+	1		...

(a) Work out the rule for the sum of the nth row.

(b) Look for the pattern of triangular numbers. Where is it?

It is a sloping diagonal, not a row or column.

(c) What pattern is there in the next diagonal?

(d) Work out a rule for the fourth term in the nth row.

7 You may have noticed that English people are very reserved. If they enter a room and have to sit down, they will choose a chair so that they do not need to sit next to anyone else. Each person that comes in will also choose a chair between two empty ones, if there is one.

You can explore this mathematically.

1 chair: There are two ways to fill the seats.

○ unoccupied, where no one is sitting down

☺ occupied

2 chairs: There are three ways to fill the seats.

○○

○☺

☺○

3 chairs: There are five ways to fill the seats.

○○○

○☺○

○○☺

☺○○

☺○☺

(a) Work out the number of ways you can fill a row of chairs when the row has:

(i) 4 chairs (ii) 5 chairs (iii) 6 chairs.

Note that the first way of 'filling' a row is the one in which no one is sitting down.

You should have started to generate the Fibonacci sequence.

(b) Without drawing, write down the number of ways you can fill 10 chairs.

Activity: An introduction to fractals

When you use a number (known, such as 2, or an algebraic unknown, such as x) to generate a sequence, you apply the same operation over and over again.

For example:

- 2, 5, 8, 11, 14, 17, ... Add 3 to each previous term.
- $2, x + 2, 2x + 2, 3x + 2, 4x + 2$ Add x to each term.

You can do the same in geometry. If you apply the same rule, over and over again, you can make a repeating pattern within a pattern. This is a **fractal**.

1 Sierpinski's gasket

You are going to shade and then rub out repeatedly in this sequence, so do the first shading very lightly.

(a) Cut out an equilateral triangle of side 16 units from a sheet of isometric paper. Divide it into four equal triangles. Lightly shade the outside three triangles. Do not shade in the central triangle. This is your first generation gasket.

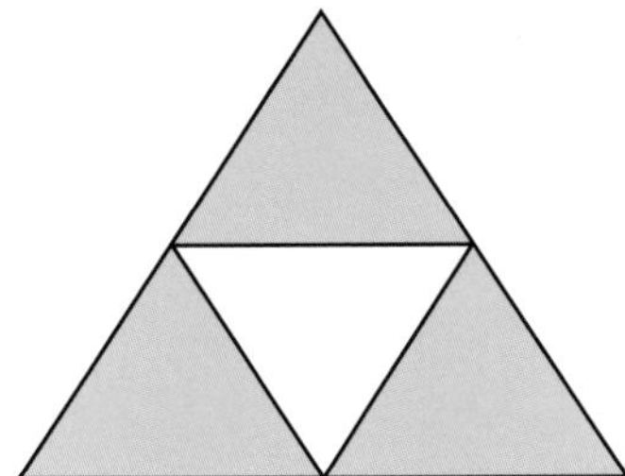

(b) Divide each shaded triangle into four and remove (rub out) the central one – this is the second generation gasket.

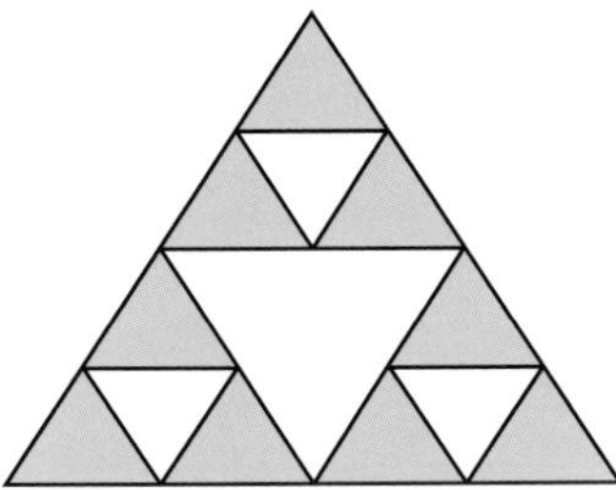

(c) Repeat this procedure as many times as you can. Shade the final result carefully.

(d) Copy and complete this table.

Generation number	1	2	3	4	5
Number of triangles (including the unshaded ones)	4	13			
Fraction of whole triangle unshaded	$\frac{1}{4}$				

(e) How many triangles (including the unshaded ones) will there be in the nth generation?

A gasket is a mechanical seal that fills the space between two or more surfaces, generally to prevent leakage. They are made of rubber or a similar material, with holes cut in them, which is the shape that you have produced here.

2 Another equilateral triangle with sides of 16 units

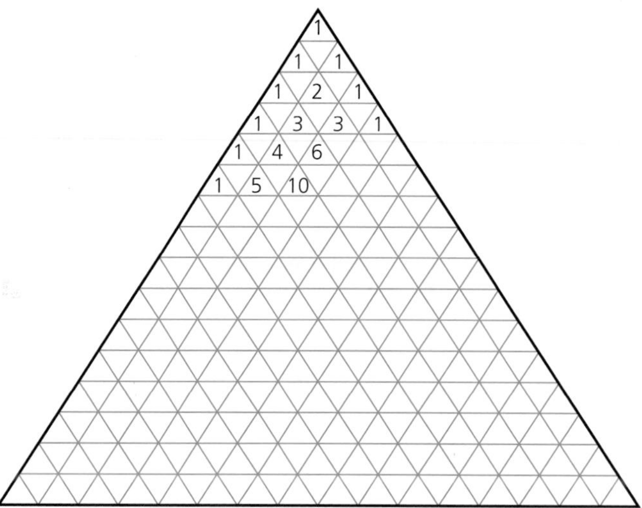

(a) Pascal's triangle has been started for you. Note that the numbers are formed by adding the number above on the left to the number above on the right ($3 + 3 = 6$, $4 + 6 = 10$, $5 + 10 = ?$). Copy and complete it so that all the 16 rows are filled in. Use a calculator if you need to!

(b) Shade all the odd numbers.

(c) Compare your two triangles (those from (a) and (b)). What do you notice? Can you explain your answer?

Now do some more research into fractals. You will look at another one at the end of Chapter 15

9 Using formulae

A **formula** is a mathematical statement of a rule or principle that is written in the form of an equation. When you found the rule for the nth term of a sequence in the last chapter, you were finding the formula for that sequence.

Writing a formula

Formulae are written using symbols and do not include any units (kg, cm, ...). As algebraic equations, they do not contain any × or ÷ signs but may use brackets and fractions.

Example

Write a formula for A, where A is the mean, in kilograms, of three masses, x kg, y kg, and z kg.

$$A = \frac{x+y+z}{3}$$

Exercise 9.1

1 Write a formula for N, where N is the total amount of money that I have in pounds, when I start with £x and I am then given £y more.

2 Write a formula for N, where N is the total amount of money that I have left, in pounds, when I start with £a and spend £b.

3 Write a formula for A, where A is the average of four lengths, w metres, x metres, y metres and z metres.

4 Write a formula for P, where P is the perimeter of this rectangle.

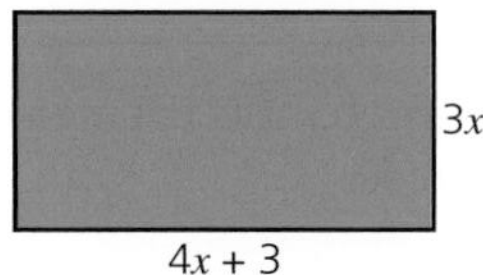

5 Write a formula for A, where A is the area of the rectangle in question 4

6 Write a formula for P, where P is the perimeter of this triangle.

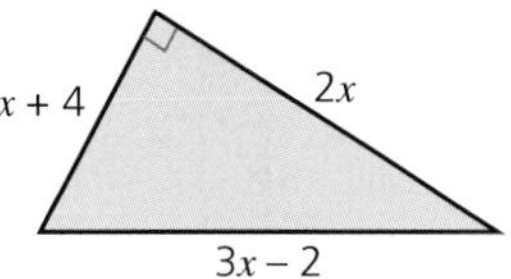

7 Write a formula for A, where A is the area of the triangle in question 6

8 Write a formula for N, where N is the total amount of money that I have, in pence, when I start with £x and am then given £y more.

9 Write a formula for N, where N is the total amount of money that I have, in pounds, when I start with x pence and am then given y pence more.

10 Write a formula for N, where N is the cost, in pounds, of buying 10 articles at £y each.

11 Write a formula for N, where N is the cost in pounds, of buying n articles at £y each.

12 Write a formula for N, where N is the cost, in pounds, of buying n articles at x pence each.

13 Write a formula for P, where P is the perimeter of this shape.

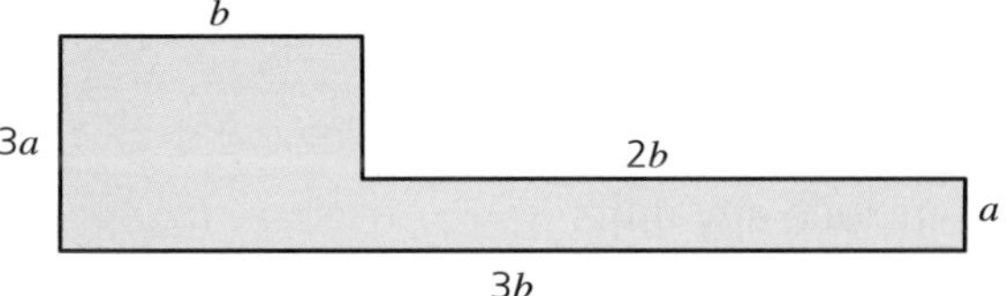

14 Write a formula for A, where A is the area of the above shape.

15 Write a formula for P, where P is the perimeter of this shape:

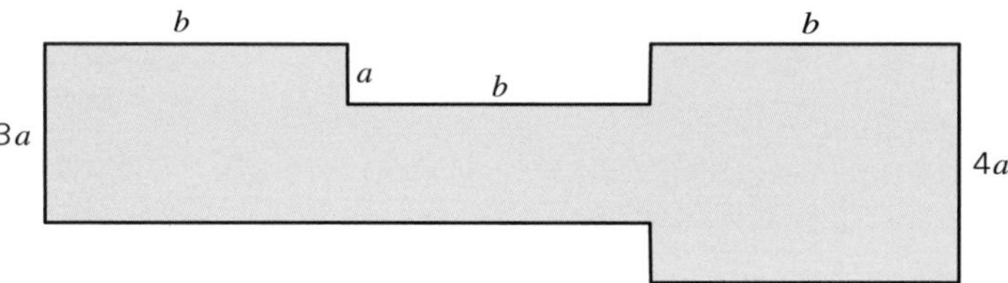

16 Write a formula for A, where A is the area of the shape in question 15

17 Write a formula for A, where A is the area of the coloured region in this square.

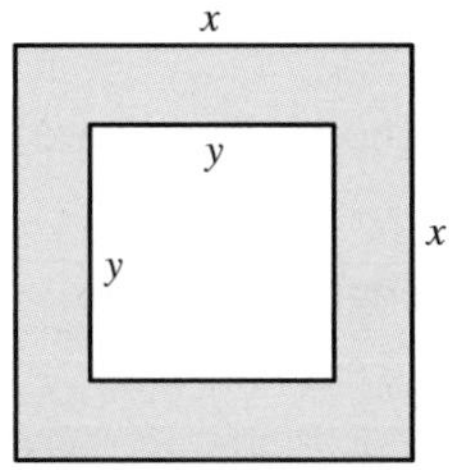

18 Write a formula for A, where $A\,\text{cm}^2$ is the area of a frame measuring x cm by y cm that is 5 cm wide.

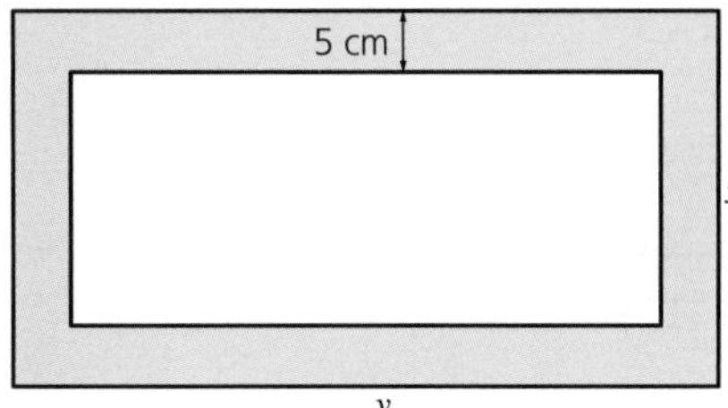

Substituting into formulae

To use a formula, you substitute numbers for the letters and calculate the result. Then you can write down the answer, with correct units. While this can often appear simple, particularly if you use a calculator, it is very important to follow certain rules. These help you to avoid making careless mistakes and allow someone else to follow your working.

You need to take particular care when substituting negative numbers into a formula. It is very easy to make a mistake with the signs, which can then lead to a wrong answer.

Example

Given that $a = {}^{-}2$, $b = {}^{-}3$ and $c = 2$, calculate the value of N when $N = ab^2 - bc$

$N = ab^2 - bc$	Formula
$= ({}^{-}2) \times ({}^{-}3)^2 - ({}^{-}3) \times 2$	Substitute
$= ({}^{-}2) \times 9 - ({}^{-}6)$	Calculate
$= {}^{-}18 + 6$	
$= {}^{-}12$	Answer

In the above example the steps were:

1 Formula

2 Substitute

3 Calculate

4 Answer

5 Units if necessary

You must conscientiously write down and perform all of these steps. You may use a calculator but always write down the calculation first.

Most mistakes made when you are using formulae occur through careless substitution. Do not try to combine substitution and calculation.

A very common mistake is to confuse ab^2 with $(ab)^2$

$ab^2 = a \times b \times b$ while $(ab)^2 = a \times b \times a \times b$

and $2a^2 = 2 \times a \times a$ while $(2a)^2 = 2 \times a \times 2 \times a$

also note that ${}^{-}a^2 = {}^{-}(a \times a) = {}^{-}a^2$ but $({}^{-}a)^2 = ({}^{-}a) \times ({}^{-}a) = a^2$

Exercise 9.2

1 Given that $a = {}^{-}2$ and $b = {}^{-}1$, find the value of N when:

(a) $N = a + b$
(b) $N = ab$
(c) $N = a - b$
(d) $N = 3a + 2b$
(e) $N = b - a$
(f) $N = 3a - 2b$

2 Given that $a = {}^{-}3$, $b = 2$ and $c = {}^{-}4$, find the value of N when:

(a) $N = a^2$
(b) $N = ab - bc$
(c) $N = a^2 + b^2$
(d) $N = a(b - c)$
(e) $N = 3a^2 - 2c^2$
(f) $N = a^2(2b - 3c)$

3 Given that $a = {}^{-}0.5$, $b = {}^{-}2$ and $c = {}^{-}0.2$, find the value of N when:

(a) $N = ac$
(b) $N = ab - bc$
(c) $N = ab + c^2$
(d) $N = a(b - c)$
(e) $N = abc$
(f) $N = b(b^2 - c^2)$

4 Given that $x = {}^{-}3$, $y = 4$ and $z = {}^{-}1$, find the value of M when:

(a) $M = \frac{x}{y}$
(b) $M = \frac{(x + y)}{(y - z)}$
(c) $M = \frac{xy}{z}$
(d) $M = \frac{(x^2 - z^2)}{(x + y)}$
(e) $M = \frac{xyz}{4}$
(f) $M = \frac{(3x^2 - 2z^2)}{(3y - 2z)}$

5 Given that $a = {}^{-}1$, $b = {}^{-}2$ and $c = 3$, find the value of N when:

(a) $N = ab^2$
(b) $N = ab - bc$
(c) $N = (ab)^2$
(d) $N = a^2b - b^2c$
(e) $N = abc$
(f) $N = a^2(4b^2 - 3bc^2)$

6 Given that $a = 0.24$, $b = 2.1$ and $c = 0.3$, find the value of N when:

(a) $N = ab^2$
(b) $N = ab - bc$
(c) $N = (ab)^2$
(d) $N = a^2b - b^2c$
(e) $N = abc$
(f) $N = a^2(4b^2 - 3bc^2)$

7 Given that $a = {}^{-}3$, $b = 2$ and $c = {}^{-}2$, find the value of N when:

(a) $N = ab^2$
(b) $N = \frac{a^2}{c}$
(c) $N = (ab)^2$
(d) $N = \frac{a(c - b)}{2c}$
(e) $N = abc$
(f) $N = b^2 - 4ac$

8 Given that $x = 3.1$, $y = {}^{-}0.07$ and $z = {}^{-}1.25$, find the value of A when:

(a) $A = x^2 + y^2$
(b) $A = \frac{xy - z^2}{4}$
(c) $A = x(y + z)$
(d) $A = \frac{2(x - 2z)}{y}$
(e) $A = x^2 - yz$
(f) $A = \frac{(x - 2y)}{1 - 4z}$

9 Given that $x = {}^{-}0.5$, $y = 2.5$ and $z = {}^{-}1.2$, find the value of:

(a) $V = x^2y$

(b) $N = \dfrac{x(y-z)^2}{5}$

(c) $V = x(y^2 + z^2)$

(d) $N = \dfrac{2xy^2 - 3yz^2}{2}$

(e) $V = x^2 - y^2z$

10 Given that $a = {}^{-}0.25$, $b = 2.1$ and $c = {}^{-}0.8$, find the value of N when:

(a) $N = ab^2 - bc^2$

(b) $N = \dfrac{b^2 - a^2}{1+c}$

(c) $N = (ab - bc)^2$

(d) $N = \dfrac{a(c-b)}{2}$

(e) $N = \sqrt{b^2 - 4ac}$

Area and volume formulae

Here are some familiar formulae for length, area and volume.

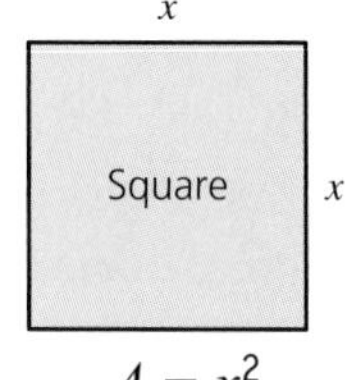

$A = x^2$

$P = 4x$

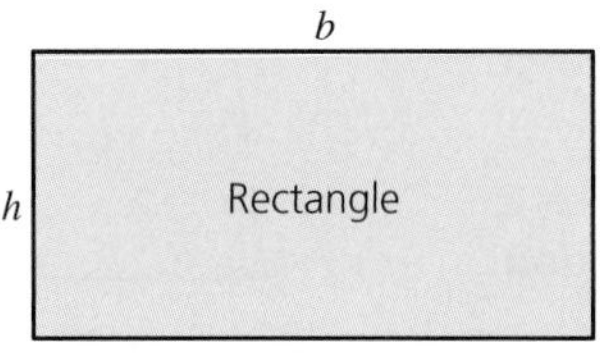

$A = bh$

$P = 2(b + h)$ or $2b + 2h$

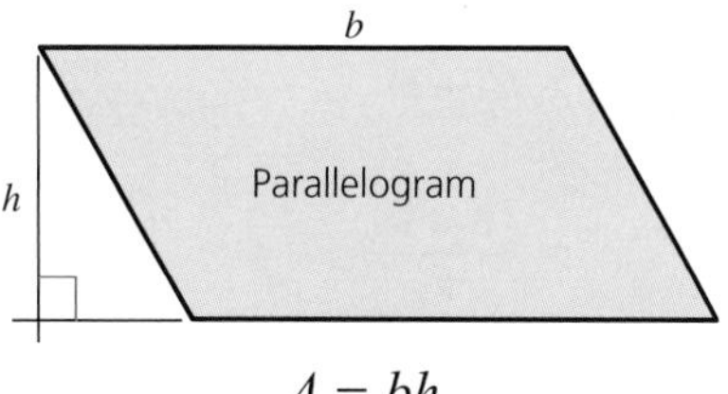

$A = bh$

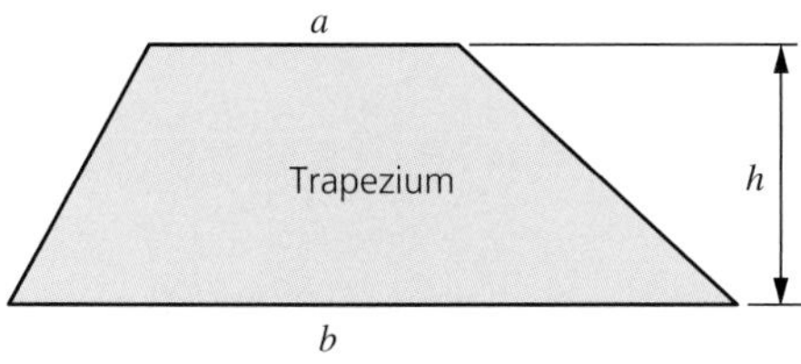

$$A = \frac{h(a+b)}{2}$$

h

Triangle

b

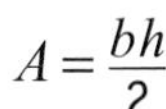

$$A = \frac{bh}{2}$$

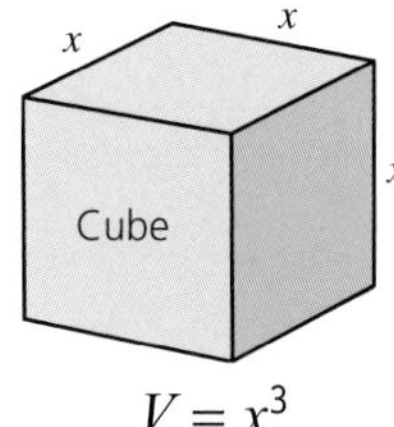

$V = x^3$

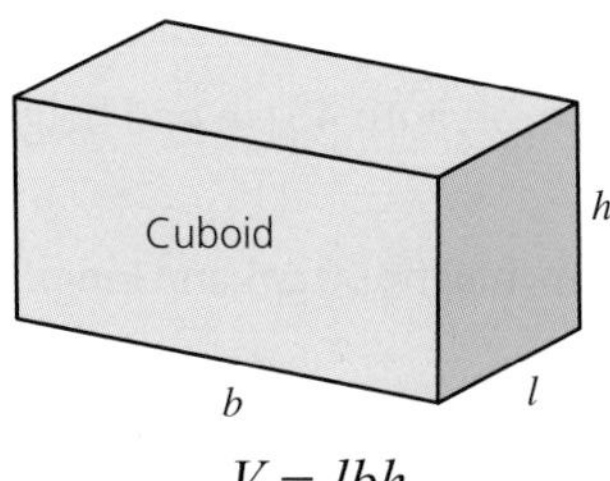

$V = lbh$

When you look at the diagrams, you can see what each unknown in the formula stands for.

However, when you use these formulae, you should not just write '$A = \dots$' but say exactly what A stands for. This applies to any formula you use. It also helps you to check you are using the correct formula.

In the next exercises you should set your working out like this.

1 Start each question with a sketch.

2 Make sure you choose the correct formula.

3 Follow the steps for substituting into the formula.

4 Even if you use a calculator, write down the stages of working and remember the units. Round non-exact answers to 3 significant figures (3 s.f.).

Example

Calculate the area of a trapezium with parallel sides of length 4 cm and 7 cm and height 6 cm

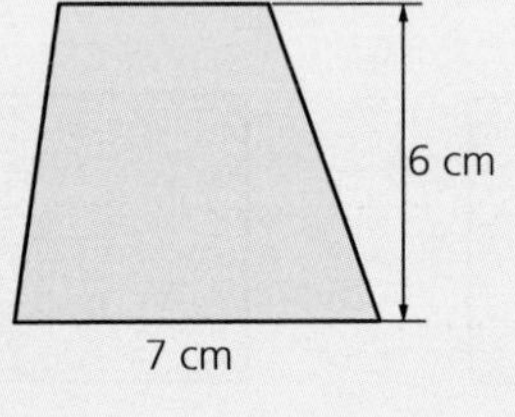

Area of trapezium $= \frac{h(a+b)}{2}$ Step 1: Formula

$= \frac{{}^{3}\not{6}(4+7)}{\not{2}_{1}}$ Step 2: Substitution

$= 3 \times 11$ Step 3: Calculation

$= 33\text{ cm}^2$ Step 4: Answer and units

The area is 33 cm^2

Exercise 9.3

1 Calculate the area of a triangle of base 5.6 cm and height 2.8 cm.

2 Find the perimeter of a rectangle of base 45 cm and height 1.4 m. Give your answer in metres.

3 Find the volume of a cube of edge 1.2 m.

4 Find the area of a parallelogram of base 1.3 m and height 55 cm. Give your answer in square metres (m^2).

5 Calculate the volume of a cuboid of length 5.2 m, breadth 45 cm and height 45 cm. Give your answer in cubic metres (m^3).

6 Work out the volume of a cuboid of width 55 cm, height 90 cm and length 1.2 m. Give your answer in litres.

7 Calculate the area of a trapezium with parallel sides of lengths 55 cm and 1.4 m and height 65 cm. Give your answer in square metres (m^2).

8 Starting with the formula for the area of a triangle, derive the formula for the area of a kite in terms of its diagonals. Then work out the area of a kite with diagonals of lengths 12 cm and 15 cm.

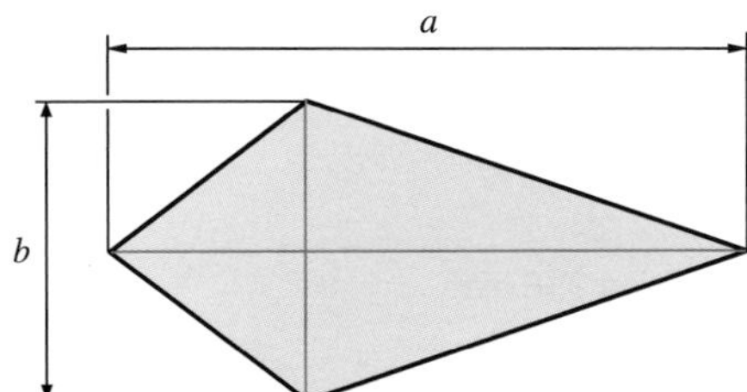

9 Starting with the formula for the area of a square, derive a formula for the surface area of a cube. Then work out the surface area of a cube of side length 12 cm.

10 Starting with the formula for the area of a rectangle, derive a formula for the surface area of a cuboid. Then work out the surface area of a cuboid of length 14 cm, breadth 20 cm and height 12 cm.

Calculating an unknown quantity

Previously you have been given the lengths of the sides of various shapes and asked to find the area, perimeter or volume. Sometimes, you will know the volume, area or perimeter and then you need to work out a length.

To calculate an unknown length, you start by substituting into the formula, just as before. Then you treat it exactly like an equation, solving it for the unknown.

Example

The area of a triangle is 24 cm^2 and the length of its base is 12.4 cm. Work out the height of the triangle.

Area of triangle $= \frac{bh}{2}$ where b is the base and h is the height — Step 1: Formula

$24 = \frac{12.4 \times b}{2}$ — Step 2: Substitute

$24 = 6.2 \times b$ — Step 3: Calculate

$\frac{24}{6.2} = b \quad (\div 6.2)$

$b = 3.870...$

$= 3.87$ cm (to 3 s.f.) — Steps 4 and 5: Answer and units

Exercise 9.4

Use the formulae given earlier to answer these questions. Give rounded answers correct to 3 s.f.

1 Find the side length of a square of area 289 cm^2

2 Find the height of a rectangle of base 12 cm and area 228 cm^2

3 Find the length of the base of a parallelogram of height 14 cm and area 238 cm^2

4 Find the length of the base of a triangle of height 5.5 cm and area 132 cm^2

5 Find the length of an edge of a cube of volume 343 cm^3

6 Find the height of a trapezium with parallel sides of lengths 10 cm and 12 cm and an area of 132 cm^2

7 Find the height of a trapezium with parallel sides of lengths 55 cm and 1.2 m and an area of 4 m^2

8 In a trapezium, one of the parallel sides is twice as long as the other and the height is 5 cm. Given that the area is 12 cm^2, find the lengths of the parallel sides.

9 Find the length of one parallel side of a trapezium if the length of the opposite side is 20 cm, the height is 12 cm and the area is 264 cm^2

10 Find the length of one parallel side of a trapezium, given that the length of the opposite side is 1.4 m, the height is 60 cm and the area is 1.5 m^2

These questions are more challenging.

11 A parallelogram has a base twice as long as its height and an area of 30 cm^2. How long is the base?

12 The height of a triangle is three times the length of its base and it has an area of 25 cm^2. What is the height?

13 The sides of a rectangle are in the **ratio** 3 : 4 and the area of the rectangle is 100 cm^2. What are the lengths of the sides?

14 The base and height of a triangle are in the ratio 3 : 5 and the triangle has an area of 150 cm^2. What are the lengths of the base and the height?

Distance, speed and time formulae

When you make a journey, the **time** you travel will depend on the **distance** travelled and the **speed** at which you are moving. The longer the distance, the greater the time it will take, the greater the speed, the shorter the journey time.

The formula for the **distance** travelled, given the **speed** and **time**, is: $d = st$

where d is the distance travelled, s is the **average speed** and t is the time taken.

From this formula you can derive the formula for the time taken: $t = \frac{d}{s}$

and the formula for the speed: $s = \frac{d}{t}$

You can remind yourself of these formulae by writing them in a triangle, like this.

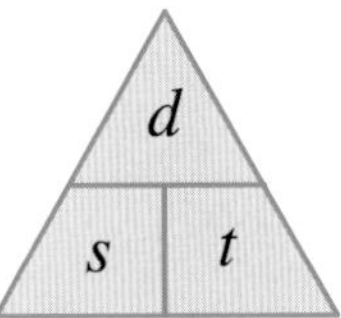

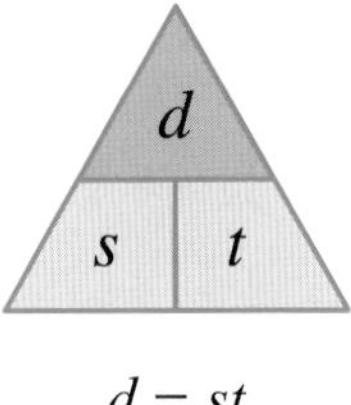

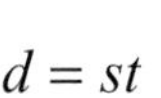

$d = st$

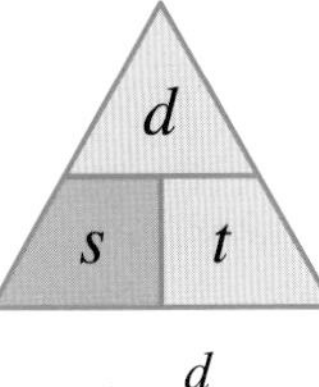

$s = \frac{d}{t}$

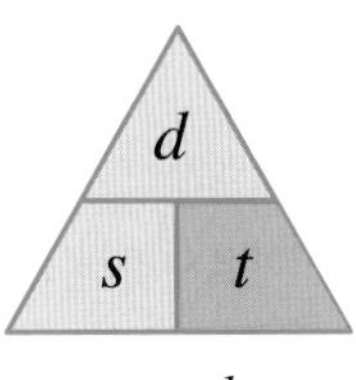

$t = \frac{d}{s}$

The next example shows how to use this speed triangle.

Example

I walk for 4 hours at 3 km/h. How far do I walk?

Distance = speed × time

= 3 × 4

= 12 km

Remember that the units of time do not follow the metric system – there are 60 seconds in a minute and 60 minutes in an hour. When time is not given as a whole number of hours you need to convert it to a fraction or decimal fraction of the unit. If speed is expressed in kilometres per hour (km/h), you must calculate with time in hours, not minutes.

25 minutes is $\frac{25}{60} = \frac{5}{12}$ hour.

If the time is given as 2 hours and 30 minutes, as a fraction it would be $2\frac{1}{2}$ hours and as a decimal it would be 2.5 hours. If you calculated time to be 3.3333... hours, this is $3\frac{1}{3}$ hours or 3 hours and 20 minutes.

Example

I travelled 12 miles in 12 minutes. What was my speed?

$d = 12$ miles $\quad t = 12$ minutes $= \frac{1}{5}$ hour $= 0.2$ hours

$$s = \frac{d}{t}$$

$$= \frac{12}{0.2}$$

$$= 60 \text{ mph}$$

If you are using a calculator then change time to a decimal. If you do not have a calculator, you may as well use fractions.

Exercise 9.5

1 I travel at 60 mph for 45 minutes. How far do I go?

2 I drive 90 miles at a speed of 60 mph. How long does the journey take?

3 I walk three-quarters of a mile in 20 minutes. What is my speed, in miles per hour (mph)?

4 A comet travels 5000 miles in 10 minutes. What is its speed, in miles per hour (mph)?

5 A space shuttle travels at 30 000 km/h for 5 minutes. How far does it go?

6 My mother drives at 40 mph for 30 minutes and then drives at 30 mph for 40 minutes. How far does she go?

7 It took us 3 hours and 20 minutes to travel 300 km. What was our speed?

8 We travelled 12 miles on the M25 at 10 mph, but then we travelled 80 miles on the M2 at 60 mph. What was our total journey time?

9 An aeroplane left Heathrow at 10:34 and arrived at Newark at 16:24. The distance is 3605 miles. What was the speed of the aeroplane?

10 A ship travelled for 6 days and 4 hours on a journey from Southampton to Gibraltar, a distance of 3219 nautical miles. What was the average daily distance covered, and what was the speed?

At sea, distance is measured in nautical miles; one nautical mile per hour is called one **knot**.

1 knot ≈ 1.852 km/h ≈ 1.151 mph

11 If a car travels twice as far as the distance between Acity and Beville, at the same speed it would have taken to travel from Acity to Beeville, how much longer or shorter is the journey time?

12 If a car travels three times as far as the distance between Acity and Beeville, in the same time it would have taken to travel from Acity to Beeville, how much greater or less is its speed?

13 If a car travels three times as far as the distance from Acity to Beeville, in half the time it would have taken to travel from Acity to Beeville, how much faster or slower is it travelling?

Average speed

Although the examples so far have referred to speed, it is almost impossible to move at a constant speed. To travel anywhere, you would start from rest, which means at zero speed. On a car journey of 60 miles, you would speed up and slow down, depending on road conditions and traffic and whether you stop for a break.

Therefore, in problems about distance, speed and time, you work with an **average speed.**

$$\text{Average speed} = \frac{\text{total distance travelled}}{\text{total time taken}}$$

When you calculate the average speed, you work out the total distance you have travelled, from start to finish. Then you work out the time taken, including any stops you had to make. This is the total time. Generally, you cannot just take the mean of the various stages of the journey.

Example

We travelled at 40 km/h for 15 minutes and then travelled at 60 km/h for 20 minutes. What was our average speed?

> For a two part journey it can help to think of t_1, t_2 for the time of each part, d_1, d_2 for distance and s_1, s_2 for speed.

$d = st$

For the first part of the journey:

$\text{speed}_1 = 40\text{ km/h}$ $\quad\quad$ $\text{time}_1 = 15\text{ minutes} = \frac{1}{4}\text{ h}$

$$\begin{aligned} d_1 &= s_1t_1 \\ &= 40 \times \frac{1}{4} \\ &= 10\text{ km} \end{aligned}$$

For the second part of the journey:

$\text{speed}_2 = 60\text{ km/h}$ $\quad\quad$ $\text{time}_2 = 20\text{ minutes} = \frac{1}{3}\text{ h}$

$$\begin{aligned} d_2 &= s_2t_2 \\ &= 60 \times \frac{1}{3} \\ &= 20\text{ km} \end{aligned}$$

For the whole journey:

$\text{total distance} = d_1 + d_2 = 30\text{ km}$ $\quad\quad$ $\text{total time} = 35\text{ minutes} = \frac{7}{12}\text{ h}$

$$\begin{aligned} \text{average speed} &= \frac{\text{total distance}}{\text{total time}} \\ &= 30 \div \frac{7}{12} \\ &= 51.428... \\ &= 51.4\text{ km/h (to 3 s.f.)} \end{aligned}$$

Exercise 9.6

1 A car travels for 15 minutes at 45 km/h and then for 30 minutes at 60 km/h.

   (a) What distance did the car travel?

   (b) What was its average speed?

2 A man walked for 15 minutes at 4 km/h and then for 10 minutes at 5 km/h.

   (a) What distance did the man walk?

   (b) What was his average speed?

3 A train travelled at 60 km/h for 20 minutes and at 120 km/h for 1 hour and 40 minutes.

   (a) What distance did the train travel?

   (b) What was his average speed?

4 An aeroplane travelled at 250 km/h for one and a half hours and then at 350 km/h for two and a half hours.

   (a) What distance did the aeroplane travel?

   (b) What was its average speed?

5 A car travelled at an average speed of 60 mph for 2 hours. In the first part of the journey, the car was being driven in a town and was travelling at 25 mph for 20 minutes. What speed did the car travel in the second part of its journey?

6 A car travelled at an average speed of 80 km/h for 100 km. In the first part of the journey the car travelled at 40 km/h for 15 minutes. What speed did the car travel in the second part of the journey?

7 A London-to-Paris train travelled from London to Dover, a distance of 120 km, at 200 km/h. It then travelled 50 km under the channel at 100 km/h, before completing the remaining 330 km to Paris at 300 km/h.

   (a) What was the average speed of the train?

   (b) What was the total journey time?

Units of formulae

Whenever you are writing formulae, or working with several formulae put together, it is important to keep asking yourself: 'Does it look right? Does it seem sensible?'

It is as easy to do this with letters representing unknown numbers as it is with known numbers. If you continually bear in mind the units of a formula it can help to check the validity of what you are doing.

The next example uses a compound unit that you may have used in science, called **density**. This is the mass of a substance, per unit volume. It is calculated as mass/volume.

Example

Given that D is the density in grams per cubic centimetre (g/cm^3), M is the mass in grams (g) and V is the volume in cubic centimetres (cm^3), work out the units of each formula and hence what quantity (if any) is being calculated.

(i) DV (ii) $\frac{V}{M}$

(i) $DV = \frac{\text{grams}}{\text{cm}^3} \times \text{cm}^3$

$= \text{grams} \rightarrow \text{mass}$

(ii) $\frac{V}{M} = \frac{\text{cm}^3}{\text{grams}}$ $\rightarrow$ cubic centimetres per gram

This is possibly the wrong formula!

Exercise 9.7

1 Given that d is a length in metres, t is a time in seconds and s is a speed in metres per second (m/s), work out units for each formula and hence the quantity that is represented.

(a) st (b) $\frac{d}{s}$

2 Given that D is the density in grams per cubic centimetre (g/cm^3), M is the mass in grams (g) and V is the volume in cubic centimetres (cm^3), work out units for each formula and hence the quantity that is represented.

(a) $\frac{M}{V}$ (b) $\frac{M}{D}$

3 Given that a, b, c and d are units of length, in centimetres, state the quantity, length, area or volume, given by each formula.

(a) $a(b+c)$ (b) $\sqrt{a^2+b^2}$ (c) $\frac{\pi a^2}{b}$ (d) $\pi a^2(b+c)$ (e) $\sqrt[3]{abc}$ (f) $\frac{abc}{\pi}$ (g) $\frac{\pi a^2(b+c)}{2a}$

4 Given that u and v are units of speed in metres per second (m/s), t is time in seconds, m is mass in grams and a, b, c and s are lengths in metres, write down the units of A, B and C.

(a) $A = \frac{m}{abc}$ (b) $B = t\sqrt{u^2 - v^2}$ (c) $D = \frac{s}{u+v}$

Extension: Rearranging formulae

When you were asked to find the unknown lengths in previous exercises, you substituted numbers into the appropriate formula and then solved the resulting equation. However, there are times when you will need to rearrange the formula. For example, you have rearranged the formula:

$d = st$

to give:

$t = \frac{d}{s}$ and $s = \frac{d}{t}$

In the first formula, d is the **subject**. In the rearranged formulae, the subjects are t and s

To solve a more difficult equation you carry on as you have done before, taking it one step at a time. Remember always to do the same to both sides and always write a summary of what you are doing on the right-hand side.

Example

Rearrange the formula $y = \frac{x}{4} + 7$ to give x in terms of y.

$y = \frac{x}{4} + 7$ (− 7)

$y - 7 = \frac{x}{4}$ (× 4)

$4(y - 7) = x$

$x = 4(y - 7)$

Note the use of brackets and the correct use of algebra. There are no × or ÷ signs in the formula.

Extension Exercise 9.8

Make x the subject of each formula.

1 $y = x + 3$

2 $y = x - 5$

3 $y = x + a$

4 $y = x - b$

5 $y = d - x$

6 $y = 2x$

7 $y = ax$

8 $y = \frac{x}{2}$

9 $y = \frac{x}{b}$

10 $y = 2x + 3$

11 $y = 3x - 4$

12 $y = 2x - b$

13 $y = c + 3x$

14 $y = ax + b$

15 $y = cx - d$

16 $y = a(x - b)$

17 $y = \frac{3x}{a}$

18 $y = \frac{ax}{b}$

19 $y = \frac{2a}{x}$

20 $y = \frac{3b}{2x}$

21 $y = \frac{(x + b)}{c}$

22 $y = \frac{2(x - 1)}{3}$

23 $y = \frac{a(x - b)}{c}$

24 $y = \frac{ab}{x - 1}$

25 $y = \frac{x}{2} + 1$

26 $y + 3 = ax - 2$

27 $\frac{y}{2} = \frac{x}{a} + b$

28 $\frac{y}{2} = \frac{a}{x}$

29 $\frac{y}{b} = \frac{a}{x - c}$

30 $\frac{y}{b} = \frac{a + d}{x - c}$

Summary Exercise 9.9

In this exercise you can use your calculator, but remember to show all stages of your working. Give any rounded answers correct to 3 s.f.

1 Write a formula for *P*, where *P* is the perimeter of this shape.

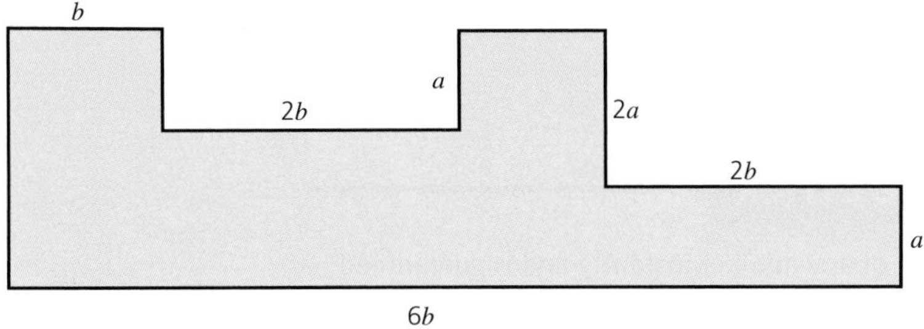

2 Write a formula for *A*, where *A* is the area of the shape in Q1

3 Given that $a = {}^-1$, $b = 2$ and $c = {}^-4$, find the value of N when:

(a) $N = a - b$

(b) $N = \frac{a^2}{c}$

(c) $N = abc$

(d) $N = \frac{a(c - b)}{2b}$

(e) $N = c^2 - a^2$

(f) $N = b^2 - 4ac$

4 Find the perimeter of a square with sides of length 8 cm.

5 **(a)** Find the area of a trapezium with height 1.2 m, and parallel sides of lengths 85 cm and 1.05 m. Give your answer in square metres (m²).

(b) A triangle has an area of 12 cm² and its base is 9 cm long. What is the height?

6 A cuboid has a volume of 500 cm³ and a base area of 81 cm². What is its height?

7 I drive 750 miles at a speed of 60 mph. How long does the journey take?

8 A car travelled at 40 km/h for 10 minutes and then at 60 km/h for 50 minutes.

(a) What was its average speed?

(b) What distance did the car travel?

9 Make x the subject of each formula.

(a) $y = a - x$ (b) $y = c + ax$ (c) $y = \frac{h(a-x)}{b}$

10 A motorbike courier spends part of his day in town and part of his time on a motorway. On the motorway he travels at an average speed of 60 mph and in town his speed is an average of 20 mph.

(a) On Monday he had a 40-mile journey, of which 30 miles were on the motorway.

(i) What distance did he travel in town?

(ii) What was the total time?

(iii) What was his average speed?

(b) On Tuesday he had to make the same trip in the same time but he was held up in town and travelled at an average speed of 15 mph. Was he able to make the delivery without breaking the 70 mph speed limit on the motorway?

Activity: The cube root trick

This trick lets you find the cube root of any number instantly and is guaranteed to impress your maths teacher.

Before you can do the trick you will have to learn the first nine cubes.

1, 8, 27, 64, 125, 216, 343, 512, 729

Now remember the last digit of each cube.

Number	Last digit of cube
1	1
2	8
3	7
4	4
5	5
6	6
7	3
8	2
9	9

They are quite easy to remember because:

1 and 9 give 1 and 9

4, 5 and 6 give 4, 5, and 6

And the others add up to 10:

2 gives 8   8 gives 2

3 gives 7   7 gives 3

Now for the trick!

Announce that you can work out the cube root of any perfect cube number. Ask the person to think of any two-digit number, calculate its cube and give you the number.

For example: 50 653   (the cube of 37) $37^3 = 50\,653$

To find the cube root, follow these two steps.

Step 1 Ignore the last three digits of the number (in this case 653) and work out the largest cube contained in 50

In this case it is $3^3 = 27$ This tells you that the tens digit is 3

Step 2 Go back to the last three digits (653) and look at the last digit, which is 3

3 is the last digit in 7^3 so your units digit is 7

You can now reveal that the cube root of 50 653 is 37

Look at one more example.

To find the cube root of 592 704

Step 1 The nearest cube to 592 is $8^3 = 512$ so the tens digit is 8

Step 2 The cube that ends in 4 is 64, which is 4^3, therefore the cube root of 592 704 is 84

Now go and amaze your teacher!

10 Geometry

Geometry involves the study of angles and shapes, both two-dimensional (**2D**) and three-dimensional (**3D**). Pilots and navigators use geometry all the time. This is because a position on a map or chart can be given by a distance and an angle from a point, which is called a **bearing**.

Bearings

Bearings are measured clockwise from north. They may be given in terms of compass directions or in degrees. For navigational purposes, bearings are given in three figures, such as 'two seven five', to be sure that the pilot or captain has the correct numerals.

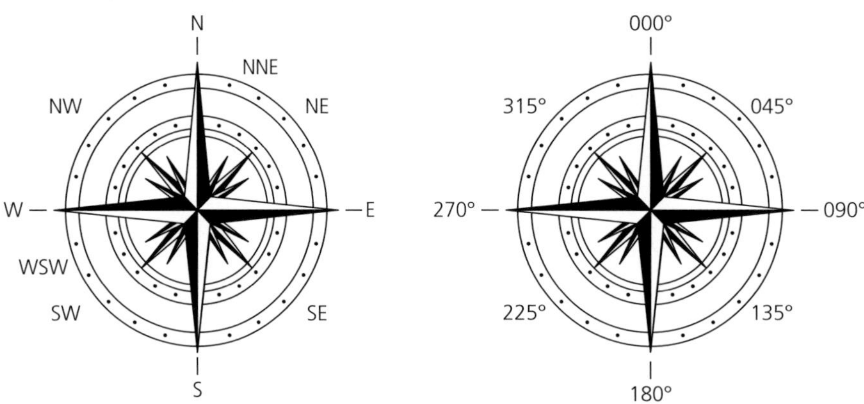

When describing a position, you need to take a bearing from something, such as a fixed point.

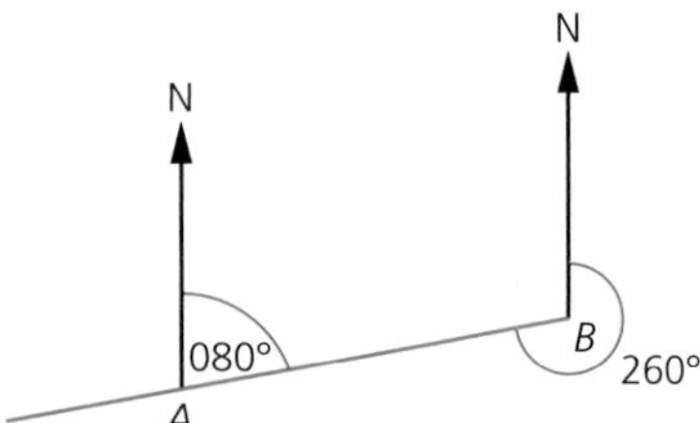

In this diagram, the bearing of *A* from *B* is 260° and the bearing of *B* from *A* is 080°

By now you will have noticed that bearings are based on angles and how they relate to a north line. Pause here and review what you know about angles at points and in parallel lines.

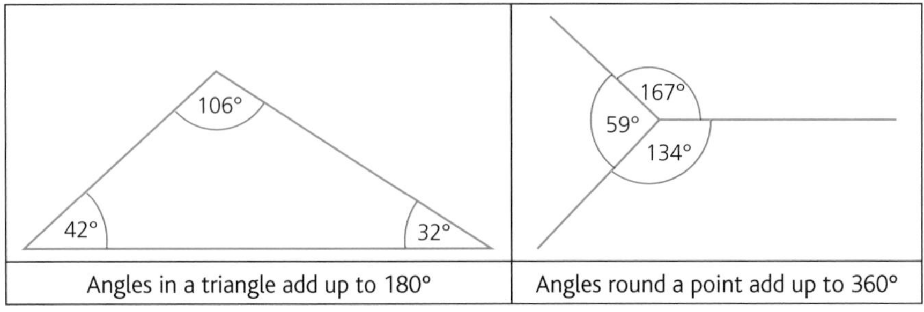

Angles in a triangle add up to 180° | Angles round a point add up to 360°

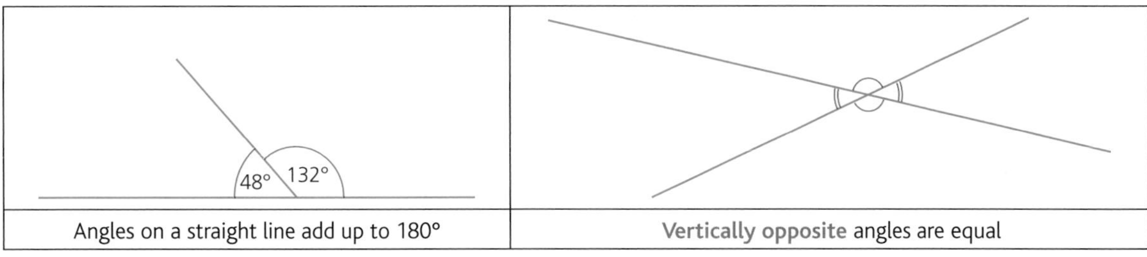

Angles on a straight line add up to 180° | Vertically opposite angles are equal

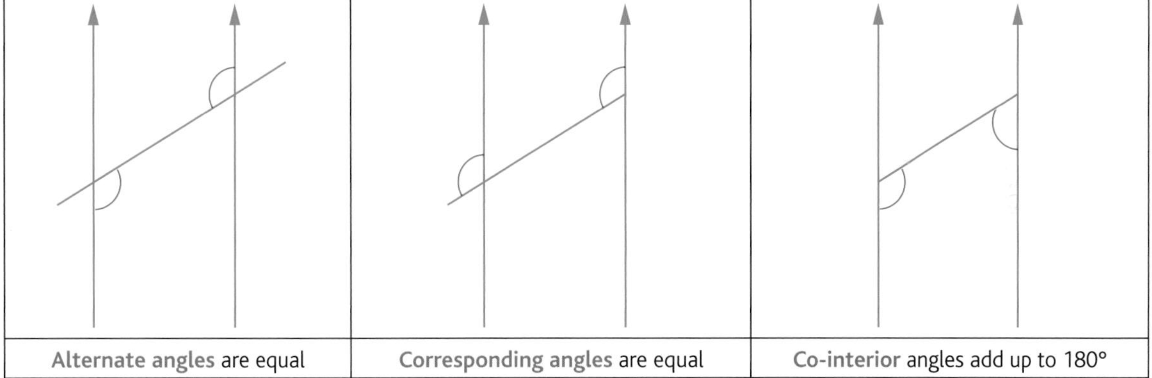

Alternate angles are equal | Corresponding angles are equal | Co-interior angles add up to 180°

Calculating angles and bearings

When you are calculating with angles and bearings, always start with a rough **sketch**. Label it with all the details you are given, to make sure that you are looking at the correct angle.

> A **construction** is a diagram drawn accurately. A **sketch** is a neat drawing that approximates the shape of a construction. You generally use geometric tools such as ruler, protractor and compasses for a construction, but you may draw a sketch freehand.

Exercise 10.1

1 Write each compass direction as a three-figure bearing.

(a) south east (c) east north east

(b) south south west (d) north north west

2 Write each three-figure bearing as a compass direction.

(a) 225° (b) $022\frac{1}{2}°$ (c) $157\frac{1}{2}°$ (d) $292\frac{1}{2}°$

3 (a) If the bearing of *A* from *B* is 045°, what is the bearing from *B* from *A*?

(b) If the bearing of *C* from *D* is 200°, what is the bearing from *D* from *C*?

(c) If the bearing of *P* from *Q* is 118°, what is the bearing from *Q* from *P*?

(d) If the bearing of *X* from *Y* is 312°, what is the bearing from *Y* from *X*?

4 In this diagram, *B* is the same distance from *A* as from *C* and the bearing of *B* from *A* is 112°

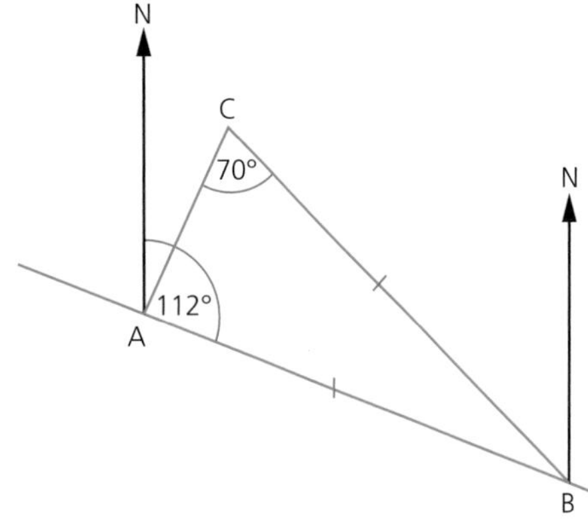

Given that $\angle ACB = 70°$ calculate, giving reasons:

(a) $\angle ABC$

(b) the bearing of *C* from *A*

(c) the bearing of *C* from *B*.

5 Construct a triangle *LMN* such that *N* is 6 cm due north of *M* and *L* is to the east of *MN*. *LM* = 7 cm and *LN* = 5 cm.

Measure the bearing of: (a) *L* from *M* (b) *L* from *N*

6 Point *Q* lies due south of point *P*. Point *S* is equidistant from points *P* and *Q* and is on a bearing of 305° from *Q*

(a) What is the bearing of *S* from *P*?

(b) What is the bearing of *P* from *S*?

7 Point A lies on a bearing of 054° from point B. Point C lies due east of A and point D lies due east of B and due south of C

(a) Draw a neat sketch to show the relative positions of A, B, C and D

(b) Given that $AC = CD$ calculate $\angle BAD$

8 Point C is the midpoint of line AB, with B being due east of A

Point D lies on a bearing of 038° from C and $DC = BC$

(a) Draw a neat sketch to show the relative positions of A, B, C and D

(b) Calculate the bearing of B from D

(c) Calculate the bearing of A from D

You will look again at bearings in Chapter 18

2D shapes

By now, you should have learnt a great deal about 2D shapes.

How much can you remember? Read through the next section and look at the diagrams. Make sure that you can recall all of the properties of the 2D shapes, and what the marks on the sides and angles mean.

Triangles

There are three main types of triangle, based upon the properties of their sides:

- **equilateral** – all sides equal
- **isosceles** – two sides equal
- **scalene** – no sides equal.

Within these categories, there are further classifications.

- **Isosceles triangles** may be **right-angled** or **obtuse-angled**.
- **Scalene triangles** may be right-angled or obtuse-angled.

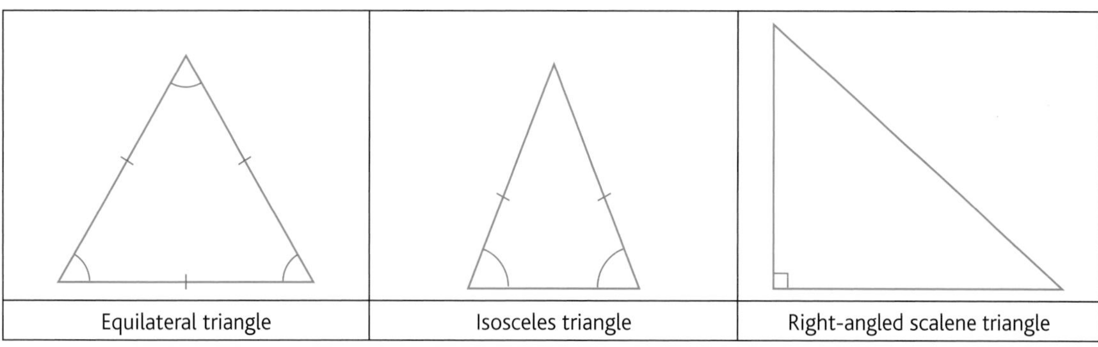

Equilateral triangle	Isosceles triangle	Right-angled scalene triangle

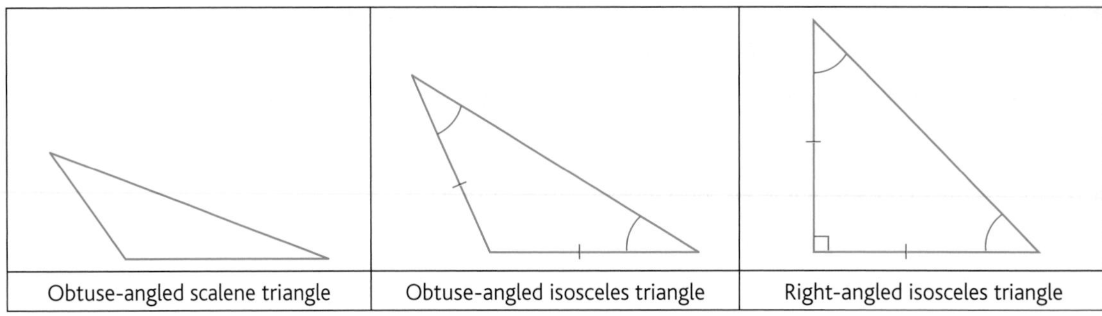

Quadrilaterals

A quadrilateral is any four-sided 2D shape. The table shows a summary of the shapes and their properties.

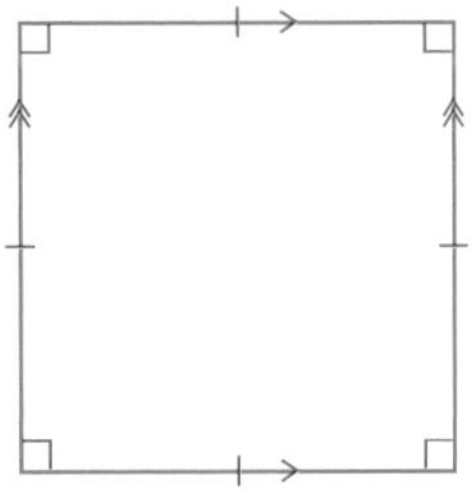 Square	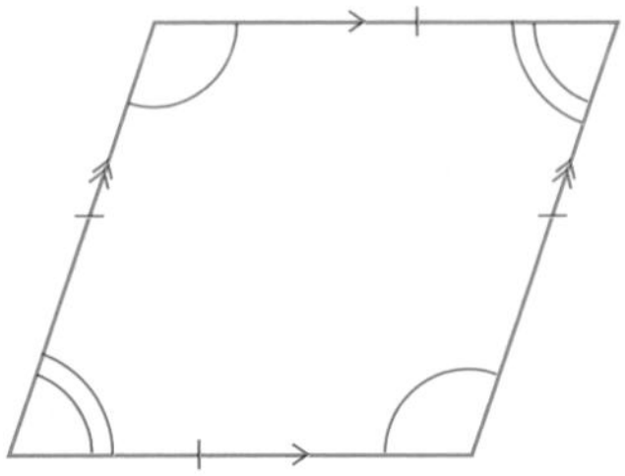 **Rhombus**	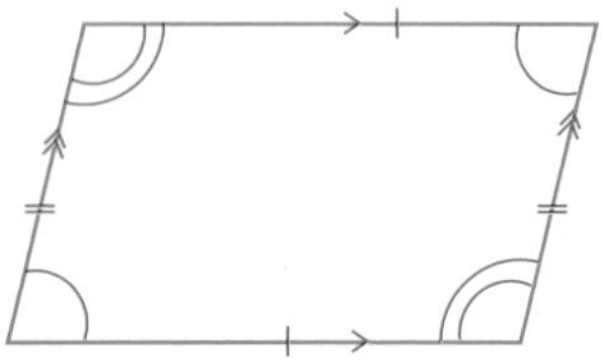 Parallelogram
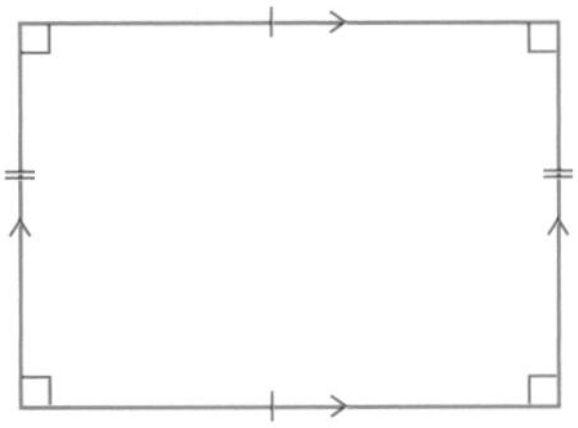 Rectangle	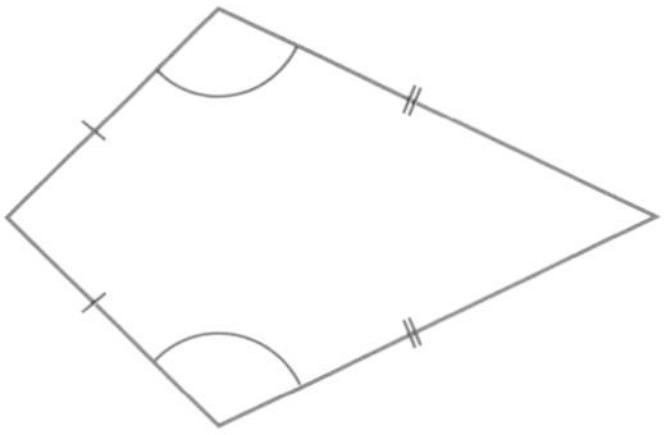 Kite	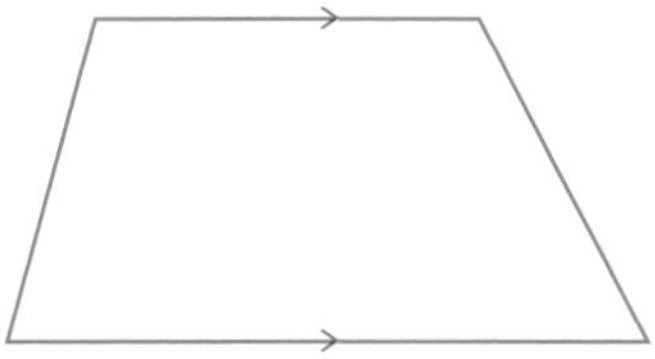 Trapezium
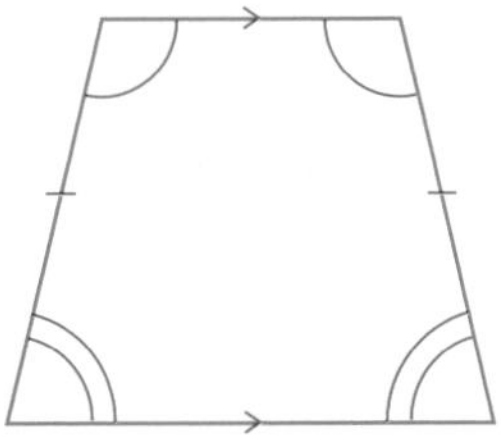 Isosceles trapezium	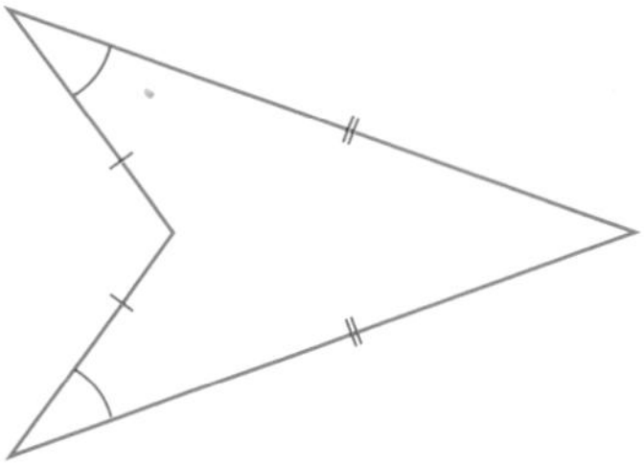 Isosceles arrowhead	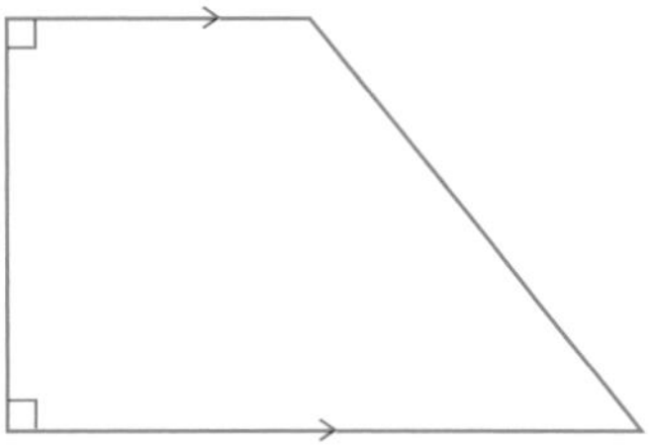 Right-angled trapezium

Polygons

A **polygon** is a 2D shape that has three or more sides. The table shows some examples.

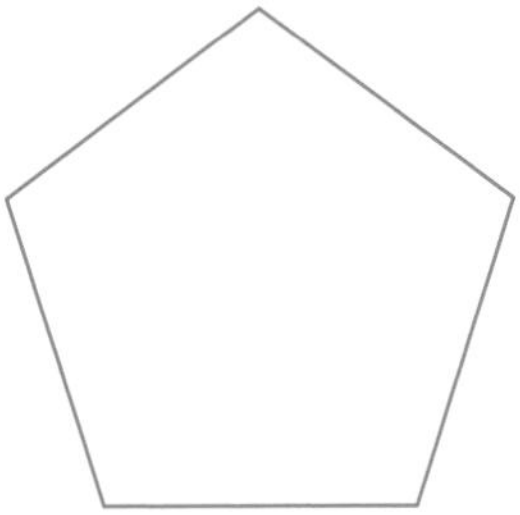	Pentagon 5 sides 5 angles	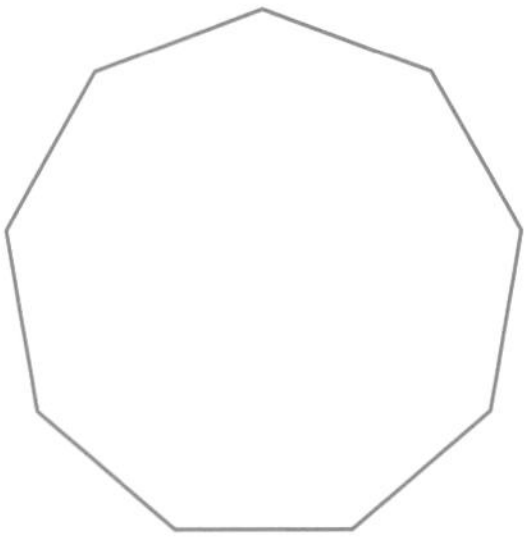	Nonagon 9 sides 9 angles
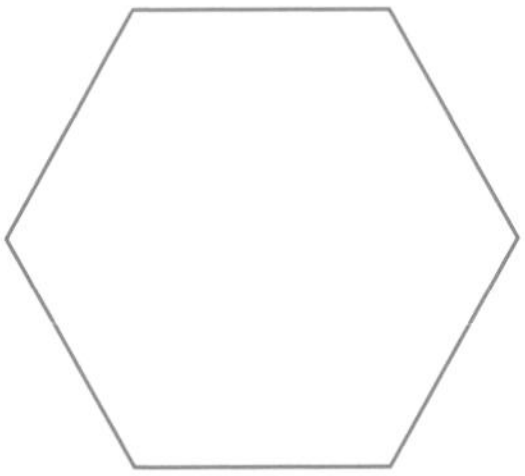	Hexagon 6 sides 6 angles	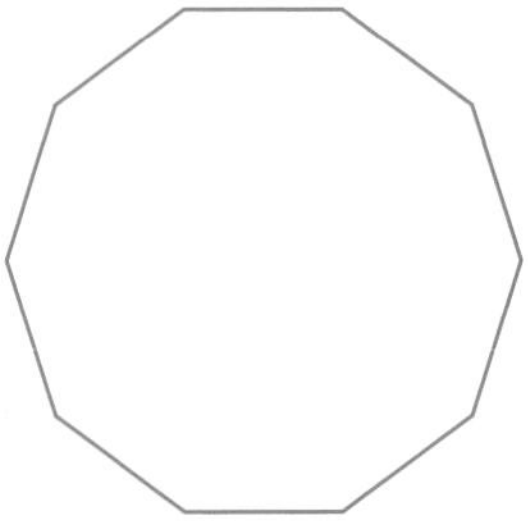	Decagon 10 sides 10 angles
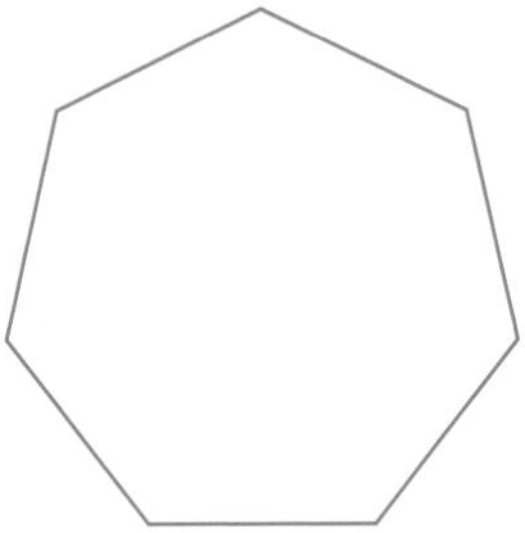	Heptagon 7 sides 7 angles	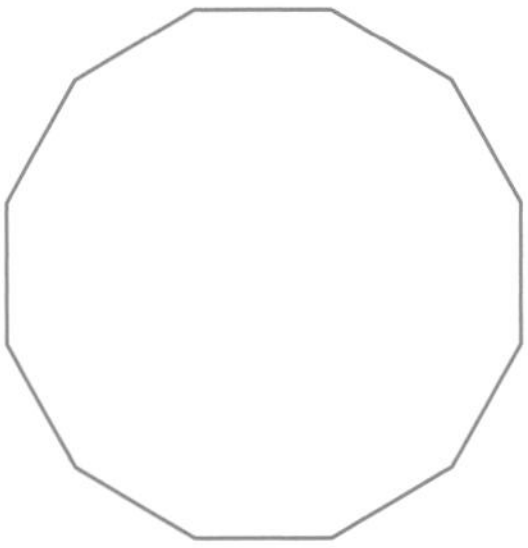	Dodecagon 12 sides 12 angles
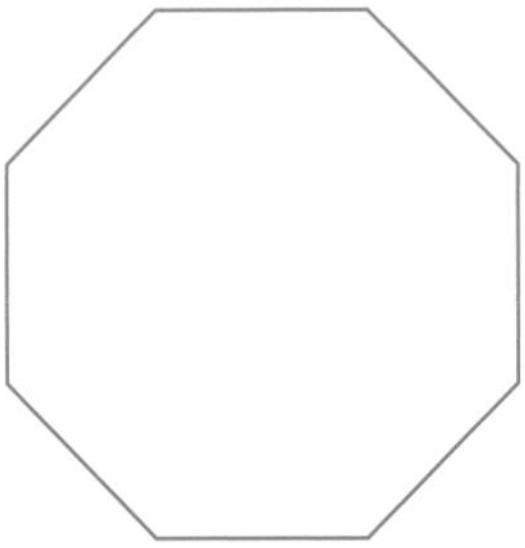	Octagon 8 sides 8 angles		

Note that in a **regular polygon** all the sides are the same length and all the angles are the same size.

Polygon formulae

There are **formulae** for finding the **interior** and **exterior** angles of polygons.

As the interior and exterior angles meet on a straight line they must **add up to 180°**

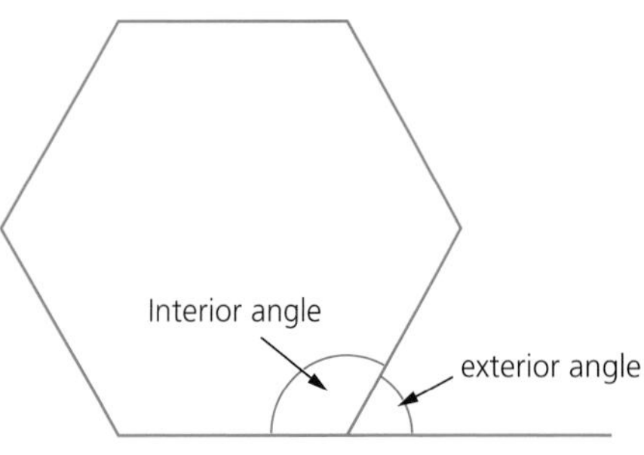

For any polygon with n sides:

- sum of exterior angles = 360°
- sum of interior angles = $180(n - 2)°$

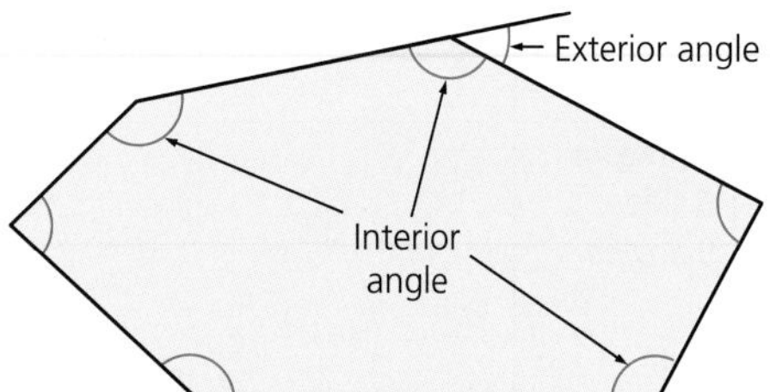

For any regular polygon with n sides:

- exterior angle = $\frac{360°}{n}$ and $n = \frac{360°}{\text{exterior angle}}$
- interior angle = 180° – exterior angle or = $\frac{180(n-2)°}{n}$

Example

(i) Work out the interior angle of a regular pentagon.

Interior angle = $\frac{180(n-2)°}{n}$

When $n = 5$:

interior angle = $\frac{180° \times 3}{5}$

$= 108°$

> Just as you have done before, substitute the values that you know into the formula and then solve it as you would any other equation.

(ii) A regular polygon has interior angles of 120°. How many sides does it have?

Interior angle = $\frac{180(n-2)°}{n}$

$120° = \frac{180(n-2)°}{n}$

$120n = 180n - 360$

$60n = 360$

$n = 6$ sides

or

Exterior angle = 180 – 120

$= 60$

$n = \frac{360°}{\text{exterior angle}}$

$n = \frac{360°}{60}$

$n = 6$ sides

Exercise 10.2

1 Calculate the sum of the interior angles of a pentagon.

2 Calculate the sum of the interior angles of a nonagon.

3 Calculate the sum of the interior angles of an octagon.

4 Calculate the exterior angle of a regular hexagon.

5 Calculate the exterior angle of a regular heptagon.

6 Calculate the exterior angle of a regular decagon.

7 Calculate the interior angle of a regular hexagon.

8 Calculate the interior angle of a regular octagon.

9 How many sides has a regular polygon with all exterior angles equal to 18°?

10 How many sides has a regular polygon with all exterior angles equal to 24°?

11 How many sides has a regular polygon with all interior angles equal to 150°?

12 How many sides has a regular polygon with all interior angles equal to 160°?

Applying the formulae

When you are calculating angles in geometric figures, you may need to apply the formulae for the angles of a polygon.

Example

The diagonal AC is drawn in the regular pentagon $ABCDE$

(a) Calculate the size of $\angle ABC$

(b) What type of triangle is ABC? Give reasons for your answer.

(c) What type of quadrilateral is $ACDE$? Give reasons for your answer.

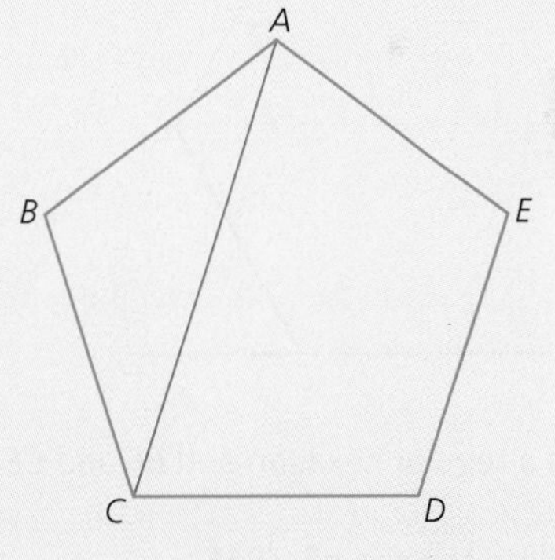

(a) $\angle ABC = \dfrac{180(n-2)^\circ}{n}$

$= \dfrac{180^\circ \times 3}{5}$

$= 108^\circ$

(b) $\angle ABC$ is greater than 90°

$AB = AC$

So ABC is an obtuse-angled isosceles triangle.

(c) AC is parallel to DE

$CD = AE$

So $ACDE$ is an isosceles trapezium.

Exercise 10.3

1 *ABCDE* is a regular pentagon.

O is the centre of the pentagon such that $AO = BO = CO = DO = EO$

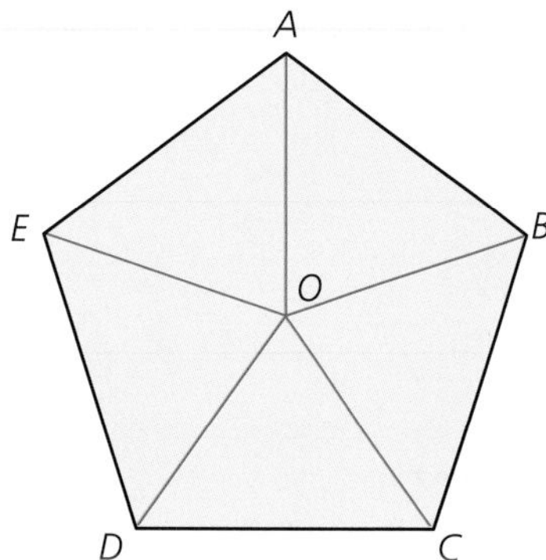

Calculate the size of: **(a)** $\angle AOB$ **(b)** $\angle OBC$ **(c)** $\angle ABC$

2 *BCDEFG* is a regular hexagon.

Calculate the size of each of these angles. Give reasons for your answers.

(a) $\angle CDG$ **(b)** $\angle CDE$ **(c)** $\angle DCF$

(d) What can you say about *CF* and *DE*?

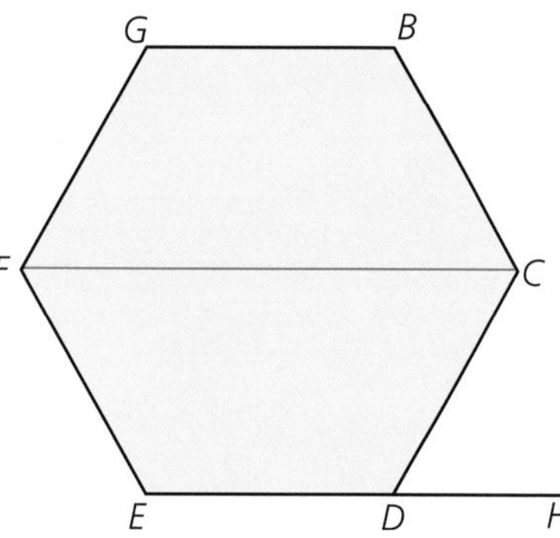

3 *ABCDEF* is a regular hexagon and *BF* and *CE* are two of its diagonals.

(a) Calculate the size of $\angle BAF$

(b) Calculate the size of $\angle ECD$

(c) What type of quadrilateral is *ABCF*? Give reasons for your answer.

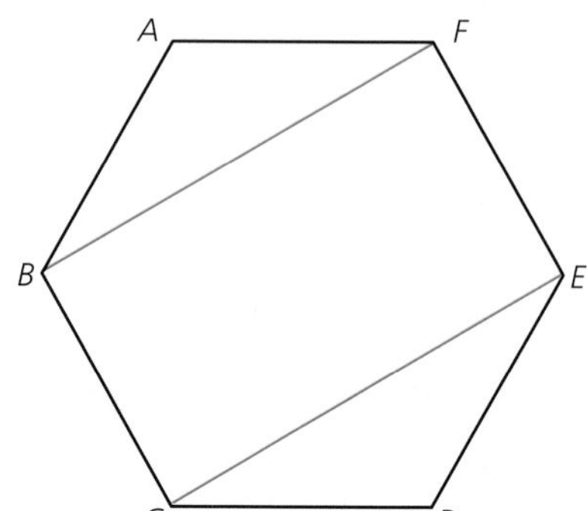

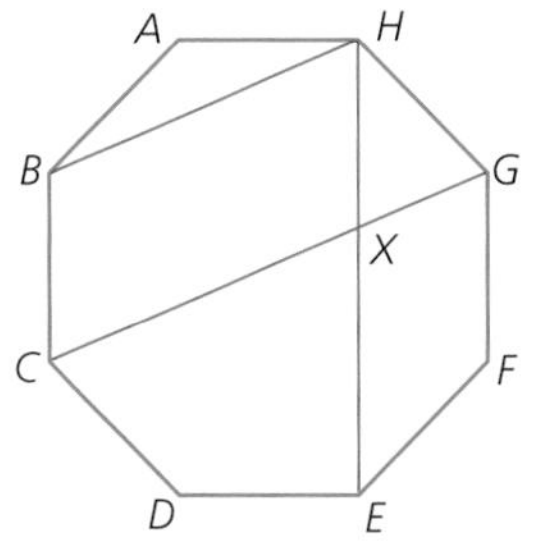

4 *ABCDEFGH* is a regular octagon with diagonals *BH*, *CG* and *EH*. *EH* and *CG* cross at *X*

(a) Calculate the size of $\angle BAH$

(b) Calculate the size of $\angle HBA$

(c) Calculate the size of $\angle HBC$

(d) What type of quadrilateral is *EFGH*? Give reasons for your answer.

(e) What type of quadrilateral is *HBCX*? Give reasons for your answer.

5 *ABCDEFGH* is a regular octagon with centre *O*

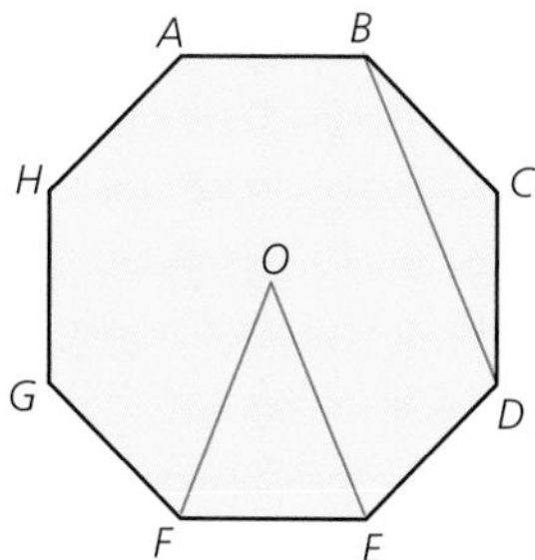

Calculate the size of each of these angles. Give reasons for your answers.

(a) $\angle EOF$ **(c)** $\angle OED$ **(e)** $\angle CDB$

(b) $\angle FED$ **(d)** $\angle BCD$ **(f)** $\angle BDE$

(g) What can you say about *BD* and *OE*?

6 *ABCDE* is a regular pentagon and *EDFGHI* is a regular hexagon.

Calculate the size of each of these angles. Give reasons for your answers.

(a) $\angle CDE$ **(c)** $\angle CED$ **(e)** $\angle CDF$

(b) $\angle EDF$ **(d)** $\angle DEF$ **(f)** $\angle ECF$

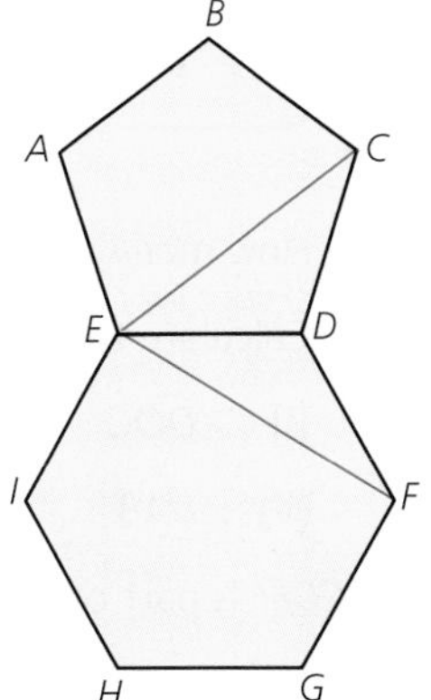

7 This is the base of a regular polygon.

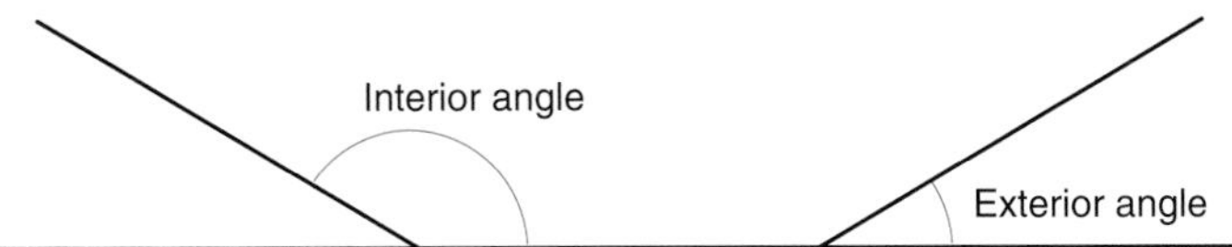

The interior angle is 11 times the size of the exterior angle. How many sides has the polygon?

8 *ABDEFGH* is regular octagon with centre *O*

(a) Calculate the size of each of these angles. Give reasons for your answers.

(i) $\angle GHA$

(ii) $\angle HGB$

(iii) $\angle GOF$

(iv) $\angle FGE$

(v) the angle marked x

(vi) the angle marked y

(b) What type of quadrilateral is *GOEF*? Give reasons for your answer.

9 *AB*, *BC* and *CD* are three sides of a regular polygon.

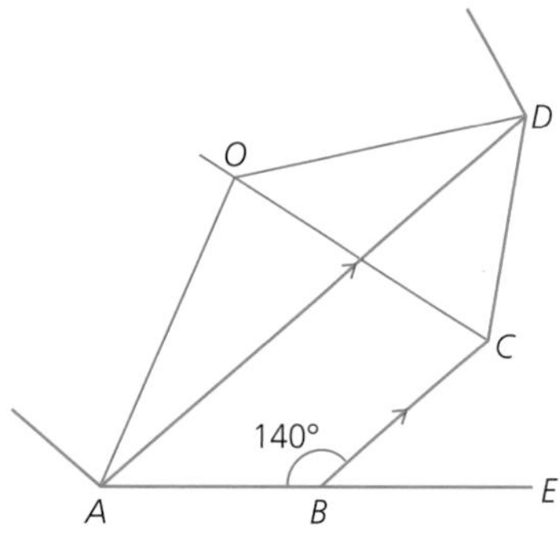

(a) How many sides has the polygon?

(b) Calculate these angles, giving reasons for your answers.

(i) $\angle DOC$

(ii) $\angle DAB$

(iii) $\angle CDO$

(iv) $\angle ADO$

10 *ABCDEF* is part of a regular polygon with 15 sides.

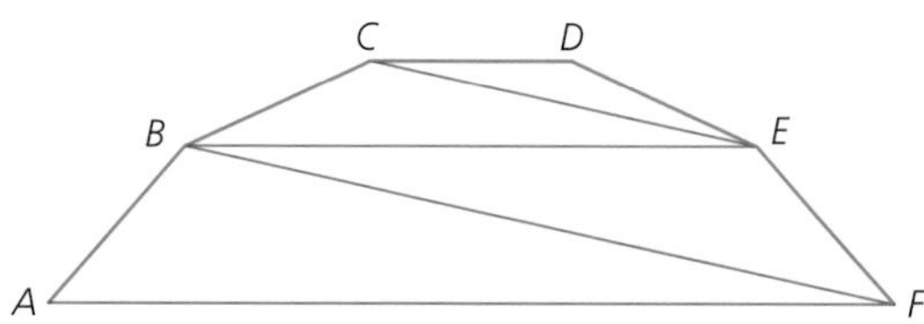

Calculate the size of each of these angles. Give reasons for your answers.

(i) $\angle BCD$

(ii) $\angle CBE$

(iii) $\angle FEB$

(iv) $\angle BAF$

(v) $\angle DCE$

(vi) $\angle AFB$

Constructions

Constructing a perpendicular

Look at this triangle.

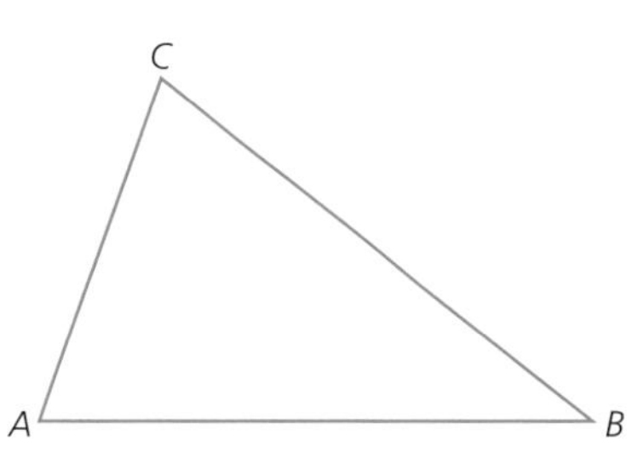

To find its area you need to know its base and its height. You can measure its base, but you need to construct the height so that you can measure it exactly.

You can construct the height by constructing a **perpendicular** from *C* to *AB*. The perpendicular will be the shortest distance from *C* to *AB*.

The method comprises four steps.

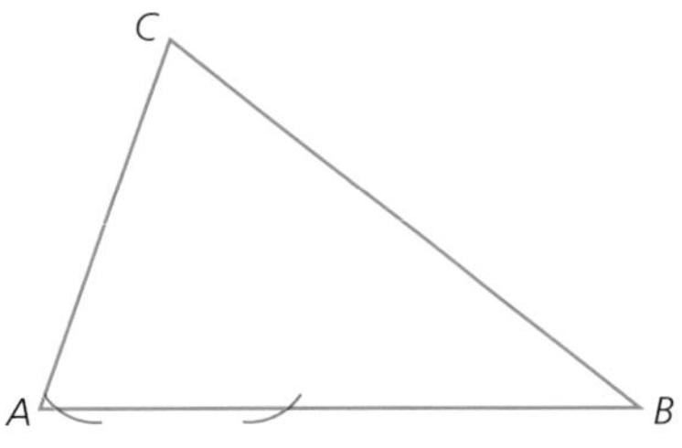 1 Set your compasses to a suitable **radius**. With the compass point on *C*, draw two **arcs** that cut *AB*.	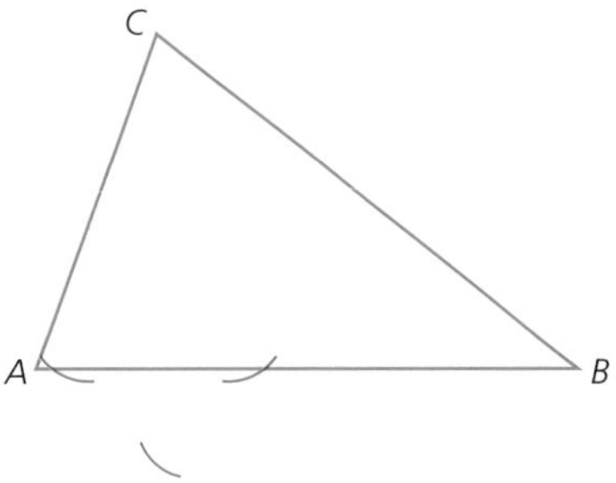 2 Place the point of your compasses on the point where one arc crosses *AB* and draw an arc below *AB*.
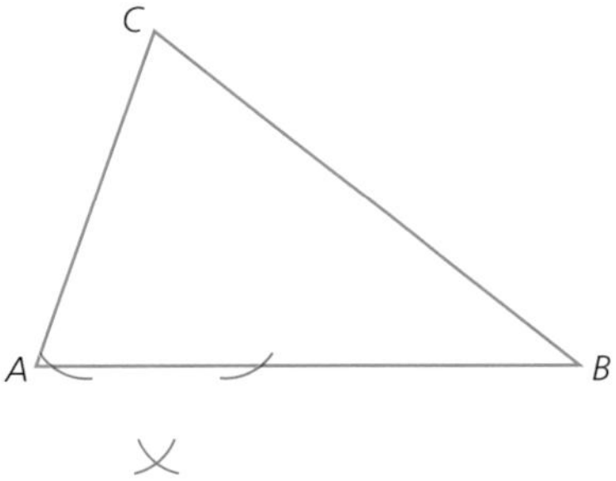 3 Without changing the setting of your compasses, place the compass point on the place where the second arc from step 1 cuts *AB*. Draw an arc to cut the arc drawn in step 2	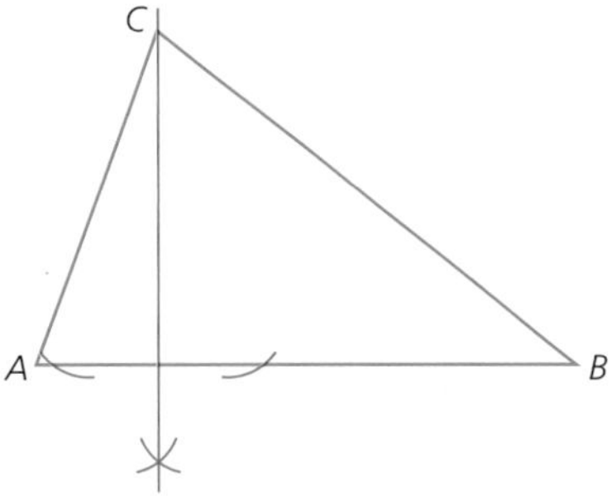 4 Join the point where the arcs intersect to point *C*.

Exercise 10.4

1 (a) Construct triangle ABC in which $AB = 8\,\text{cm}$, $BC = 7\,\text{cm}$ and $AC = 6.5\,\text{cm}$.

  (b) Construct a perpendicular from C to AB, meeting AB at D

  (c) Measure CD

  (d) Calculate the area of the triangle.

2 (a) Construct triangle DEF in which $DE = 9\,\text{cm}$, $DF = 8\,\text{cm}$ and $\angle FDE = 54°$

  (b) Construct a perpendicular from F to DE, meeting DE at X

  (c) Measure FX

  (d) Calculate the area of the triangle.

3 (a) Construct triangle PQR such that $PQ = 7.5\,\text{cm}$, $\angle RPQ = 42°$ and $\angle PQR = 63°$

  (b) Construct a perpendicular from R to PQ, meeting PQ at X

  (c) Measure RX

  (d) Calculate the area of the triangle.

Bisecting an angle

To **bisect** is to divide exactly in two, so an **angle bisector** divides the angle into halves.

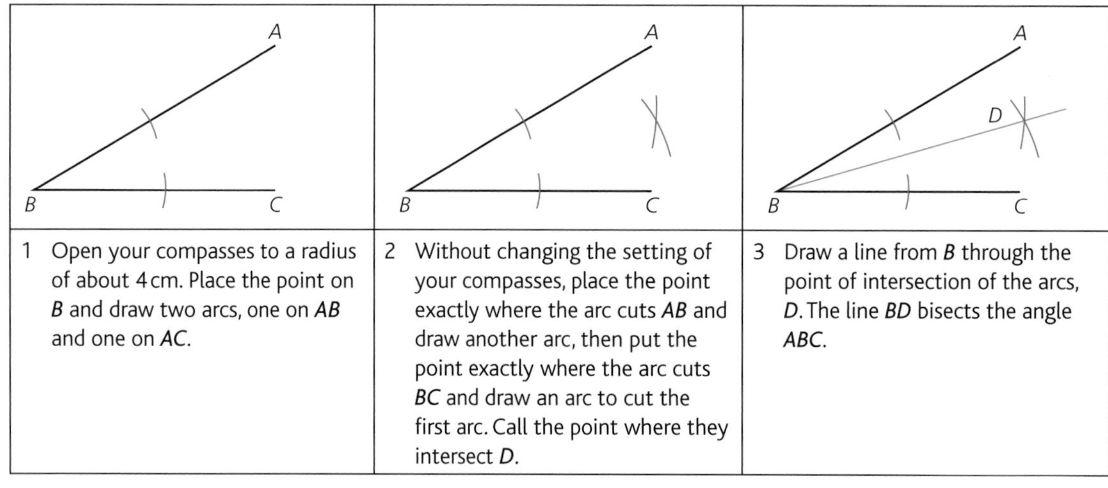

1 Open your compasses to a radius of about 4 cm. Place the point on *B* and draw two arcs, one on *AB* and one on *AC*.	2 Without changing the setting of your compasses, place the point exactly where the arc cuts *AB* and draw another arc, then put the point exactly where the arc cuts *BC* and draw an arc to cut the first arc. Call the point where they intersect *D*.	3 Draw a line from *B* through the point of intersection of the arcs, *D*. The line *BD* bisects the angle *ABC*.

Why does this construction work?

Label the points where the arcs cut the lines *AB* and *BC* as *P* and *Q*. Join *DP* and *DQ*

As $BP = BQ = DP = DQ$, the quadrilateral *BPDQ* is a rhombus. The diagonals of a rhombus bisect the angles.

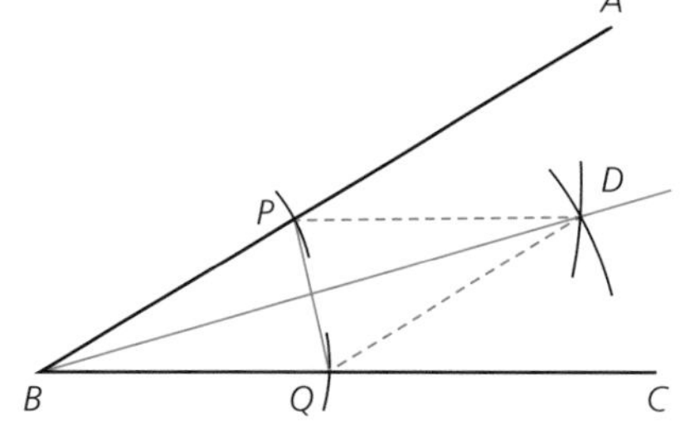

Perpendicular bisector of a line

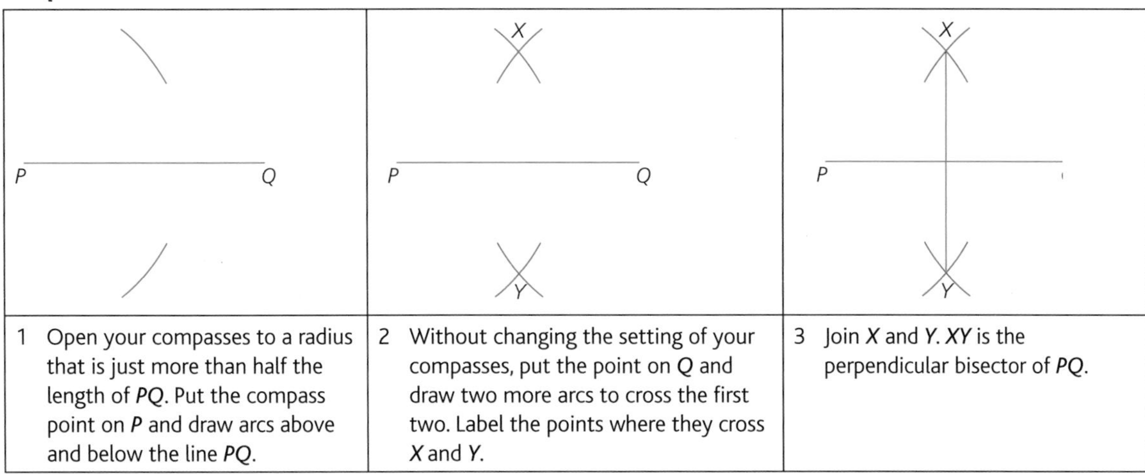

1 Open your compasses to a radius that is just more than half the length of *PQ*. Put the compass point on *P* and draw arcs above and below the line *PQ*.	2 Without changing the setting of your compasses, put the point on *Q* and draw two more arcs to cross the first two. Label the points where they cross *X* and *Y*.	3 Join *X* and *Y*. *XY* is the perpendicular bisector of *PQ*.

In the next exercise you are going to construct shapes and bisect angles and lines. It helps to have two pencils, one in your compasses and one to draw lines. When you need to mark a specific length during a construction, you should adjust your compasses so that the compass point and the sharp point of your pencil are exactly positioned in the dents of the rule to the required length.

> If you draw the quadrilateral *PXQY* it will be a rhombus, and the diagonals of a rhombus bisect each other at **right angles**.

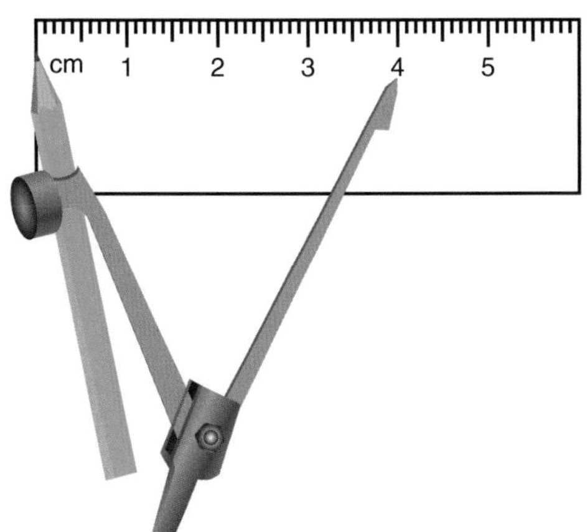

Exercise 10.5

Before you start each construction, draw a sketch of the shape and mark on it all known lengths and angles.

1 (a) Construct triangle ABC with $AB = 7$ cm, $BC = 7$ cm and $\angle ABC = 65°$

(b) Bisect angle BAC

(c) Use a ruler and a pair of compasses to mark a point D on the angle bisector so that $CD = 7$ cm.

(d) Join C to D and A to D

(e) Describe $ABCD$. What are its properties?

2 (a) Construct the perpendicular bisector of a line AB, 6 cm long.

(b) With a pair of compasses set to the required length, mark a point P on the perpendicular bisector so that $AP = 4$ cm.

(c) With a pair of compasses, mark a point Q on the perpendicular bisector on the opposite side of AB to P so that $AQ = 5.5$ cm.

(d) Join A to P and Q. Join B to P and Q

(e) Describe $APBQ$. What are its properties?

3 Repeat Q2 but this time draw P and Q on the same side of AB. Describe $APBQ$ and list its properties.

4 (a) Construct a regular hexagon, $ABCDEF$, with sides of length 5 cm. Do this by constructing equilateral triangles of side 5 cm.

(b) Bisect $\angle ABC$

(c) Where does the angle bisector cross the hexagon?

(d) What does that tell you about the angle bisector?

5 Follow these steps to construct a hexagon $ABCDEF$ with sides $AB = DE = 5$ cm and sides $BC = CD = AF = EF = 4$ cm and $\angle ABC = \angle BAF = \angle FED = \angle EDC = 130°$

(a) Construct triangles ABC and BAF. Join F to C

(b) Drop a perpendicular from A to cross CF and extend it. With your compasses, mark point E

(c) Drop a perpendicular from B to cross CF and extend it. With your compasses mark point D

(d) Join C to D, D to E and E to F

6 Construct an octagon $ABCDEFGH$ with sides $AB = CD = EF = GH = 6$ cm, sides $BC = DE = FG = HA = 4$ cm and $\angle ABC = 150°$. Use what you know about the properties of an octagon and its related triangles and design your own construction.

Summary Exercise 10.6

1 If the bearing of *A* from *B* is 21°, what is the bearing of *B* from *A*?

2 Find the value of x in the diagram. Give reasons for your answer. You may wish to identify and calculate some other angles first.

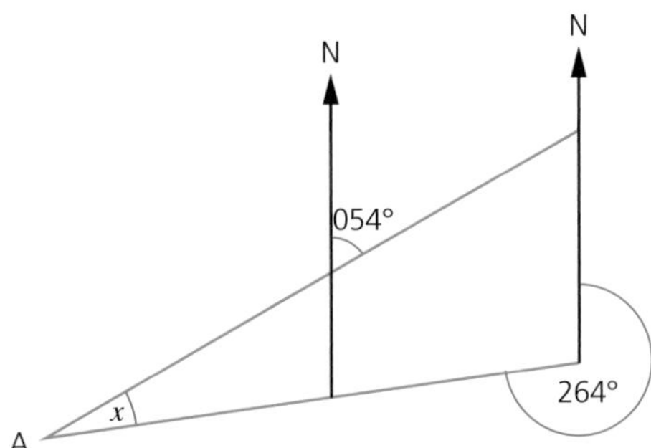

3 Calculate the interior angle of a regular decagon.

4 How many sides has a regular polygon with interior angles of 157.5°?

5 *ABCDEFG* is a regular octagon.

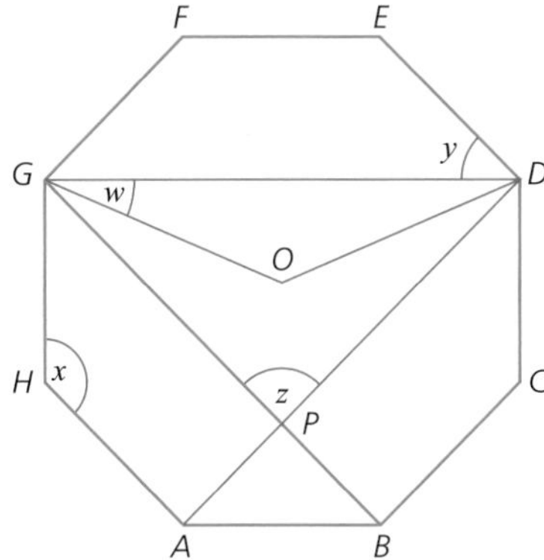

(a) Calculate the size of the angles marked w, x, y and z. Give reasons for your answers.

(b) What type of quadrilateral is *APGH*? Give as many reasons for your answer as you can.

6 (a) Construct triangle *ABC* with $AB = 9$ cm, $BC = 7$ cm and $\angle CBA = 65°$

(b) Construct a line from *C* to meet *AB* at right angles at point *D*

(c) Measure *CD* and hence find the area of the triangle.

Activity: Perigal's dissection

You will need a sheet of plain A3 paper.

Draw a right-angled scalene triangle near the middle of your sheet of paper. It does not matter exactly what its dimensions are. Draw your triangle askew like this.

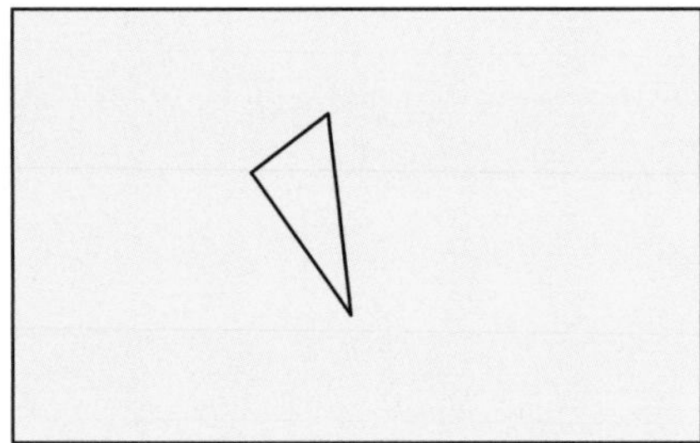

Now construct a square on each side of the triangle. Your paper will look like this.

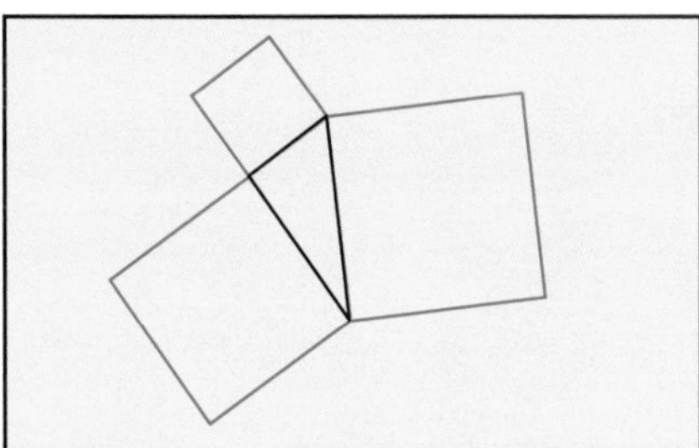

You now have three squares, one large, one small and one middle-sized. **Dissect** the middle-sized square by first drawing the two diagonals very lightly to find its centre.

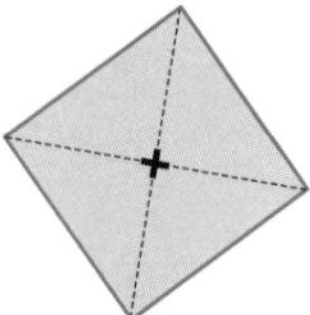

The longest side of a right-angled triangle is the side opposite the right angle. It is called the **hypotenuse**. Using a set square and ruler, draw a line, parallel to the hypotenuse, through the centre of the middle-sized square.

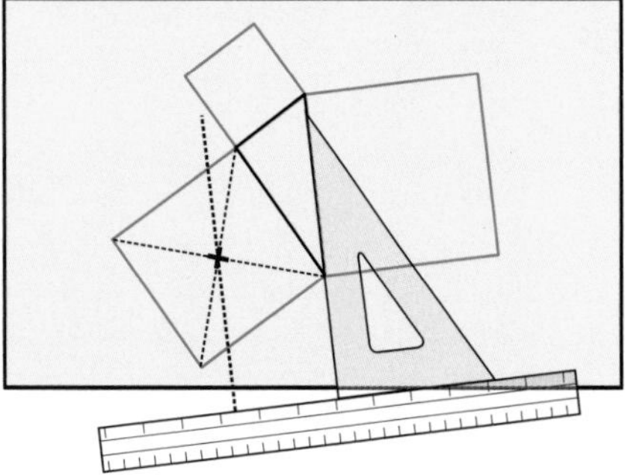

You will need to slide your set square along the ruler to draw this parallel line.

Now draw a line at right angles to the line you have just drawn, also passing through the centre of the middle-sized square.

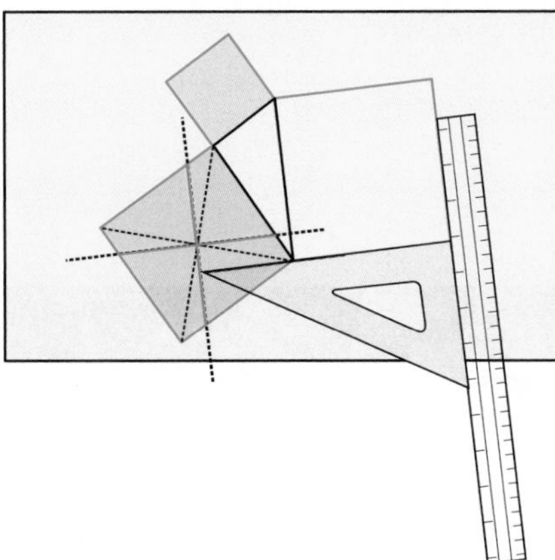

Again, you will need to slide your set square along the ruler to draw this parallel line.

Next, trace over the small square and cut out the tracing. Then trace over the middle-sized square and cut out the four pieces.

Can you fit all five pieces together in the big square?

Does the area of the square on the hypotenuse equal the sum of the areas of the other two squares?

Try repeating this activity for a different right-angled scalene triangle.

11 Pythagoras' theorem

Pythagoras was a Greek philosopher and mathematician. He was born on the island of Samos around 560BC and travelled extensively as a young man. His contribution to mathematics was enormous. He was the first in the Western world (rather than the Eastern world of Ancient China and the Arabic world) to use letters on geometric shapes. This enabled him to deduce and prove many geometric and algebraic **theorems**.

While Pythagoras' exploration of number theory has been the starting point for much mathematical development, he is best known for the theorem that takes his name.

■ *Pythagoras in The School of Athens*, Raffael

Right-angled triangles

In a **right-angled triangle** the **hypotenuse** is the longest side – the side opposite the right angle.

For any right-angled triangle the square of the hypotenuse is equal to the sum of the squares of the other two sides.

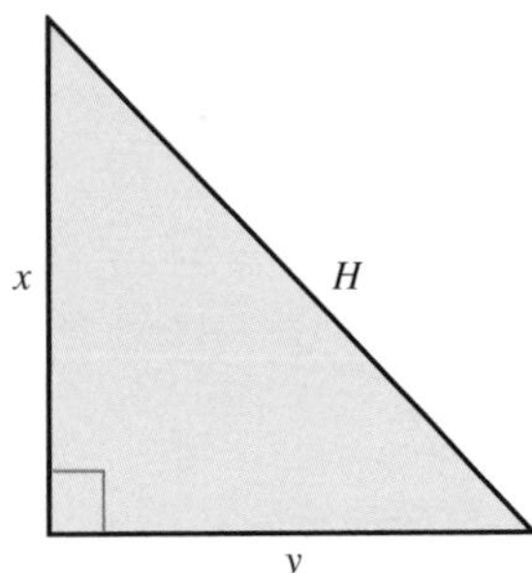

$H^2 = x^2 + y^2$

Using the capital H for hypotenuse avoids confusion with a lower-case h, commonly used for height. Many calculations concerning right-angled triangles involve both the height and the hypotenuse.

Exercise 11.1

Copy each of these triangles with a neat sketch and mark the hypotenuse with a capital H.

1

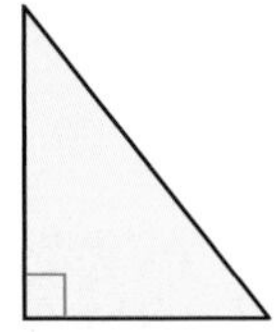

3

5

2

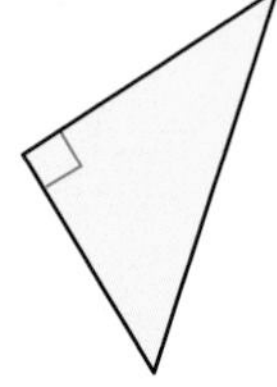

4

6

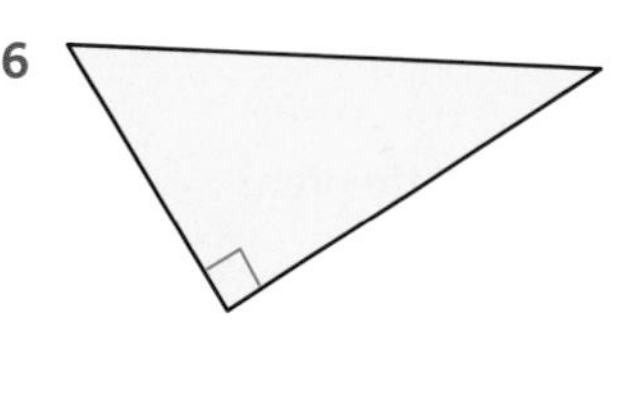

Calculating the hypotenuse

You can use **Pythagoras' theorem** to calculate the length of the hypotenuse of any right-angled triangle. As usual, there are five steps in solving each problem.

Step 1: Formula

Step 2: Substitute

Step 3: Calculate

Step 4: Answer

Step 5: Units

For each question you should draw a sketch of the triangle and label the hypotenuse H.

Example

Calculate the length of the hypotenuse of this triangle.

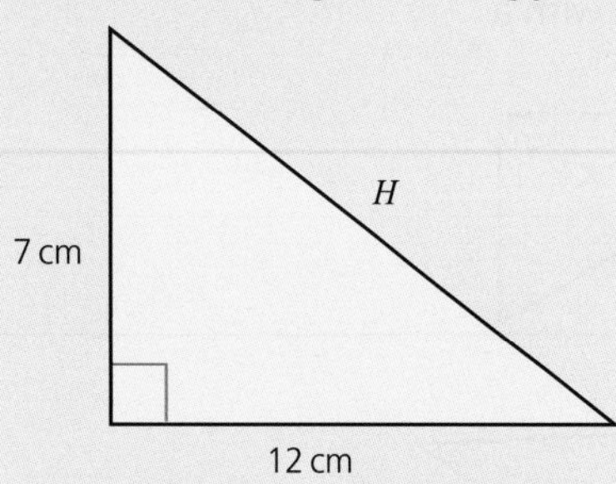

$H^2 = x^2 + y^2$ Pythagoras' theorem

$= 7^2 + 12^2$ Substitute

$= 49 + 144$ Calculate

$= 193$

$H = \sqrt{193}$

$= 13.892 \ldots$ Answer

The length of the hypotenuse is 13.9 cm (to 3 s.f.).

Remember to write more digits than you need before you round your answer.

Note that when writing down your calculations:

$H^2 = 193$ and $H = \sqrt{193}$

Do not write
$H^2 = 193$
$= \sqrt{193}$
$= 13.892...$

Exercise 11.2

Calculate the length of the hypotenuse of each right-angled triangle. Round your answers to 3 s.f. if necessary.

1

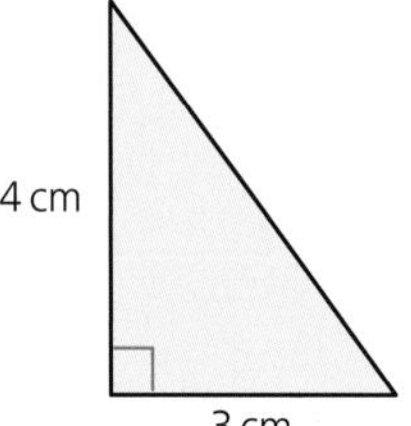

2

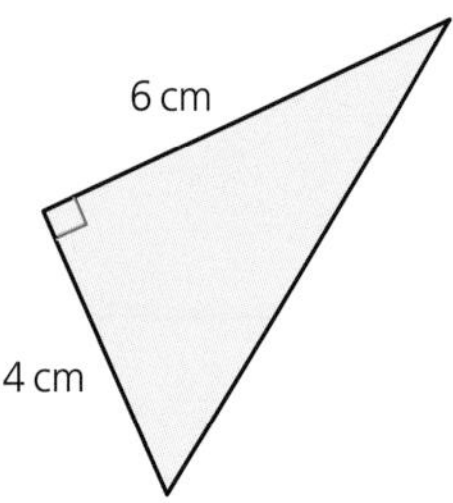

3

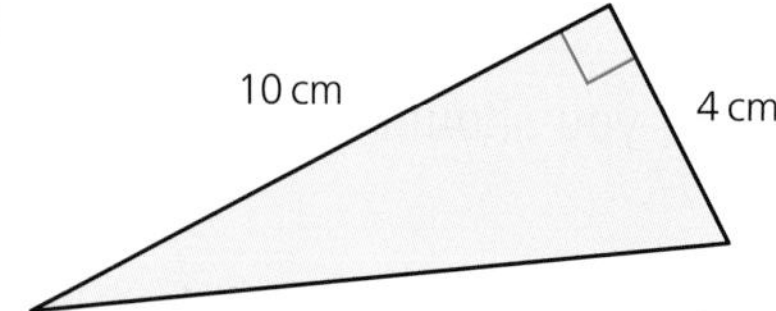

4

7 m

6 m

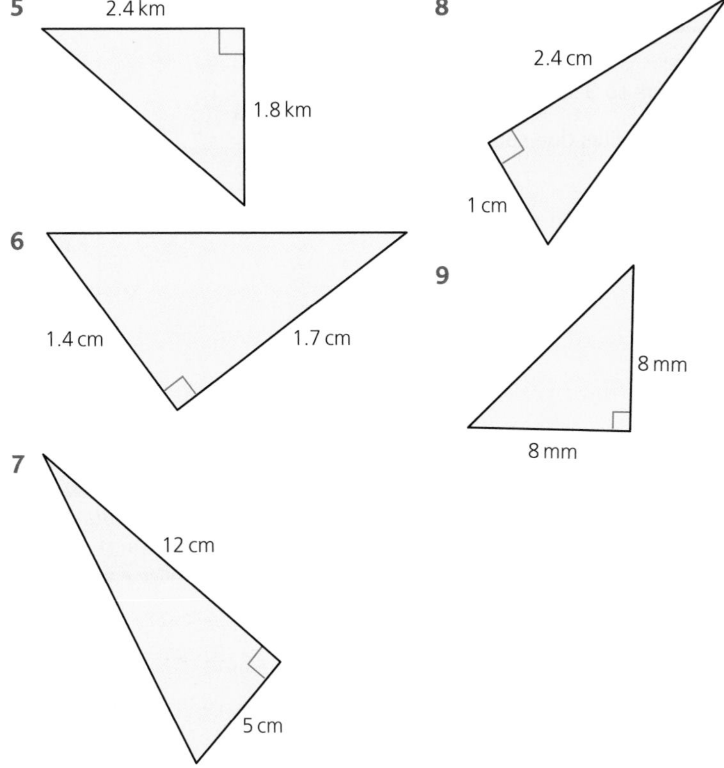

Using Pythagoras' theorem to solve problems

Now that you can use Pythagoras' theorem to find the length of a hypotenuse in a right-angled triangle, you can use it to answer problems in everyday contexts.

Example

A man walked 400 m due north and then 500 m due west. By then, how far was he from his starting point?

$H^2 = x^2 + y^2$ Pythagoras' theorem

$= 400^2 + 500^2$

$= 160\,000 + 250\,000$

$= 410\,000$

$H = \sqrt{410\,000}$

$= 640.312\,42\ldots$

$= 640$ m (to 3 s.f.)

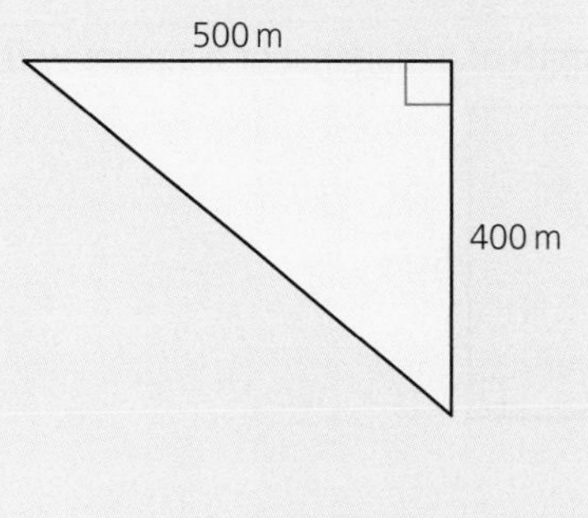

He was 640 m from his starting point.

Exercise 11.3

Now solve these problems, rounding your answers to 3 s.f. if necessary.

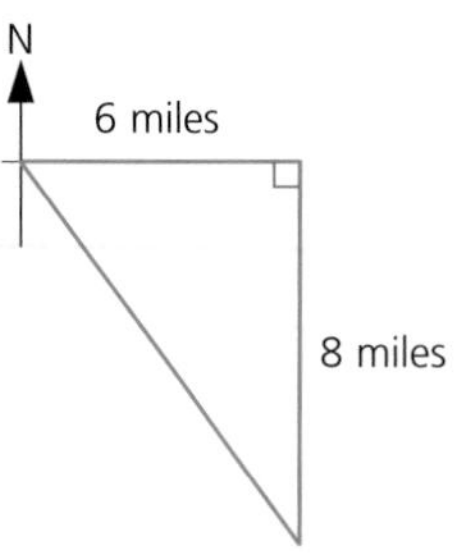

1 An aeroplane flew 6 miles due east and then 8 miles due south. How far was the aeroplane from its starting point?

2 A ship sailed 240 km south-east and then 320 km north-east. By now, how far was the ship from its starting point?

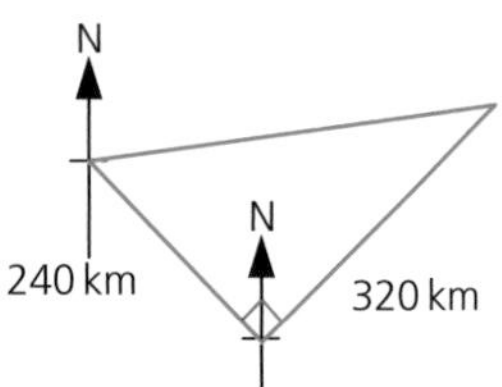

3 A hunter set out from home at *A* and walked 1.4 km on a bearing of 030° to a point *B*. Then he walked 2.7 km on a bearing of 120° to a point *C*. How far did he have to walk back home?

You must calculate angle *ABC* first!

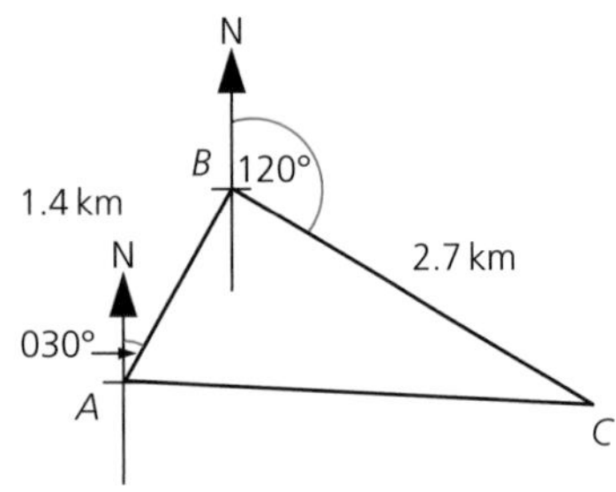

4 A school playground is in the shape of a rectangle 100 m by 50 m. John has to run around the whole perimeter of the rectangle and Janet has to run along the diagonal three times. Who runs further, Janet or John?

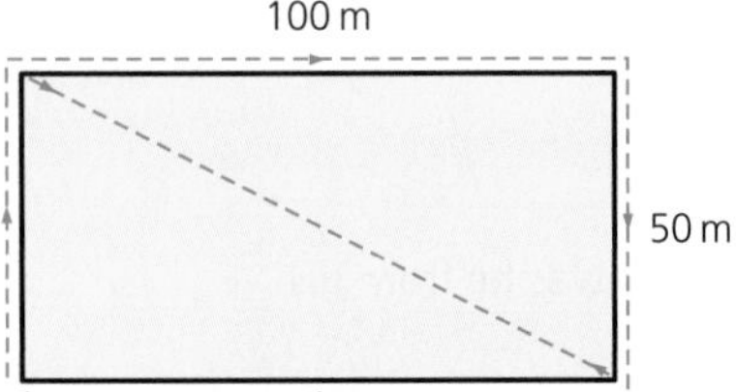

5 Find the length of a diagonal of a square with sides of 5 cm.

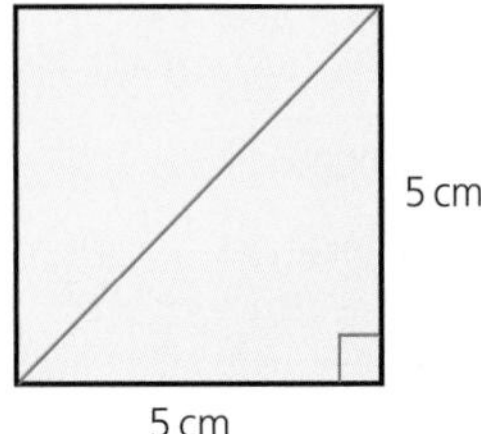

6 A doorway is 2 m tall and 1 m wide. Can I get a square wooden board of side 2.3 m through the doorway? If not, how much must I shave off one side?

7 Freddie and Angus have a new ladder. Freddie reads the instructions and puts the foot of the ladder 2 m away from the base of the wall, on level ground. The top of the ladder reaches a point 4.6 m above the ground.

(a) How long is the ladder?

Angus complains that he cannot reach high enough up the wall. He wants to move the ladder 50 cm towards the wall and says that then he will be able to reach 50 cm higher than before.

(b) Is Angus right?

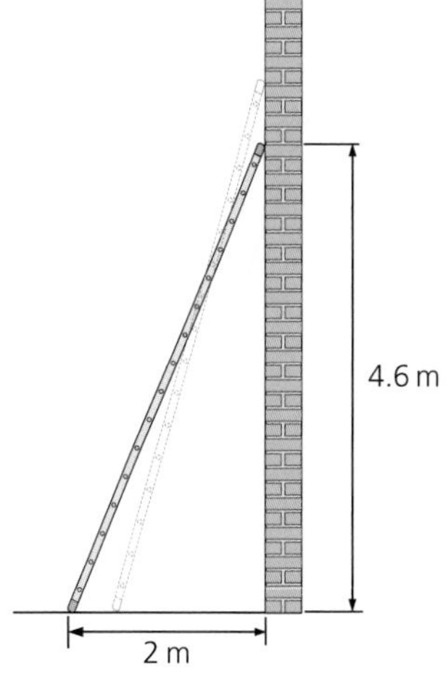

Check the length the ladder would have to be.

Finding the length of a side other than the hypotenuse

If you know the lengths of the hypotenuse and one other side of a right-angled triangle, you can use Pythagoras' theorem to find the length of the third side. However, take care to substitute correctly into the formula.

Example

Find the value of x in this triangle, giving your answer correct to 2 decimal places.

$H^2 = x^2 + y^2$ Pythagoras' theorem

$45^2 = x^2 + 7^2$

$2025 = x^2 + 49$

$2025 - 49 = x^2$ (– 49)

$x^2 = 1976$

$x = \sqrt{1976}$

$= 44.4522...$

$= 44.45$ cm (to 2 decimal places)

45 cm H 7 cm x cm

Exercise 11.4

Find the value of x in each triangle. Give any rounded answers correct to 2 decimal places if necessary.

1

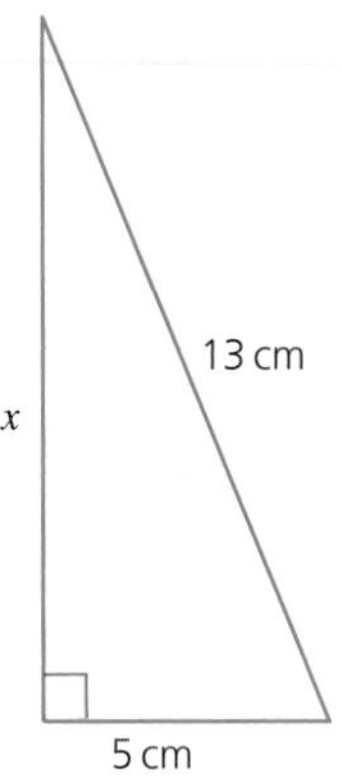

2

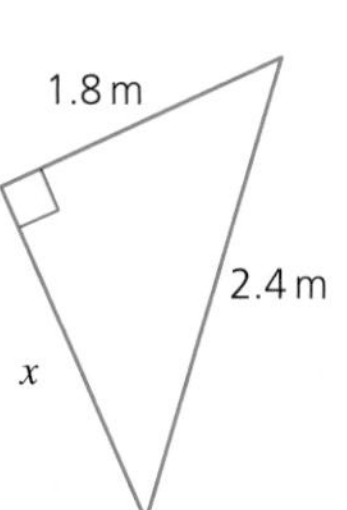

3

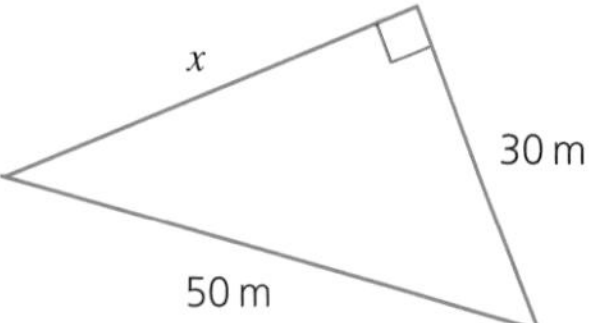

4

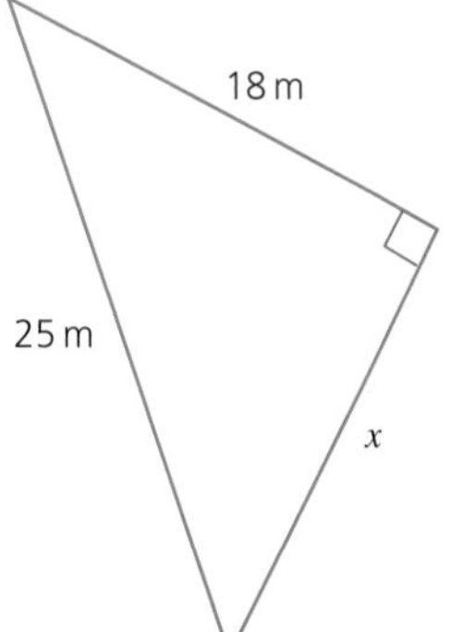

5

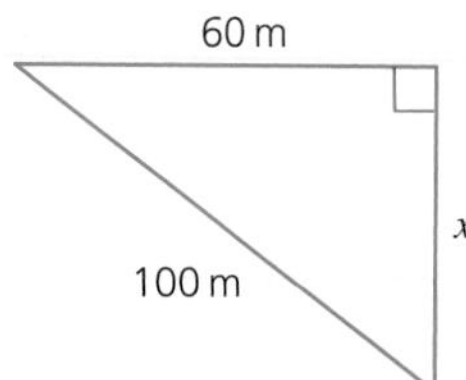

6

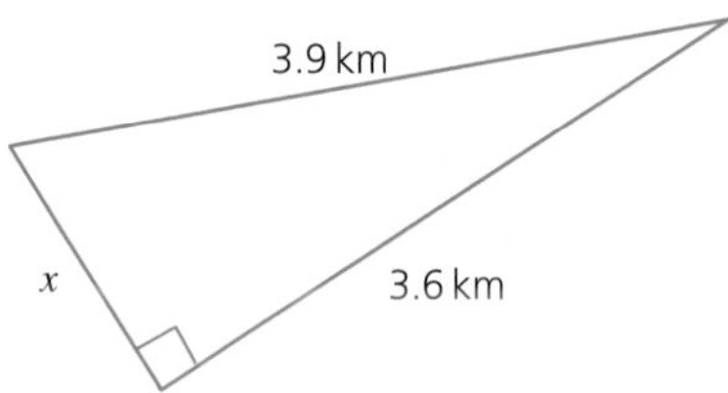

7

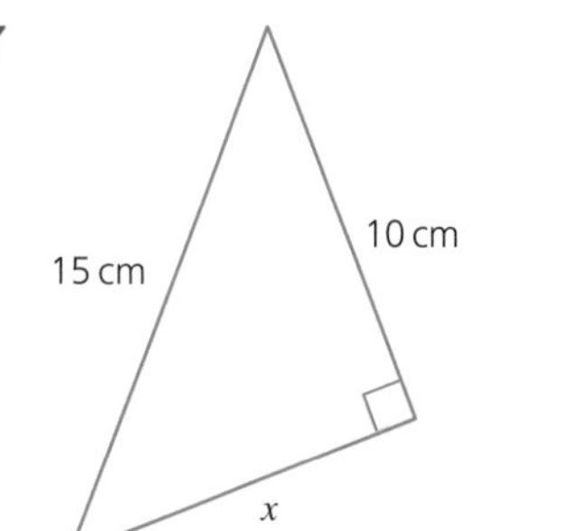

8

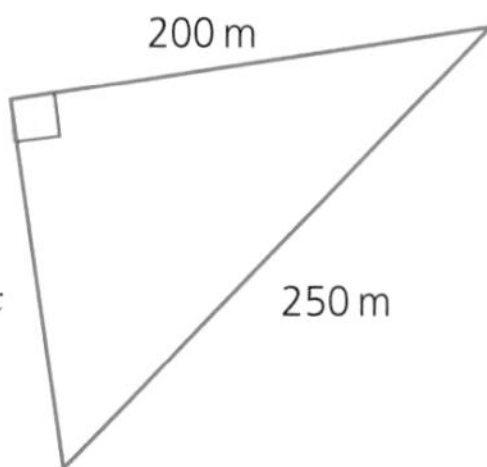

9

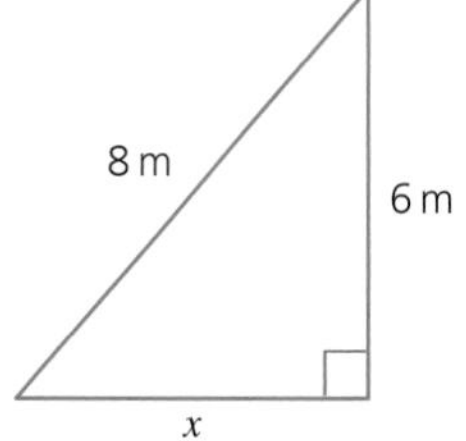

Problem solving

When you are solving geometric problems, you should always start with a sketch and add any information you are given. For questions about Pythagoras' theorem, draw a sketch of the right-angled triangle and mark the hypotenuse. Always give rounded answers correct to three significant figures (3 s.f.), unless you are asked for a different degree of accuracy.

Example

A rectangle of base length 24 cm has diagonals of length 32 cm. What length are the other sides of the rectangle? Give your answer correct to 2 decimal places.

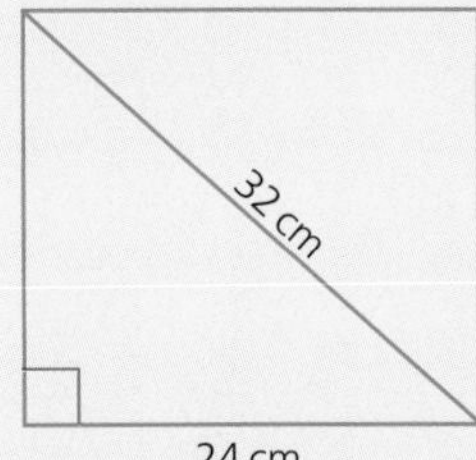

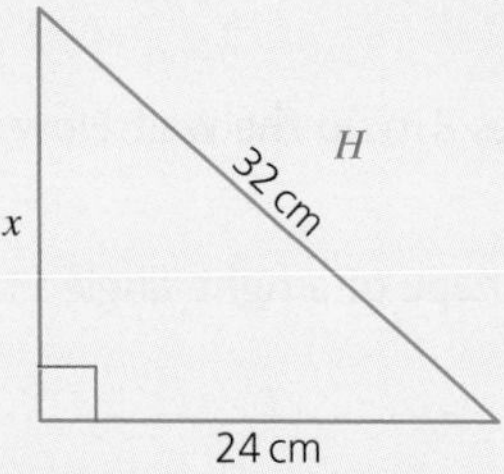

Let the length of the other side of the rectangle be x.

$H^2 = x^2 + y^2$ Pythagoras' theorem

$32^2 = x^2 + 24^2$

$1024 = x^2 + 576$

$1024 - 576 = x^2$ (– 576)

$x^2 = 448$

$x = \sqrt{448}$

$x = 21.166...$

$x = 21.17$ cm (to 2 decimal places)

Exercise 11.5

Solve these problems, giving any rounded answers correct to 2 decimal places.

Remember to start with a sketch.

1 A rectangle of base length 15 cm has diagonals of length 18 cm. What length are the other sides of the rectangle?

2 A ship sails 15 miles due north and she then sails due east until it is 30 miles from its starting point. How many miles did it sail due east?

3 After a rambler had walked 1.5 km north-west, he dropped his camera. He then walked south-west before he noticed. By then he was 2.4 km from his starting place. How far did he have to walk back to collect his camera?

4 A ladder 4 m long is leaning against a wall. When the foot of the ladder is 1 m from the base of the wall, how far up the wall does the ladder reach?

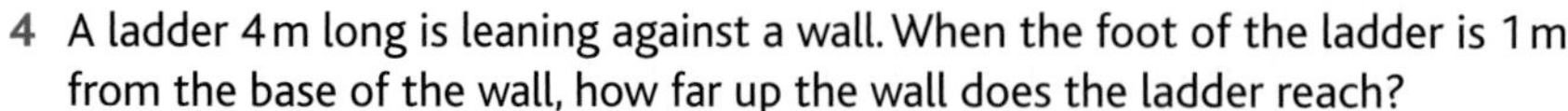

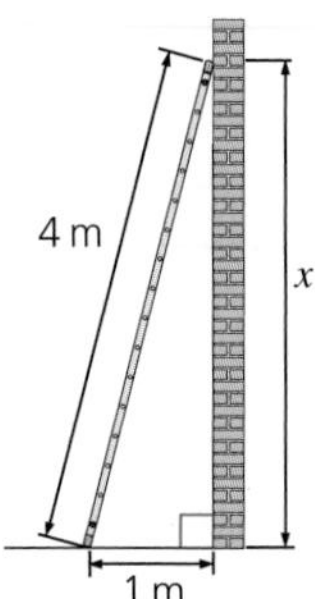

5 Another ladder is 3 m long and reaches 2 m up the wall. How far is the foot of this ladder from the base of the wall?

6 The bracket for a hotel sign is in the shape of a right-angled triangle. How long is the top of the bracket?

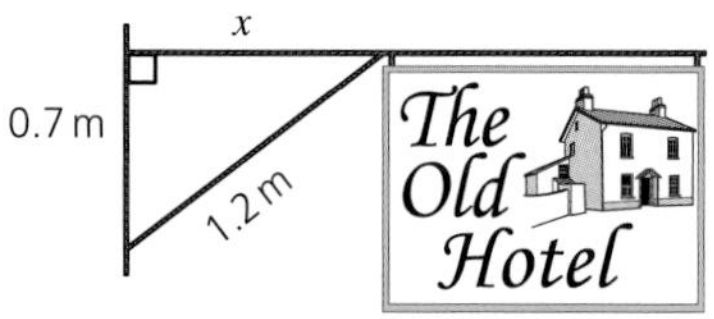

7 A square has diagonals of length 5 cm.

What is the length of a side of the square?

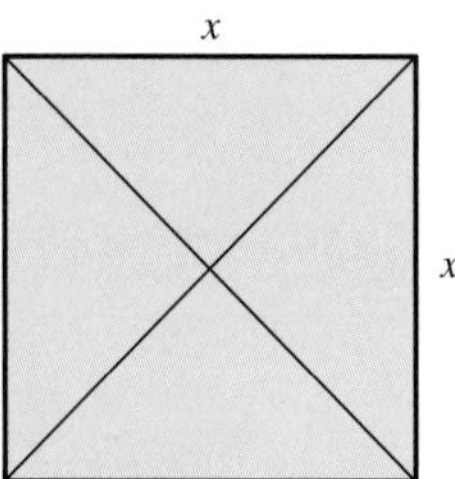

8 A rectangle has a diagonal of 12 cm and its long sides are twice the length of its short sides. What are the lengths of the sides of the rectangle?

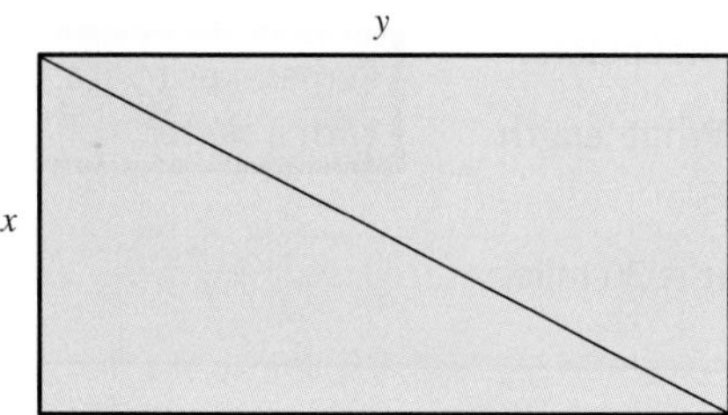

Isosceles triangles

You can use Pythagoras' theorem to find the height of an isosceles triangle, when you know the lengths of the sides. Again, it is important to start with a sketch, to be sure that you have the correct dimensions.

Example

Find the height of an isosceles triangle ABC in which $AB = AC = 12$ cm and $BC = 10$ cm.

$H^2 = x^2 + y^2$ Pythagoras' theorem

$12^2 = x^2 + 5^2$

$144 = x^2 + 25$

$144 - 25 = x^2$ (– 25)

$x^2 = 119$

$x = \sqrt{119}$

$x = 10.908...$

$x = 10.9$ cm (to 3 s.f.)

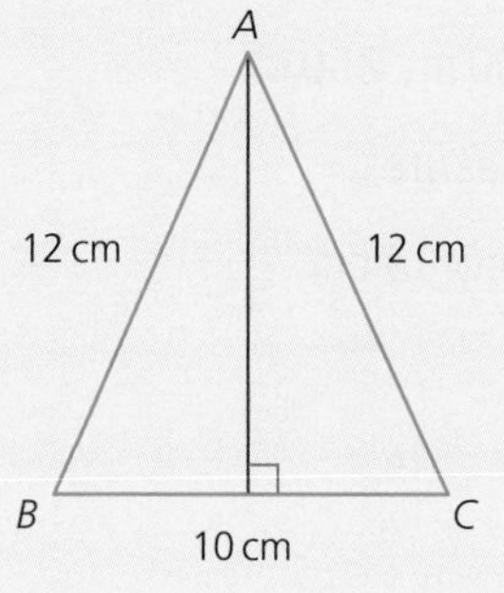

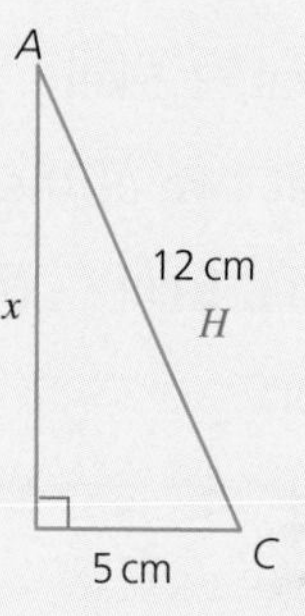

Exercise 11.6

1 Calculate the height AD of an isosceles triangle ABC in which $AB = AC = 8$ cm and $BC = 7$ cm.

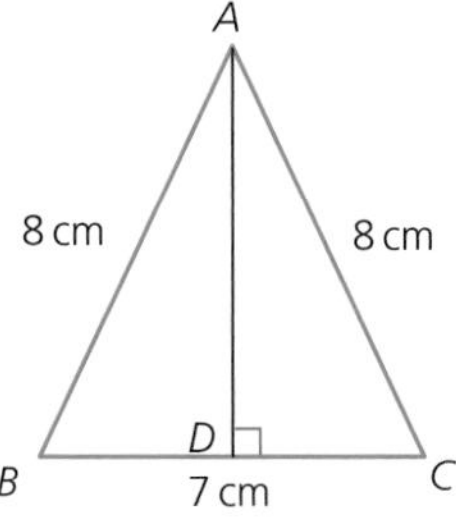

2 Find the height of an equilateral triangle of side 6 cm.

3 A tent has the dimensions shown in the diagram. What is the height of the tent pole?

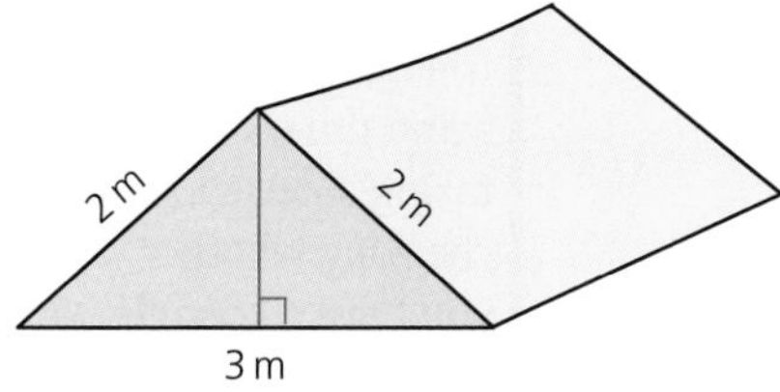

4 An isosceles triangle XYZ has height $AX = 12$ cm and sides $XY = XZ = 13$ cm. What is the length of YZ?

5 The height of an equilateral triangle is 8 cm. What is the length of a side?

Special triangles

In the last few exercises a few triangles had sides with lengths that did not need rounding. The numbers were integers or terminating decimals. Some sets of numbers, or multiples of them, come up again and again. Here are some that you may have spotted.

3 cm, 4 cm, 5 cm	1.8 km, 2.4 km, 3.0 km
5 cm, 12 cm, 13 cm	6 miles, 8 miles, 10 miles
30 m, 40 m, 50 m	60 m, 80 m, 100 m
3.9 km, 3.6 km, 1.5 km	150 m, 200 m, 250 m

Look again at two of these sets of measures.

(i) 3 cm, 4 cm, 5 cm (ii) 5 cm, 12 cm, 13 cm

Now consider:

$3^2 + 4^2 = 9 + 16$ $\quad 5^2 + 12^2 = 25 + 144$

$= 25$ $\quad = 169$

Both 25 and 169 are **perfect squares.**

$25 = 5 \times 5$ and $169 = 13 \times 13$

The sum of the squares of the two smaller numbers equals the square of the largest number. Groups of three numbers that have this property are known as **Pythagorean triplets.**

While there are many Pythagorean triplets, the two with the smallest numbers are 3, 4, 5 and 5, 12, 13 and this makes the 3 : 4 : 5 triangle and the 5 : 12 : 13 triangle very special. They frequently occur in problems, either in this form or scaled up or down, as in the examples below.

You will look at Pythagorean triplets in more detail in the activity at the end of the chapter.

A triangle with sides:

1.8 km, 2.4 km, 3.0 km is a	3 : 4 : 5 triangle × 0.6
6 miles, 8 miles, 10 miles is a	3 : 4 : 5 triangle × 2
30 m, 40 m, 50 m is a	3 : 4 : 5 triangle × 10
60 m, 80 m, 100 m is a	3 : 4 : 5 triangle × 20
150 m, 200 m, 250 m is a	3 : 4 : 5 triangle × 50
3.9 km, 3.6 km, 1.5 km is a	5 : 12 : 13 triangle × 0.3

In the last example, the lengths were not in increasing order. Always check, in case this happens in a question that you are answering.

Spotting a 3 : 4 : 5 triangle or a 5 : 12 : 13 triangle can save you some time, so it is worth taking a close look and checking whether or not you have a triangle with sides that form one of these triplets.

Example

A flagpole is 2.4 m tall and is held up by wires 2.6 m long. How far from the base of the pole do the wires reach the ground?

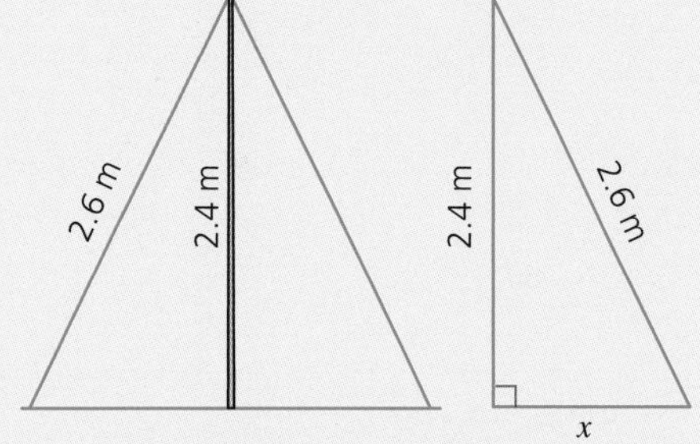

Let the distance along the level ground be x

Write down your working like this.

Ratio of sides is $x : 2.4 : 2.6$

which is $5 : 12 : 13 \times 0.2$

therefore $x = 5 \times 0.2$

$x = 1$

The distance between the base of the pole and the point where the wires reach the ground is 1 m.

> The hypotenuse 2.6, is a multiple of 13, so check to see if it is a 5 : 12 : 13 triangle.
>
> $(13 \times 0.2 = 2.6)$, so $5 : 12 : 13 \times 0.2$ is equivalent to $1.0 : 2.4 : 2.6$
>
> You have two sides that are 2.4 and 2.6, and you can now say that this is a 5 : 12 : 13 triangle. The third side is therefore 1 m long.

Exercise 11.7

State if these triangles are 3 : 4 : 5 triangles or 5 : 12 : 13 triangles. If they are, write down the scale factor and find the value of x.

1

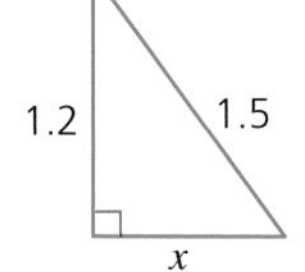

3

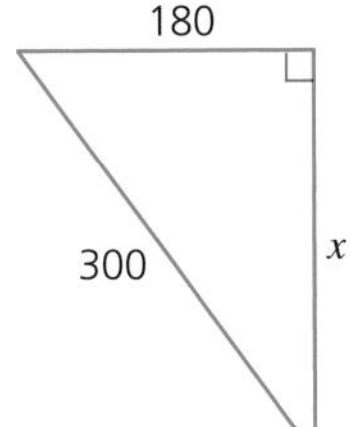

2

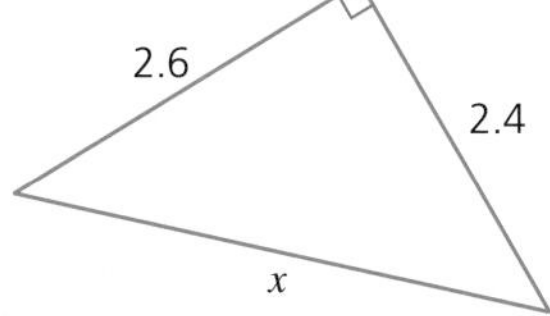

4

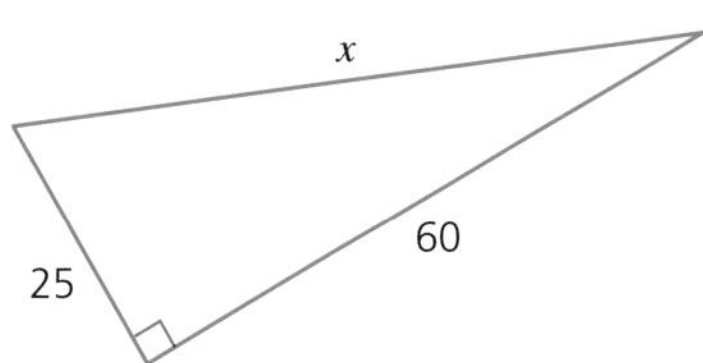

5

2.5

x

2.0

6

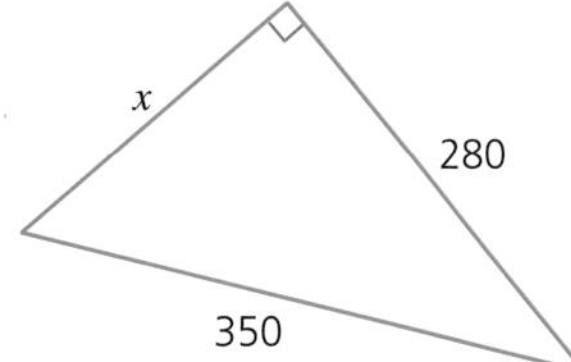

7

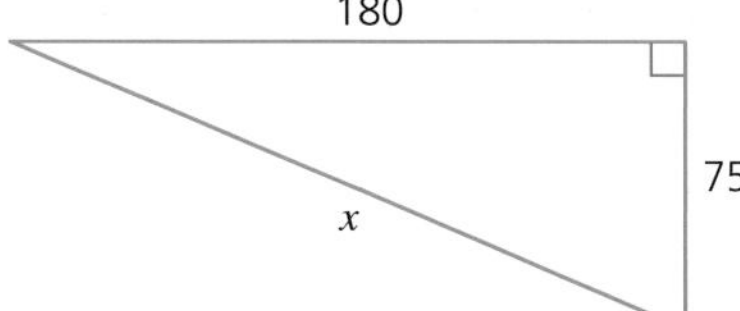

8

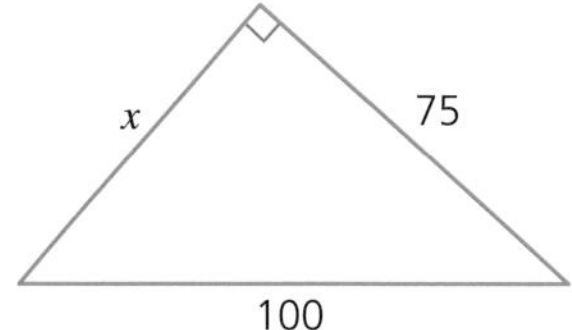

Problem solving

Use what you have learnt to try some problems.

Exercise 11.8

1 This is cross-section through a porch. How long is the roof section AD?

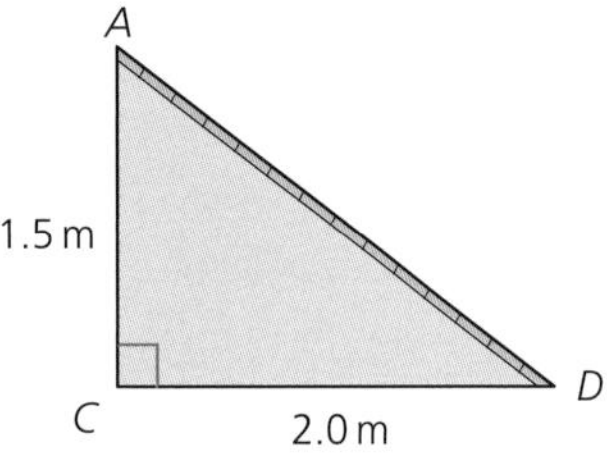

2 This is a radio aerial. It is held up by three wires attached to its top. The wires are 15 m long. How far from the base of the aerial are the wires attached to the ground?

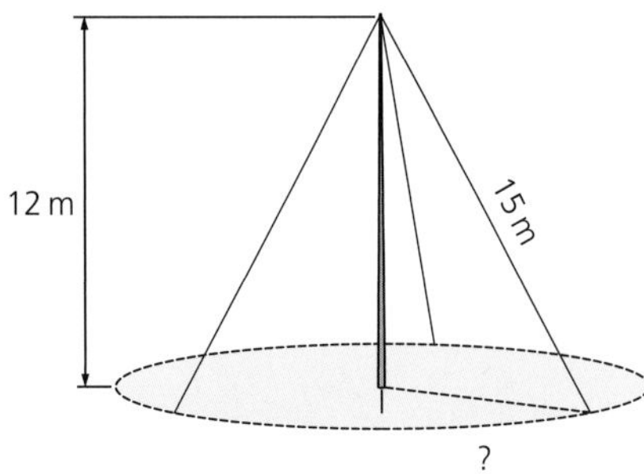

3 (a) A flagpole 18 m high is held up by wires that come $\frac{2}{3}$ of the way up the pole. How high up from the ground is this?

(b) The wires meet the ground 5 m from the base of the pole. How long are the wires?

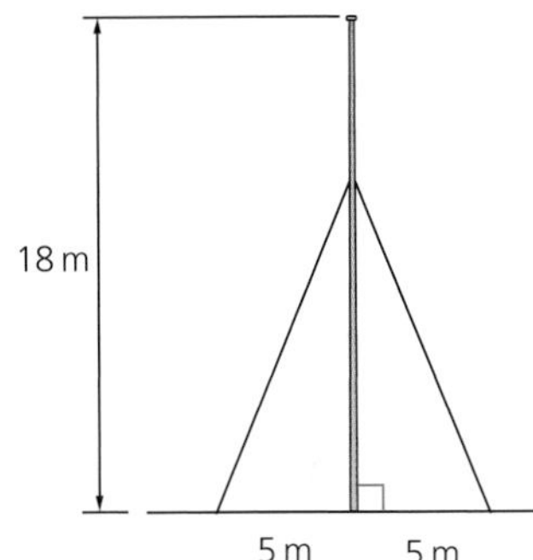

4 A hunter set out from home. He followed tracks 1200 m due north and then 500 m due west. The tracks then disappeared! How far did he have to walk home?

5 The hunter's wife, starting at home, tracked a bear 600 m north-east and then 800 m south-east, where she then lost its tracks. How far did she have to walk home?

6 The hunter's son was out collecting firewood. He walked north-west for a while and then walked 600 m north-east before walking 650 m home. How far to the north-west did he walk?

7 Calculate the height AX of an isosceles triangle in which $AB = AC = 15$ m and $BC = 18$ m.

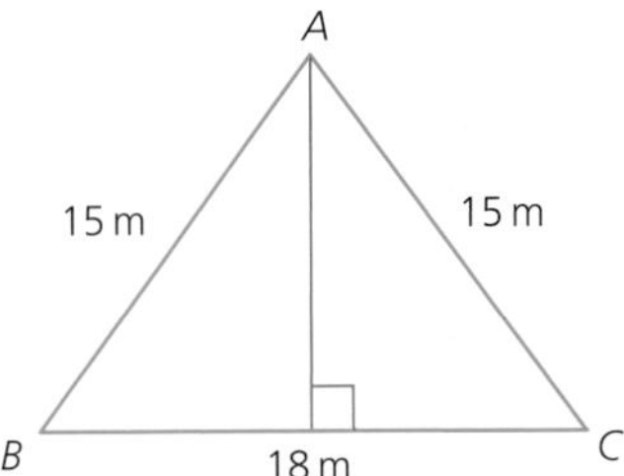

Extension: Mixed problems

Sometimes you will need to use an earlier result to complete the answer to a later part of a question. Remember that you should never calculate with a rounded answer but should always use the full calculator display. However, it can sometimes be useful to leave answers in square-root form.

When you are solving problems that require several stages, it can be helpful to refer to the lengths in terms of letters, for example, AB rather than introducing x.

Example

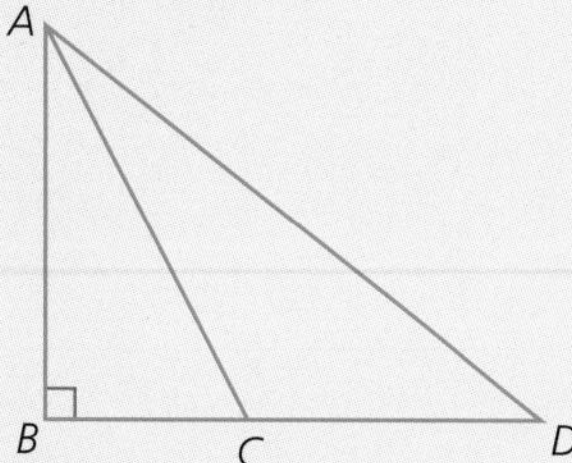

$BD = 10$ cm, $AD = 15$ cm, $BC = 4$ cm

Find the length of: (i) BC (ii) AC

(i) $H^2 = x^2 + y^2$ (Pythagoras' theorem, H is the length of the hypotenuse.)

$15^2 = AB^2 + 10^2$

$225 = AB^2 + 100$

$225 - 100 = AB^2$ (– 100)

$AB^2 = 125$

$AB = \sqrt{125}$

$= 11.1803...$

$AB = 11.1803...$ cm

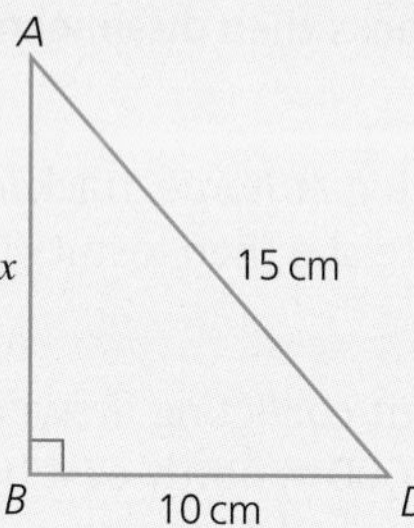

(ii) Now that you know that the length of AB is about 11.1803 you can calculate AC

$H^2 = x^2 + y^2$ (Pythagoras' theorem, H is the length of the hypotenuse.)

$AC^2 = 4^2 + AB^2$

$= 16 + 125$

$= 141$

$AC = \sqrt{141}$

$= 11.874...$

$= 11.9$ cm (to 3 s.f.)

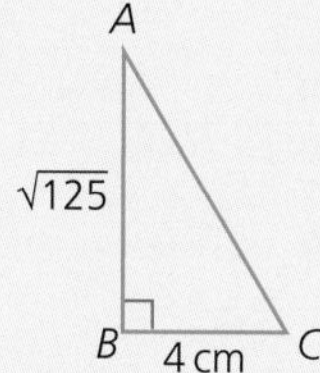

Extension Exercise 11.9

Give all rounded answers correct to 3 s.f.

1 $PR = 8$ cm, $PS = 12$ cm and $QR = 6$ cm

Calculate the lengths of PQ and RS

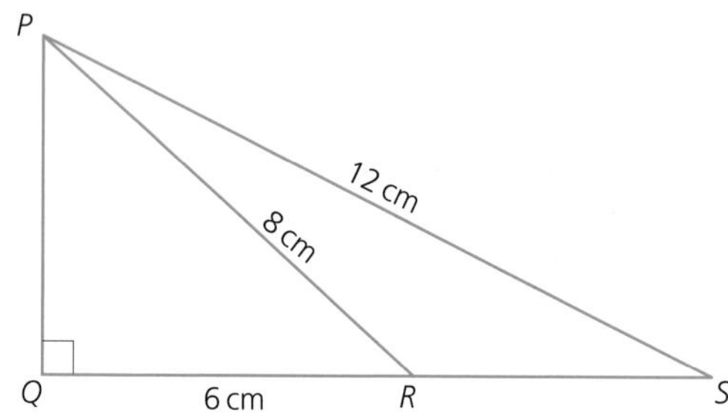

2 The lengths of the diagonals of a kite are 40 cm and 60 cm. The shorter diagonal cuts the larger one a third of the way along its length.

Calculate the lengths of the sides of the kite.

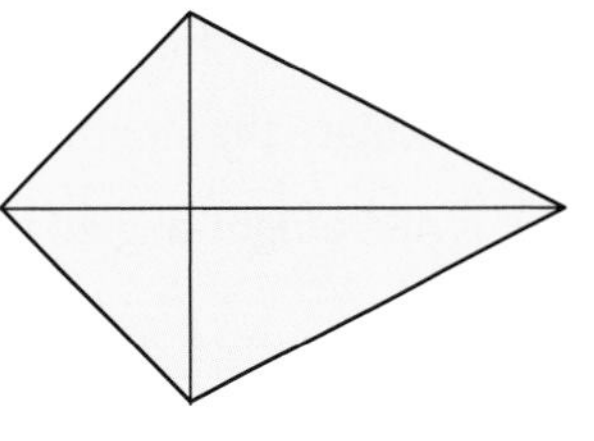

3 $ABC = 90°$ and $ADB = 90°$

$AB = 22$ cm, $AD = 19$ cm and $BC = 12$ cm

Calculate the lengths of CD and BD

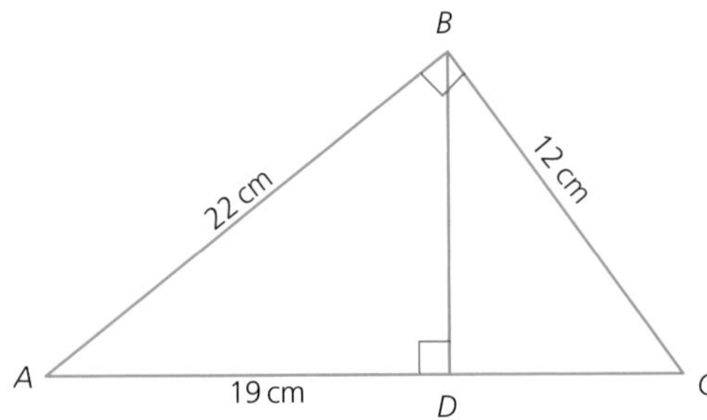

4 **(a)** A prince has a ladder 5 m long and instructions that the base of the ladder must be 2 m away from the base of the wall. Is the ladder able to reach the princess's cell window which is 4.7 m above the ground?

(b) How far forward must he move the base of the ladder if he is to reach the window?

5 $ABCD$ is a square with diagonal AC 10 cm long.

F is the midpoint of CD and E is the midpoint of BC

G is the point where EF cuts AC

Calculate:

(a) CD **(b)** CF **(c)** EF **(d)** CG

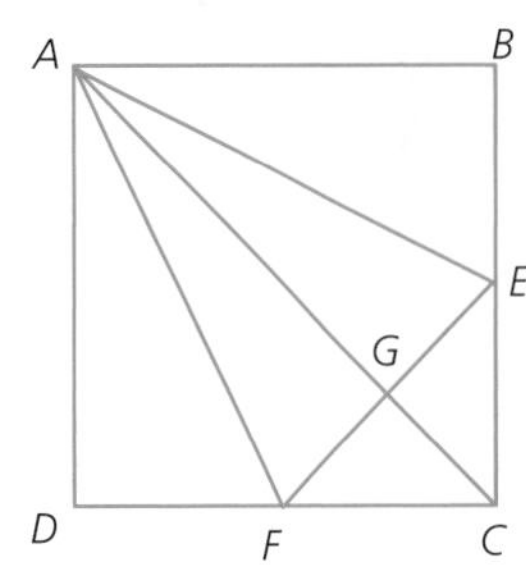

6 Look at this cuboid. It is an open-topped box with a base measuring 10 cm by 7 cm and a height of 5 cm.
A spider sitting at A spies a bug tucked inside the corner of the box at B. The spider wants to take the most direct route to the bug.

To find out the spider's route you have to draw a net of the box. Mark the positions A and B and then draw the spider's route. How far does the spider have to go?

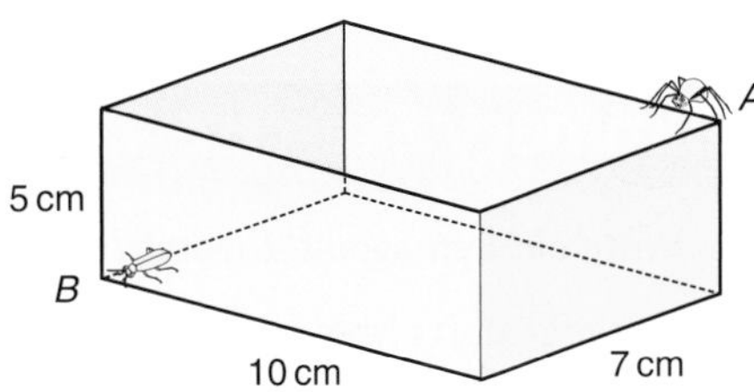

7 A is the point (5, 5), B is the point (2, 4) and C is the point (4, $^-1$)

(a) Calculate the lengths of AB, AC and BC.

(b) Is ABC a right-angled triangle?

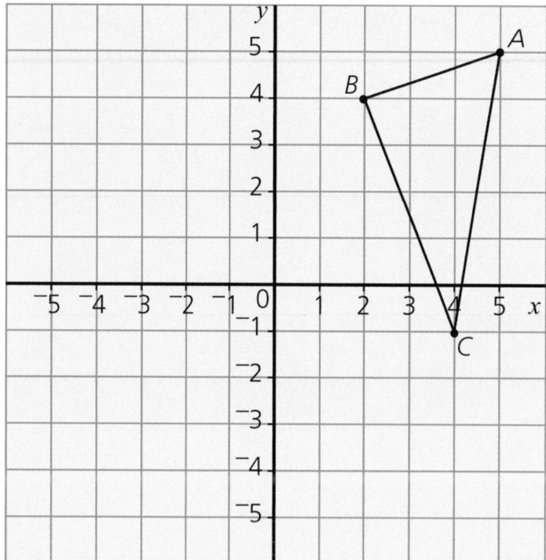

8 The mist came down on the moor in the middle of our Duke of Edinburgh expedition. My group had walked 5 km from our starting point on a bearing of 310° and then we walked another 3.75 km on a bearing of 220°

It was lucky that we had Ella with us. She managed to work out the distance we were from our starting point without using a calculator. How did she do it and what was her answer?

9 The square $ABCD$ has sides of length 12 cm. F is the midpoint of AD. Calculate:

(a) the length of AC

(b) the length of FC

(c) the areas of triangles AFB, BCF and AFC

(d) the areas of triangles GBC and AGF. Hint: Are triangles GBC and AGF similar? What is the ratio of their heights?

10 $ABCD$ is a rectangle in which $AB = 12$ cm and $AD = 8$ cm. F is the midpoint of AD and G is the point where BF crosses AC. Work out the areas of triangles GBA and GBC.

Summary Exercise 11.10

1 Write out Pythagoras' theorem in words.

2 A hunter starts from home and travels 4 km due east and then 2.5 km due north. She then shoots a pheasant, which falls at her feet. How far does she have to carry the pheasant home?

3 In isosceles triangle ABC the length of the base BC is 32 cm and the lengths of the two equal sides AB and AC are 63 cm. Calculate the height and then the area of the triangle.

4 This diagram shows the cross-section of our roof, which is in the shape of an isosceles triangle.

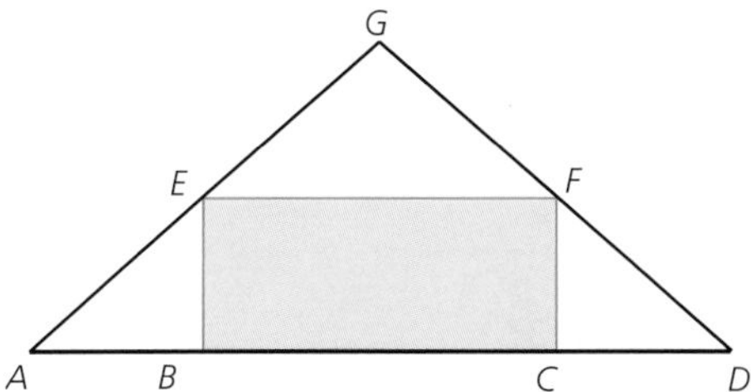

The total height of the roof is 2.6 m and the heights *BE* and *CF* are both 1.3 m.

The sloping lengths *AG* and *GD* are both 4 m.

Calculate:

(a) the length *AD*

(b) the total cross-sectional area of the roof

(c) the length *AE* and thus the length *AB*

(d) the rectangular area of useable roof space *BCFE*.

Compare the total height to height *BE*.

5 A similar roof with height *CF* of 2.6 m and base *AB* of 7 m has a dormer window inserted. The height of the window *DE* is 1.5 m and the length *CD* is 2 m. Calculate the length *BE*.

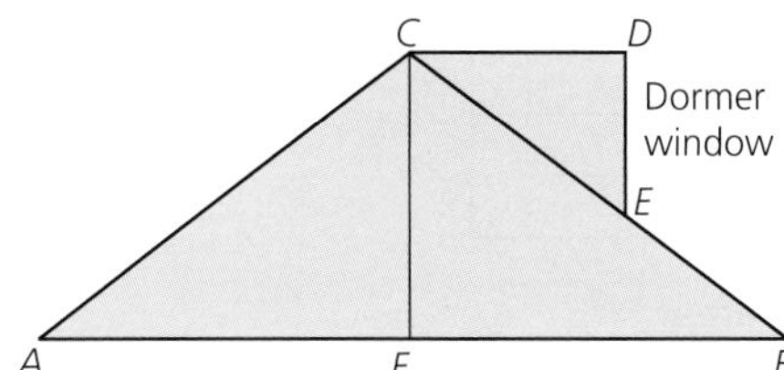

6 A company logo is in the form of two triangles, as shown. The total width of the logo is 5 cm and the height is 3 cm. The ratio of *BC* : *CE* and thus the lengths *AB* : *DE* is 3 : 2

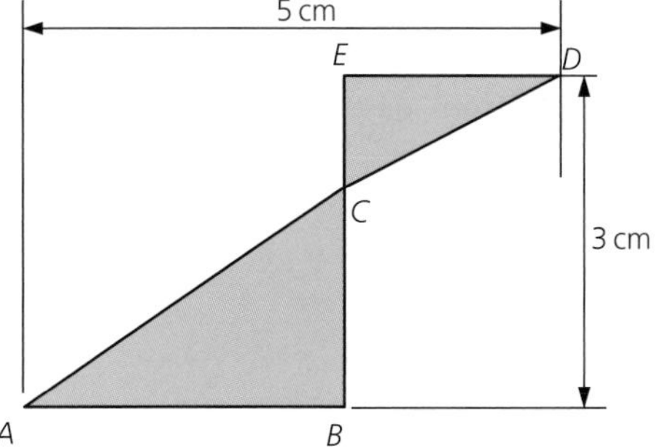

Calculate:

(a) the length of *AD*

(b) the areas of the two triangles *ABC* and *CDE*.

Activity: Pythagorean triplets

The 3 : 4 : 5 triangles and the 5 : 12 : 13 triangles are special because they have integer sides and the sum of the squares of the smaller two numbers is the square of the largest number.

Remember that **any** group of three integers that has this property is a **Pythagorean triplet**.

How many more can you find, excluding multiples of 3 : 4 : 5 and 5 : 12 : 13?

You could use the spreadsheet application on a computer to investigate this problem. If you do, you will need to find the correct formulae for finding squares and square roots.

Step 1 Start by making a table of numbers and their squares. You will need to go up to the squares of 40 or even 50

Number	Square	Subtract the previous square	Difference between the squares
1	1		
2	4	4 – 1	3
3	9	9 – 4	5
4	16	16 – 9	7
5	25	25 – 16	$9 = 3^2$
6			
7			
8			
9			
10			

Step 2 Then look at the differences between the consecutive squares. For example,

$17^2 - 16^2 = 33$

See if any of these differences are perfect squares.

Step 3 Next try looking at the differences between non-consecutive squares and see if any of those are perfect squares.

Step 4 Look for a pattern in your results. Can you find and repeat a pattern, or is this a random property of certain sets of numbers?

You have used calculators or computers to do this search, but spare a thought for the ancient Greeks who found their triplets without such aids to calculation!

12 Circles, cylinders and prisms

You are familiar with **formulae** for area and volume of some plane shapes and solids. In this chapter you will build on what you learnt in *Mathematics for Common Entrance Book Two* about the special formulae for **circles**.

Circles

Can you recall the names of the parts of a circle?

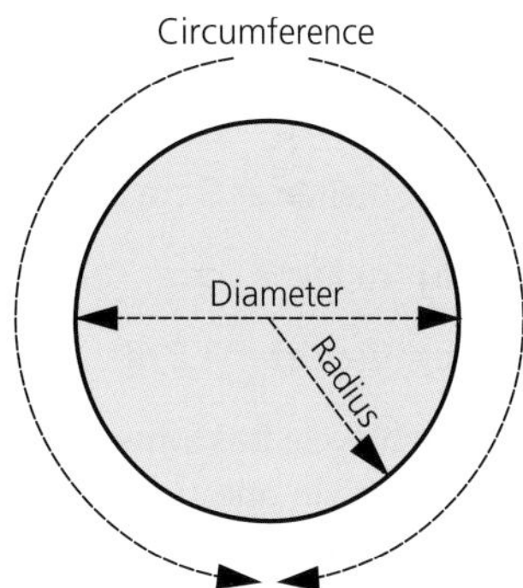

- The **circumference** is the name for the line round the outside of the circle. The perimeter of the circle is also called the circumference.
- The **radius** is the straight line from the centre of the circle to the circumference. The distance from the centre to the circumference is also called the radius.
- The **diameter** is the straight line between two points on the circumference, through the centre. The distance from two points on the circumference, through the centre, is also called the diameter.

Diameter = 2 × radius

Do you remember the formulae for calculating the circumference and **area** of a circle?

Circumference $C = \pi d$ or $C = 2\pi r$ Area $A = \pi r^2$

The symbol π is the Greek letter pi, the constant that describes the ratio of diameter to circumference.

Find the π on your calculator. It should give you 3.141592654...

You should use the full value of π when using a calculator, if not you can use 3.14 or the fraction $\frac{22}{7}$

Example

Calculate the circumference of a circle of diameter 14 cm.

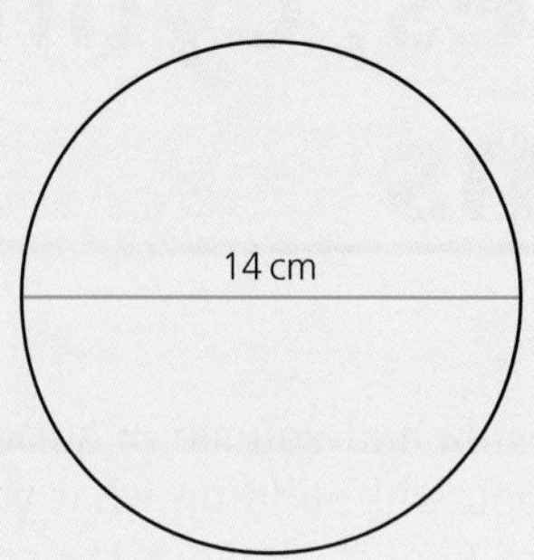

$d = 14$ cm

$C = \pi d$

$= \pi \times 14$

$= 43.982...$

$= 44.0$ cm (to 3 s.f.)

As usual, it is a good idea to start with a quick sketch, to make sure that you have the correct dimensions and do not confuse radius and diameter.

Exercise 12.1

Use the π button on your calculator for this exercise and give rounded answers correct to 3 s.f.

1 Calculate: (i) the circumference (ii) the area of each circle.

(a) diameter 8 cm

(b) radius 31 cm

(c) diameter 1.2 m

(d) radius 4.5 m

(e) diameter 50 cm

(f) radius 12 m

2 My bicycle has wheels of diameter 95 cm. How far will my bicycle move forward in one turn of the wheel?

3 The diameter of this table mat is 14 cm. Work out its area and circumference.

4 I have a glass with a base diameter of 8 cm. Find the area of the base of my glass.

5 The radius of my frisbee is 9 cm. What is the circumference?

6 I bought a large sheet of plywood measuring 1.25 m by 2.5 m. I cut from it the largest circle that I could. What area of plywood is left?

Fractions of circles

Perimeter and area of fractions of circles

Some of the shapes you will meet may not be whole circles but parts of circles.

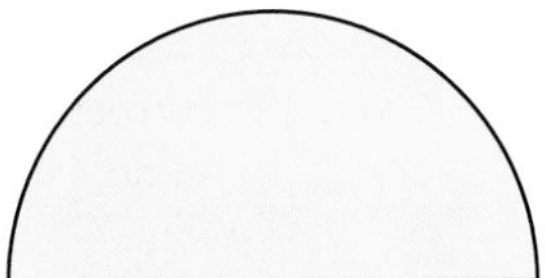

A half-circle is a **semi-circle**.

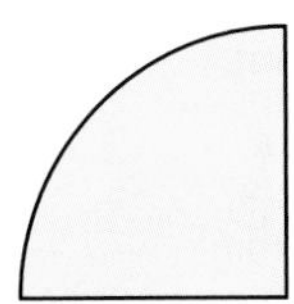

A quarter-circle is a **quadrant**.

To find the perimeter of a semi-circle you have to first find half the circumference and then add on the length of the straight side.

Example

Calculate: (i) the area (ii) the perimeter of this semi-circle.

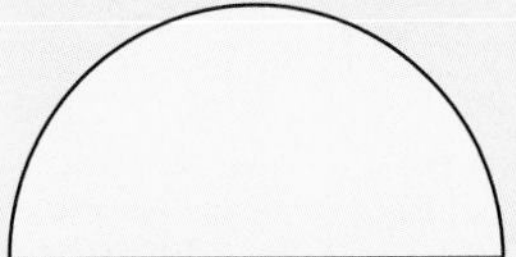

$d = 14\text{cm}$

$r = 7\text{cm}$

(i) Remember that this is half of a circle, so you must halve the area formula.

Area $= \frac{1}{2}\pi r^2$

$= \frac{1}{2}\pi \times 7^2$

$= \frac{1}{2} \times \pi \times 49$

$= 76.969\ldots$

$= 77.0\text{cm}^2$ (to 3 s.f.)

(ii) Curved length $= \frac{1}{2}\pi d$

$= \frac{1}{2} \times \pi \times 14$

$= 21.991\ldots$

The straight side is the diameter measuring 14 cm

Perimeter $= 21.991\ldots + 14$

$= 35.991\ldots$

$= 36.0\text{cm}$ (to 3 s.f.)

Note you are working with the full display, not with the rounded answers.

Here are some more parts of a circle you should know.

An **arc** is a part of the circumference.

A **sector** is a slice formed by two radii and the arc between them.

The angle at the centre of a sector, between the two radii, is the **sector angle**.

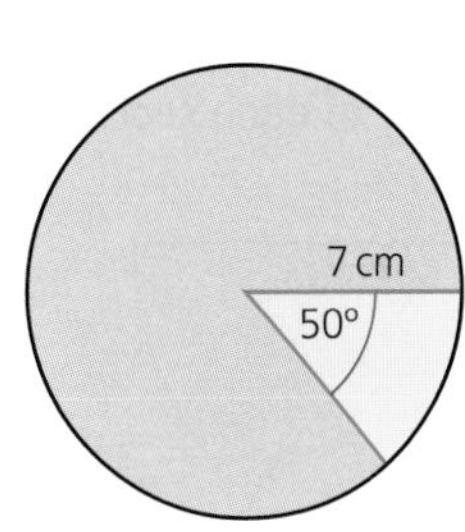

Exercise 12.2

For question 1–6 use the π button on your calculator and give rounded answers correct to 3 s.f.

1 Calculate the perimeter of this semi-circular carpet.

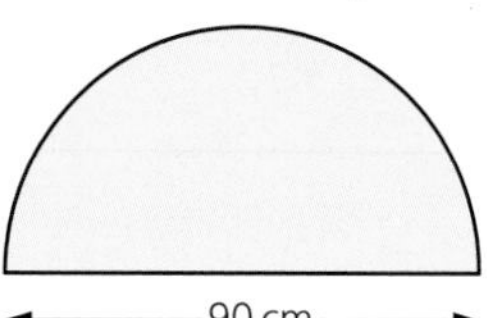

2 Calculate the area and perimeter of this quadrant.

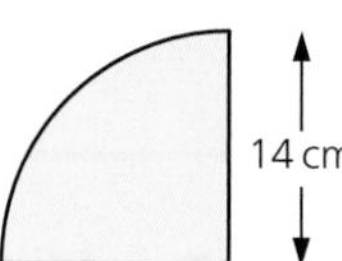

3 Calculate the area of this three-quarter circle.

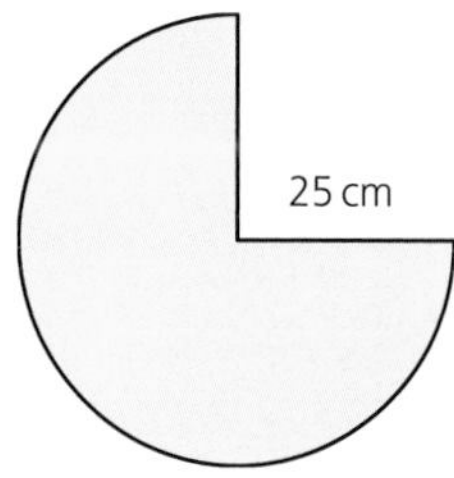

4 **(a)** Calculate the distance round the outside of this running track.

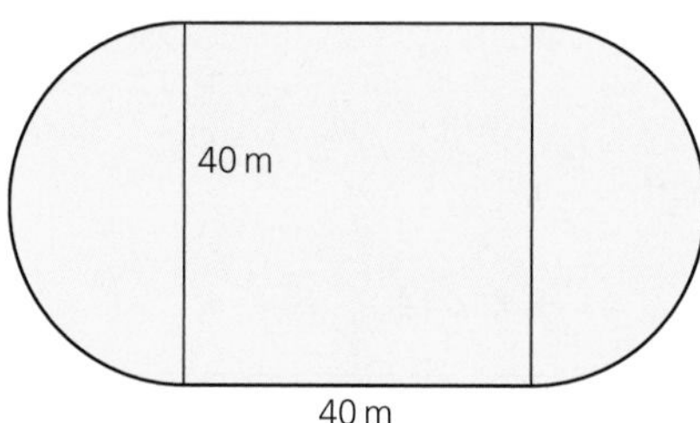

(b) What is the area enclosed by the running track?

5 Find the area of this lily pad.

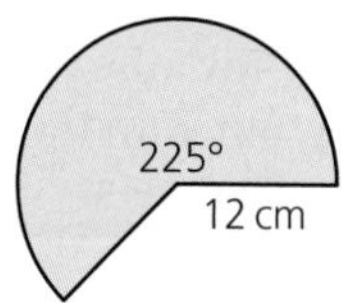

6 Look at these shapes. Each is a sector of a circle. Work out the area and perimeter of each sector.

(a)

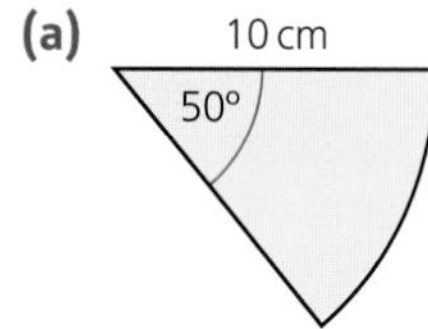

(b)

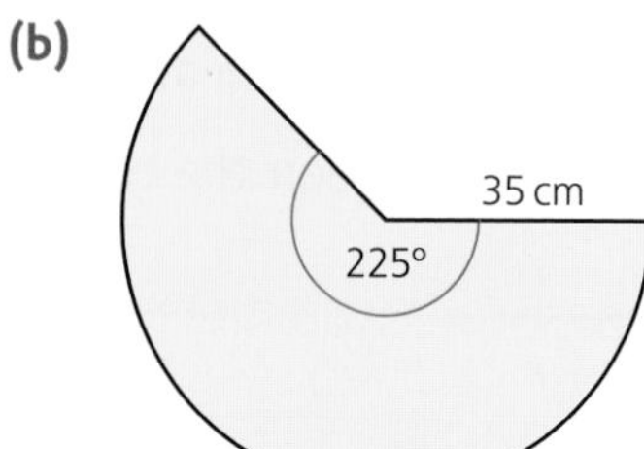

For the next few questions use $\pi = \frac{22}{7}$

7 This is the cross-sectional view of the building that won this year's architectural prize. Calculate the area of the cross-section.

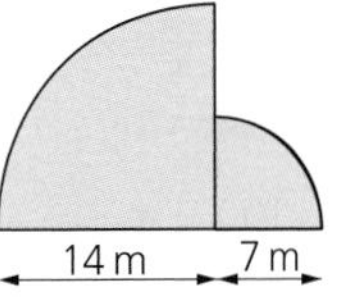

8 This is the net of a conical hat for the school play. What length of ribbon do I need to trim the whole outside edge of the net?

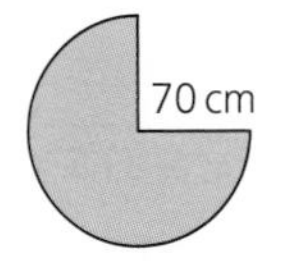

9 This is the vertical cross-section through a spinning toy. The top semi-circle has a diameter of 49 mm and the bottom semi-circle a diameter of 98 mm. What is the area of the cross-section?

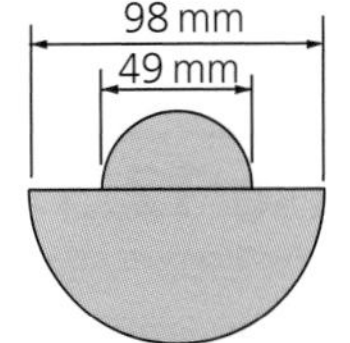

10 Look at Kim's design. It is made from four semicircles of diameter 14 cm.

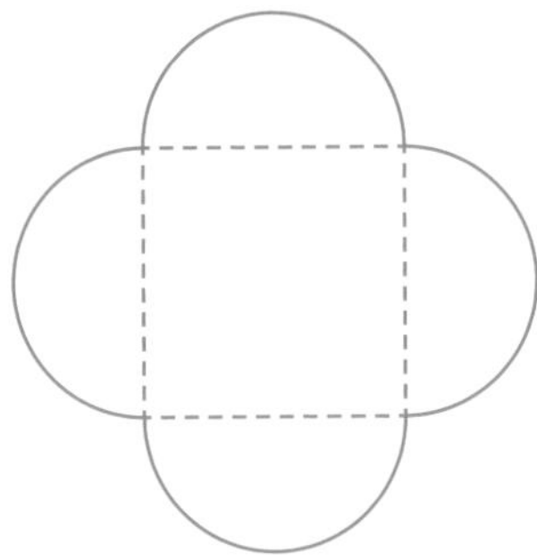

(a) What is the perimeter of the design?

(b) What is the area of the design?

(c) Kim draws the design on a piece of card that is 28 cm by 28 cm and then cuts it out. What area of card is left?

Calculating the radius and diameter

Given the radius or diameter of a circle, you can calculate its perimeter (circumference) or area.

It follows that, given the circumference or area, you can calculate the radius or diameter.

Example

Work out the radius of a circle of area $100\,\text{cm}^2$.

Area of circle $= \pi r^2$

$100 = \pi r^2$

$100 \div \pi = r^2$

$r^2 = 31.8309...$

$r = \sqrt{31.8309}$

$= 5.6418...$

The radius is 5.64 cm (to 3.s.f.).

Exercise 12.3

1 Calculate the diameter of a circle of circumference 14 cm.

2 Work out the radius of a circle of area $100\,\text{cm}^2$.

3 Calculate the radius of a circle of circumference 12 m.

4 Work out the diameter of a circle of area $250\,\text{cm}^2$.

5 Calculate the radius, in centimetres, of a circle of area $4\,\text{m}^2$.

6 I have a length of wooden trim measuring 2 m. What is the radius of the largest circle that I could trim with it?

7 I have a circular tablecloth of area $5\,\text{m}^2$. What is the radius of the largest table that it could cover?

8 The perimeter of a semi-circle is 20 cm. What is the diameter?

Always write down the dimensions that you are given first, to make sure that you use the correct formula and substitute the correct value.

More circle problems

Some questions need a little more thought. For some of the following problems you may need to use Pythagoras' theorem. Be sure to set out your working clearly.

Exercise 12.4

Use the π on your calculator for this exercise and give rounded answers correct to 3 s.f.

1 (a) Calculate the diameter of the circle **inscribed** in a square of side 10 cm.

(b) Now work out the length of the diagonal of the square.

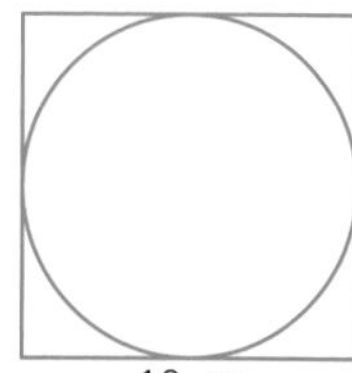

The **inscribed circle** is inside the square and just touches the sides.

2 Calculate the diameter and thus the area of the **circumscribed** circle for a square of side 10 cm.

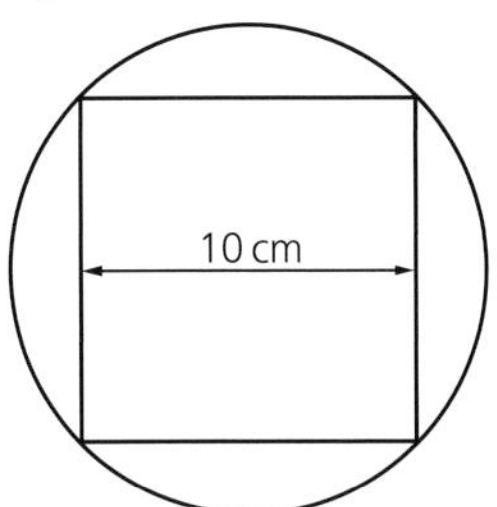

The **circumscribed circle** is the smallest circle that can be drawn around the outside of the square (or any other 2D shape). It passes through all of the vertices of the shape.

3 Calculate the area of the shaded part of this circle.

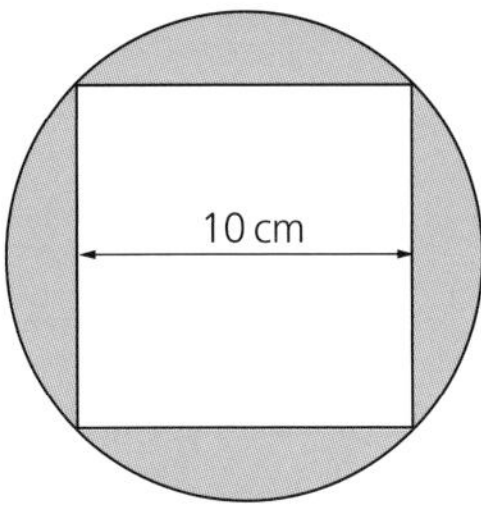

4 **(a)** This square is inscribed inside a circle of diameter 22 cm. Calculate the length of a side of the square.

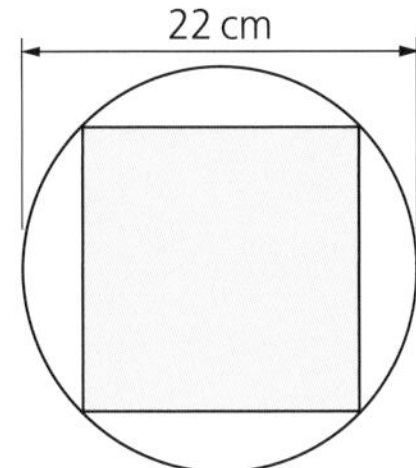

(b) Now find the shaded area in the second diagram.

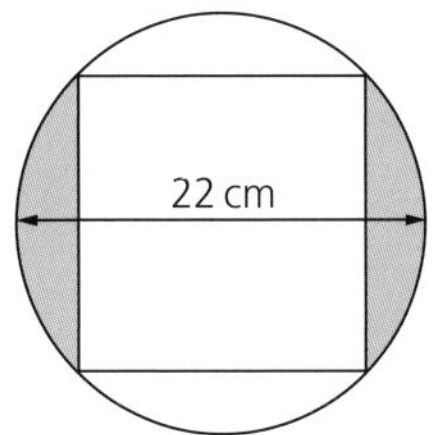

5 A square is inscribed in a circle of radius 7 cm. What is the area of the square?

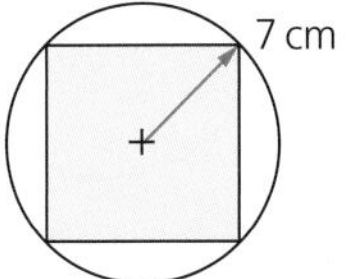

6 A circle of radius 12 cm is inscribed in a square. What is the area of the square?

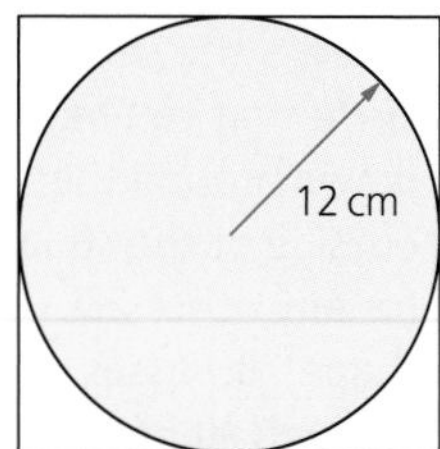

7 A circle of diameter 25 cm is inscribed inside a square. What is the length of a diagonal of the square?

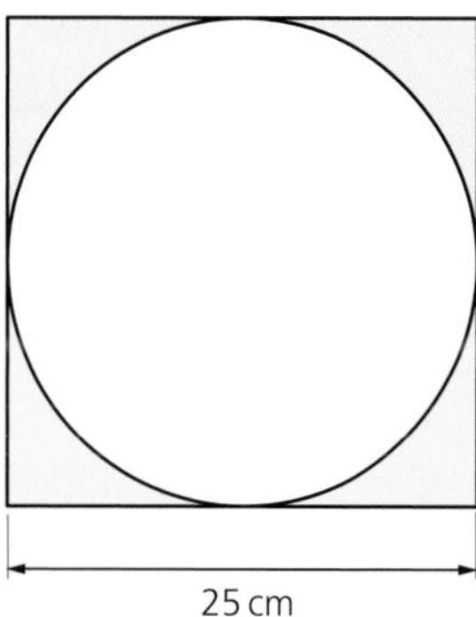

8 Leave your answers to these questions in terms of π.

(a) A circle is inscribed inside a square of diagonal $2x$. Write down an expression for the area of the circle, in terms of x.

(b) A square is inscribed inside a circle of diameter $2x$. What is the area of the square?

(c) A square of area $4x^2$ is inscribed inside a circle. What is the area of the circle?

(d) A circle of area πx^2 is inscribed inside a square. What is the area of the square?

9 An equilateral triangle of side 4 cm is drawn between the centres of three adjacent circles as shown.

Radius of circles = 2 cm

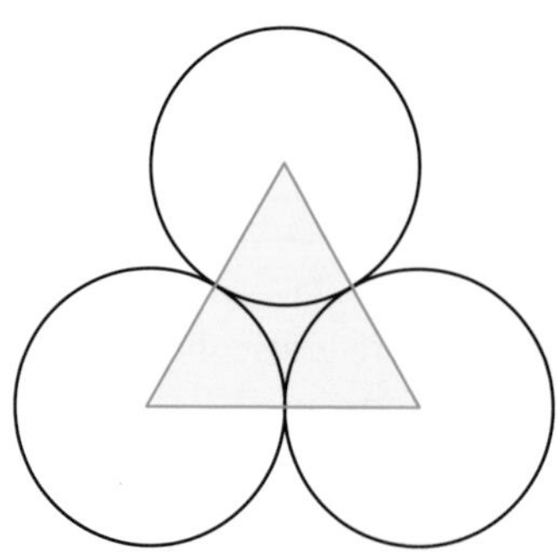

(a) What is the height of the triangle?

(b) What is the area of the triangle?

(c) What is the area of one circle?

(d) What is the area of the part of one circle that is in the triangle?

(e) From your answers to **(b)** and **(d)**, find the percentage of the area of the triangle that does not lie in a circle.

Draw the triangle and then use Pythagoras' theorem.

10 Silver discs of diameter 5 cm are stamped out of a strip of metallic foil. Assuming there is minimum waste, how many discs can be stamped out of a strip of foil, 1 m by 5 cm, and what is the percentage of foil wasted?

Volumes of prisms

A **prism** is a shape that has a constant cross-section throughout its length. This means that you can slice it anywhere, perpendicular to its length, and the cut slice will be **congruent** to the end face.

In science, you may have used a glass prism to separate white light into its spectrum of coloured lights.

The prism probably looked like this. It is called a **triangular prism**.

Here are some more examples of prisms.

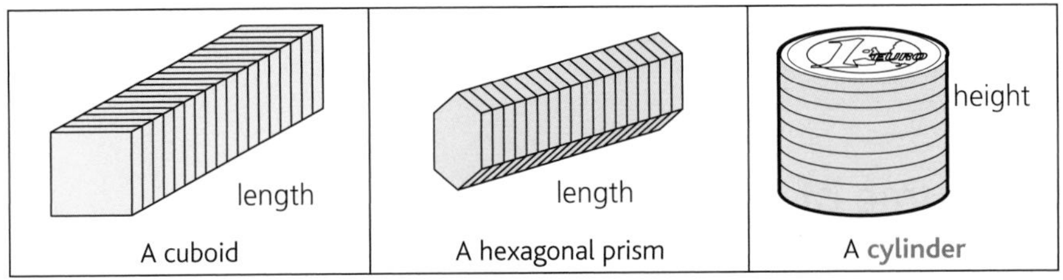

A cuboid | A hexagonal prism | A **cylinder**

These are all prisms. Note that the slices all have the same cross-section and are parallel to the ends of the prism and perpendicular to its length.

When you derived the volume of a cuboid, you considered how may centimetre cubes would fill one layer of the cuboid.

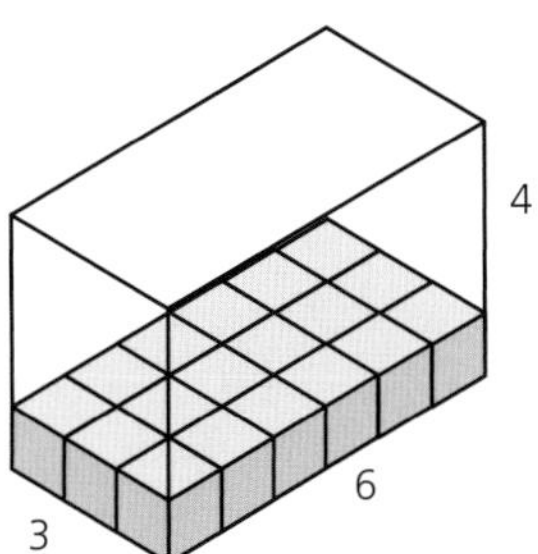

This gives the area of the base of the cuboid.

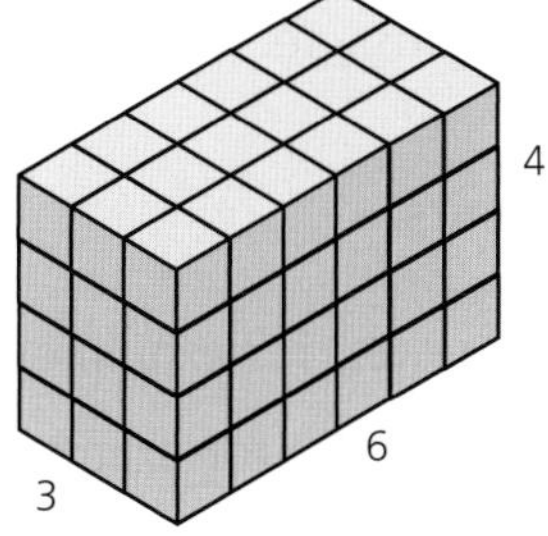

Then you multiplied this area by the number of layers.

So the volume is the area of the base multiplied by the height.

A cuboid is one type of prism, so can you use the same method to find the volume of any prism?

Work through the next exercise to find out.

Exercise 12.5

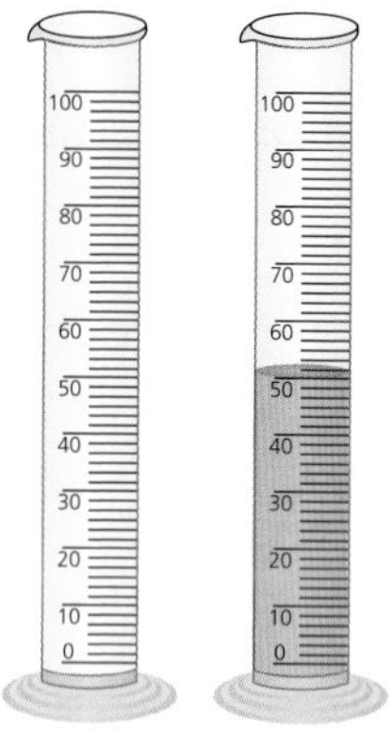

1 Examine a measuring cylinder.

   (a) Measure the diameter of the top, and calculate the radius.

   (b) Calculate the area of the top. This is the cross-sectional area.

   (c) Pour exactly 50 cm^3 of water into the measuring cylinder.

   If the cylinder is marked in millilitres remember $1\,cm^3 = 1\,ml$.

   Measure the height of the water in the cylinder.

   (d) Multiply the height by the area that you calculated in part **(b)**. What do you notice?

2 Repeat question 1 with some measuring cylinders with different diameters. Try using different amounts of water.

3 Repeat question 1 with a hollow triangular prism. Start by calculating the cross-sectional area.

Calculating the volume of a prism

You have demonstrated that the formula to calculate the volume of a prism is:

volume of a prism = **area of cross-section** × **length** (or **height** or **depth**)

As with any formula, start by making sure that all your dimensions are in the same units.

It is a good idea to sketch the cross-section, especially if you need to calculate the area.

Remember to take care with units.

- The units of area are square units: for example, cm^2
- The units of volume are cubic units: for example, cm^3

Example

Work out the volume of a prism of length 15 cm and a triangular cross-section of base 8 cm and height 6 cm.

Always start with a diagram of the cross-sectional face.

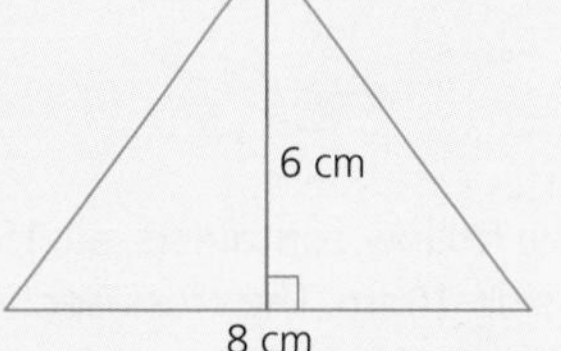

Area of triangle $= \frac{1}{2}bh$

Next, calculate the cross-sectional area.

$= \frac{1}{\not{2}_1} \times \not{8}^4 \times 6$

$= 24\,\text{cm}^2$

Volume of prism = area of cross-section × length

$= 24 \times 15$

Now use the formula to work out the volume.

$= 360\,\text{cm}^3$

Remember the cubic units.

Exercise 12.6

1 Calculate the volume of each prism.

(a) A water tank with cross-sectional area of $2.5\,\text{m}^2$ and depth 1.4 m

(b) A mug with cross-sectional area $8\,\text{cm}^2$ and height 12 cm

(c) The roof of a barn with cross sectional-area $6\,\text{m}^2$ and length 12 m

(d) A swimming pool with cross-sectional area $28\,\text{m}^2$ and width 8 m

2 Calculate the volume of a triangular prism of length 18 cm. The triangular face has height 2.5 cm and base 3 cm.

3 A wooden bar has cross-sectional area $5\,\text{cm}^2$ and length 2 m. What is its volume, in cubic centimetres (cm^3)?

4 The cross-section of a hexagonal paving stone is made up from two trapezia, each with base 12 cm, top 6 cm and height 5.5 cm. The paving stone is 3 cm thick. What is its volume?

As the paving stone has a constant cross-section, it is a prism.

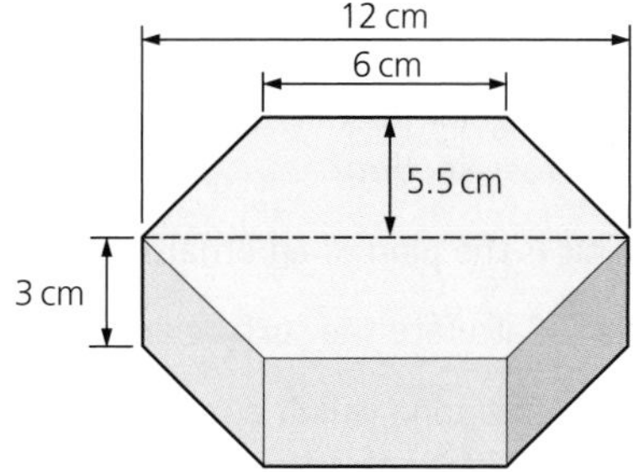

5 A prism has a cross-sectional area in the shape of a parallelogram of height 95 cm and base 1.2 m. The depth of the prism is 1.4 m. What is the volume of the prism, in cubic metres (m^3)?

6 This builder's skip is 3 m wide. What volume of rubbish will it hold?

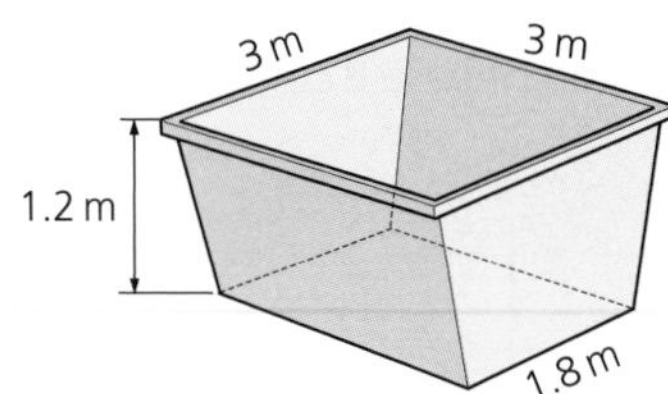

7 I have three hollow containers, all 15 cm tall. The cross-section of one is a square of side 10 cm. The cross-section of another is a rectangle of width 8 cm and length 12 cm. The cross-section of the last is a triangle with base 14 cm and height 12 cm.

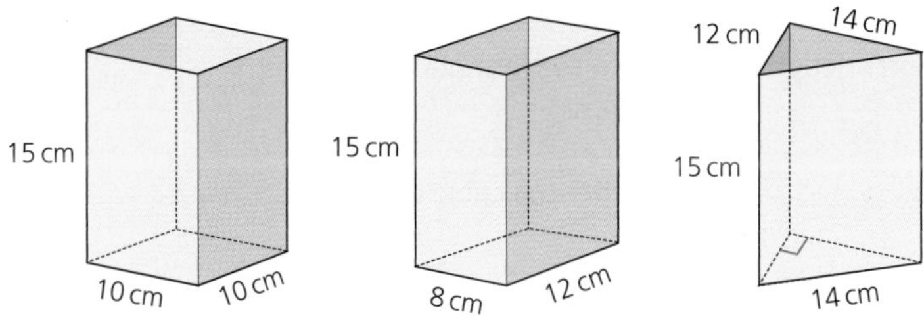

(a) Which container has the greatest capacity?

(b) If I were to pour 1.5 litres of water into each prism, which ones would overflow?

8 A bird nesting-box is made up of five pieces, as shown.

Calculate the volume of the box.

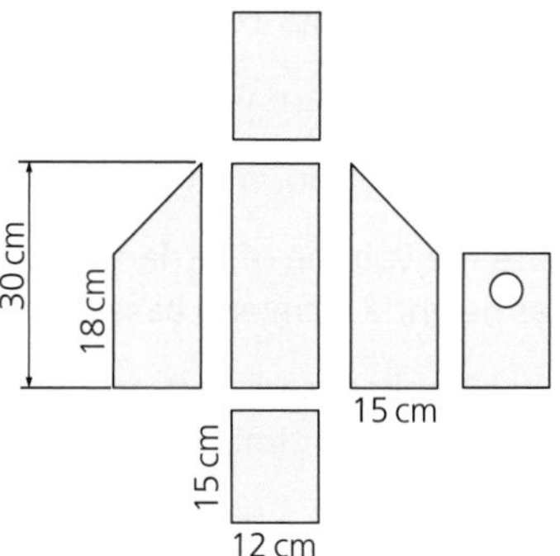

9 A triangular prism has volume 120 cm^3 and length 15 cm. What is the area of its cross-section?

10 This is the plan of an ornamental pond.

(a) Calculate the surface area of the pond.

(b) The pond is half a metre deep. Each goldfish requires 10 litres of water. What is the maximum number of goldfish that I could keep in the pond?

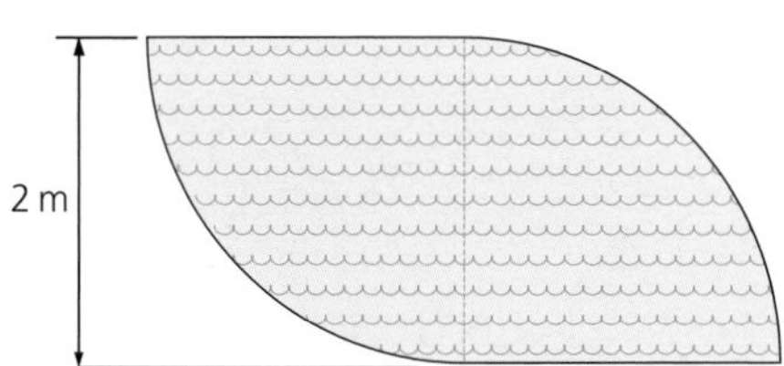

Volume of a cylinder

You know that the volume of a prism is given by the formula:

volume of a prism = area of cross-section × height (or length or breadth)

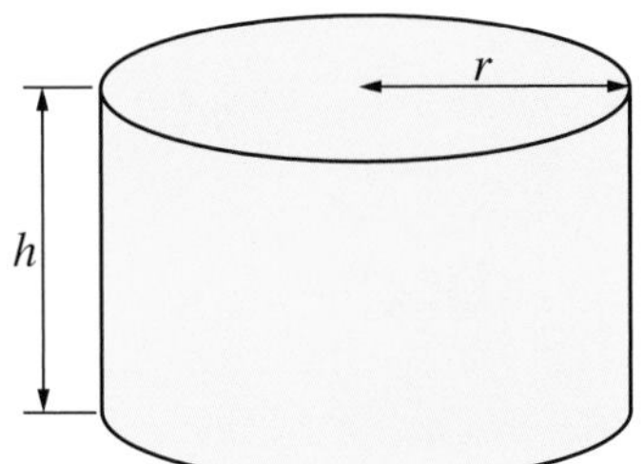

The cross-section of a **cylinder** is a circle, so you can write the formula for the volume of a cylinder as:

volume of cylinder = $\pi r^2 h$

Example

Calculate the volume of a cylinder of radius 5 cm and height 10 cm. Give your answer in litres.

$r = 5$ cm $h = 10$ cm $1000 \text{ cm}^3 = 1$ litre

Volume $= \pi r^2 h$

$= \pi \times 5^2 \times 10$

$= 785.398...$

$= 785 \text{ cm}^3$

$= 0.785$ litres

Remember to write your answer with more digits than you need before you round it.

Exercise 12.7

Use the π button on your calculator for this exercise. Give rounded answers correct to 3 s.f.

1 Calculate the volume of each cylinder, giving your answer in:

(i) cubic centimtres (cm^3) **(ii)** litres.

(a) radius 3 cm and height 5 cm

(b) radius 4 m and height 5 m

(c) diameter 60 cm and height 50 cm

(d) height 20 cm and radius 9 cm

(e) diameter 15 cm and height 8 cm

(f) height 1.2 m and radius 0.75 m

2 Work out the volume of a cylinder of radius 80 cm and height 2.4 m, giving your answer in cubic metres (m^3).

3 Find the volume of a cylinder of diameter 110 cm and height 1.2 m, giving your answer in litres.

4 I have a glass of base diameter 6 cm and height 8 cm. How many glasses can I fill from a full jug containing 2 litres of water?

5 A tin of *WOOF* dog food has a radius of 5 cm and a height of 12 cm.

What volume of *WOOF* is in the can, assuming it is full to the top?

Surface area of a cylinder

In question 5 above you considered the volume of a can of dog food.

Now suppose you cut through the label on the tin and unwrapped it. What shape would it be?

The label is a rectangle.

In fact, it is a rectangle with length equal to the **circumference** of the cylinder.

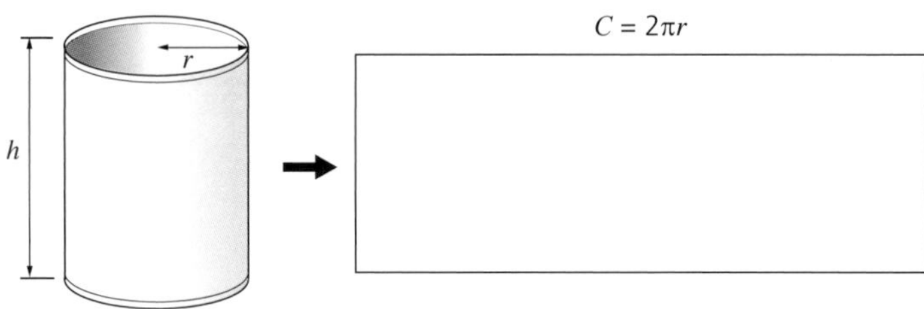

$C = 2\pi r$

Therefore the area of the curved surface of a cylinder is given by the formula:

curved surface area $= 2\pi rh$

But a solid cylinder also has two ends (two circles):

Area of each circular end $= \pi r^2$

So the formula for the complete surface area of a cylinder, including top and bottom, is:

$$SA = 2\pi rh + 2\pi r^2$$

or $$SA = 2\pi r(h + r)$$

Until you are confident in working out the surface area of a solid it is best to work out the parts separately then add them together. Always look carefully at what you are being asked to do. Some cylinders are hollow, some are solid (and have volume rather than capacity) and some are open at one end.

Example

Find the surface area of a closed cylinder of radius 5 cm and height 10 cm.

$r = 5$ cm $\quad h = 10$ cm

Area of curved surface $= 2\pi rh$

$= 2 \times \pi \times 5 \times 10$

$= 314.159...$

Area of circular ends $= 2\pi r^2$

$= 2 \times \pi \times 5^2$

$= 157.079 ...$

Total $SA = 314.159... + 157.079 ...$

$= 471.23...$

$= 471$ cm^2 (to 3 s.f.)

If you calculate with rounded values you will get wrong answers.

Exercise 12.8

Use the π button on your calculator for this exercise. Give rounded answers correct to 3 s.f.

1 What are the dimensions of the rectangular label from the *WOOF* can above? What is its area?

2 (a) I have a cylindrical can of radius 5 cm and height 10 cm. What is the area of the label that wraps around the can?

(b) What is the volume of the can?

3 Here is the top of a hat box. The radius of the circle is 25 cm and the height is 15 cm. What is the external surface area of the top of a hat box?

4 You can unwrap an empty toilet roll into a parallelogram.

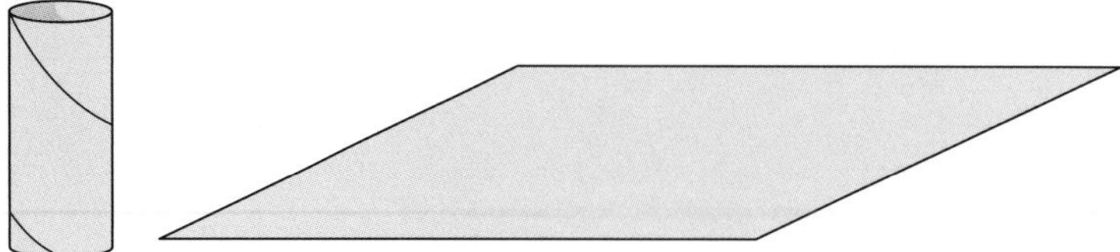

(a) If the parallelogram has base 15 cm and height 10 cm, what is the surface area of the cylinder?

(b) What do you think the advantages are of a parallelogram rather than a rectangle?

5 This is a cylindrical drum. It has diameter 15 cm and height 7 cm. What is its surface area?

6 Which has the greater surface area, and by how much, a cube of side 10 cm or a cylinder of diameter and height 10 cm?

7 Which has the larger volume, a cylinder with radius 5 cm and height 6 cm or a cylinder with a radius of 6 cm and a height 5 cm? Try to answer the question without actually calculating the volumes of the two cylinders.

8 A can of tomato juice has a radius of 5 cm and a height of 12 cm. What volume of tomato juice is contained in a tray of 24 tins? Give your answer in litres.

9 My little sister has a cylindrical paddling pool of radius 1.2 m, filled to a depth of 14 cm. I had to fill up the pool using a cylindrical bucket of radius 12 cm and height 30 cm. How many bucket loads did I have to carry?

10 A prism has a cross-section in the shape of a circle of circumference 15 cm. The volume of the prism is 268 cm^3. What is the length of the prism? (Clue: find r from the circumference first.)

Units of area and volume

All the calculations you have done so far have used just one unit of area in each question. These have been square millimetres (mm^2), square centimetres (cm^2), square metres (m^2) or square kilometres (km^2).

There are times when you start out with one unit of area and then need to change to another. This is more complicated than it looks.

Look at these two squares.

You know that $1\,\text{m} = 100\,\text{cm}$.

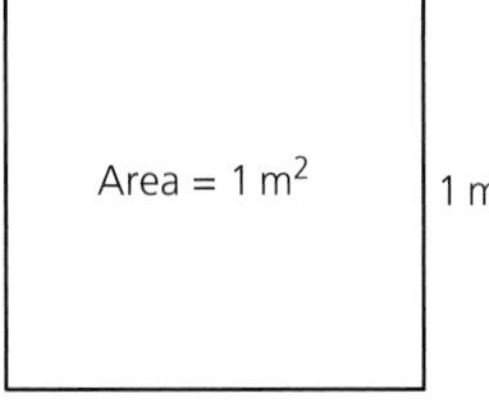

Area = $1\,\text{m}^2$
= $10\,000\,\text{cm}^2$
100 cm
100 cm

Therefore $1\,\text{m}^2 = 10\,000\,\text{cm}^2$

There are also occasions when you need to change units of volume.

Look at these two cubes.

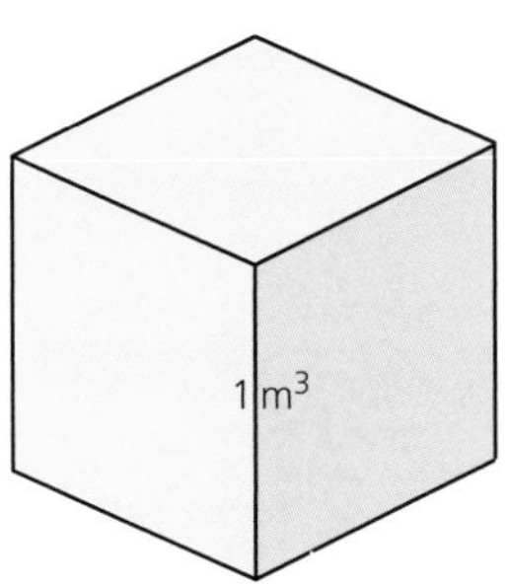

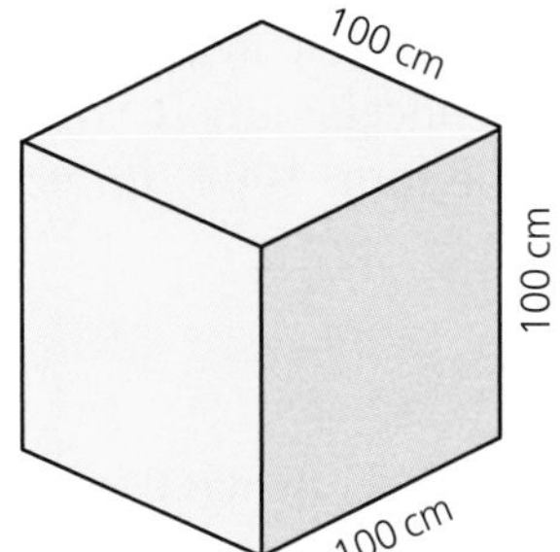

The volume of the second cube is

$100 \times 100 \times 100 = 1\,000\,000\,\text{cm}^3$

Therefore $1\,\text{m}^3 = 1\,000\,000\,\text{cm}^3$

Exercise 12.9

1 Draw squares like the two above to find how many:

(a) square millimetres there are in a square centimetre

(b) square millimetres there are in a square metre

(c) square metres there are in a square kilometre

(d) square metres there are in a square centimetre

(e) square metres there are in a square millimetre

(f) square kilometres there are in a square metre.

2 Draw cubes like the two above to find how many:

(a) cubic millimetres there are in a cubic centimetre

(b) cubic millimetres there are in a cubic metre

(c) cubic metres there are in a cubic kilometre

(d) cubic metres there are in a cubic centimetre

(e) cubic metres there are in a cubic millimetre

(f) cubic kilometres there are in a cubic metre.

3 **(a)** How many litres are there in a cubic metre?

(b) How many cubic millimetres (mm^3) are there in a litre?

Extension: More volume problems

When you are calculating with π, leave it in your answer until the last possible moment – it frequently cancels out. It is perfectly acceptable to leave a length or volume in the form 100π, for example, and only multiply out the final answer.

Example

A cylindrical glass of radius 4 cm and height 8 cm is filled with water.

All the water is poured into an empty cylindrical jug of radius 8 cm.

What is the depth of water in the jug?

$$\begin{aligned}\text{Volume of glass} &= \pi r^2 h\\ &= \pi \times 4^2 \times 8\\ &= 128\pi\ \text{cm}^3\end{aligned}$$

$$\begin{aligned}\text{Volume in jug} &= \pi r^2 h\\ &= \pi \times 8^2 \times h\ \text{cm}^3\\ &= 64\pi h\ \text{cm}^3\end{aligned}$$

Therefore $128\pi = 64\pi h$ (h = depth of water in the jug)

$h = 2$ cm

Extension Exercise 12.10

Solve these problems. You may need to use Pythagoras' theorem to find some of the lengths. If the answer is not exact, give it correct to 3 s.f.

1 A cylindrical jug of radius 9 cm is filled with squash to a depth of 20 cm. All the squash is to be equally divided into 10 small cylindrical glasses of internal diameter 6 cm. What depth of squash should be poured into each glass?

2 A cube, 1 m by 1 m by 1 m, is filled with water. A cylinder with diameter 1 m contains the same amount of water. How high is the water in the cylinder?

3 A cylindrical glass of radius 4 cm and height 8 cm is filled with water. All the water is poured into an empty cylindrical jug of radius 8 cm. What is the depth of water in the jug?

4 A fish tank has a rectangular base 20 cm by 35 cm and is filled with water from two cylindrical buckets of diameter 24 cm and depth 15 cm. What is the depth of water in the fish tank?

5 A rectangular block of clay, 5 cm by 6 cm by 10 cm, is fashioned into a cylinder of diameter 6 cm. How long is this cylinder?

6 A cylinder has a volume of 1 litre. Another cylinder has the same height as the first but twice the radius. What is its volume?

7 I have to pack a cylindrical tube of circumference 21.5 cm and length 1.2 m into a rectangular box.

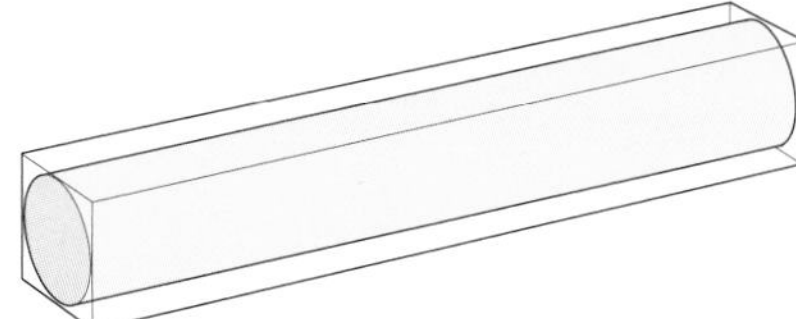

(a) What is the volume of the smallest box that I could use?

(b) Sketch the net of the box and work out the surface area.

8 A fly walks around the inside of a cylindrical glass of height 12 cm and diameter 8 cm. The fly starts at the bottom and finishes at the top of the glass immediately above its starting point, but it has travelled twice around the glass. How far has the fly walked?

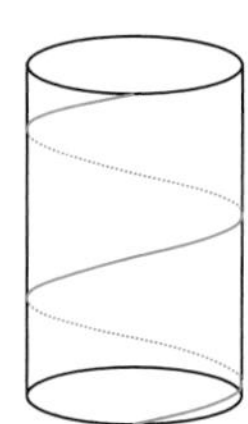

9 Six cylindrical cans are tightly packed into a rectangular box of base 12 cm by 18 cm and height 10 cm.

(a) What is the volume of one can?

(b) What is the volume of the box?

(c) What percentage of the volume of the box is not filled?

10 Here is my birthday cake, before and after it was iced.

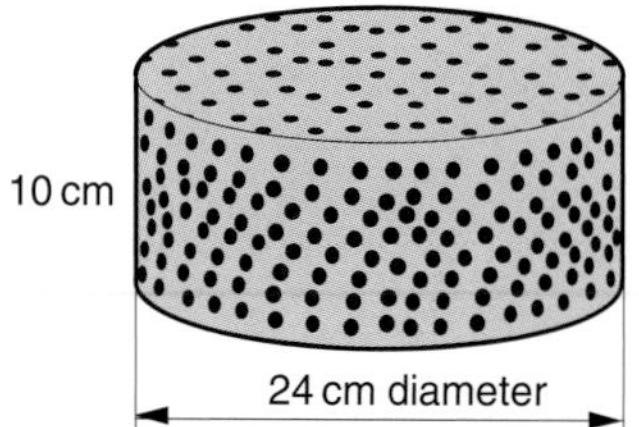

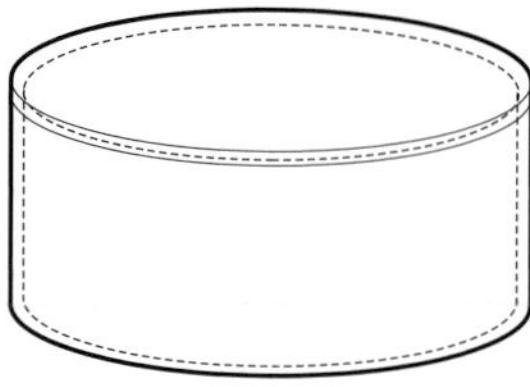

(a) The cake without the icing is in the shape of a cylinder 10 cm high and of diameter 24 cm. What is its volume, to 3 s.f?

(b) The icing is 0.5 cm thick and is made in two parts, a circle for the top, and a long rectangle to go round the sides. What is the diameter of the circle of icing?

(c) What are the height and length of the rectangle of icing?

(d) What is the total volume of the icing?

(e) I mixed icing sugar and water in the ratio 10 : 1. What volume of icing sugar did I use?

Summary Exercise 12.11

Use a calculator to solve these problems. Make sure you show all formulae and working. Use the value of π given by your calculator and give rounded answers to 2 decimal places.

1 Find the area and circumference of a circle of diameter 1.3 m.

2 Find the area and perimeter of this fan-shaped garden pond.

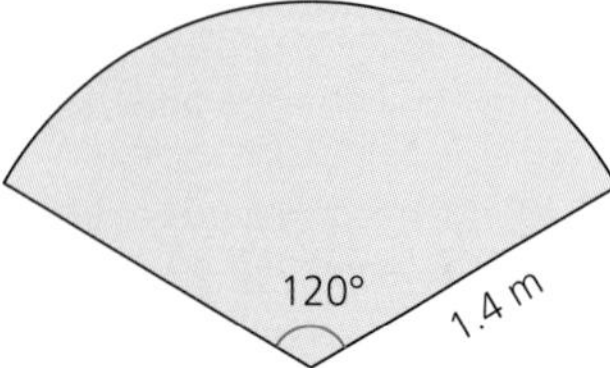

3 I put a £2 coin in a charity box. The coin rolls down two slopes each of 15 cm before it falls into a hole. How many times does the coin rotate on its journey? The diameter of a £2 coin is 28 mm.

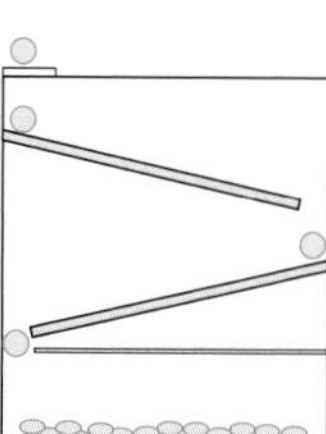

4 Find the volume of a prism with cross-sectional area of 15 cm^2 and length 1.2 m. Give your answer in cubic centimetres (cm^3).

5 Find the diameter of a circle with an area of 15 cm^2.

6 (a) A prism has a volume of 500 cm^3 and a cross-sectional area of 81 cm^2. What is its height?

(b) If the cross-section is a triangle of base 18 cm what is the height of the triangle?

7 I pour 5 litres of water into a pan of radius 12 cm. How far does the water come up the pan?

8 Gasometers are large cylindrical containers holding domestic gas, used to feed the domestic supply. Gasometers are constructed so that as the gas is drawn out of the gasometer the height of the whole cylinder drops.

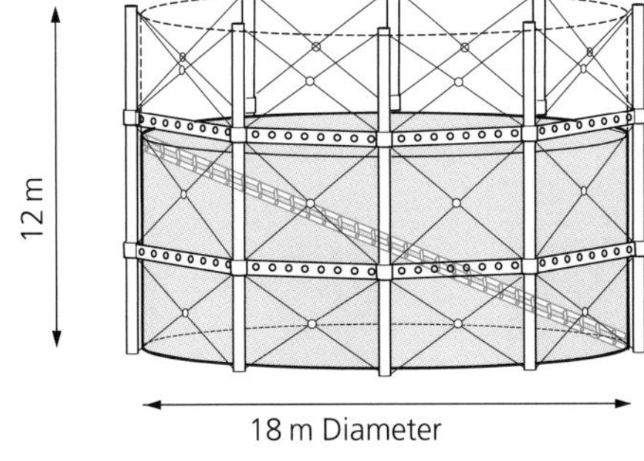

(a) A gasometer is a cylinder with a diameter of 18 m and when it is full it stands 12 m high. What volume of gas is contained in it when it is full? Give your answer to the nearest 1000 litres.

(b) 2 million litres of gas are drawn off the gasometer during the week and its height decreases accordingly. How tall is it now?

(c) The rest of the gas drained out of the gasometer but something has gone wrong! The gasometer is stuck at the height in part **(b)**. The repair man has to put a ladder across the inside of the gasometer. How long is his ladder?

9 This is a tin of *BowWow* dog food.

The radius of the tin is 6 cm and the height is 12 cm.

(a) The labels round the can overlap by 1 cm. Sketch a label and calculate its dimensions.

(b) In the dog-food factory several labels are printed on each sheet of A0 paper and then cut up by machine before the individual labels are stuck on the cans of *BowWow*. If a sheet of A0 paper is 84 cm by 118.8 cm, how many labels are there on every sheet?

10 This is the new logo for a record company.

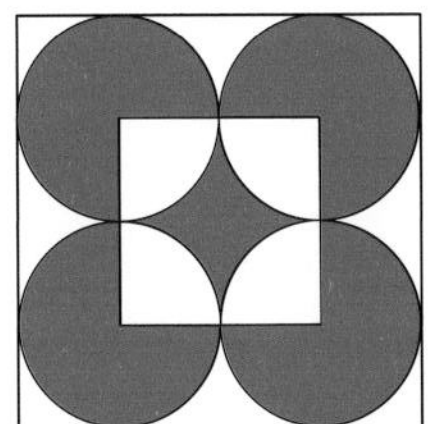

The larger square has sides of length 25 cm. Calculate:

(a) the area of one whole circle

(b) the red area of one circle

(c) the total red area of the shape

(d) the percentage of red area in the square logo.

Activity: Packaging the litre

The litre is the most common unit of volume now in use. Petrol is sold in litres. In the supermarket you will see orange juice, milk, wine, shampoos and other fluids are also measured in litres or millilitres.

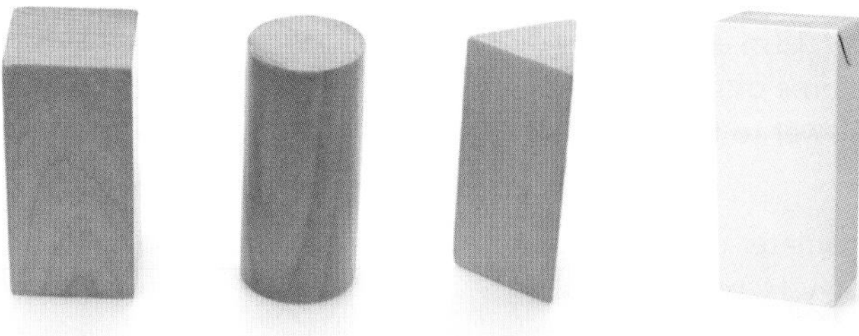

How many different packages with a volume of exactly one litre can you find?

Although the cube is an obvious shape for a container it is not usually used. Can you think why?

Can you design some prisms with a volume of exactly one litre? Their cross-sections could be circular, rectangular, triangular, trapezoid or any regular or irregular shape that you like.

Step 1 First decide what it is that you are going to package: a bright green fizzy drink, a herbal shampoo, a new chocolate bar, orange juice, talcum powder or just a pretty container to keep on your bedside table.

Step 2 Next think about the shape you want your package to be: long and thin, small and squat.

Step 3 Now think about putting hundreds of these packages together. To do this efficiently and economically, they must fit closely together. In fact this could be part of your design – put several together and make a new shape (like triangular prism chocolate bars).

The net of your package is important too. How are you going to cut hundreds of these from one long strip of cardboard?

Step 4 Now calculate the dimensions of your package – you could use a spreadsheet program to help you – making sure that you include the print out with your finished design.

Simultaneous equations

What is an equation?

An **equation** is a **statement** that one quantity or **expression** is **equal** to another quantity or expression.

These are examples of the types of equation you have worked with.

$y = x^2$ $\quad a + 3 = 5 \quad 4 - 2x = 3x - 1$

$3(t + 1) = 1 - 2(2t + 4) \quad 2u + 3v = 2 \quad \frac{a + 4}{3} = 4a$

Equations may include powers, fractions and brackets.

You have derived and solved equations in one variable, which was often x but could equally have been y, h, p, s or a

You solved each equation by simplifying, then adding, subtracting, multiplying and dividing, making sure that you always did the same to both sides.

Now you are going to look at writing and solving equations with two variables. You will find that the methods you use are similar to those you have already been using.

Consider this problem:

I double one number and add another and get the answer 12
What are my numbers?

Suppose your numbers are u and v. Then you can write this as an equation.

$2u + v = 12$

Drawing up a table of values, you can see that there are several possible values of u and v.

u	v	$2u + v$
$^{-}1$	14	$^{-}2 + 14 = 12$
0	12	$0 + 12 = 12$
1	10	$2 + 10 = 12$
2	8	$4 + 8 = 12$
3	6	$6 + 6 = 12$
10	$^{-}8$	$20 - 8 = 12$

The table includes just a few of the countless possibilities.

Problems in two variables

Writing equations in two variables

In the previous example, the two unknown numbers were defined as u and v. When writing an equation to solve a problem, always start by defining the variables.

Example

I spend exactly £5 buying some apples and some pears. Apples cost 25p each and pears cost 30p each.

Write this as an equation.

Let the number of apples be a and the number of pears be p

$25a + 30p = 500$

£5 has been written as 500p

Exercise 13.1

1 I am thinking of two numbers with a sum of 24. Write this as an equation.

2 I am thinking of two numbers with a difference of 8. Write this as an equation.

3 I am thinking of two numbers. I double one and add this to the other. The answer is 20. Write this as an equation.

4 My mother sends me to buy 15 assorted cans of drink. I can buy cola or orangeade. Show this as an equation.

5 I spend exactly £3 on some pencils and rulers. Pencils cost 25 pence each and rulers cost 30 pence each. Show this as an equation.

Drawing graphs to solve problems in two variables

Once you have an equation, one simple way to solve it is by drawing a graph.

Example

I want to buy some avocados and some mangoes. Avocados cost 60 pence each and mangoes cost 80 pence each.

(a) Let the number of avocados I buy be a and the number of mangoes I buy be m. I spend exactly £12 altogether. Show how this can be given by the equation $3a + 4m = 60$.

(b) Plot suitable points and draw a graph of $3a + 4m = 60$. Use your graph to show how many of each fruit I can buy.

(a) The cost of a avocados at 60 pence each $= 60a$

The cost of m mangoes at 80 pence each $= 80m$

The total cost is £12 or 1200 pence.

Therefore:

$60a + 80m = 1200$

$3a + 4m = 60$ $(\div 20)$

(b) To plot the graph, choose $a = 0$ for the first point and $m = 0$ for the second.

Substitute these values into the equation.

When $a = 0$, $m = 15$ and when $m = 0$, $a = 20$

Now choose a third value of a or m as a check, say, $a = 8$

When $a = 8$: $3 \times 8 + 4m = 60$

$24 + 4m = 60$ (-24)

$4m = 36$ $(\div 4)$

$m = 9$

To draw a graph of a **linear** relationship (a straight-line graph), you need to calculate and plot three points. You can draw a straight line with two points but the third point provides a useful check.

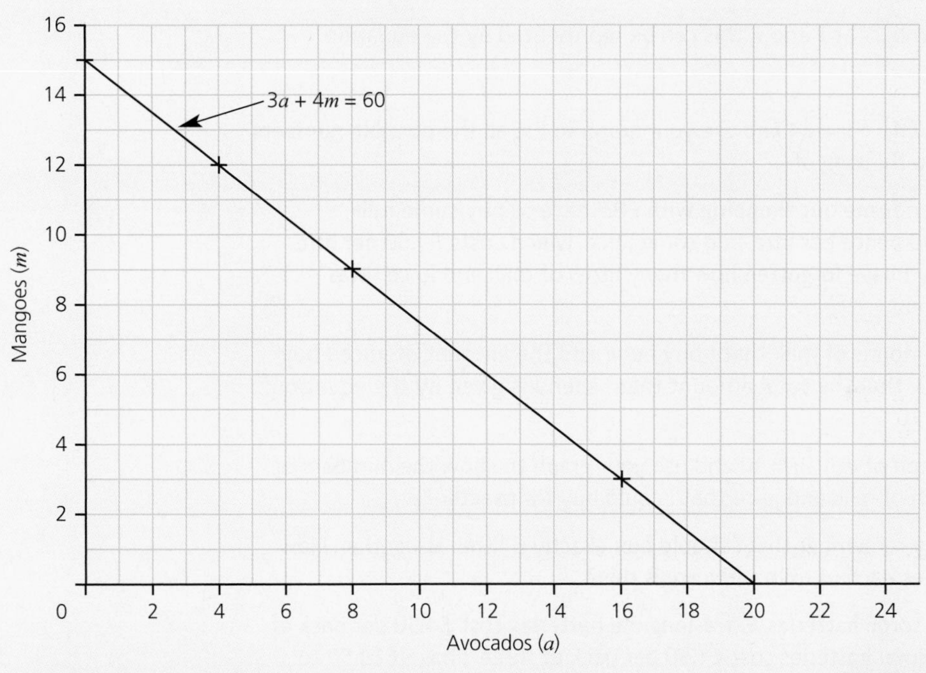

Clearly, I can only buy whole numbers of each fruit, so from the graph I could buy:

20 avocados and 0 mangoes

or 16 avocados and 3 mangoes

or 12 avocados and 6 mangoes

or 8 avocados and 9 mangoes

or 4 avocados and 12 mangoes

or 0 avocados and 15 mangoes

Remember to label the **axes** and the origin.

Exercise 13.2

1 (a) Plot a graph of $3x + 5y = 15$

(b) Draw a table to show the integer values of x and y that lie on the line.

2 (a) Plot a graph of $2x + 7y = 28$

(b) Draw a table of the integer values of x and y that lie on the line.

3 I am thinking of two integers greater than 0. If I double one of them and add it to the other the result is 20. If my numbers are x and y this can be shown by the equation $2x + y = 20$

Plot a graph of $2x + y = 20$ and use your graph to list all the possible numbers that I could be thinking of.

4 I am thinking of two integers, both greater than 0. If I double one of them and add it to half the other the answer is 12

Taking my numbers as x and y, this can be represented by the equation:

$2x + \frac{y}{2} = 12$

Plot a graph of $4x + y = 24$ and use your graph to list all the possible numbers that I could be thinking of.

5 My mother sends me out shopping with £8. I have to buy some milk, which costs 80 pence per litre, and some juice, which costs £1.60 per litre. Unfortunately I have forgotten how many litres of milk and juice I was supposed to buy.

(a) Let the amount of milk that I buy be m and the amount of juice I buy be j. Show that the total amount that I spend is given by the equation: $m + 2j = 10$

(b) Plot a graph of $m + 2j = 10$ and use your graph to show the numbers of litres each of milk and juice that I could buy for exactly £8

(c) I suddenly remember that I should buy exactly 6 litres altogether. How many litres each of milk and juice is this?

6 I have to buy some batteries. Extra-long life batteries cost £4.50 per pack of five, while normal batteries cost £1.50 per pack of three. I have £13.50 to spend.

(a) Let the number of packs of extra-long life batteries I buy be x and the number of packs of normal batteries I buy be y. Show that the total amount that I spend can be shown by the equation: $3x + y = 9$

(b) Plot a graph of $3x + y = 9$

(c) Use your graph to show how many packs of each type of battery I could buy for exactly £13.50

(d) I decide to buy as near as possible the same number of batteries of each type. How many of each pack do I buy?

Solving simultaneous equations

Think back to the original example.

I double one number and add another and get the answer 12
What are my numbers?

This can be written as an equation:

$2u + v = 12$

for which there are several possible values of u and v

To find a **unique solution**, you need another fact about the two numbers.

For example, the difference between them is 9

This leads to another equation:

$u - v = 9$

From the previous table of values, the numbers must be 1 and 10

A pair of equations such as

$2u + v = 12$

$u - v = 9$

that can be solved together to give values that satisfy both equations are called **simultaneous equations**.

Look up 'simultaneous' in a dictionary: the definition is 'happening or being done at exactly the same time'.

It is not always practical to solve simultaneous equations from a table of values. There are various other methods you can use. The method you choose depends on the wording of the question and the format of the equation.

The graphical method

As you have already seen, it is often easier to understand a visual version (a graph) and, although the graphical method of solving equations can take quite a long time to complete, it is a good place to start.

Example

The sum of two numbers is 13 and the difference between the numbers is 3
Work out the two numbers.

Let the two numbers be x and y.

$x + y = 13$

The difference between the two numbers is 3. Assume x is the larger and write another equation.

$x - y = 3$

To solve the problem, draw the graphs of both equations.

Calculate three points that lie on the line. You should not need to write down an equation and solve it to find corresponding values of x and y, you can do this in your head. Put your results in a neat table.

As before, you need three points. It is useful to take $x = 0$ as one point and $y = 0$ for another, and then calculate a third point.

$x + y = 13$

x	0	13	6
y	13	0	7

$x - y = 3$

x	0	3	6
y	$^-3$	0	3

$x - y = 3$ may be written in a more recognisable form as $y = x - 3$

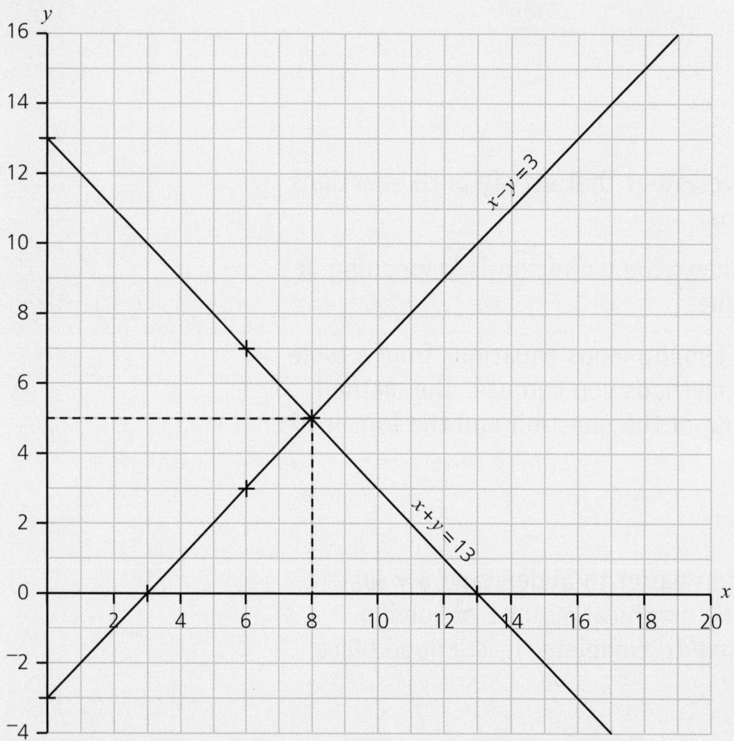

The solution to the equations is given by the point where the two lines cross. The solution is therefore $x = 8$ and $y = 5$

From the graph you can see that there is one, and only one, point that lies on both lines (8, 5)
The solution is **unique**.

13 Simultaneous equations

Exercise 13.3

1 Use the graphical method to find the solution to each pair of simultaneous equations.

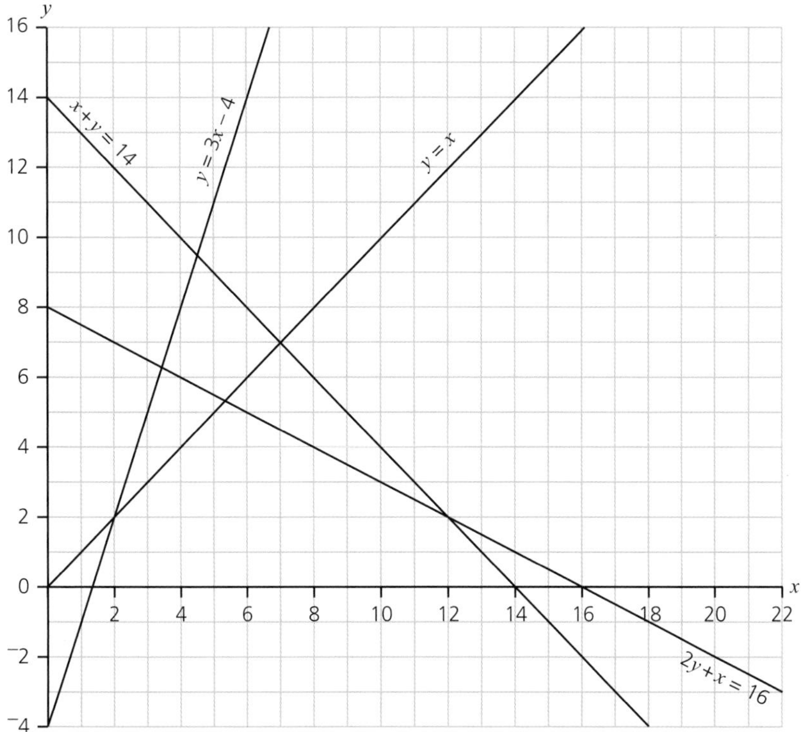

(a) $x + y = 14$

$y = x$

(b) $x + y = 14$

$y = 0$

(c) $y = 3x - 4$

$y = x$

(d) $2y + x = 16$

$x + y = 14$

(e) $2y + x = 16$

$x = 0$

(f) $y = 3x - 4$

$x + y = 14$

(g) $2y + x = 16$

$y = 3x - 4$

(h) $2y + x = 16$

$y = x$

2 For each pair of simultaneous equations, draw a set of co-ordinate axes and label both axes (x and y) from $^-5$ to 5. Draw the graphs to solve the equations.

(a) $x + y = 3$

$x - y = {}^-5$

(b) $2x + 3y = 0$

$x - y = {}^-5$

(c) $x - 2y = 2$

$2x - y = 4$

(d) $3x + y = 8$

$2x - y = 7$

3 For each pair of simultaneous equations, draw a set of coordinate axes and label both axes (x and y) from $^-4$ to 15. Draw the graphs to solve the equations.

(a) $x + y = 2$
$x - y = 4$

(b) $x + 2y = 10$
$x - y = 7$

(c) $x + y = 10$
$2x - y = 8$

(d) $3x + y = 15$
$2x - y = 0$

4 For each pair of simultaneous equations, draw a set of coordinate axes with a scale of 1 cm to 1 unit. Label the x-axis from $^-8$ to 8 and the y-axis from $^-5$ to 12. Draw the graphs to solve the equations. The answers to these equations may not always be whole numbers. Read them from your graph carefully and give them in decimal form.

(a) $x + 2y = 6$
$3x - 4y = 4$

(b) $7x + 2y = 5$
$x - 4y = 11$

5 Choose your own scale and axes for these pairs of equations.

(a) $2x + y = 1$
$x - y = {}^-7$

(b) $x - 3y = 9$
$x + y = {}^-5$

6 Draw graphs for each pair of equations. What is different about them?

(a) $x + y = {}^-1$
$x + y = 3$

(b) $y = 2x + 1$
$2x - y = 3$

The elimination method

Drawing graphs accurately can be quite a time-consuming process. Most of the answers to the previous exercise were either whole numbers or quite simple decimals.

There is a quicker way to solve simultaneous equations.

Look again at this pair of equations.

$x + y = 13$

$x - y = 3$

Notice that there are the same number of xs in each equation and the same number of ys, but the sign is different.

If you add y to ^-y you get zero. Therefore if you add these two equations together the y-terms will disappear, leaving:

$2x = 16$

and so $x = 8$

Why does this work? Why can you add the equations?

Remember that in each equation, the quantities on both sides are the same, so you are, effectively, adding the same quantity on both sides.

As always in mathematics, it is very important to explain clearly to anyone reading your work exactly what you are doing. There is a conventional way of writing out the solution to a pair of simultaneous equations. It is important that you follow these conventions so that your work will be understood.

In the first of the next examples the equations are added together to eliminate the y-terms. In the second, one equation is subtracted from the other to eliminate the x-terms.

The next step is to substitute the first solution into one of the original equations to work out the other variable. Finally, you can check your answers in the second equation. Note the convention of numbering each equation to show your working method.

Examples

(i) Solve these equations.

	$2x + y = 5$	(1)
	$3x - y = 10$	(2)
(1) + (2)	$5x = 15$	
	$x = 3$	(÷ 5)
Sub in (1)	$6 + y = 5$	
	$y = {}^{-}1$	(− 6)
Check in (2)	$9 - ({}^{-}1) = 10$	

$x = 3$ and $y = {}^{-}1$

(ii) Solve these equations.

	$2x + 3y = 10$	(1)
	$2x - y = 2$	(2)
(1) − (2)	$4y = 8$	
	$y = 2$	(÷ 4)
Sub in (1)	$2x + 6 = 10$	
	$2x = 4$	(− 6)
	$x = 2$	(÷ 2)
Check in (2)	$4 - 2 = 2$	

$x = 2$ and $y = 2$

Note the final check at the end of each solution. You then know your answer is correct!

Exercise 13.4

Use the elimination method to solve each pair of simultaneous equations.

1 $3x + y = 7$
$x - y = 1$

2 $2x + y = 10$
$3x - y = 5$

3 $2x + y = 12$
$2x - 3y = 4$

4 $x + 2y = 7$

$x + y = 4$

5 $3x + 2y = 15$

$x + 2y = 9$

6 $3x - y = 8$

$3x + y = 10$

7 $x + 2y = 7$

$x - y = 1$

8 $x + 2y = 10$

$3x - 2y = 6$

9 $3x + y = 7$

$3x - 2y = {}^{-}5$

The scale factor method

In the above exercise, in each pair of equations, either the **coefficients** of x or the coefficients of y were the same. Sometimes you will need to solve pairs of simultaneous equations when neither unknown has the same coefficient in both equations. In such cases, you will need to add in another stage of working.

You need to multiply either one or both of the equations by a scale factor so that one of the variables has the same coefficient.

In the first of the next examples only one of the equations has to be multiplied by a scale factor. In the second, both equations do. Again, Note the convention of numbering each equation to show your working method.

Examples

(i) Solve these equations.

	$2x + y = 5$	(1)
	$3x - 2y = 4$	(2)
(1) × 2	$4x + 2y = 10$	(3)
(2)	$3x - 2y = 4$	
(3) + (2)	$7x = 14$	
	$x = 2$	(÷ 7)
Sub in (1)	$4 + y = 5$	
	$y = 1$	(− 4)
Check in (2)	$6 - 2 = 4$	

$x = 2$ and $y = 1$

(ii) Solve these equations.

	$2x + 7y = 10$	(1)
	$3x - 2y = {}^{-}10$	(2)
(1) × 3	$6x + 21y = 30$	(3)
(2) × 2	$6x - 4y = {}^{-}20$	(4)
(3) − (4)	$25y = 50$	
	$y = 2$	(÷ 25)
Sub in (1)	$2x + 14 = 10$	
	$2x = {}^{-}4$	(− 14)
	$x = {}^{-}2$	(÷ 2)
Check in (2)	${}^{-}6 - 4 = {}^{-}10$	

$x = {}^{-}2$ and $y = 2$

It is important to check your answers by substituting into the **original** equations and **not** into the one that you have multiplied. This will give you easier numbers to work with and, if you have made a mistake, will quickly show up any errors.

Exercise 13.5

Solve each pair of simultaneous equations.

1 $3x + y = 5$
$x + 3y = 7$

2 $3x + 2y = 8$
$2x + y = 5$

3 $5x - 2y = 11$
$x + 4y = 11$

4 $2x - y = 5$
$x + 3y = 13$

5 $5x - 3y = {}^{-}5$
$2x + y = 9$

6 $5x + 2y = 22$
$3x + y = 13$

7 $3x + 2y = 7$
$2x - 3y = 3$

8 $2x + 3y = 11$
$3x + 4y = 14$

9 $5x - 2y = 1$
$3x + 5y = {}^{-}18$

The rearrangement and substitution methods

Sometimes the equations you are asked to solve are given in different forms. Then there are two options.

- Rearrange the equations so that they are in the same form.
- Substitute from one equation into the other.

The next examples show the same pair of equations. In the first, one equation is rearranged. In the second, one equation is substituted into the other.

Examples

(i) Solve these equations.

	$3x + 2y = 6$	(1)
	$y = 5 - 2x$	(2)
(2) + $2x$	$2x + y = 5$	(3)
(3) × 2	$4x + 2y = 10$	(4)
	$3x + 2y = 6$	(1)
(4) – (1)	$x = 4$	
Sub in (1)	$12 + 2y = 6$	
	$2y = {}^{-}6$	(– 12)
	$y = {}^{-}3$	(÷ 2)
Check in (2)	${}^{-}3 = 5 - 8$	

$x = 4$ and $y = {}^{-}3$

(ii) Solve these equations.

	$3x + 2y = 6$	(1)
	$y = 5 - 2x$	(2)
Sub (2) in (1)	$3x + 2(5 - 2x) = 6$	
	$3x + 10 - 4x = 6$	
	$10 - x = 6$	
	$10 = 6 + x$	$(+x)$
	$4 = x$	(– 6)
Sub in (2)	$y = 5 - 8$	
	$y = {}^{-}3$	
Check in (1)	$12 - 6 = 6$	

$x = 4$ and $y = {}^{-}3$

Exercise 13.6

Solve these pairs of simultaneous equations either by rearrangement or by substitution.

1 $3x + y = 6$
$y = x + 2$

2 $2x + 3y = 25$
$x = y - 5$

3 $3x = y - 9$
$2y = 4 - x$

4 $y - 4x = 1$
$3x = y$

5 $12 = 2x - 3y$
$4x = 3 - y$

6 $2x + y = 1$
$x = 2 + 7y$

7 $y - 6x = 4$
$2y = 18 + 4x$

8 $\frac{x}{2} = {}^{-}4 - 3y$
$x + 2y = 2$

9 $4y - 2x = 15$
$y = x + 3$

10 $x - y = 4$
$3x = {}^{-}4y$

11 $5x - y = 3$
$3y = 10x + 9$

12 $2x + y = 3$
$3y = 2 - 4x$

Solving problems with simultaneous equations

Many story problems are made easier to solve by using simultaneous equations. You must explain every step of your working as you solve these problems, otherwise it will be very difficult for anyone else to follow what you are doing. Start by defining your variables, for example, x and y.

Example

I buy 15 pencils. Coloured pencils cost 35p each and ordinary graphite pencils cost 22p each. If I receive 92p change from a £5 note, then how many of each type of pencil did I buy?

First identify and define the two equations:

Let the number of coloured pencils be x and the number of graphite pencils be y.

The total cost = £5 – £0.92

= £4.08 = 408p

The two equations are:

	$x + y = 15$	(1)
	$35x + 22y = 408$	(2)
(1) × 22	$22x + 22y = 330$	(3)
(2) – (3)	$13x = 78$	
	$x = 6$	(÷ 13)
Sub in (1)	$6 + y = 15$	
	$y = 9$	(– 6)

Check in (2) $35 \times 6 + 22 \times 9 = 408$

$x = 6$ and $y = 9$ I bought 6 coloured pencils and 9 graphite pencils.

When you have finished your solution, always check the original problem to make sure that you have answered the question.

Exercise 13.7

Solve these problems by forming simultaneous equations and solving them.

1 The sum of two numbers is 25 and the difference between the two numbers is 5. What are the numbers?

2 I have two brothers. One of them is four years older than the other. The sum of their ages is 28. How old are they?

3 I have saved up £25 more than my sister has. We decided to pool our money to buy a CD player and found that we had £145 between us. How much had each one of us saved?

4 On a walking holiday I walked 4 miles further on the first day than I did on the second. I walked a total of 17 miles in two days. How far did I walk each day?

5 **(a)** Solve this pair of simultaneous equations.

$$c + g = 20$$

$$24c + 30g = 564$$

(b) I have to buy 20 apples. I buy some Cox's at 24p each and some Granny Smith's at 30p each. I spend £5.64 in total. Use your answer to part **(a)** to find out how many of each type of apple I bought.

6 **(a)** Solve this pair of simultaneous equations.

$$4p + s = 84$$

$$2p + 2s = 84$$

(b) My little sister collects stickers. For 84p she can either buy four sheets of plain stickers and one sheet of shiny ones, or she can buy two sheets of plain stickers and two sheets of shiny ones. Use your answer to part **(a)** to find out what it would cost her to buy three sheets of plain stickers and two sheets of shiny ones.

7 **(a)** Solve this pair of simultaneous equations.

$$3c + m = 195$$

$$2c + 3m = 270$$

(b) If I buy three cartons of juice and one muesli bar, it will cost me £1.95

If I buy two cartons of juice and three muesli bars, it will cost me £2.70

Use your answers to part **(a)** to find the cost of one carton of juice and one muesli bar.

8 **(a)** Solve this pair of simultaneous equations.

$$y = x + 4$$

$$2y + 2x = 56$$

(b) The length of a rectangle is 4 cm greater than its width. The perimeter is 56 cm. What is the area of the rectangle?

9 A straight line, given by an equation in the form $y = mx + c$, passes through point $A(2, 4)$ and point $B(1, 1)$. Form a pair of simultaneous equations and solve them to find m and c. Write down the equation of the line.

10 In my new computer game I have to shoot down asteroids and alien star ships. I shot 12 asteroids and five alien ships and scored 465 points on level one. Then I shot 15 asteroids and four alien ships and scored 480 points on level two. How many points did I score on level three, when I shot down 20 asteroids and six alien ships?

Extension: Equations with more than two unknowns

You have been solving pairs of simultaneous equations to find two unknown quantities. Suppose you have three unknown quantities with three equations. The equations need not all include all three variables.

Example

The sum of two numbers is 15 One of these numbers added to a third number gives 17 and the other number added to the same third number gives 14

What are the numbers? Let the numbers be a, b and c

The three given facts lead to three equations.

	$a + b = 15$	(1)	Write the equations with the letters in the same columns.
	$a + c = 17$	(2)	
	$b + c = 14$	(3)	

It does not matter which pair of equations you take first.

Subtract (2) – (3)	$a - b = 3$	(4)	to eliminate c
	$a + b = 15$	(1)	
Add (4) + (1)	$2a = 18$	(÷ 2)	
	$a = 9$		
Substitute for a in (1)	$9 + b = 15$	(– 9)	
	$b = 6$		
Substitute for b in (2)	$9 + c = 17$	(– 9)	
	$c = 8$		
Check in (3)	$6 + 8 = 14$		

$a = 9$, $b = 6$ and $c = 8$

Extension Exercise 13.8

1 Solve these three simultaneous equations.

$x + y = 4$ $x + z = 8$ $y + z = 2$

2 Solve these three simultaneous equations.

$a + b + c = 7$ $a + b - c = 6$ $a - b - c = 2$

3 Solve these three simultaneous equations.

$2a + b - c = 1$ $4a + b - 3c = 5$ $a - c = 2$

4 I have two brothers. The sum of our three ages is 41

The difference between the eldest and the youngest of us is 14

I am closer to my younger brother's age than my elder brother's age by two years. How old am I?

5 My mother sent me out to buy 10 pieces of fruit, of three different varieties.

If I buy three apples, six bananas and one coconut it will cost me £1.59

However if I buy two coconuts, seven bananas and one apple it will cost me £2.18

If I buy one coconut, two apples and seven bananas it will cost me £1.55

(a) Write three simultaneous equations and solve them to find the cost of the three types of fruit.

(b) How can I buy my 10 pieces of fruit at the minimum cost?

6 I am thinking of three numbers. The sum of two of them is 24

If I multiply the smallest number by the remaining number I have 49

If all my numbers are prime numbers, what are the numbers?

7 **(a)** **(i)** Show that it is impossible to solve these simultaneous equations.

$x + 2 = y$

$y - 1 = z$

$z - 1 = x$

(ii) Is there a limit to the possible solutions of these three equations?

(b) **(i)** Show that it is impossible to solve these simultaneous equations.

$x - 3 = y$ $y + 6 = z$ $z - 4 = x$

(ii) Is there a limit to the possible solutions of these three equations?

8 Solve these three simultaneous equations. (Think about what you know about special index numbers.)

$x = (2y)^z$ $y = 2^x$ $x = 3^z$

Summary Exercise 13.9

1 Use this graph to solve each pair of simultaneous equations.

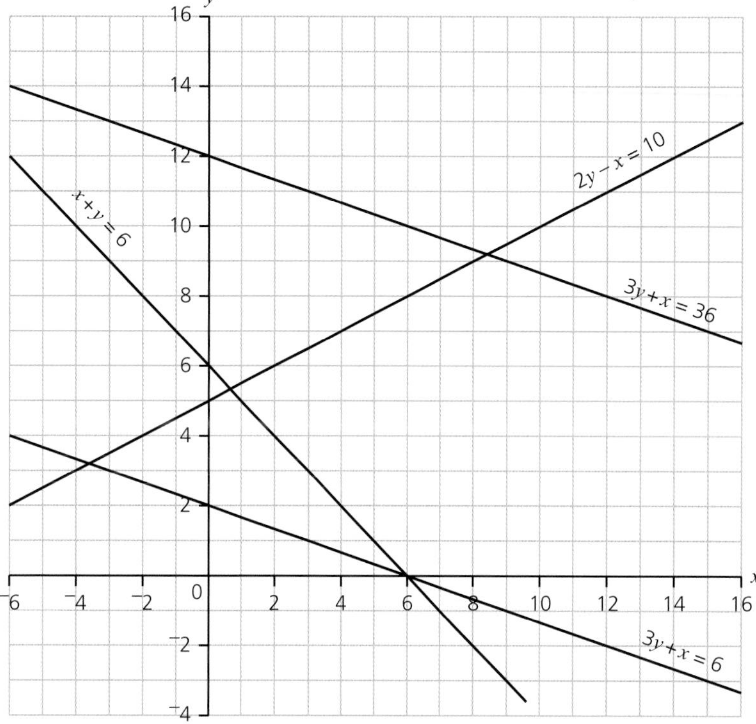

(a) $x + y = 6$
$2y - x = 10$

(b) $3y + x = 36$
$2y - x = 10$

(c) $x + y = 6$
$3y + x = 6$

(d) Explain why you cannot find a solution to this pair of simultaneous equations.
$3y + x = 6$ $\qquad$ $3y + x = 36$

2 Solve each pair of simultaneous equations.

(a) $x + 2y = 5$
$x - y = 2$

(b) $x - y = 6$
$x + y = 4$

(c) $x + 4y = 10$
$4x - 5y = {}^{-}23$

(d) $2x - 3y = 7$
$5x + 2y = 8$

(e) $y = 1 - 2x$
$x + 2y = {}^{-}1$

(f) $x = y + 4$
$2x - 3y = 7$

3 I was supposed to buy my mother three yellow dusters and four white dishcloths, which would have cost £3.10

By mistake I bought four yellow dusters and three white dishcloths and they cost me £3.20. What is the cost of a yellow duster and a white dishcloth?

4 My parents bought 10 packets of sparklers for Guy Fawkes Night. Plain sparklers cost £1.20 per packet and coloured sparklers cost £1.50 per packet. If they spent £12.90 in all, how many packets of coloured sparklers did they buy?

Activity: Trigon dragon patrol

You will need triangular isometric paper for this activity.

Dragons rule on the planet Trigon. If you were unlucky enough to find yourself on the planet Trigon, you would probably be caught and thrown into a dungeon. Dragons guard the dungeons carefully. It is not an easy job and so the dragons have to be trained.

A learner dragon is known as a (1, 1). 'Why?', you may ask.

On Trigon the dungeons are arranged on a triangular grid. The dragons are known by the instructions they are given, and they can only turn right. So a (1, 1) dragon will go: 1 unit, turn right, 1 unit, turn right, 1 unit, turn right. So it will walk round and round an equilateral triangle.

Once the dragon has mastered this patrol, he is promoted to a (1, 2) dragon. He then has to patrol as follows.

1 unit, turn right, 2 units, turn right, 1 unit, turn right, 2 units, turn right, 1 unit, turn right, 2 units, turn right.

His patrol will look like this.

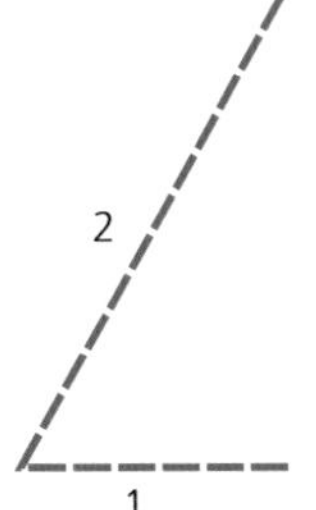

■ **1 unit,** turn right, 2 units, turn right

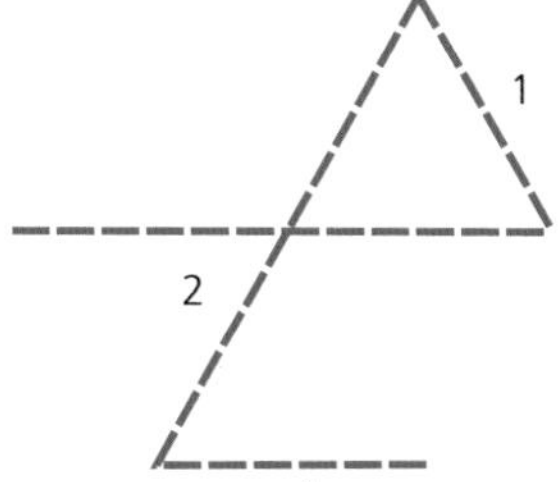

■ **1 unit,** turn right, 2 units, turn right.

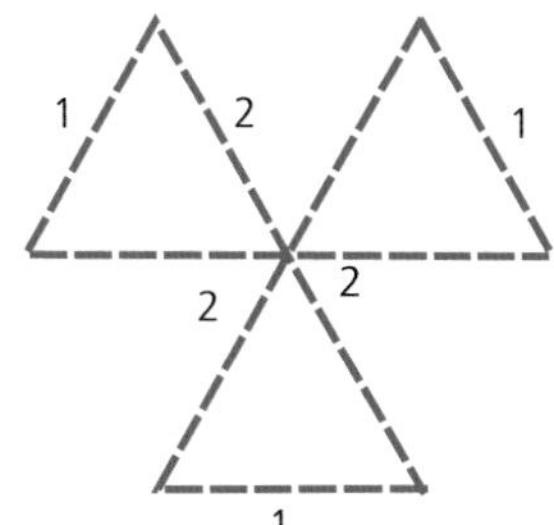

■ **1 unit,** turn right, 2 units, turn right.

So the (1, 1) dragon guards one dungeon and the (1, 2) dragon guards three dungeons.

1 Applying the same principle as the one described above, use triangular isometric paper to draw the paths of:

(a) a (1, 3) dragon

(b) a (1, 4) dragon

(c) a (1, 5) dragon

(d) a (1, 6) dragon.

The dungeons are all 1 unit in length, so if a dragon walks round a triangle of sides 2 units, he is cleverly guarding four dungeons.

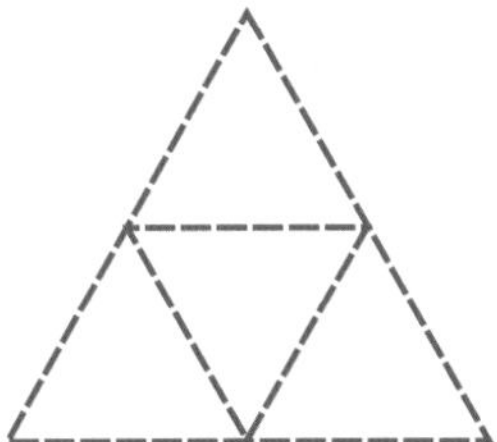

2 Copy and complete this table.

Dragon	Units walked in one circuit	Dungeons guarded
(1, 1)	3	1
(1, 2)	9	3
(1, 3)		
(1, 4)		
(1, 5)		

3 Without drawing, try to work out the numbers in the next two lines.

4 Now draw and check your answers.

5 To become a megadragon, you have to work out how many dungeons a (1, 10) dragon will guard.

6 What is the formula to show how many a (1, n) dragon will guard?

7 Once a dragon becomes a megadragon, his training follows the pattern described below.

First he is given the command (2, 1)

When he has mastered that he becomes a (2, 2) dragon and then is promoted to (2, 3) dragon and so on.

Just as before, draw the patrol for the first few commands. Now copy and complete the table below and fill in the results.

Dragon	Units walked in one circuit	Dungeons guarded
(2, 1)	9	
(2, 2)	6	
(2, 3)		
(2, 4)		
(2, 5)		

8 Work out the (2, 10) results and then write the formula for a megadragon.

9 Even dragons have ambition. To become a megamegadragon, you have to work out the formula that tells you how many dungeons a (m, n) dragon can patrol and how far he walks in one circuit.

14 Graphs

A **graph** is a pictorial representation of a relationship. It may be a bar graph, a column graph, a **line graph** or a curve. At the start of this chapter, you will look further at **straight-line graphs**.

A straight-line graph is exactly what it sounds like, a straight line through the plotted points. It represents a **linear relationship** between the two **variables** on the axes. If the graph goes through the **origin** (0, 0), the two variables are **directly proportional** to one another.

Examples of this type of relationship include the **conversion graphs**, such as foreign exchange, Celsius to Fahrenheit temperatures, miles to kilometres, that you have seen before in this course.

Travel graphs

In Chapter 9 you considered formulae for speed, distance and time. Showing a journey as a graph on a grid is a useful way of seeing what is happening.

A **travel graph** shows the relationship between distance travelled and time taken.

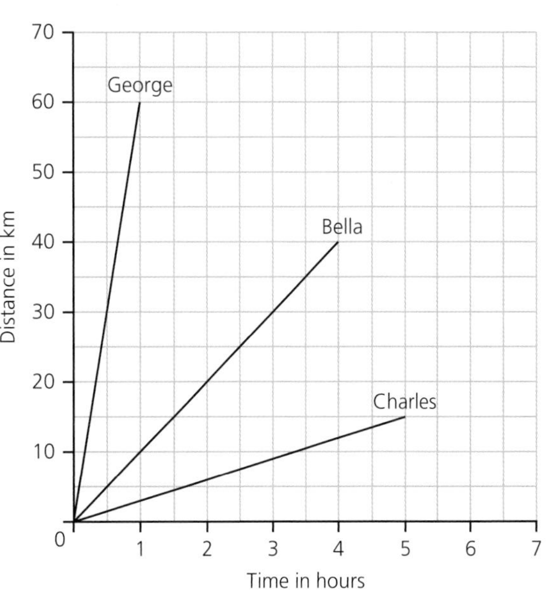

These graphs show that Charles travelled 15 km in 5 hours, Bella travelled 40 km in 4 hours and George travelled 60 km in one hour.

From the bottom graph can see that Charles travelled 15 km in 5 hours. His speed was 3 km/h, which means he was probably walking. Similarly, from the middle graph, Bella travelled at 10 km/h, possibly on a bicycle and George, at the top, travelled at 60 km/h, probably by car.

Exercise 14.1

1 Look at the three graphs on this grid.

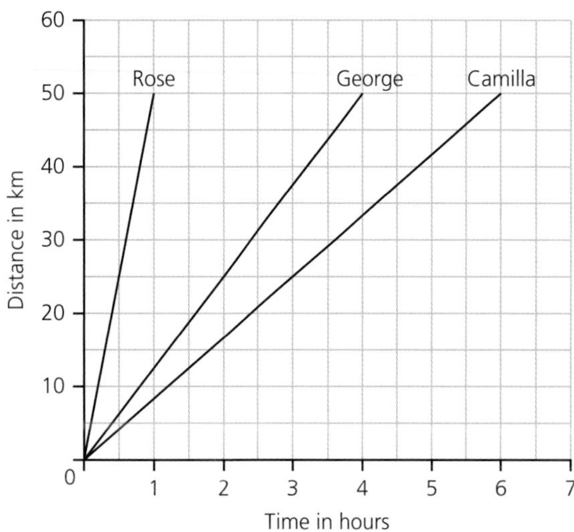

Rose, George and Camilla have all travelled 50 km but in different times.

From the graphs, write down:

(a) Rose's speed **(b)** George's speed **(c)** Camilla's speed.

Say how do you think each was travelling.

2 Here is the graph of another journey.

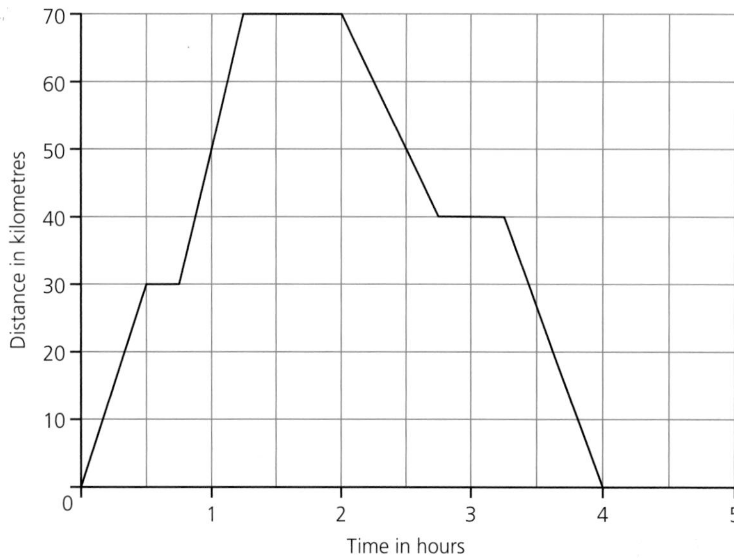

Describe this journey. Include the time and different speed for each part of the journey.

3 These graphs show two trains leaving Adamstown and Beesville at the same time.

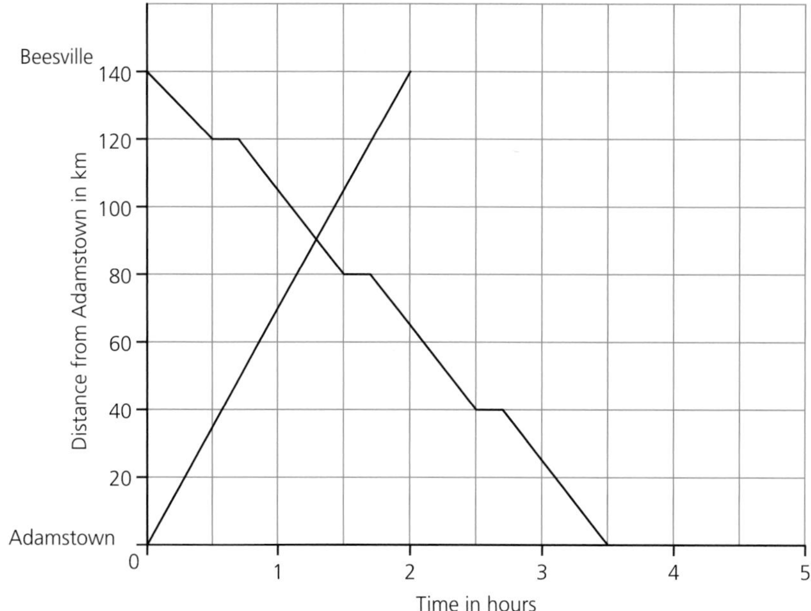

(a) What is the difference between the journeys of the two trains?

(b) How long after the start of the journeys do the two trains pass?

(c) How far from Beesville is this?

(d) At what speed does the Adamstown to Beesville Express travel?

(e) What is the greatest speed at which the Beesville to Adamstown train travels?

4 The headmaster is going to a conference. He travels at 100 km/h along the motorway for one and a half hours. He then stops at a Jolly Muncher restaurant for 45 minutes before continuing his journey.

The traffic is now heavier and so the headmaster travels for 30 minutes at 40 km/h before coming off the motorway and travelling for 15 minutes at 60 km/h.

Draw a travel graph to show the journey, taking 1 cm to represent 30 minutes on the horizontal (time) axis and 1 cm to represent 50 km on the vertical (distance) axis. How far was the journey?

5 **(a)** Mr Mattix's car leaves Ammersmith School at 10 a.m. and travels 100 km at 80 km/h. Mr Mattix then stops for 30 minutes while he has an Elfy Eating salad. He then travels another 80 km at 60 km/h to Bighton. Draw a travel graph to show the journey. Use your graph to find out the time at which Mr Mattix arrives at Bighton.

(b) Miss Peinter leaves Bighton at 10.45 a.m. and travels at a steady 70 km/h to Ammersmith School. Add a graph of this car's journey. Use your graph to find out when Miss Peinter reaches Ammersmith School and at what time the two cars passed.

6 Alfie and Bella set off from school at 4.00 p.m. to visit the local museum. Alfie walks at 4 km/h for 15 minutes and then catches a bus, which travels at 30 km/h for 20 minutes, directly to the museum. Bella cycles at 15 km/h for 44 minutes until she gets to the museum.

Draw travel graphs of these two journeys and find out at what time the bus overtakes the bicycle.

Everyday graphs

A graph is a pictorial representation of the relationship between two variables. This means that graphs can be used to represent other events, as well as journeys.

Study these two graphs of the monthly sales totals for two companies.

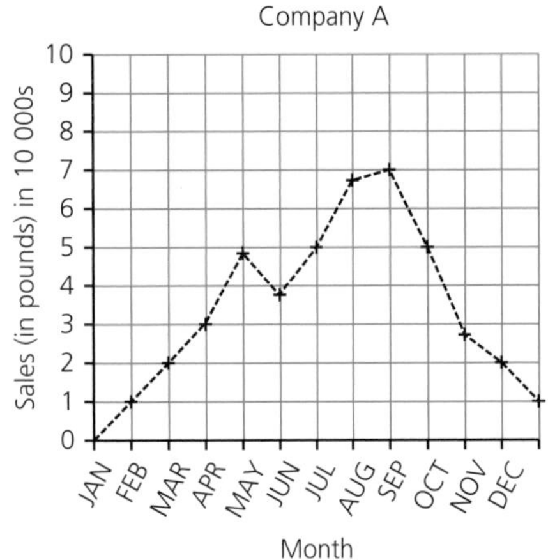

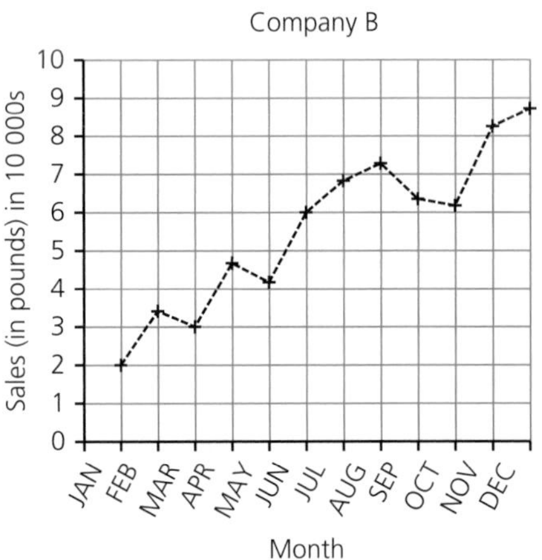

These graphs show the general pattern of rise and fall of the total sales. Such patterns are called **trends**. At first glance it would seem that the prospects for Company B look a lot better than those for Company A. But what else do the graphs tell you?

On each graph there is a point for each monthly total and these points are joined by dotted lines. The line is dotted because there is no absolute value for the sales between the points.

Although Company A's sales have declined rapidly in the winter months they climbed from a low position at the start of the year to peak around June, July and August. This could suggest that the business is seasonal and may depend on good weather in the summer.

Company B had a steady rise in sales. Although there was a slight fall during September and October, it did not affect the overall growth in sales; indeed it probably reflects fewer purchases during and immediately after the holiday months.

Exercise 14.2

1 (a) Suggest the types of business that Company A and Company B might be.

(b) How would you explain the rise in Company A's sales in April?

2 Consider the possible pattern of sales for a company that makes umbrellas and draw a monthly sales graph for an umbrella manufacturer. Your drawing only needs to be a sketch. Explain any trends in your graph.

3 These are four sales graphs for companies selling ski-clothes, swimwear, bicycles and computer software. Describe the trends for each graph and write down what you think each company sells and why.

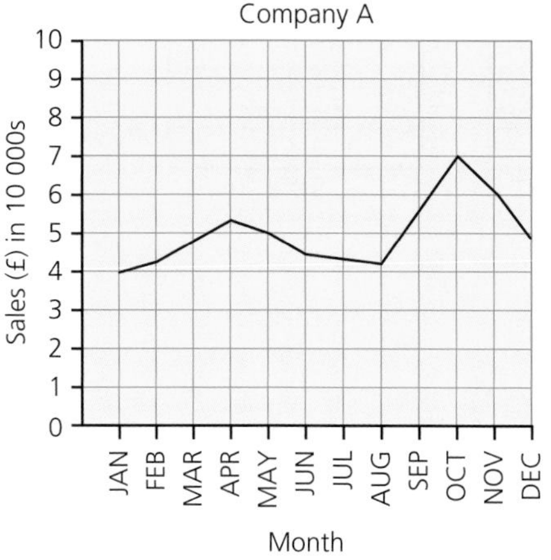

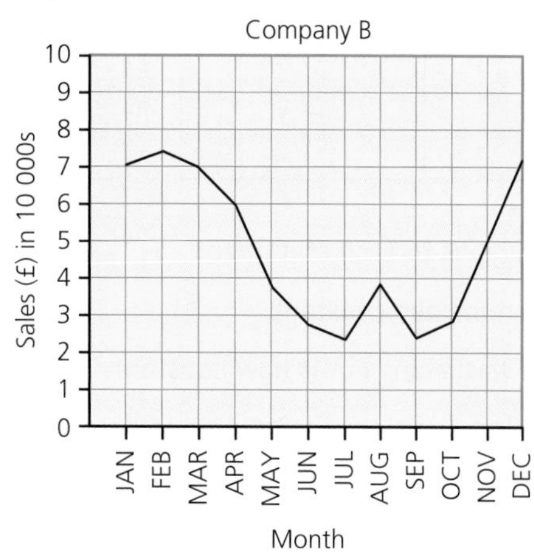

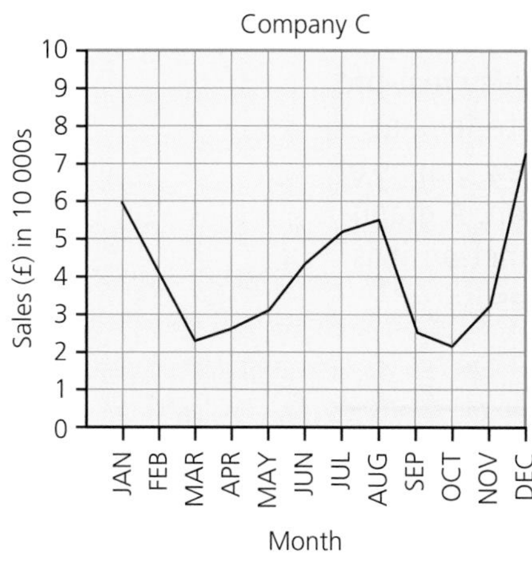

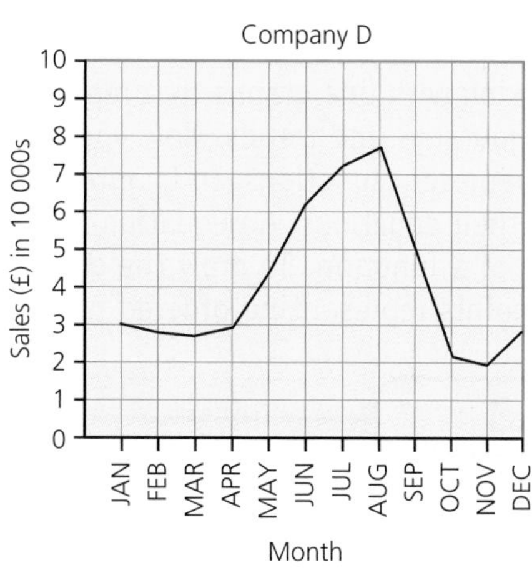

4 Look at these four distance–time graphs.

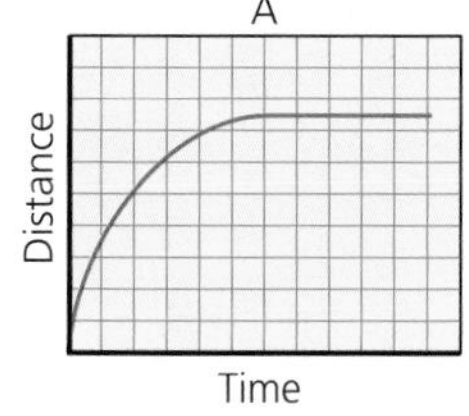

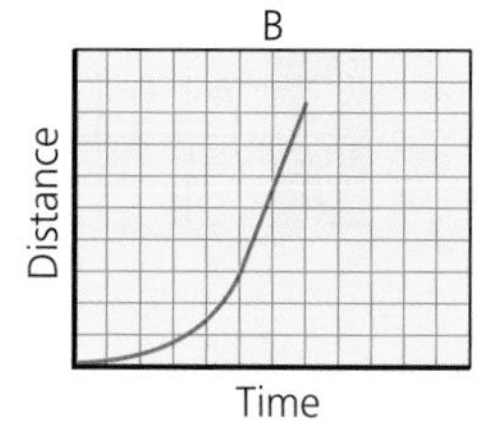

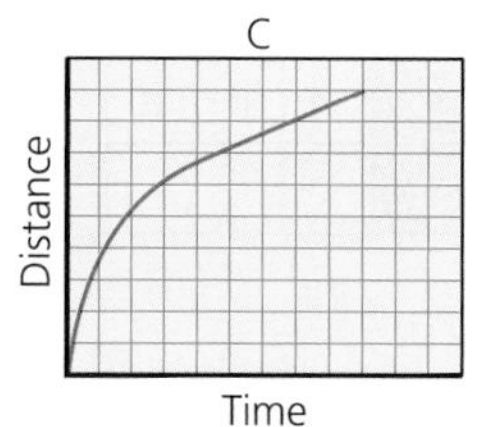

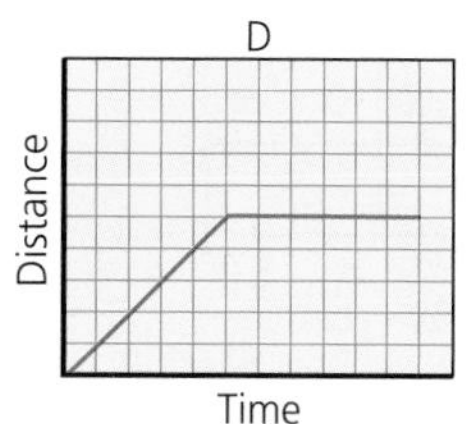

Match one of the graphs to each of these situations.

(a) The car accelerated steadily for the first 5 minutes and then travelled at a steady speed.

(b) The car travelled at a steady speed for 20 minutes and then stopped.

(c) The car decelerated steadily for 20 minutes and then travelled at a steady speed.

(d) The car decelerated for 20 minutes and then stopped.

5 Look at these four graphs.

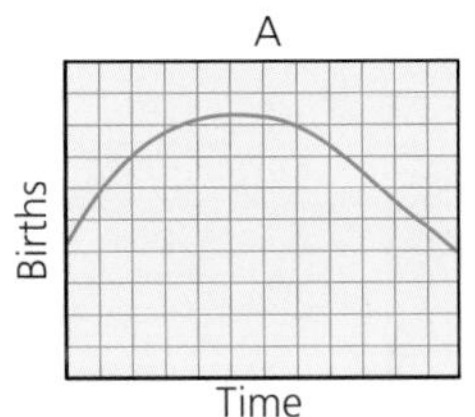

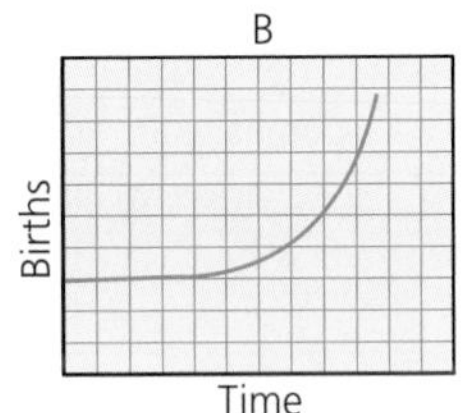

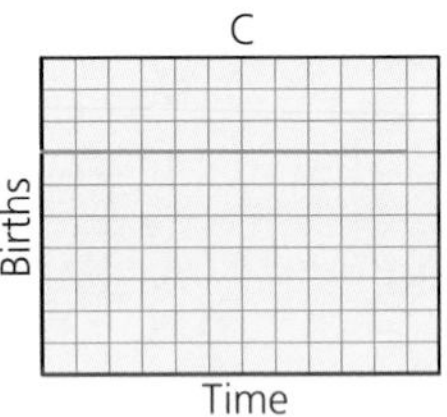

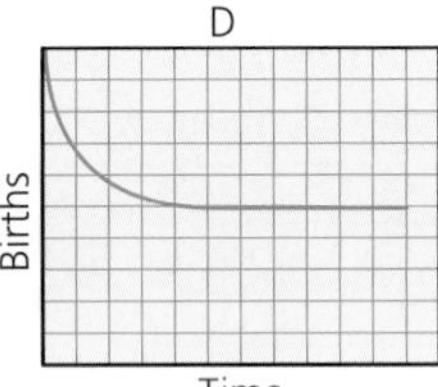

Match one of the graphs to each statement.

(a) The birth rate remained constant.

(b) The birth rate was falling but is now constant.

(c) The birth rate is now rising much more rapidly than before.

(d) The birth rate was rising but is now falling.

From functions to graphs

You have been working with line graphs that represent everyday real-life situations such as journeys and trends. Now you are going to look at straight lines that represent functions. In Chapter 12 you drew graphs of straight lines from their equations. An equation has a solution. A graph is a representation of a function. To draw the graph of a function it is necessary to plot points representing ordered pairs of values.

Exercise 14.3

Use graph paper for this exercise.

1 (a) Copy and complete the table of values for each function.

(i) $y = 2x$

x	$^-2$	0	5
y			

(ii) $y = {^-3}x$

x	$^-3$	0	1
y			

(iii) $y = \frac{x}{2}$

x	$^-4$	0	10
y			

(iv) $y = 5x$

x	$^-1$	0	2
y			

(v) $y = \frac{^-x}{4}$

x	$^-4$	0	8
y			

(b) Draw a set of co-ordinate axes with appropriate values of x and y. Draw and label the graphs of the five functions on your grid.

(c) Draw the graphs of $y = x$ and $y = {}^{-}x$ on the same grid.

2 What is the relationship between the coefficient of x and the angle and steepness of the graph, in the functions in question 1?

3 (a) Copy and complete the table of values for each function.

(i) $y = 2x + 4$

x	$^{-}4$	0	3
y			

(ii) $y = 3x - 2$

x	$^{-}1$	0	3
y			

(iii) $y = \frac{x}{2} + 3$

x	$^{-}4$	0	10
y			

(iv) $y = 5x + 2$

x	$^{-}1$	0	2
y			

(v) $y = \frac{x}{4} - 3$

x	$^{-}4$	0	8
y			

(b) Draw a set of co-ordinate axes with appropriate values of x and y. Look at your tables of values to help you decide. Draw and label the graphs of the five functions on your grid.

In question 2 you should have noticed that all the equations in which the coefficient of x is positive slope up from left to right and those in which the coefficient of x is negative slope down from left to right.

You should also notice that the larger the coefficient of x, the steeper the slope, so $y = 5x$ has a very steep slope and $y = \frac{^{-}x}{4}$ has a very gentle slope.

In question 3 you should have noticed that the lines cut the y-axis at the value of the number added or subtracted in the function. If you think about it, this makes sense because it is that number which moves the graph up and down.

Graphs of quadratic or non-linear functions

All of the graphs you have been drawing were made up of straight lines. However, not all functions lead to straight-line graphs, many will produce curves.

You have established that, to draw a straight-line graph, you only need two points, although it is sensible to work out at least a third, in case of errors in calculations. This is not the case when you need to draw an accurate curve. You need to plot far more than just two points.

The lines in the previous exercise were all straight lines because they had a linear relationship between x and y. Both x and y are to the power 1 (i.e. no index number).

Think about the function $y = x^2$ for the range of whole-number values of x such that $^{-}3 \leqslant x \leqslant 3$

Draw a table of values.

x	$^-3$	$^-2$	$^-1$	0	1	2	3
y	9	4	1	0	1	4	9

y is equal to 9 when x is equal to either $^-3$ or 3

y is equal to 4 when x is equal to either $^-2$ or 2

y is equal to 1 when x is equal to either $^-1$ or 1

Any function that contains a term in x^2 will give the same value of y for two values of x. For example, in the case of $y = x^2$, when $x = {}^-2$ or $x = 2$ then y will be equal to 4. This is why the graph is curved. This is an example of a **quadratic function**.

This is how to draw the graph of $y = x^2$

Mark the points from the table of values with small, neat marks. As you need to be very accurate when plotting points, it is best to use a + or a × to do this. You should never use a large dot, as it is just not accurate enough.

Join the points with a smooth, continuous curve.

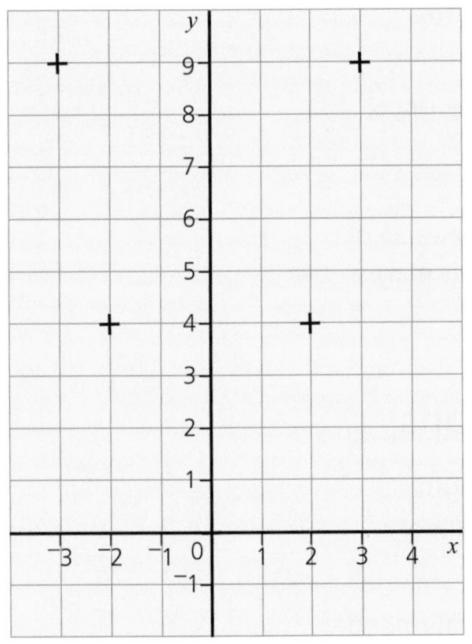

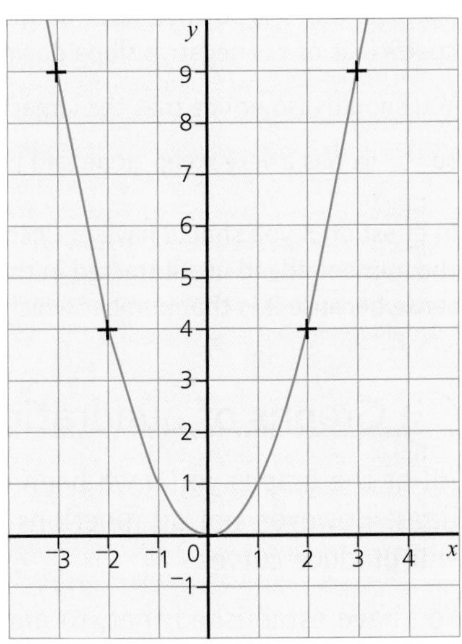

The shape of this particular curve is very distinctive. It is always symmetrical. It is called a **parabola**. If the equation was of the form $y = {}^-x^2$ the parabola would be the other way up.

Exercise 14.4

Use graph paper for this exercise.

Copy and complete the table of values for x and y for each function, then draw the graph. Use integer values of x in the range $^{-}3 \leqslant x \leqslant 3$

1 $y = x^2 - 1$

x	$^{-}3$	$^{-}2$	$^{-}1$	0	1	2	3
x^2	9	4		0			
y	8	3		$^{-}1$			

2 $y = x^2 + 2$

x	$^{-}3$	$^{-}2$	$^{-}1$	0	1	2	3
x^2	9						
y	11	6		2			

3 $y = 2x^2$

x	$^{-}3$	$^{-}2$	$^{-}1$	0	1	2	3
x^2		4					
y	18	8		0			

4 $y = \frac{x^2}{2}$

x	$^{-}3$	$^{-}2$	$^{-}1$	0	1	2	3
x^2	9	4		0			
y	4.5	2		0			

5 $y = 2x^2 - 3$

x	$^{-}3$	$^{-}2$	$^{-}1$	0	1	2	3
x^2		4					
y							

When the range of values for y is greater than the range of values for x you should change the scale on the y-axis.

Points of intersection

In the last two exercises you have drawn just one graph on each grid. Sometimes you may need to draw two graphs on the same grid. When you do this, the graphs may or may not cross each other. A point where two graphs cross is called a **point of intersection**.

Example

Find the point (or points) of intersection of the graphs of the functions $y = x^2 - 2$ and $y = 2x + 1$

Start with a table of values for each function.

$y = x^2 - 2$

x	$^-3$	$^-2$	$^-1$	0	1	2	3
x^2	9	4	1	0	1	4	9
y	7	2	$^-1$	$^-2$	$^-1$	2	7

$y = 2x + 1$

x	$^-2$	0	2
$2x$	$^-4$	0	4
x	$^-3$	1	5

Now draw the two functions on the same pair of axes.

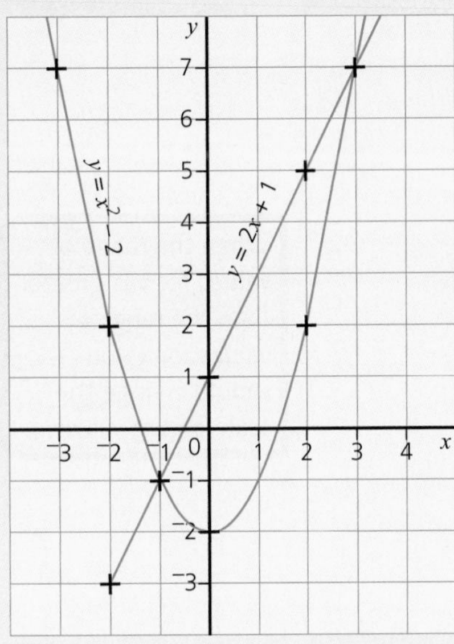

The two lines intersect at the two points ($^-1$, $^-1$) and (3, 7)

Exercise 14.5

Draw graphs of each pair of functions and find the points of intersection. You will need to complete tables of values for x and y for each function first.

1 $y = x^2$

$y = x + 2$

2 $y = x^2 + 2$

$y = x + 4$

3 $y = x^2 - 1$

$y = x - 1$

4 $y = \frac{1}{2}x^2 + 2$

$y = x + 1\frac{1}{2}$

5 $y = x^2 - 4$

$y = 2 - x$

6 $y = x^2 + 1$

$y = 1 - 2x$

Extension Exercise 14.6: The reciprocal curve

1 Copy and complete this table of values for $y = \frac{1}{x}$

x	$^-5$	$^-3$	$^-1$	$^-0.5$	$^-0.25$	0	0.25	0.5	1	3	5
y											

The value of y for $x = 0$ has been blocked out. Try this on your calculator and see what answer it gives you.

Try calculating values of y for smaller and smaller values of x. What do you notice?

You should notice that as x gets smaller the value of y gets closer to 0 but never actually reaches it.

Draw a **co-ordinate grid** with a scale of 1 cm to 1 unit on the x-axis for values of x in the range $^-5 \leqslant x \leqslant 5$, and a scale of 1 cm to 1 unit on the y-axis for values of y in the range $^-5 \leqslant y \leqslant 5$ Draw a graph of $y = \frac{1}{x}$

Your graph should approach the axes, but not touch them. The axes in this case are **asymptotes**, which are lines that the curve approaches but does not touch. The shape of the reciprocal curve is called a **hyperbola**.

2 Draw a graph of each equation.

(a) $y = \frac{4}{x}$

(b) $y = \frac{1}{x-4}$

(c) $y = \frac{1}{x^2}$

(d) $y = \frac{1}{2x}$

(e) $y = \frac{1}{2-x}$

(f) $y = \frac{^-1}{x^2}$

Extension Exercise 14.7: Other curves

1 Copy and complete this table of values for the function $y = x^3$
Then draw the graph of the function.

x	$^-5$	$^-4$	$^-3$	$^-2$	$^-1$	0	1	2	3	4	5
y											

2 Copy and complete this table of values for the function $y = x^2 - x$
Then draw the graph of the function.

x	$^-5$	$^-4$	$^-3$	$^-2$	$^-1$	0	1	2	3	4	5
x^2											
y											

3 Copy and complete this table of values for the function $y = x^2 + 2x$
Then draw the graph of the function.

x	$^-5$	$^-4$	$^-3$	$^-2$	$^-1$	0	1	2	3	4	5
x^2											
y											

4 Copy and complete the table of values for the function $y = \sqrt{x}$ or $x = y^2$
Then draw the graph of the function.

x	⁻5	⁻4	⁻3	⁻2	⁻1	0	1	2	3	4	5
y	*	*	*	*	*						

You cannot have the square root of a negative number!

Summary Exercise 14.8

1 This is the graph of a car journey.

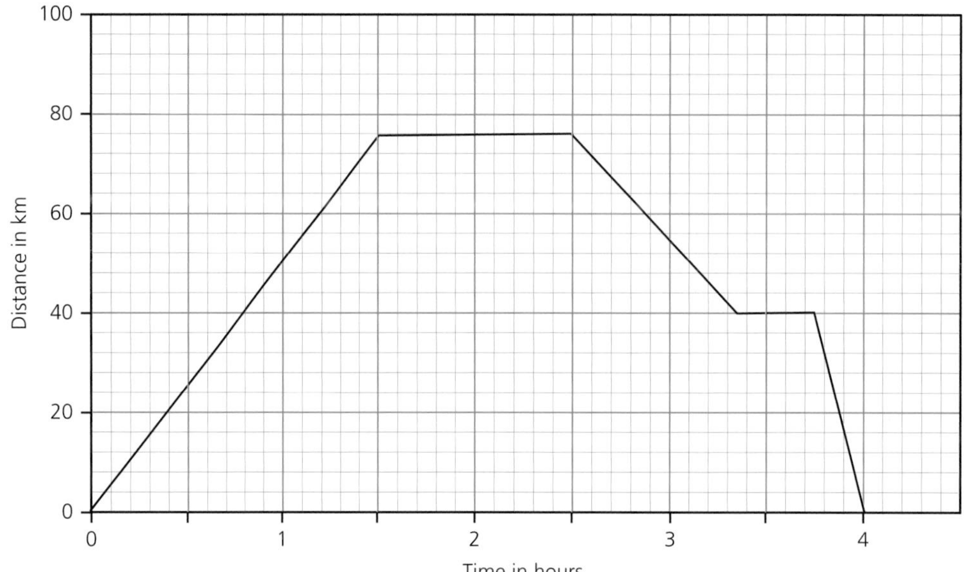

(a) At what speed was the car travelling for the first hour and a half?

(b) What did the car do after the first hour and a half?

(c) At what speed did the car travel after that?

(d) At what speed did the car travel for the last quarter of an hour of the journey?

(e) Describe what you think the purpose of this car journey was.

2 (a) Copy and complete this table of values for the function $y = 2x - 4$

x	⁻2	⁻1	0	1	2
x^2					
y					

(b) Draw a co-ordinate grid with the x-axis numbered from ⁻2 to 2 and the y-axis numbered from ⁻8 to 1. Draw a graph of this function on your grid.

(c) Where does this graph cross:

(i) the x-axis

(ii) the y-axis

(iii) the line $x = {}^-1$

(iv) the line $y = {}^-6$?

3 **(a)** Complete a table of values for the function $y = x^2 - 1$ for integer values of x in the range $^-3 \leqslant x \leqslant 3$ and for the function $y = x + 1$ for integer values of x in the range $^-2 \leqslant x \leqslant 1$

(b) Draw a co-ordinate grid with the x-axis numbered from $^-3$ to 3 and a scale of 2 cm to 1 unit and the y-axis numbered from $^-2$ to 10 with a scale of 1 cm to 1 unit.

(c) Draw the graphs of both functions from part (a).

(d) Give the co-ordinates of the points where the two graphs intersect.

Activity: Experiments and graphs

Are there any experimental results that will produce a straight line when you plot the results?

You know that if you draw a graph of distance travelled against time for a car travelling at a constant speed, that graph will be a straight line. Are there any other situations which can be investigated over a period of time to give a straight line?

Here are some examples that you could investigate.

1 The distance travelled by the tip of the minute hand of a clock

2 The length of your shadow on a sunny day

3 The number of pupils in the school from an hour before school starts to the start of school

4 The height of a bean plant over three weeks

5 The temperature of a cup of tea in the first 30 minutes from when it was brewed

6 The height of an ice cube when it is left out of the fridge

Since the minute hand of a clock travels at a constant rate you know that this will give a straight line graph, but what about the other examples?

Look at each experiment and state what other variables, apart from those you are recording, might affect the result of your experiment. Write down the steps you would take to ensure that your experiment is a fair test.

Here is an example for Experiment 6: Measuring the height of an ice cube.

Step 1 Make a big block of ice so that it is easier to measure. Take a clean, empty yoghurt pot, fill it with tap water and place it in the freezer for 48 hours before you carry out the experiment.

Step 2 Take the pot out of the freezer and turn it upside down on a flat plate. Put the plate in a position so that any melted water can drain away.

Step 3 Keep testing the pot every 5 minutes until you can lift the pot off the ice. Measure the height of the ice block.

Step 4 Measure the height of the ice block every 10 minutes until it is too small to be measured. Record your results.

Step 5 Draw a graph of height against time.

Equations and brackets

Brackets

You have been using brackets in your calculations for quite a while but, until now, you have only had to multiply a term in brackets by a single number or variable. In this chapter, you are going to revise the use of one or more sets of brackets in an expression, and then look at how to multiply two terms in brackets.

In a calculation, brackets indicate that the expression inside them must be worked out before the rest of the calculation.

$3 \times (4 + 5) = 3 \times 9$ Work out 4 + 5 first.

$= 27$

In algebra it is not always possible to simplify the term inside the brackets. In this case, you must multiply each term inside the brackets by the number or variable before the opening bracket.

Example

Multiply: $3(2x + 4)$

$3(2x + 4) = 3 \times 2x + 3 \times 4$

$= 6x + 12$

The 3 before the brackets has first multiplied the $2x$ and then the + 4

When an expression includes a second set of brackets, you multiply out both sets and then simplify the whole expression.

Remember to take care with minus signs and negatives.

Example

Multiply out the brackets and simplify the expression: $3(2x + 4) - 4(2 - x)$

$3(2x + 4) - 4(2 - x) = 3 \times 2x + 3 \times 4 - 4 \times 2 - 4 \times (^-x)$

$= 6x + 12 - 8 + 4x$

$= 10x + 4$

Keeping the ^-x in brackets helps you to work out what to do with the signs.

$^-4 \times (^-x) = {}^+4x$

Exercise 15.1

Multiply out these brackets.

1 $3(3x + 1)$

2 $4(2x - 5)$

3 $2(5 - 3x)$

4 $7(3 + x)$

5 $6(2x + 5)$

6 $x(3x + 1)$

7 $2x(4x - 3)$

8 $a(5a - 2b)$

9 $a(5b + c)$

10 $3x(4 - 3x)$

Multiply out the brackets and simplify the expression, if possible.

11 $2(x + 3) + 3(2x - 2)$

12 $2(x + 2) - 3(x - 2)$

13 $2(4x - 3) + 4(2x + 1)$

14 $4(3 - x) - 3(x - 3)$

15 $5(2x - 1) - (2 - 5x)$

16 $2(x + 3) + 3x(x + 3)$

17 $3a(a - b) + 4(a - b)$

18 $a(a - b) + b(a - b)$

19 $3x(1 - 2x) + 3(1 - 2x)$

20 $x(2x - y) - 2y(2x - y)$

Two sets of brackets

Look carefully at Q16–20 from the last exercise. In each question, the expression within both sets of brackets is the same.

$2(x + 3) + 3x(x + 3)$

This could be written as $(2 + 3x)(x + 3)$ because $(x + 3)$ is a **common factor** in both terms.

Therefore, if you have to multiply out two sets of brackets, you multiply the expression in the second set of brackets by each term in the first set, in turn, and then simplify.

$$(a + b)(c + d) = a(c + d) + b(c + d)$$

$$= ac + ad + bc + bd$$

You can think of this as being like the multiplication you would do to find the area of a rectangle.

	$a + b$	
c	ac	bc
$+$ d	ad	bd

Work through these examples, following the method step by step.

Examples

(i) Multiply and simplify: $(2 + x)(x + 1)$

(ii) Multiply and simplify: $(2x - 2)(x - 1)$

(i) $(2 + x)(x + 1) = 2(x + 1) + x(x + 1)$

$= 2x + 2 + x^2 + x$

$= x^2 + 3x + 2$

(ii) $(2x - 2)(x - 1) = 2x(x - 1) - 2(x - 1)$

$= 2x^2 - 2x - 2x + 2$

$= 2x^2 - 4x + 2$

Exercise 15.2

Multiply out these brackets and simplify.

1 $(x + 1)(x + 4)$

2 $(x + 3)(x + 2)$

3 $(x + 4)(x + 6)$

4 $(x + 7)(x + 7)$

5 $(x + 1)(x + 1)$

6 $(x + 3)(x + 4)$

7 $(x + 2)(x + 4)$

8 $(x + 3)(x + 3)$

9 $(x + 8)(x + 3)$

10 $(x + 2)(x + 7)$

Once you are confident with this method, you could leave out the first line of the working by remembering this mnemonic.

First pair Outer pair Inner pair Last pair

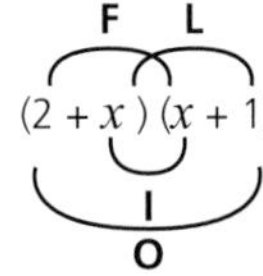

Check that it works, by reworking a few of the previous questions.

Then use the FOIL method to expand these brackets and then simplify the expressions.

11 $(x + 1)(x - 2)$

12 $(x + 3)(x - 2)$

13 $(x + 1)(x - 5)$

14 $(x + 4)(x - 4)$

15 $(x - 1)(x + 3)$

16 $(x - 2)(x + 6)$

17 $(x + 7)(x + 4)$

18 $(x - 3)(x + 3)$

19 $(x + 5)(x - 4)$

20 $(x + 1)(x - 1)$

21 $(x - 1)(x - 2)$

22 $(x - 4)(x - 2)$

23 $(x - 3)(x - 5)$

24 $(x - 7)(x - 1)$

25 $(x - 2)(x - 2)$

26 $(x + 4)(x - 2)$

27 $(x - 3)(2 - x)$

28 $(x + 3)(x + 2)$

29 $(3 - x)(3 - x)$

30 $(x - 2)(x + 2)$

Squares and differences

In some of the questions in the last exercise, the two brackets had the same expression inside them. These could have been written as squares.

$$(x + 7)(x + 7) = (x + 7)^2$$

$$(x - 2)(x - 2) = (x - 2)^2$$

$$(3 - x)(3 - x) = (3 - x)^2$$

These can be multiplied out just as before.

Example

Expand these brackets. (i) $(x + 7)^2$ (ii) $(x - 2)^2$

(i) $(x + 7)^2 = (x + 7)(x + 7)$

$= x(x + 7) + 7(x + 7)$

$= x^2 + 7x + 7x + 49$

$= x^2 + 14x + 49$

(ii) $(x - 2)^2 = (x - 2)(x - 2)$

$= x(x - 2) - 2(x - 2)$

$= x^2 - 2x - 2x + 4$

$= x^2 - 4x + 4$

Note that the final expression starts and ends with a perfect square, and the coefficient of the x-term is an even number (twice the constant term inside the brackets). The x^2 term and the number term are always positive.

That is because all squares are positive.

Therefore in general terms:

$(x + a)^2 = x^2 + 2ax + a^2$ $(x - a)^2 = x^2 - 2ax + a^2$

$(a + x)^2 = a^2 + 2ax + x^2$ $(a - x)^2 = a^2 - 2ax + x^2$

Exercise 15.3

Multiply out the brackets.

1 $(x + 2)^2$

2 $(x + 5)^2$

3 $(x - 6)^2$

4 $(3 + x)^2$

5 $(4 - x)^2$

6 $(1 + x)^2$

7 $(x + 4)^2$

8 $(x - 2)^2$

9 $(x + 10)^2$

10 $(x - 8)^2$

Factorising a squared bracket

In earlier work you looked for common factors in algebraic expressions.

$16x^2 + 4xy - 8x = 4x(4x + y - 2)$

In an expression such as $x^2 + 6x + 9$, there are no common factors but notice that the first and last terms are both **perfect squares.**

You may be able to factorise the expression into a perfect square by splitting the middle term.

$$\begin{aligned} x^2 + 6x + 9 &= x^2 + 3x + 3x + 9 \\ &= x(x + 3) + 3(x + 3) \\ &= (x + 3)(x + 3) \\ &= (x + 3)^2 \end{aligned}$$

When you need to factorise an expression, look at it carefully, to see whether it follows the pattern for a perfect square.

- The first and last terms are positive and squares.
- The coefficient of the middle term is an even number.

If it does, you can use the pattern for squaring an expression in brackets in reverse.

$x^2 + 2ax + a^2 = (x + a)^2$ $\qquad$ $x^2 - 2ax + a^2 = (x - a)^2$

$a^2 + 2ax + x^2 = (a + x)^2$ $\qquad$ $a^2 - 2ax + x^2 = (a - x)^2$

Example

Factorise these expressions. (i) $x^2 + 4x + 4$ (ii) $x^2 - 6x + 9$

(i) $x^2 + 4x + 4 = (x + 2)(x + 2)$ 2 is the square root of 4 and the sign must be +

(ii) $x^2 - 6x + 9 = (x - 3)(x - 3)$ 3 is the square root of 9 and the sign must be –

Exercise 15.4

Factorise each expression.

1 $x^2 - 4x + 4$

2 $x^2 + 6x + 9$

3 $x^2 + 8x + 16$

4 $x^2 - 2x + 1$

5 $x^2 + 14x + 49$

6 $25 - 10x + x^2$

7 $100 + 20x + x^2$

8 $b^2 - 2bx + x^2$

9 $b^2 - 2bc + c^2$

10 $x^2 + 2xy + y^2$

The next questions may require a little more thought.

Check your factorising by multiplying out the brackets in your answer.

11 $4x^2 - 4x + 1$

12 $16x^2 + 8x + 1$

13 $9x^2 + 6x + 1$

14 $4x^2 - 8x + 4$

15 $49x^2 + 98x + 49$

16 $100 - 20x + x^2$

17 $100 + 40x + 4x^2$

18 $4b^2 - 4bx + x^2$

19 $9b^2 - 6bc + c^2$

20 $4x^2 + 8xy + 4y^2$

The difference between two squares

Look back at Exercise 15.2 again. In some of the questions, the middle term cancelled out when you combined the terms in x.

$(x + 4)(x - 4) = x^2 - 16$

$(x + 1)(x - 1) = x^2 - 1$

$(x - 3)(x + 3) = x^2 - 9$

$(x - 2)(x + 2) = x^2 - 4$

The result in each case is one perfect square subtracted from another perfect square.

An expression in this form is known as the **difference between two squares** or the **difference of two squares**.

Exercise 15.5

Multiply out these brackets.

1 $(x - 10)(x + 10)$

2 $(x - 9)(x + 9)$

3 $(11 - x)(11 + x)$

4 $(2x + 5)(2x - 5)$

5 $(3x - 3)(3x + 3)$

6 $(2a - x)(2a + x)$

7 $(6 + ax)(6 - ax)$

8 $(8 - \frac{x}{2})(8 + \frac{x}{2})$

9 $(a - \frac{x}{2})(a + \frac{x}{2})$

10 $(y - \frac{x}{4})(y + \frac{x}{4})$

Factorising the difference of two squares

When an expression is made up of two squares separated by a minus sign, you can factorise it by taking the square roots of the terms.

Example

Factorise these expressions. (i) $x^2 - a^2$ (ii) $x^2 - 16$ (iii) $25x^2 - 16$

(i) $x^2 - a^2 = (x - a)(x + a)$

(ii) $x^2 - 16 = (x - 4)(x + 4)$

(iii) $25x^2 - 16 = (5x - 4)(5x + 4)$

Exercise 15.6

Factorise each expression, if possible.

1 $x^2 - 9$	6 $x^2 - y^2$	11 $x^2 + 1$	16 $25x^2 - y^2$
2 $x^2 - b^2$	7 $4x^2 - 1$	12 $4x^2 - b^2$	17 $x^2 - 9y^2$
3 $x^2 - 81$	8 $9x^2 - 1$	13 $9x^2 - 25$	18 $x^2 - 49y^2$
4 $x^2 - 16$	9 $16x^2 - 1$	14 $144 - x^2$	19 $x^2 - 16y^2$
5 $x^2 - 100$	10 $x^2 - 4a^2$	15 $81 + x^2$	20 $36x^2 - 121a^2$

Solving equations by factorising

When an expression is factorised, the result is a product of factors – one number or expression multiplied by another.

However consider these products.

$7 \times 0 = 0$ $\quad 0 \times x = 0$ $\quad 4x^2 \times 0 = 0$

You should remember that any number multiplied by 0 is 0

So if $xy = 0$ you know that $x = 0$ or $y = 0$

and if $(x + 3)(x - 4) = 0$ therefore $x = {}^-3$ or $x = 4$

then $(x + 3) = 0$ or $(x - 4) = 0$ and $x = {}^-3$ or ${}^+4$

Example

Solve these equations. (i) $9x^2 + 3x = 0$ (ii) $x^2 - 9 = 0$

(i) $9x^2 + 3x = 0$

$3x(3x + 1) = 0$

Either $3x = 0$ or $3x + 1 = 0$

$x = 0$ or $3x = {}^-1$

$x = 0$ or $x = \frac{^-1}{3}$

(ii) $x^2 - 9 = 0$

$(x - 3)(x + 3) = 0$

Either $x - 3 = 0$ or $x + 3 = 0$

$x = 3$ or $x = {}^-3$

To understand why this is so, look back to Chapter 14 Check where the graph of the equation $y = x^2 - 4$ meets the x-axis. It happens twice, both when $y = 0$, showing that there are two solutions to the equation $y = x^2 - 4$ These are $x = 2$ and $x = {}^-2$

Quadratic equations

An equation that includes an x^2 term, but no higher powers of x, is a **quadratic equation**. A quadratic equation has two solutions. When the quadratic expression is a perfect square these two solutions are the same.

Exercise 15.7

Factorise the left hand side of these equations and hence solve the equations.

1 $2x^2 - 8x = 0$

2 $x^2 - 4x = 0$

3 $12x^2 - 15x = 0$

4 $x^2 - 16 = 0$

5 $x^2 - 4x + 4 = 0$

6 $x^2 - 10x + 25 = 0$

7 $4x^2 - 16x = 0$

8 $x^2 - 25 = 0$

9 $15x^2 - 25x = 0$

10 $x^2 - 100 = 0$

11 $x^2 + 8x + 16 = 0$

12 $5x^2 - 15x = 0$

13 $12x^2 + 27x = 0$

14 $36 - x^2 = 0$

15 $36x - 60x^2 = 0$

16 $x^2 + 14x + 49 = 0$

17 $10x - 16x^2 = 0$

18 $9x^2 - 36 = 0$

19 $81 - 18x + x^2 = 0$

20 $35x + 49x^2 = 0$

To solve these equations, you may need to rearrange them before you can factorise. You need all of the non-zero terms on one side of the equals sign.

21 $x^2 + 16 = 8x$

22 $9x^2 = 15x$

23 $x^2 = 121$

24 $6x = 9 + x^2$

25 $36x = 4x^2$

26 $1 = 4x^2$

27 $16x + x^2 = {}^{-}64$

28 $10x + x^2 = 25x$

29 $4(2x - 4) = x^2$

30 $x(x + 6) = {}^{-}9$

Solving problems by factorising and brackets

Some problems can be solved by letting an unknown quantity be x and forming an equation.

If the equation is **linear**, you can solve it by rearrangement.

If the equation is **quadratic**, you need to solve it by factorising. This may give you two answers, in which case you must consider both. Then you may discard one because it doesn't make sense.

Example

In a rectangle, one side is three times as long as the other and the area is 27 cm². How long are the sides? Let the length of the short side be x cm.

x

$3x$

$$3x \times x = 27$$

$$3x^2 = 27$$

$$3x^2 - 27 = 0$$

$$(\div 3)$$

$$x^2 - 9 = 0$$

$$(x-3)(x+3) = 0$$

Either $x - 3 = 0$ or $x + 3 = 0$

$x = 3$ or $x = {}^{-}3$

A length cannot be negative, therefore discard $x = {}^{-}3$ and accept $x = 3$

The lengths of the sides are 3 cm and 9 cm.

Exercise 15.8

1 One side of a rectangle is twice as long as the other and the area of the rectangle is 72 cm². Work out the lengths of the sides.

2 One side of a rectangle is four times as long as the other and the area of the rectangle is 100 cm². Work out the lengths of the sides.

3 Two numbers have a difference of 6. Their squares have a difference of 120 What are the two numbers?

4 Two numbers have a sum of 20. Their squares have a difference of 40. What are the two numbers?

5 The sum of two numbers is 15. If the difference between their squares is 45, what are the two numbers?

6 The lengths of the sides of a rectangle are $(7 - x)$ cm and $(x + 3)$ cm respectively. The area of the rectangle is 25 cm². Work out the lengths of the sides.

7 A square of side x cm and a square of side $(x + 3)$ cm have a difference in area of $9x$ cm². Work out the lengths of the sides of the squares.

8 Two consecutive numbers can be written as n and $n + 1$

(a) **(i)** Write down the sum of these two consecutive numbers.

(ii) Explain if the sum is always odd, always even or if it is not possible to tell.

(b) **(i)** Write down the difference between these two consecutive numbers.

(ii) Explain if the difference is always odd, always even or if it is not possible to tell.

(c) **(i)** Write down the product of these two consecutive numbers.

(ii) Explain if the product is always odd, always even or if it is not possible to tell.

9 Three consecutive numbers can be written as $n - 1$, n and $n + 1$

(a) **(i)** Write down the sum of these three consecutive numbers.

(ii) What are the factors, if any, of the sum of any three consecutive numbers?

(b) **(i)** Write down the product of these three consecutive numbers.

(ii) Explain if the product is always odd, always even or if it is not possible to tell.

10 **(a)** Multiply out $(p + q)(p - q)$

(b) You know that $5^2 - 4^2 = 3^2$

Given that $(p + q)(p - q) = 9$, what are the values of p and q?

(c) What values of p and q give a difference of two squares of:

(i) 16 **(ii)** 25?

(d) Write your answers above in the form of a Pythogorean triplet: $x^2 + y^2 = z^2$

Then use the same method to find one more.

Summary Exercise 15.9

1 Multiply out the brackets and simplify the result if possible.

(a) $2x(3 - 3x)$ **(c)** $2(a - 5) - 3(a - 2)$

(b) $3(b + 2) + 2(2b - 1)$ **(d)** $2x(x + 6) - 3(4x - 3)$

2 Multiply out the brackets.

(a) $(x + 1)(x + 3)$ **(c)** $(2 + b)(5 - b)$

(b) $(x - 4)(x + 7)$ **(d)** $(a - b)(5 - a)$

3 Multiply out the brackets.

(a) $(x + 5)^2$ **(c)** $(5 - a)^2$

(b) $(x - 6)^2$ **(d)** $(2a - b)^2$

4 Factorise each expression.

(a) $x^2 - 6x + 9$ **(b)** $a^2 + 10x + 25$

5 Multiply out the brackets.

(a) $(x + 5)(x - 5)$ **(c)** $(6 - a)(6 + a)$

(b) $(x - 7)(x + 7)$ **(d)** $(2a - b)(2a + b)$

6 Factorise each expression.

(a) $x^2 - 36$

(b) $a^2 - 144$

7 I take a number and square it. I add 2 to the original number and then square the result. The difference between my two numbers is 144

What was my first number?

8 Two squares, one of which has sides 3 cm longer than the other, have a difference in area of 57 cm^2. What are the lengths of the sides of the two squares?

Activity: The dragon curve

This fascinating pattern was first discovered by NASA scientists in the 1960s. It is quite simple to get the pattern started but you may wish to carry it through by using some suitable software on a computer.

The **dragon curve** is a fractal, like those you looked at it Chapter 8. It is formed by a series of repeated tasks, called an **iteration**. As with all fractals, the next iteration or generation has self-similarity to the first.

Start with a long strip of paper. Fold it in half and then open it out so that it makes a right angle. This is the first iteration.

Fold it up again and halve it once more, then open it up. This is the second iteration. Do this again and then again. This diagram shows the first four iterations.

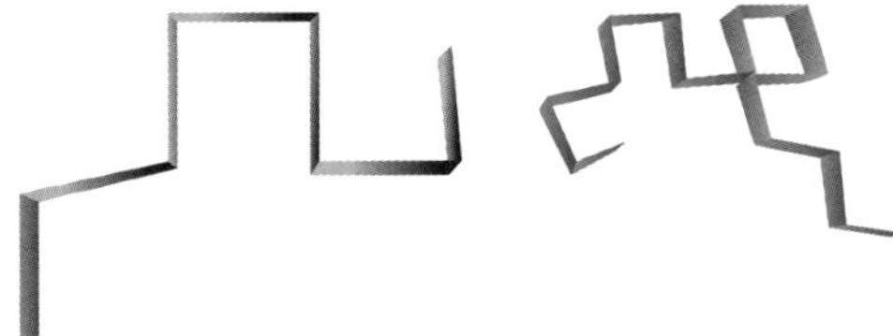

From here, it is probably easier to draw them rather than carry on folding.

With real paper there is a physical limit regarding how many times one can fold a paper in half. Even though in theory there is no real limit in a computer, the limit becomes the amount of memory and the processor. Even though this is one of the slowest growing fractals, you probably won't be able to go past iterations 13 or 14

Go ahead and give it a try.

How quickly do the numbers of points (ends and corners) grow?

You want to find out the general formula to predict the number of points at any iteration. As a hint, start by figuring out the number of lines at each iteration. You may also want to fill in this table.

Iteration	Number of lines	Numberofpoints
0	1	2
1	2	3
2	4	
3		
4		
5		
6		

You might also want to consider right and left L-bends. How do you define them?

Now use strips of paper or pipe cleaners to make the next iterations.

Iteration 7

If you could fold the paper about 50 times, it would look like this.

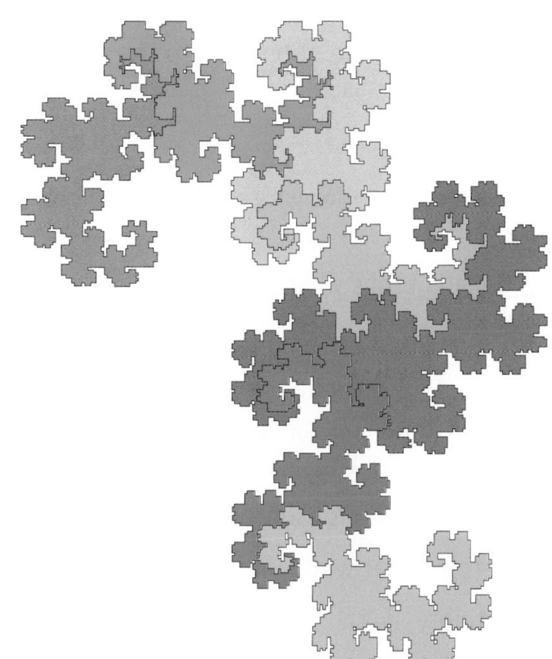

But of course, you can't fold the paper 50 times, so you have to let the mathematics take over the paper-folding process.

16 Probability

Fred's end of term report read: 'Fred hands his homework in on time once in a blue moon.'

'Once in a blue moon' is an expression you may have heard. Very occasionally, the moon does appear to be blue. The expression therefore implies that an event is possible but unlikely or infrequent.

In mathematics, the calculation of likelihood of something happening is known as **probability**.

What can you recall about earlier studies of probability? Here is a quick review of what you have already covered.

Calculating probability

The probabilities associated with an **event** can be calculated by considering the possible **outcomes** of that event, assuming that all outcomes of the event are **equally likely**.

For example, if you throw a normal die the possible outcomes are 1, 2, 3, 4, 5 and 6; there are six equally likely outcomes. Scoring a 6 is one of the six possible outcomes, so the probability of scoring a six is $\frac{1}{6}$
This is written as:

$P(6) = \frac{1}{6} \qquad P(3) = \frac{1}{6}$

The plural of die is **dice**; some people talk of one dice but this is incorrect.

A **fair** die is one for which all possible scores or outcomes are equally likely.

In general terms when all the possible outcomes are equally likely, the probability of an outcome can be calculated as:

$$P(\text{outcome}) = \frac{\text{frequency of the outcome}}{\text{number of equally likely outcomes}}$$

You can also write a probability as a percentage or a decimal, but in mathematics you generally write a probability as a fraction.

From this rule you can see that the probability of an outcome must lie between 0 and 1

The sum of the probabilities of all possible outcomes is 1

Something that will definitely happen is a **certainty**.

P(certainty) = 1

Something that will definitely not happen is an **impossibility**.

P(impossibility) = 0

Since an outcome must either happen or not happen:

P(outcome not happening) = 1 – P(outcome happening)

Examples

When throwing a normal die what is the probability of throwing:

(i) an odd prime number (ii) 7 (iii) a number less than 7?

(i) Possible outcomes are 1, 2, 3, 4, 5 and 6

Two of these are odd primes.

P(odd prime) $= \frac{2}{6} = \frac{1}{3}$

(ii) None of the numbers is 7

P(7) = 0

(iii) All six of the numbers are less than 7

P(less than 7) $= \frac{6}{6} = 1$

Many games including those with a pack of cards depend on chance. Questions on probability sometimes refer to dice or packs of cards. In case you were not sure, note that in a pack of cards there are 52 playing cards and two jokers. There are four **suits**; two are red: hearts and diamonds, and two are black: spades and clubs. Each suit has three royal cards: **king**, **queen** and **jack** (or **knave**), an **ace** and numbers 2 to 10

When you take a card from a pack, without knowing what it will be, you are taking a card at **random**.

Examples

A bag contains 12 balls. Five are blue, four are green, two are white and one black. If one ball is taken out of the bag at random, what is the probability that it is:

(i) blue (ii) white (iii) not green?

(i) P(blue) $= \frac{5}{12}$

(ii) P(white) $= \frac{2}{12} = \frac{1}{6}$

(iii) P(green) $= \frac{4}{12} = \frac{1}{3}$

P(not green) $= 1 - \frac{1}{3} = \frac{2}{3}$

Remember that you should always write fractions in their **lowest terms**.

Exercise 16.1

1 A normal pack of 52 cards is cut and one card is taken at random. Write down the probability the card is:

(a) black

(b) a heart

(c) not a royal card

(d) a king

(e) not a diamond

(f) the ace of hearts.

2 A normal die is rolled. Write down the probability that the score is:

(a) three

(b) a square number

(c) an even number

(d) less than 6.

3 A letter is picked at random from the alphabet. Write down the probability that the letter is:

(a) a vowel

(b) not a vowel

(c) one that appears in the word MATHEMATICS.

4 A letter is chosen at random from the letters in the word PROBABILITY. Write down the probability that the letter is:

(a) a vowel

(b) the letter I

(c) the letter L

(d) the letter S.

5 A bag contains three orange sweets, five red sweets, six green sweets and four purple sweets. If I select one sweet at random, write down the probability that it is:

(a) red or green

(b) not orange or purple?

6 Another bag of sweets contains only orange sweets and lemon sweets.

(a) If the probability of picking a lemon sweet is $\frac{4}{7}$, what is the probability of picking an orange sweet?

(b) If there are 12 lemon sweets in the bag, how many orange ones are there?

7 (a) I have four pairs of white socks, three pairs of black socks and five pairs of grey socks. I take one pair of socks at random. What is the probability that I pick a pair of grey socks?

(b) If my socks are not in pairs but are lying loose in my sock drawer, and I take one sock at random, what is the probability that it is a grey sock?

8 I am asked to pick a number from one to 20 at random. Give the probability that I pick:

(a) a prime number

(b) a multiple of 5

(c) a square number

(d) a negative number

(e) a number with more than two factors

(f) a number that is not a multiple of 3

Using theoretical probability

You have been working out probabilities, based on the number of possible outcomes and the assumption that they are all equally likely. You were using **theoretical probability**.

You can use this to solve problems such as question 6 in the last exercise. This next exercise looks at how theoretical probability may work in some practical situations.

Example

A bag contains red and white balls. My teacher tells me that if I pick one ball at random the probability of it being a white ball is $\frac{2}{3}$. If there are 12 red balls in the bag, how many white balls are there?

If P(white) $= \frac{2}{3}$ then P(red) $= \frac{1}{3}$

There are twice as many white balls as red balls.

Number of white balls $= 2 \times 12$

$= 24$

Exercise 16.2

1 A bag contains green balls and red balls. My teacher tells me that if I pick one ball at random the probability of it being a green ball is $\frac{3}{4}$. If there are 12 red balls in the bag, how many green balls are there?

2 A bag contains peppermints and toffees. My friend tells me that if I pick one sweet at random the probability of it being a toffee is $\frac{4}{5}$. If there are 12 peppermints in the bag, how many toffees are there?

3 I buy a packet of 20 seeds. The instructions warn that only $\frac{2}{3}$ of the seeds can be expected to germinate. How many seedlings can I expect?

4 In the tombola at the School Fair, the winning numbers all end in 0 or 5 and all the numbers from 1 to 500 are in the draw.

(a) If I buy 30 tickets, how many prizes might I expect to win?

(b) How many tickets must I buy to be sure of winning a prize?

5 (a) If I toss a coin 20 times how many times would I expect it to land on heads?

(b) If I toss a hairbrush 20 times, can I expect it to land bristles up 10 times? Explain your answer.

6 You roll a die 60 times. Write down how many times you should expect to score:

(a) a 6

(b) a number greater than 3

(c) a number less than 3

7 In the school raffle 1000 tickets were sold.

(a) If I bought 20 tickets, what is the probability of my winning first prize?

(b) If there were 20 prizes, how many tickets would I have to buy to be sure of winning a prize, in theory?

(c) How many tickets would I have to buy to be absolutely sure of winning a prize?

8 The company that makes Luckychoc bars say that every hundredth chocolate bar that they make contains a lucky token. If I buy a bag of 12 Luckychoc bars, what is the probability that I will be lucky? If I buy nine bags of Luckychocs, can I be sure that I will get a lucky token?

The moral of that last exercise is that probability is theoretical – you cannot depend on it to win games of chance!

Probability with two events

Two events can be either **dependent** or **independent.**

For example, picking a king or a 10 from a pack of cards are independent events. To calculate the probability, in this case, you add the probability of one outcome to the probability of the other.

Example

What is the probability of picking a king or a 10 from a pack of cards?

P(king) $\frac{4}{52}$ = and P(10) = $\frac{4}{52}$

P(king or 10) $\frac{4}{52} + \frac{4}{52}$

$= \frac{8}{52}$

$= \frac{2}{13}$

However, if you are asked for the probability of picking a black card or an ace from a pack of cards, there is a slight complication because two of the black cards are aces. Half the pack, comprising 26 cards, is black, and this includes the two black aces. There are also two red aces.

Therefore there are 28 cards that satisfy the criterion.

P(black card or ace) = $\frac{28}{52}$

$= \frac{7}{13}$

The probabilities of picking a black card and of picking an ace are **not independent** (but are **dependent**), so you cannot just add them.

There is no simple rule you can apply here. You must judge each situation on its own merits.

Exercise 16.3

1 A card is drawn at random from a full pack of 52 cards. Write down the probability that it is:

(a) a two or a three

(b) a red card or a knave

(c) an ace or a king

(d) a red ace or a heart

(e) a black queen or a red knave

(f) a black card or a royal card.

2 I pick a number from 1 to 30 at random. Give the probability that I pick:

(a) 5

(b) a multiple of 5

(c) a prime number

(d) a multiple of 5 or a prime number

(e) an odd number or a prime number.

3 A bag contains eight green sweets, six red sweets and four yellow sweets.

(a) Given that the first sweet I take out at random is red, give the probability that the second sweet is: (i) red (ii) yellow.

(b) Given that the first sweet I take out at random is green, give the probability that the second sweet is: (i) green (ii) yellow.

(c) Given that the first sweet I take out at random is yellow, give the probability that the second sweet is: (i) yellow (ii) red.

4 A mixed bag of snack bars contained five caramel bars, four chocolate bars and three orange-flavoured bars. I was allowed to choose one bar at random every day for my break time snack.

(a) On Monday, what is the probability that the bar I picked was caramel?

(b) In fact the bar I picked on Monday was an orange-flavoured bar. What was the probability that I would chose a caramel bar on Tuesday?

(c) In fact the bar I picked on Tuesday was a chocolate bar. What is the probability that I would choose a caramel bar on Wednesday?

(d) In fact the bar I picked on Wednesday was an orange-flavoured bar. How many bars would I have to take out of the bag now to be sure of getting a caramel bar?

5 I am dealt five cards from a pack of cards. These are three kings and two queens. If no other cards have been taken from the pack, give the probability that the next card:

(a) will be a royal card

(b) will not be a royal card.

6 I am dealt five cards from a pack of cards. These are three hearts and two diamonds. If no other cards have been taken from the pack, give the probability that the next card will be:

(a) a heart (b) a spade.

7 I have a packet of candy balls. Twelve are red, six are green, five are yellow and four are orange.

(a) I offered the packet to my little sister. What is the probability that she took a green candy ball? Assume the green candy ball is then put back in the bag.

(b) My little sister does not like green so she put the green candy ball back and then told me she had taken a red candy ball. What is the probability that when I offer the bag to my mother she will take a red candy ball too?

(c) Before I offered the bag to my mother, I found that my little sister had actually taken all the orange candy balls! What is the probability now that my mother will take a red one?

8 There are 240 pupils in the school and they are grouped so that there are equal numbers in each of four houses: Austen, Churchill, Nightingale and Wellington.

(a) The headmaster chooses one pupil at random to run an errand. What is the probability that the pupil is from Churchill?

(b) What is the probability that the next pupil the headmaster chooses will also be from Churchill?

(c) (i) If half the pupils in each house are boys and half are girls, what is the probability that the first pupil to be chosen was a boy from Churchill?

(ii) What is the probability that the second pupil to be chosen was a girl from Churchill?

9 Have you heard of the bosun's locker? This is where the bosun (a ship's officer in charge of equipment and the crew) keeps his secret store of food supplies. Unfortunately the locker is wet and so all the labels have fallen off. The bosun knows that he has 15 tins of rice pudding, five tins of fruit salad and 12 tins of emergency rations for the ship's cat. The bosun takes two tins at random.

Give the probability that:

(a) the first is rice pudding

(b) if the first was rice pudding the second is fruit salad

(c) if the first was cat food the second is also cat food.

10 In Aladdin's cave there were 10 bags of gold, 12 bags of silver, 13 bags of emeralds and two bags of diamonds.

(a) Aladdin had to leave in a rush and could only carry one bag. What was the probability that he took a bag of gold?

(b) The genie followed him out with another bag. If Aladdin had taken a bag of gold, what was the probability that the genie also took a bag of gold?

(c) Actually no one knows which bag Aladdin took, but the bag that the genie took had a probability of $\frac{1}{18}$ of being selected. Can you tell who took which bag?

(d) If the genie took a bag that had a probability of $\frac{1}{3}$ of being selected, work out who took which bag.

Possibility space diagrams for combined events

When you toss two coins together, the result could be two heads, two tails or one head and one tail. It looks as though there are three possibilities, but there are in fact four possible combinations.

(head, head)   (head, tail)   (tail, head)   (tail, tail)

It is easier to see all the possibilities if you put the possible outcomes in a table like this.

		First coin	
		H	T
Second coin	H	(H, H)	(T, H)
	T	(H, T)	(T, T)

This table is called a **possibility space** because it clearly shows all the possibilities. It is now clear that there are four possibilities, not three, as the combination of one head and one tail can be achieved in two ways.

Exercise 16.4

1 Copy and complete this possibility space to show the possible outcomes when two dice are thrown.

		First die					
		1	2	3	4	5	6
Second die	1	(1, 1)	(2, 1)	(3, 1)			
	2	(1, 2)	(2, 2)	(3, 2)			
	3	(1, 3)	(2, 3)	(3, 3)			
	4	(1, 4)	(2, 4)				
	5	(1, 5)	(2, 5)				(6, 5)
	6	(1, 6)	(2, 6)				(6, 6)

Write down the probability of throwing two dice and scoring:

(a) a total of 4

(b) a total more than 6

(c) a double

(d) a total that is an even number.

2 Use the possibility space in question 1 to find the probability that:

(a) the total score is prime number

(b) there is a prime number on at least one die.

3 Draw a possibility space to show all the outcomes when you throw together a normal die and a die with its faces numbered 1, 1, 1, 2, 2, 3

Use this possibility space to find the probability that:

(a) the total score is 2

(b) the total score is more than 4

(c) a double is thrown

(d) there is a multiple of 3 on each die

(e) the total score is a prime number

(f) the total score is 6 or more.

4 I throw a die with eight faces, numbered from 1 to 8, at the same time as I throw a die with six faces, numbered from 1 to 6

(a) Draw a possibility space to record all the possibilities.

(b) Use this probability space to find the probability that:

(i) the total score is 12

(ii) the total score is more than 12

(iii) a double is thrown

(iv) there is a multiple of 2 on each die

(v) the total score is a prime number.

(c) What is the most likely total score?

5 These are two spinners from the game of *Tops*. For each move they are spun together. The score is the sum of the two numbers.

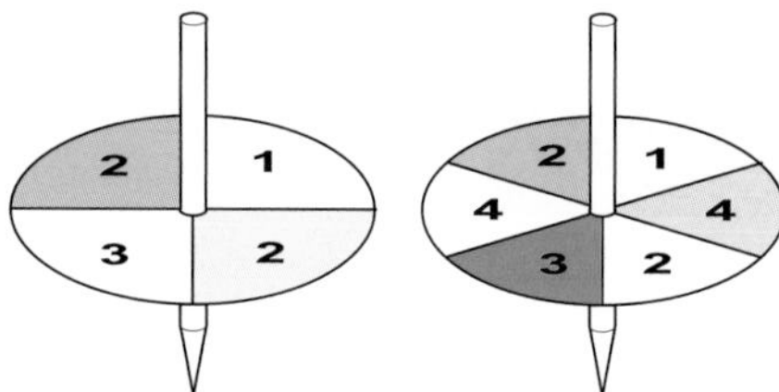

(a) Draw a possibility space to show all the possible outcomes from the two spinners.

(b) From the possibility space find:

(i) the highest and lowest possible scores

(ii) the most likely score

(iii) the probability of throwing a score that is even

(iv) the probability of throwing a score that is odd

(v) the probability of a score of 4

(vi) the probability of a score of 6

6 I have the four aces from a pack of cards in one pile and the four kings in another.

(a) Draw a possibility space to show all the possible outcomes from selecting a card from each pile.

(b) If I take one card from each pile give the probability of selecting:

(i) two red cards

(ii) a red card and a black card

(iii) two cards of the same suit

(iv) two kings.

Extension: Tables and Venn diagrams

When you have to work with lots of information it can be useful to put the numbers in a table or diagram.

Example

There are 24 students in my class. 16 are boys and 12 play the violin. Six girls play the violin. What is the probability that a pupil chosen at random is a boy that plays the violin?

	Girls	Boys	Total
Violin	**6**	6	**12**
No violin	2	10	12
Total	8	**16**	**24**

$$\text{P(boy that plays violin)} = \frac{6}{24}$$

$$= \frac{1}{4}$$

In the table, the numbers in bold are the figures you have been given. From these you can work out all the missing numbers.

Another useful way to show information is a **Venn diagram**. You may have used these to find common factors and common denominators. For example, from this Venn diagram showing all the factors of 84, 260 and 330 you can see that the highest common factor of all three numbers is 2.

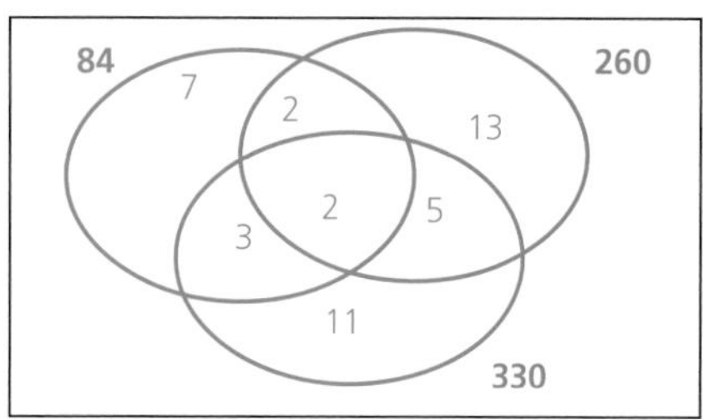

You can also use a Venn diagram to show the total numbers of objects in a group or set and how many belong in two or more of the groups or sets.

When drawing a Venn diagram follow these steps.

- Draw the Venn diagram to show 2 or more intersecting sets.
- Fill in any information you have been given in the correct section.
- Carefully calculate other values and fill in all the section.
- Answer the question.

Example

There are 24 pupils in the class. 12 of them learn the piano and 11 of them learn the violin. Five pupils learn neither the violin nor the piano.

Draw a Venn diagram to illustrate this.

What is the probability that a pupil picked at random plays the piano but not the violin?

If 5 do not play either instrument $24 - 5 = 19$ do. Of these, 12 play the piano, therefore $19 - 12 = 7$ play the violin but not the piano. Write 7 in the appropriate part of the Venn diagram. Therefore 4 learn both the violin and the piano. Write 4 in the intersection of the sets. Eight pupils must play the piano only.

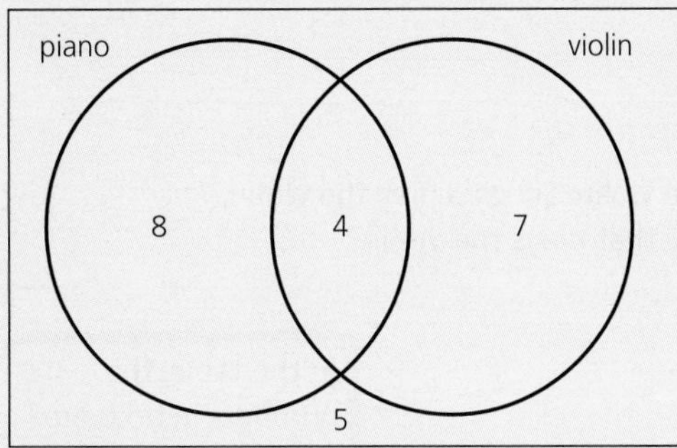

$$\text{P(piano and not violin)} = \frac{8}{24} = \frac{1}{3}$$

Extension Exercise 16.5

Use a table or a Venn diagram to help solve these problems.

1 In our class there are 10 boys and 12 girls. 16 of us have pets and the rest do not. Seven of the pet owners are girls. If one of the class is picked at random, give the probability that it is:

(a) a girl **(b)** a pet owner **(c)** a boy that owns a pet.

2 In a school of 240 pupils there are 70 boys that board and 90 day girls. 130 pupils board altogether.

(a) Draw a table to show this information.

(b) If a pupil is picked at random, what is the probability that it will be a day boy?

(c) All the boarders went to Long Hall to do prep. Matron then picked a day pupil at random. What was the probability that she picked a girl?

3 On a school trip to France we ate in a restaurant. We had to choose a main course and a pudding. 43 of us chose coq au vin and the rest chose an omelette. 49 chose crème caramel and the rest chose a glace. 8 of us had coq au vin and a glace. 29 of those who had the omelette did not have crème caramel.

(a) How many of us had coq au vin and a glacé (comme moi!)?

(b) One pupil was sick on the way home. What was the probability that this pupil had omelette and glace?

4 This Venn diagram shows how many pupils in the class own a cat and how many own a dog.

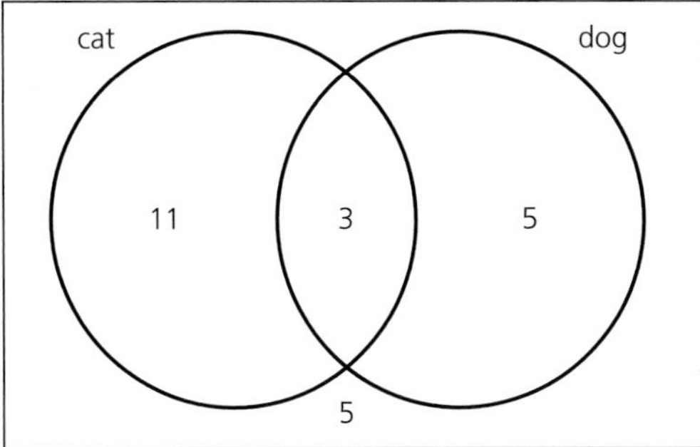

(a) How many pupils are there in the class?

(b) If a pupil is picked at random what is the probability that they own a cat?

5 In my school there are 350 pupils. 120 of them board and 145 of them have music lessons. 105 pupils neither board nor have music lessons.

(a) Show this information on a Venn diagram.

(b) What is the probability that a pupil picked at random boards but does not have music lessons?

6 There are 72 boys in my year. In the games lesson 24 boys do not play a ball game, 45 play cricket and 36 play tennis.

(a) Show this information on a Venn diagram.

(b) What is the probability that a boy picked at random plays cricket but not tennis?

7 My class did a survey about where everyone went for their summer holidays. The results are shown on this Venn diagram.

Britain
Rest of Europe
Outside Europe
7 4 5
1
3 2
2
2

(a) How many pupils are there in my class?

(b) How many had holidays in three different places?

(c) How many visited both Britain and Europe?

(d) What is the probability that a pupil picked at random has a holiday in Britain?

8 This Venn diagram shows the number of girls in my class who have a cat, a dog or a rabbit as a pet.

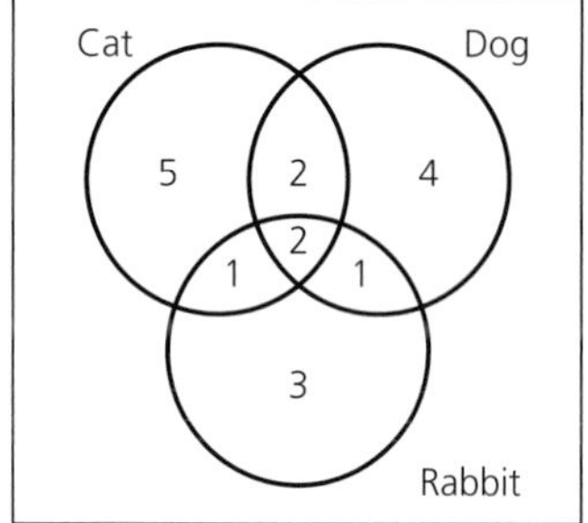

(a) How many girls are there in my class?

(b) If one girl is selected at random what is the probability that she has a cat and a rabbit but not a dog?

(c) If another girl is selected at random what is the probability that she has a dog?

9 There are 360 girls in the school. 300 of them learn languages. 200 learn French, 120 learn Latin and 110 learn Italian. Ten girls study all three languages, but none learn Italian only. Of those learning Latin, 40 also learn Italian, but not French.

(a) Show this information on a Venn diagram.

(b) If one girl is selected at random, what is the probability that she is studying French and Italian?

(c) If another girl is selected at random, what is the probability that she is studying French and Latin?

10 Last month was April. Eight of the days fell on weekends and it rained on four of them. Let the number of weekdays that were fine be x.

(a) Write an expression in x for the number of weekdays that were wet.

(b) Show this information on a Venn diagram.

(c) If a weekday were selected at random what is the probability, in terms of x, that it would be: **(i)** wet **(ii)** dry?

(d) If any day were selected at random what is the probability, in terms of x, that it would be wet ?

(e) In fact the probability that any day selected at random would be wet was the same as the probability that a day at a weekend selected at random would be dry. From this information, form an equation in x and solve it to find the number of weekdays that were fine.

11 In my school there are 320 pupils. 95 of them board and 135 of them have music lessons. 140 pupils neither board nor have music lessons.

Let the number of pupils that board and have music lessons be x.

(a) In terms of x, how many pupils board and do not have music lessons?

(b) In terms of x, how many pupils have music lessons but do not board?

(c) Show this information on a Venn diagram.

(d) Form an equation in x and solve it to find the number of pupils that board and have music lessons.

12 There are 72 boys in my year and they all do at least one after-school sports activity. 36 play tennis. Of the 45 boys that play cricket, 12 play tennis but not badminton and 9 play badminton but not tennis.

Let x be the number of boys that play cricket but not tennis or badminton.

(a) Write an expression in x for the number of boys that play tennis, cricket and badminton.

(b) Fill all the information that you can on a Venn diagram.

(c) Given that eight boys play badminton but not tennis or cricket, form an equation in x and solve it.

(d) Seven boys play tennis only. Complete your Venn diagram.

(e) If a boy is picked at random, what is the probability that he plays badminton and tennis but not cricket?

Summary Exercise 16.6

1 I cut a normal pack of cards and select one card at random. Write down the probability that this card will be:

(a) an ace

(b) a diamond

(c) the ten of hearts

(d) either an ace or a king

(e) either a heart or a queen.

2 There are eight tins of soup in my cupboard: three tomato, two chicken, two beef and one farmhouse vegetable. Given that I pick one tin at random, write down the probability that it is:

(a) tomato

(b) suitable for vegetarians

(c) not beef.

3 I roll an ordinary die and a die numbered 1, 2, 3, 3, 5, 6

(a) Draw a possibility space to show all possible results.

(b) Use the possibility space to find the probability that I throw:

(i) a double

(ii) a six on either die

(iii) a total greater than 5

(iv) a total less than 4

(c) If I rolled both the dice together 30 times, how many doubles would I expect?

4 A box contains three red balls and seven white balls. Two balls were taken from the box.

(a) What is the probability that the first ball was red?

(b) If the first ball was red, what is the probability that the second ball was also red?

(c) If the first ball was white, what is the probability that the second ball was red?

(d) How many balls would I have to take out to be sure of removing one ball of each colour?

5 I offer a bag containing a mixture of sherbet lemons and mint humbugs to my sister. There is a $\frac{3}{5}$ chance that she will pick a mint humbug. If there are six sherbet lemons in the bag, how many mint humbugs are there?

6 (a) My maths master, Mr Chance, is very absent minded. There is a 20% chance that he will forget to set us any maths prep and a 30% chance that he will forget to ask for it to be given in. However, if Mr Chance does remember to ask for it and you have not done it (regardless of whether it was set or not), then the whole class gets a detention. Write down the probability that:

(i) no prep was set and none was asked for

(ii) prep was set but you were not asked to give it in

(iii) the class got a detention although no prep was set.

(b) If there are 20 nights in a term when the class is supposed to have maths prep, how many detentions could they expect to get in a term (assuming everyone does their homework when it is set)?

7 I have a collection of 100 geometrical shapes. 25 of them are blue and 15 of them are blue triangles.

Let the number of triangles that are not blue be x.

(a) Write an expression in terms of x for the number of shapes that are not blue and are not triangles.

(b) Show this information on a Venn diagram.

(c) If a shape is selected at random, the probability that it is neither triangular nor blue is the same as the probability that a blue shape selected at random is a triangle. Use this information to find the number of triangles.

Activity: Random cricket

Using the random number key

On your calculator you should find a button marked RAN (usually a second function). Press this button and you should be presented with a three-figure number preceded by a decimal point.

Ignore the decimal point and record the number. Do this again and again until you have recorded 20 numbers, or 60 single digits.

If these numbers are produced in a truly random fashion, how many of each digit from 0 to 9 would you expect to find in your 60 digits?

It is quite likely that you do not have the number that you expected. It is probable that you will have more of some digits than others. This is not a mistake. It is because random events in real life do not spread themselves out evenly but can bunch together, which explains the commonly held belief that accidents happen in threes. This is an important fact to remember when planning something using random events.

Random cricket

You can make a model of a cricket game by using the random number generator on your calculator.

In this case you will use the first digit for the bowler and the second digit for the batsman. Ignore any numbers with fewer than three digits.

For example:

0.312 3: the bowler 1: the batsman

0.784 7: the bowler 8: the batsman

And now to cricket: First, consider the bowler. He could bowl a 'true' ball, or a 'no ball' or could bowl the batsman out. Allocate the bowler's randomly generated numbers as follows:

0 – 5 to a 'true' ball

6 – 8 to a 'no ball'

9 is bowling the batsman out.

Second, look at the batsman. He could make runs, be caught, be run out or be LBW. Allocate his randomly generated numbers as follows:

0–1 to 1 run

2–6 to the equivalent number of runs

7 is caught out

8 is run out

9 is LBW

Now to play: Use a score card like the one shown in this activity, to record the results of your game of cricket.

Assume you generate these random numbers: 3, 9, 0, 6, 4, 1, 9, 4, 7, 2, 2, 8

Ball 1: 3 means the bowler bowled true

9 means that batsman 1 was out LBW

Ball 2: 0 means the bowler bowled true

6 means that batsman 2 made 6 runs

Ball 3: 4 means the bowler bowled true

1 means that batsman 2 made 1 run

Ball 4: 9 means the bowler bowled batsman 2 out

4 has no effect because the batsman was bowled out

Ball 5: 7 means the bowler bowled a no ball and the batting team get 1 "Extra" run

2 means that batsman 2 made 2 runs

Ball 6: 2 means the bowler bowled true

8 means that batsman 3 is run out

Your score card for the first over looks like this.

First over							
Ball	Random number	Result	Batsman number	Random number	Runs	Total runs	Out?
1	3	True	1	9	LBW	0	Out
2	0	True	2	6	6	6	
3	4	True	2	1	1	7	
4	9	Out	2		0	7	Out
5	7	No ball	3	2	3	10	
6	2	True	3	8	Run out	10	Out

You can see that, in this over (6 balls), batsman 1 was out LBW for a golden duck (i.e. out on the first ball with no runs), batsman 2 was bowled out with 7 runs and batsman 3 was run out with 2 runs (the run given as a result of the no ball goes towards the batting teams score).

1 Try some more overs of your own and see how soon the batting side gets out.

2 It seems from the first over that the bowling team have the advantage. Do the statistics of your own team's results look like this? Do you think you should adjust the allocation of the random numbers? Try a variation and see if that changes the outcome of the game.

3 Look carefully at your own team's statistics and allocate the random numbers in a completely different way. Then see if you get similar results to your own.

4 Look carefully at a test match team's statistics and allocate the random numbers in an appropriate way. Then see if you get similar results to the test match team.

5 Take another game: rounders, tennis, netball, or anything else you fancy (Quidditch?) and use a random number simulation to generate the results.

17 Transformation geometry

A **transformation** is a change. In mathematics, a transformation maps one point onto another point. The transformations that you have learnt about in *Mathematics for Common Entrance* Books *One* and *Two* are **reflections**, **rotations**, **translations** and **enlargements**.

Under a transformation in which the point P is the **object**, P is mapped onto its **image**. This may be identified as P' or by another letter, such as Q. If it is the first of a series of transformations the images may be known as P_1, P_2, P_3, …

In this chapter you will **construct** transformations and so you will need your ruler, compasses and protractor.

Reflections

When you **reflect** an object you produce its **mirror image**. The object is reflected in a **mirror line** or a **line of reflection**. On a coordinate grid this could be:

- a horizontal or a vertical line, such as the x-axis or the y-axis
- a horizontal or a vertical line, such as $x = 2$, or $y = {}^{-}3$
- a sloping straight line, such as $y = x$ or $y = {}^{-}x$ or $y = 3x - 2$

If you are working on a reflection that is not on a coordinate grid, you will need to construct the image.

In this reflection of $ABCD$ in the mirror line PQ:

- the point A maps onto A'
- the point B maps onto B'
- the point C maps onto C'
- the point D maps onto D'

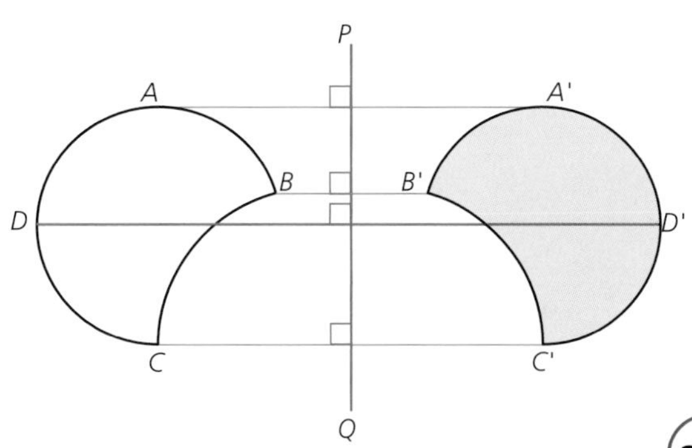

Note that the lines *AA′*, *BB′*, *CC′*, *DD′* are **perpendicular** to *PQ* and are **bisected** by *PQ*. If you take any other line from a point on *ABCD* to its reflection on *A′B′C′D′*, you will see that this is always true.

Also note that *AA′*, *BB′*, *CC′*, *DD′* are parallel.

To construct a reflection of a line *PQ* in a line *AB*

Construct a perpendicular from *P* to meet *AB* at a point *X*.

Look back to Chapter 10 if you need to remind yourself how to do this.

Extend the line *PX* to the point *P′* on the opposite side of the *AB*, so that *XP′* is equal in length to *PX*. The point *P′* is the reflection of *P* in *AB*.

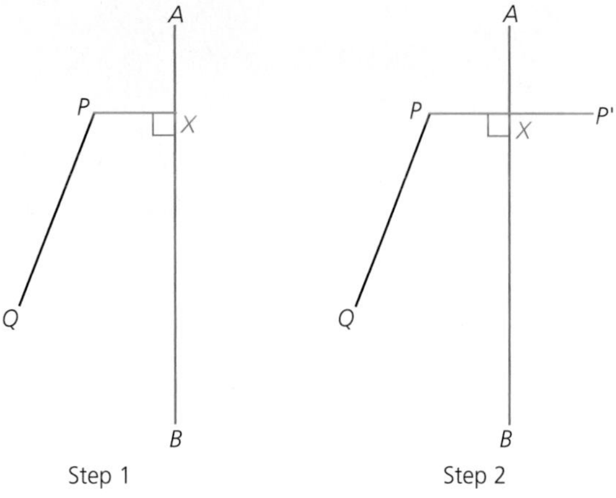

Step 1 Step 2

In the same way, construct a perpendicular from *Q* to *AB* and extend the line to point *Q′*. The line *P′Q′* is the reflection of *PQ* in the line *AB*.

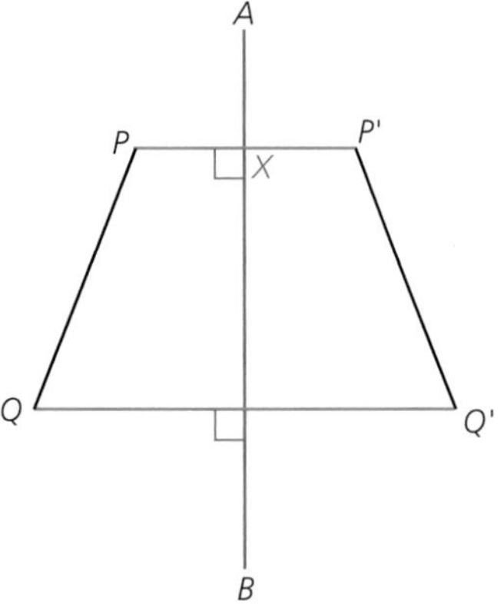

Exercise 17.1

1 Trace this diagram into your book. Some of these triangles may have a reflected image and some may not.

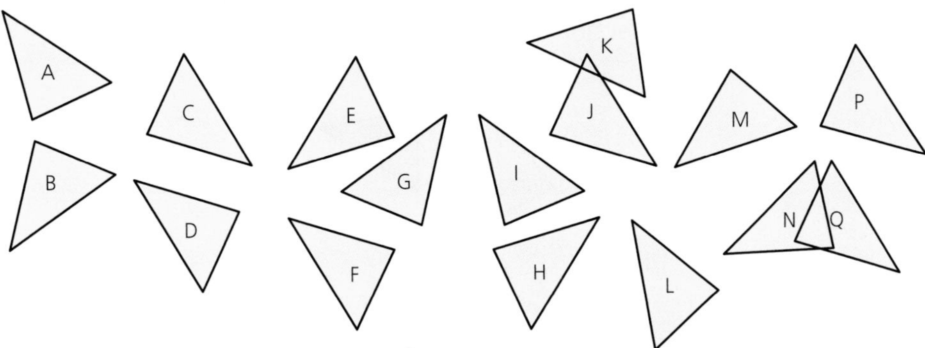

(a) On your tracing, draw any mirror lines that lie between one triangle and its image.

(b) List any pairs of triangles and their reflected images.

2 Draw a line across a page in your exercise book to divide it in two areas. Draw a line perpendicular to the first, to divide your page into quarters. In the top-right quarter, copy this shape. Construct the image of the shape after a reflection in the vertical mirror line. Then construct the image of both the original shape and its reflection in the horizontal mirror line.

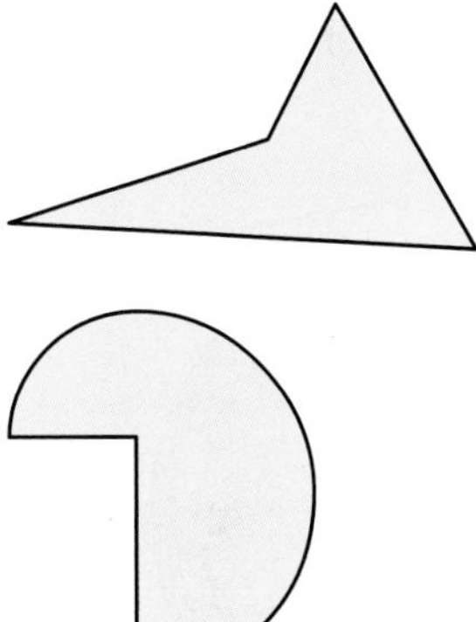

3 Repeat question 2 for this shape. You will need to construct both the original image and then the reflections by using a pair of compasses.

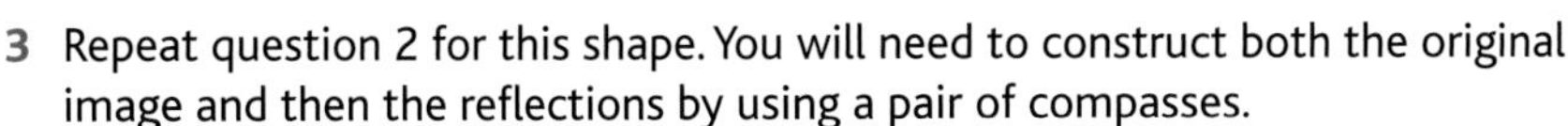

When a shape is reflected in two mirror lines, the object is first reflected in one line, and then the object and the images are reflected in the second line, to give four congruent shapes.

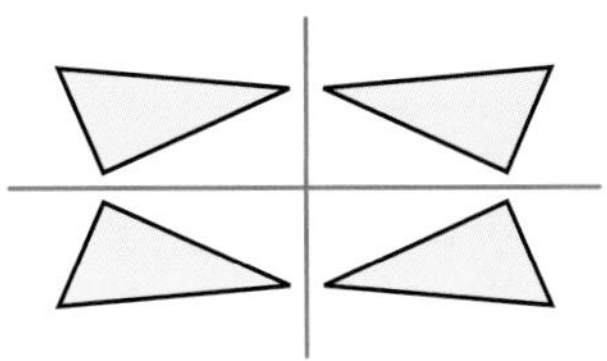

4 Construct two mirror lines perpendicular to each other. Copy each shape into one corner and then construct all three reflections.

(a)

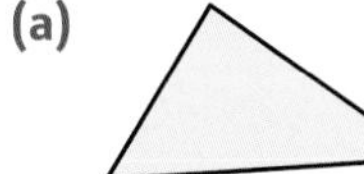

(b)

5 The design for a new logo for a computer company is in the form of a shape and its three reflections. Design the logo.

Rotations

A **rotation** is a turn. Under the rotation transformation, an object is rotated about a point. This may be either clockwise or anticlockwise. A rotation is described in terms of the **centre of rotation** and by the size of the **angle of rotation** and the direction of **turn**.

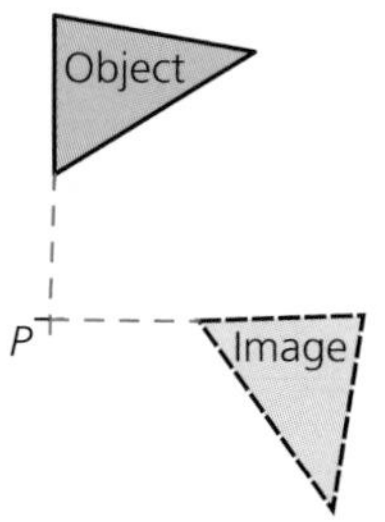

A rotation of 90° clockwise about point *P*

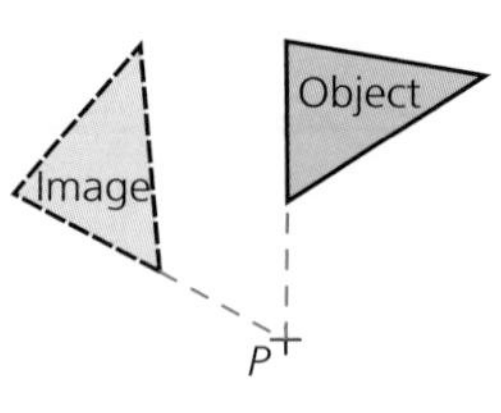

A rotation of 60° anticlockwise about point *P*

To construct the image of an object after a rotation, you need a pair of compasses and a protractor.

To construct a rotation of 90° clockwise about a point *P*

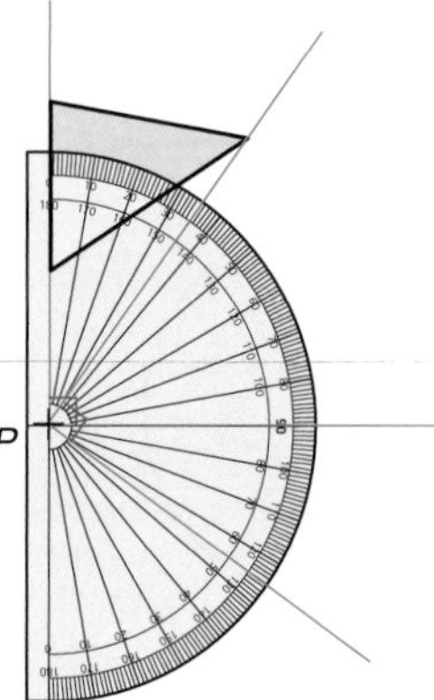

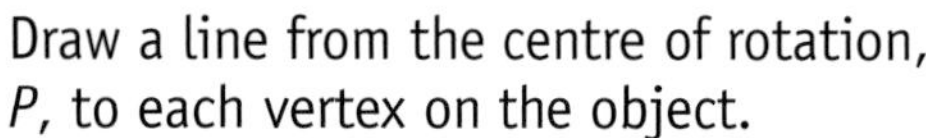

Draw a line from the centre of rotation, *P*, to each vertex on the object.

Construct the perpendicular to each of these lines, from the point *P*.

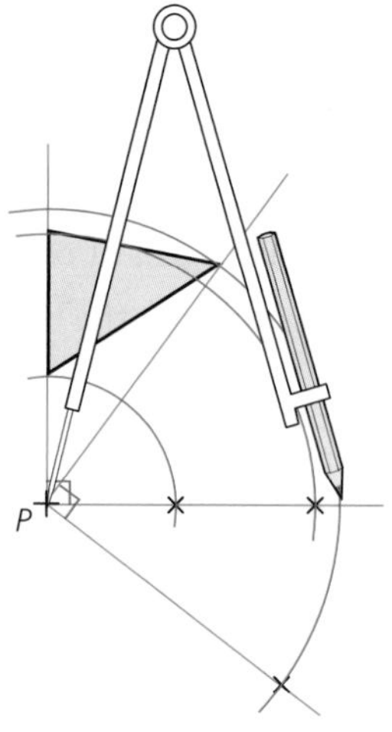

With compasses set to the distance from one vertex to *P*, and centred on *P*, draw an **arc** to cross the construction lines. Repeat for the other two vertices.

Join the points where the arcs cross the perpendiculars, to draw the image.

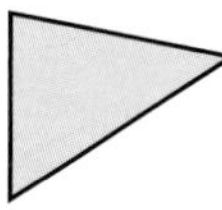

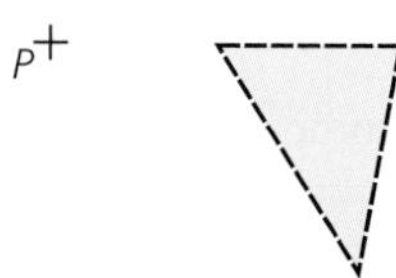

Exercise 17.2

You will need about half a page in your exercise for each question in this exercise. For each question, copy or draw the shape into the top right-hand side of the space you have available.

1 Copy this shape.

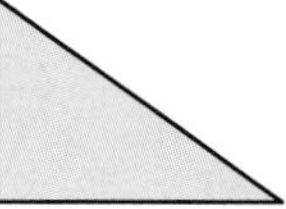

Mark a point, P, in the centre of your page.

Draw the image of the shape after a rotation of:

(a) 90° clockwise about point P

(b) 180° about P

(c) 270° clockwise about P

2 Copy this shape.

Mark a point, P, in the centre of your page.

Draw the image of the shape after a rotation of:

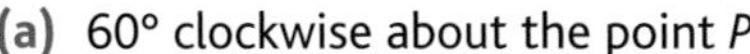

(a) 60° clockwise about the point P

(b) 120° anticlockwise about P

(c) 60° anticlockwise about P

3 Copy this shape.

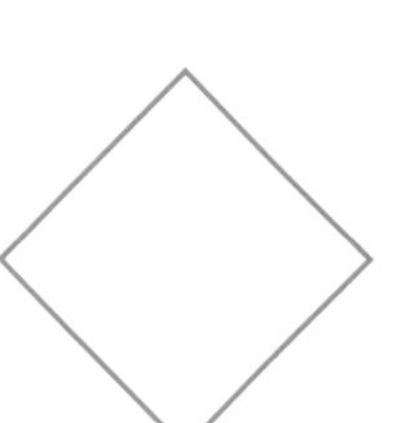

Mark a point, P, in the centre of your page.

Draw the image of the shape after a rotation of:

(a) 45° clockwise about point P

(b) 135° anticlockwise about P

(c) 135° clockwise about P

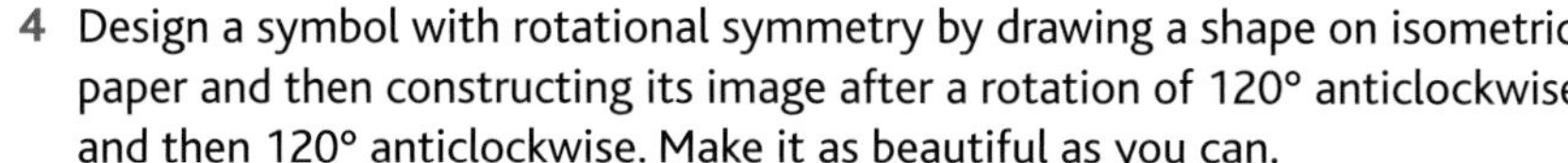

4 Design a symbol with rotational symmetry by drawing a shape on isometric paper and then constructing its image after a rotation of 120° anticlockwise and then 120° anticlockwise. Make it as beautiful as you can.

This is the symbol of the Isle of Man.

Rotational symmetry

When you rotate some shapes about their own centres, you may produce images that are identical to the original shape. These shapes have **rotational symmetry**.

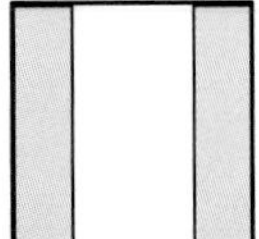

- Rotational symmetry of order 2

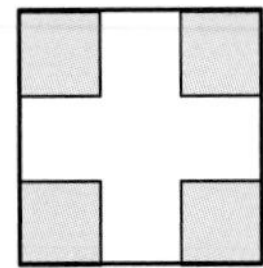

- Rotational symmetry of order 4

- Rotational symmetry of order 6

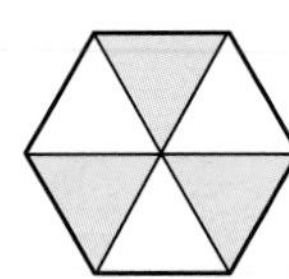

- Rotational symmetry of order 3

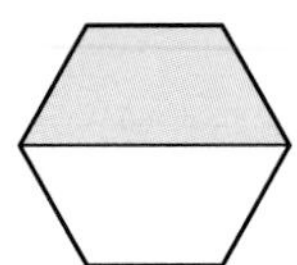

- No rotational symmetry

Exercise 17.3

You cannot have rotational symmetry of order 1, that would be no rotational symmetry.

Use tracing paper to trace the diagrams, to help you find the lines of symmetry and order of rotational symmetry.

1 Write down the order of rotational symmetry of each shape.

(a) (b) (c) (d) (e)

Now write down the number of lines of symmetry for each shape if they have any.

2 Write down the order of rotational symmetry of each shape if they have any.

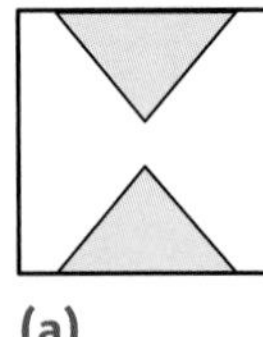

(a)

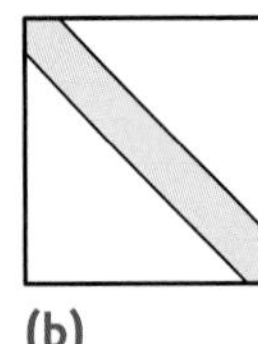

(b)

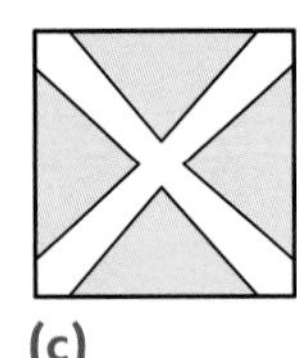

(c)

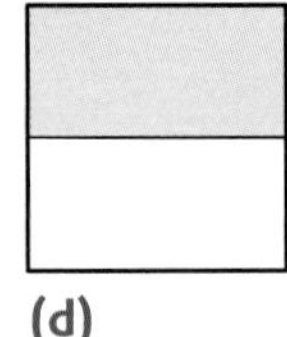

(d)

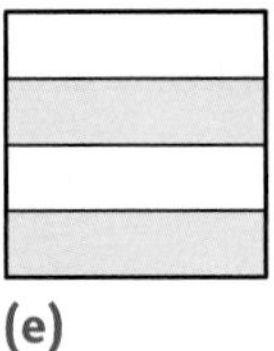

(e)

Now write down the number of lines of symmetry for each shape if they have any.

3 Write down the order of rotational symmetry of each shape.

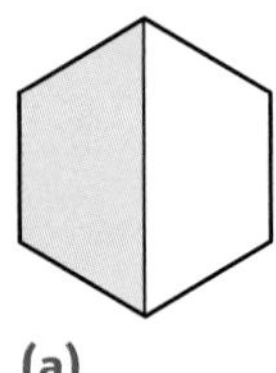

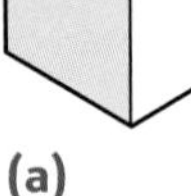

(a)

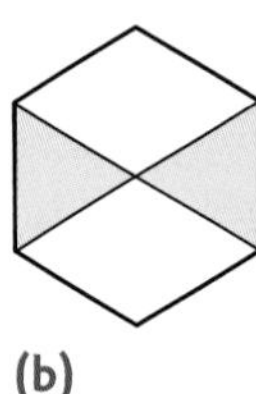

(b)

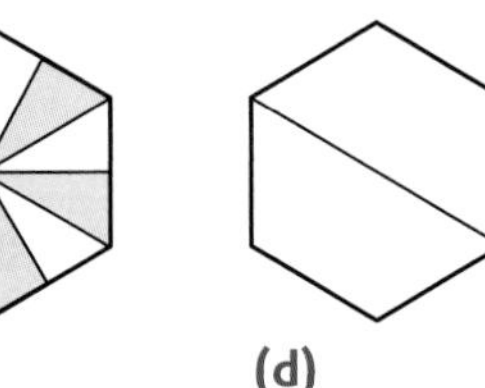

(c) (d)

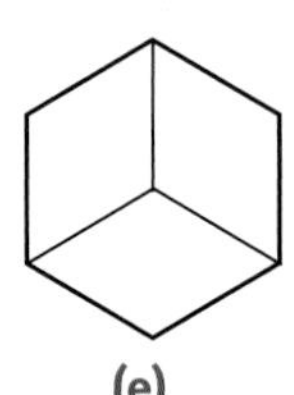

(e)

Now write down the number of lines of symmetry for each shape.

This may not possible for all of the shapes!

For Q4–6 copy each object and complete it so that the image has the number of lines of symmetry and order of rotational symmetry given in the question.

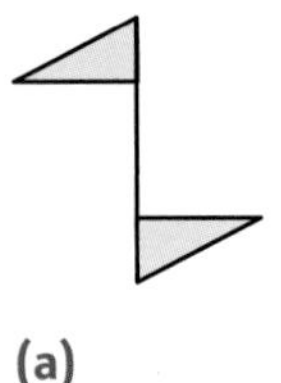

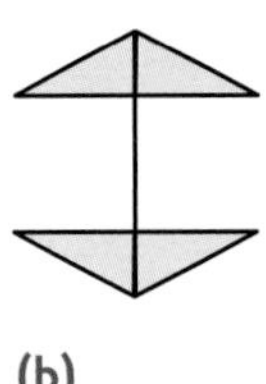

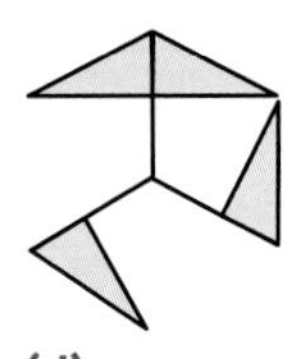

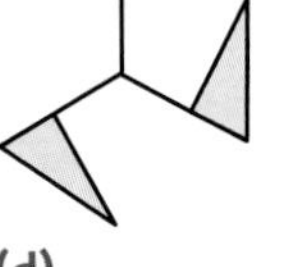

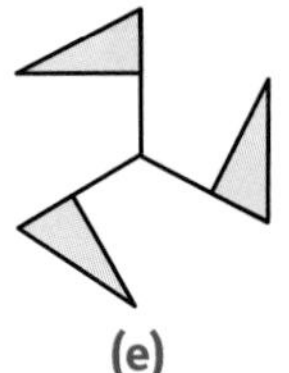

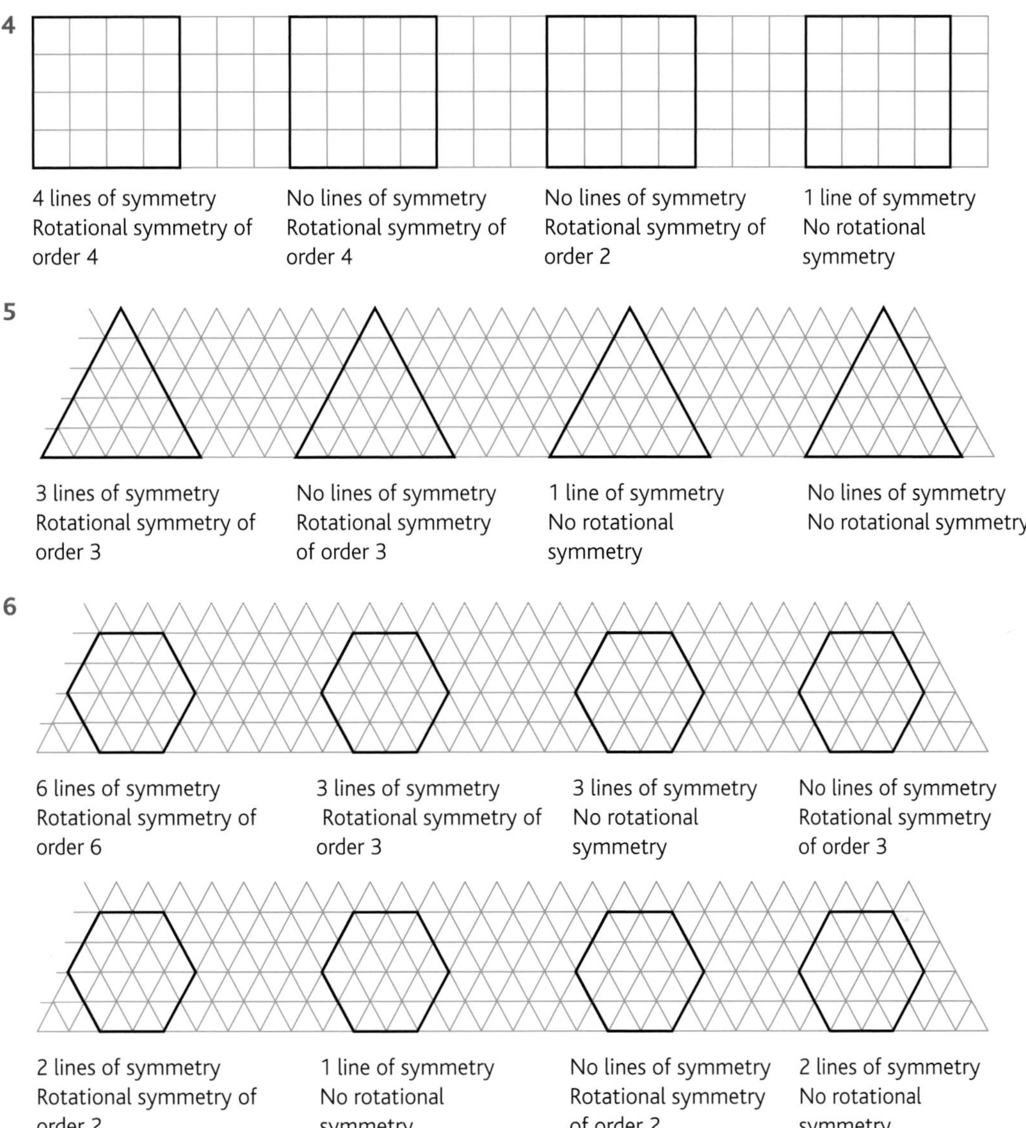

4

4 lines of symmetry
Rotational symmetry of order 4

No lines of symmetry
Rotational symmetry of order 4

No lines of symmetry
Rotational symmetry of order 2

1 line of symmetry
No rotational symmetry

5

3 lines of symmetry
Rotational symmetry of order 3

No lines of symmetry
Rotational symmetry of order 3

1 line of symmetry
No rotational symmetry

No lines of symmetry
No rotational symmetry

6

6 lines of symmetry
Rotational symmetry of order 6

3 lines of symmetry
Rotational symmetry of order 3

3 lines of symmetry
No rotational symmetry

No lines of symmetry
Rotational symmetry of order 3

2 lines of symmetry
Rotational symmetry of order 2

1 line of symmetry
No rotational symmetry

No lines of symmetry
Rotational symmetry of order 2

2 lines of symmetry
No rotational symmetry

Translations

A **translation** is a transformation that does not change the shape or orientation of an object but just moves it. A translation needs to be described in terms of moves in two directions, **horizontal** and **vertical**.

As with Cartesian coordinates, the horizontal movement (x-direction) is written first. A movement to the right is positive and a movement to the left is negative.

The vertical movement (y-direction) is written second. A movement up is positive and a movement down is negative.

This grid shows a movement of 5 units right and 2 units up. The arrow shows the direction of movement.

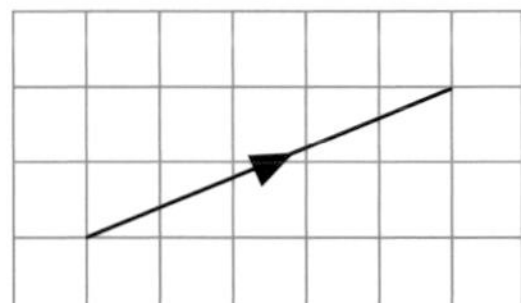

When a shape is transformed by a translation the whole object moves. This movement can be thought of as the result of a horizontal movement followed by a vertical movement. In this diagram, triangle *PQR* is mapped onto the triangle *P'Q'R'* by a translation of 9 units right and 2 units up.

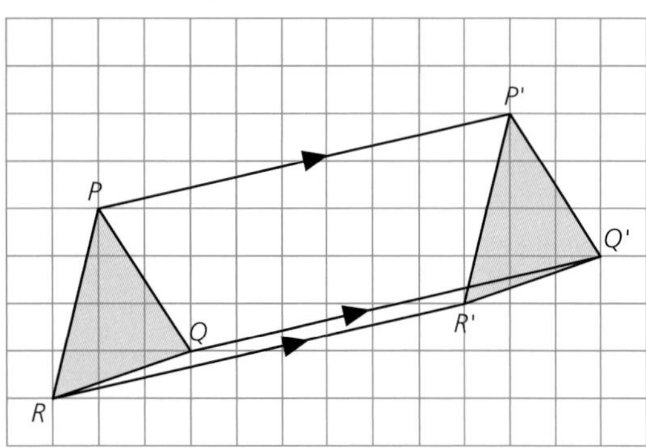

Exercise 17.4

You will need centimetre-squared paper for this exercise.

1 Copy this diagram.

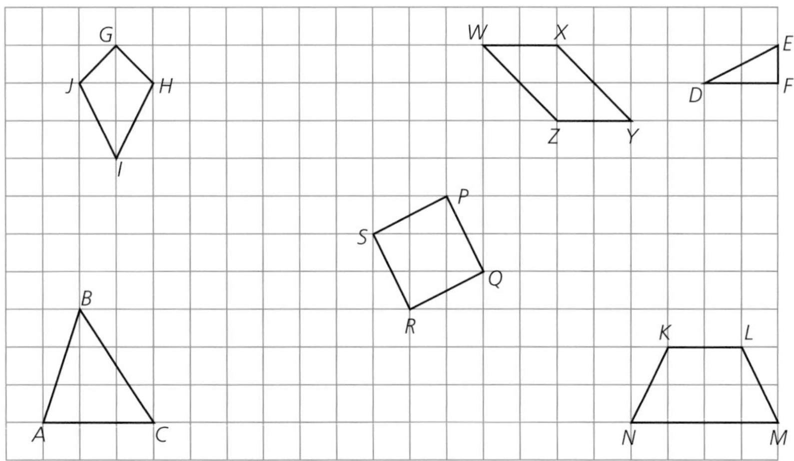

(a) Draw the image of triangle *ABC* after a translation of 3 units right and 5 units up.

(b) Draw the image of quadrilateral *PQRS* after a translation of 4 units left and 2 units down.

(c) Draw the image of *GHIJ* after a translation of 4 units right.

(d) Draw the image of triangle *DEF* after a translation of 2 units down.

(e) Draw the image of parallelogram *WXYZ* after a translation of 3 units left and 1 unit down.

(f) Draw the image of *KLMN* after a translation of 4 units left and 2 units up.

2 (a) Draw a set of co-ordinate axes with values of x and y from $^{-}6$ to 6. Draw triangle A with vertices at ($^{-}4$, 5), ($^{-}2$, 3) and ($^{-}5$, 1)

(b) Draw the image of A after a translation of 6 units right and 4 units down. Label the image B and write down the coordinates.

(c) Draw the image of B after a translation of 4 units left and 2 units up. Label the image C and write down the coordinates of its vertices.

(d) Write down the translation that will map C on to A.

3 Without drawing, write down the co-ordinates of the image of these points after the translation.

(a) $A(^{-}1, 3)$ to A' by a translation of 2 units right and 3 units up.

(b) $B(0, ^{-}3)$ to B' by a translation of 2 units left and 4 units up.

(c) $C(2, 4)$ to C' by a translation of 3 units left and 5 units down.

(d) $D(^{-}1, ^{-}2)$ to D' by a translation of 2 units left and 5 units up

(e) $E(^{-}4, 0)$ to E' by a translation of 6 units right and 5 units down

Enlargements

An **enlargement** changes the size of the object and thus its position, but its shape stays the same. The object and image are mathematically **similar**.

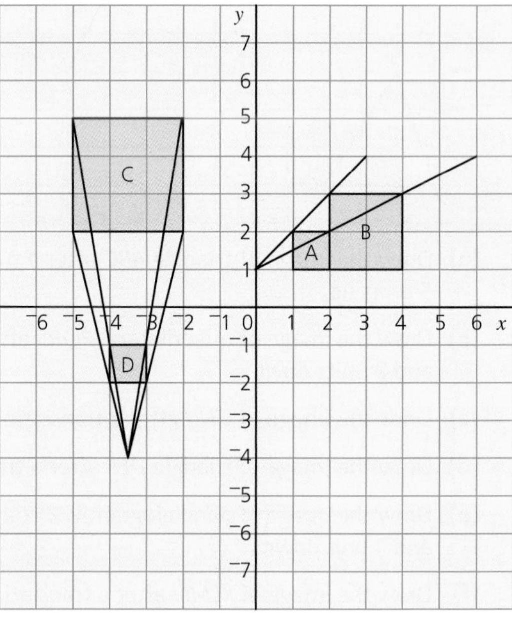

The enlargements that you have produced so far all had **scale factors** that were positive whole numbers. Now you will look at enlargements that have **fractional scale factors**.

However scale factors can be negative and they can be less than one.

Look at this diagram.

You should see that B is the enlargement of A by a scale factor 2 and centre of enlargement (0, 1)

But each side of A is half the length of the corresponding side of B.

A is the enlargement of B by a scale factor $\frac{1}{2}$ and centre of enlargement (0, 1)

You should see that C is the enlargement of D by a scale factor 3 and

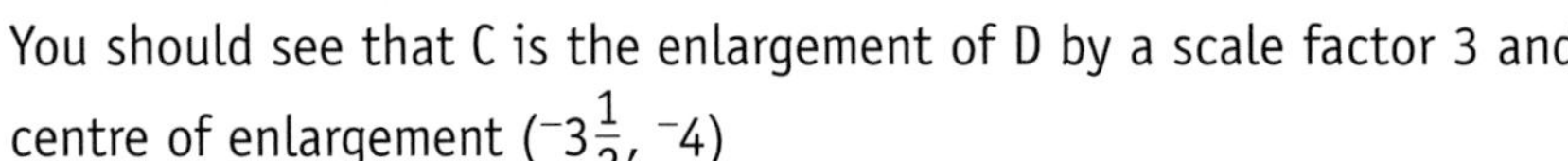
centre of enlargement $(^{-}3\frac{1}{2}, ^{-}4)$

Each side of D is a third the length of the corresponding side of C.

D is the enlargement of C by a scale factor $\frac{1}{3}$ and centre of enlargement $(^{-}3\frac{1}{2}, ^{-}4)$

A fractional scale factor less than 1 means that the lengths in the image are reduced.

Note that even though this is the case, the transformation is still called an enlargement.

Exercise 17.5

You will need squared paper and may need tracing paper for this exercise.

For each question, draw a set of co-ordinate axes with values of x and y from $^-6$ to 6

For question1–4, copy object *ABCD* and its image *A′B′C′D′* (or use tracing paper) and join the corresponding vertices. Hence find the centre of enlargement and the scale factor.

1

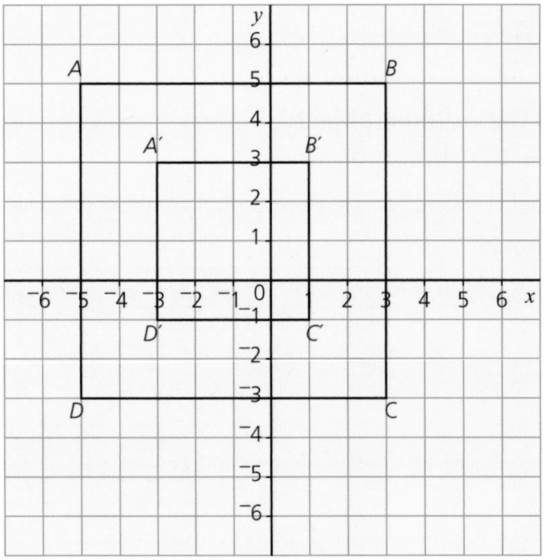

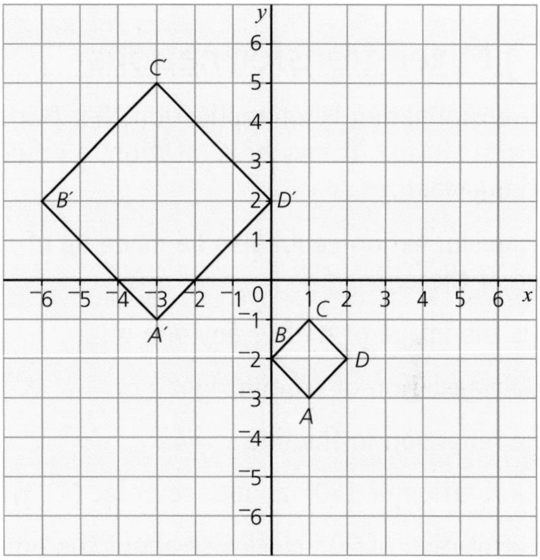

2

3

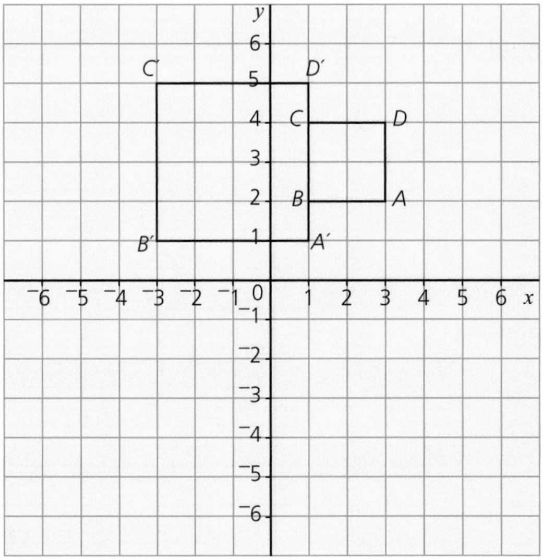

4

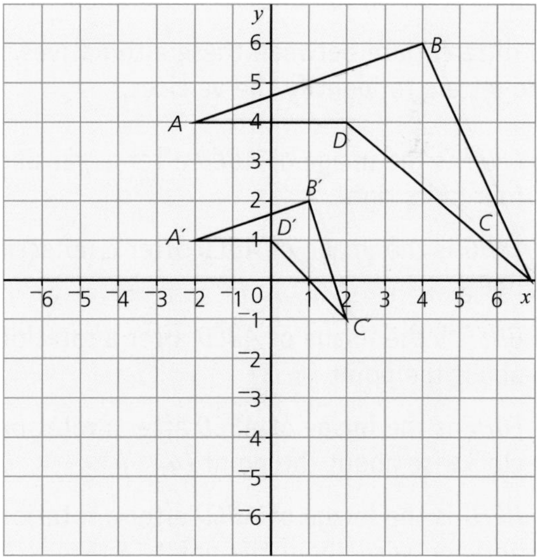

5 On your co-ordinate grid, draw *ABCD* with vertices *A*(2, 3), *B*(3, 2), *C*(3, 1) and *D*(2, 1) Draw *A′B′C′D′*, the enlargement of *ABCD* by scale factor 2 and centre of enlargement (0, 0)

6 On your co-ordinate grid, draw *ABCD* with vertices *A*(1, 3), *B*(3, 3), *C*(3, 1) and *D*(1, 1) Draw *A′B′C′D′*, the enlargement of *ABCD* by scale factor 3 and centre of enlargement (3, 3)

7 On your co-ordinate grid, draw *ABCD* with vertices *A*(2, 6), *B*(6, 6), *C*(6, 2) and *D*(2, 2) Draw *A′B′C′D′*, the enlargement of *ABCD* by scale factor $\frac{1}{2}$ and centre of enlargement ($^-2$, $^-2$)

8 On your co-ordinate grid, draw *ABCD* with vertices *A*($^-3$, 6), *B*($^-6$, 3), *C*($^-3$, $^-3$) and *D*(0, 3). Draw *A′B′C′D′*, the enlargement of *ABCD* by scale factor $\frac{1}{3}$ and centre of enlargement ($^-3$, $^-3$)

Mixed transformations

A transformation is an application that transforms the original object onto its image. It may be a rotation, a reflection, a translation or an enlargement.

A transformation could also be made up of more than one of these.

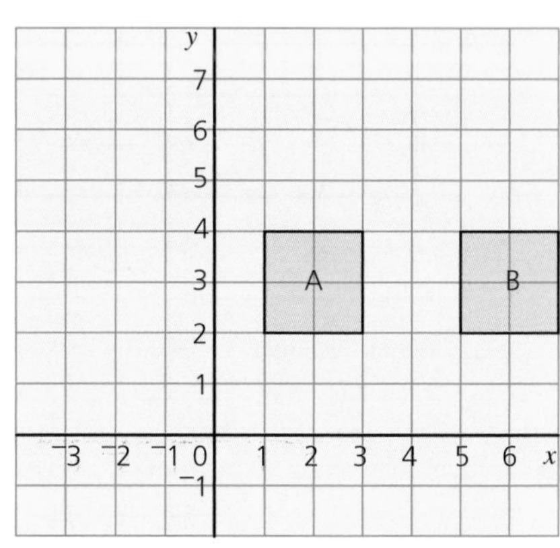

B is the image of A after any one of:

- a translation of 4 units right
- a reflection in the line $x = 4$
- a rotation of 180° about the point (4, 3)
- a rotation of 90° clockwise about the point (4, 1)
- a rotation of 90° anticlockwise about the point (4, 5)

To differentiate between these alternatives, you could add letters to identify the vertices.

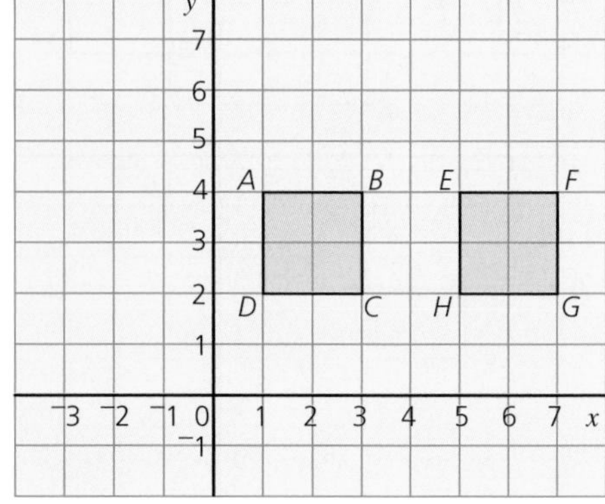

- *EFGH* is the image of *ABCD* after a translation by four units right.
- *FEHG* is the image of *ABCD* after a reflection in the line $x = 4$
- *GHEF* is the image of *ABCD* after a rotation of 180° about the point (4, 3)
- *FGHE* is the image of *ABCD* after a rotation of 90° clockwise about the point (4, 1)
- *HEFG* is the image of *ABCD* after a rotation of 90° anticlockwise about the point (4, 5)

The order of the letters is important. Compare the last three examples.

In the first rotation $A \to G$, $B \to H$, $C \to E$ and $D \to F$

In the second rotation $A \to F$, $B \to G$, $C \to H$ and $D \to E$

In the third rotation $A \to H$, $B \to E$, $C \to F$ and $D \to G$

Note the description of each transformation. It is important to describe these in full, taking care not to miss out any piece of information.

A reflection *in* a *line*

A translation *by units right/left and then up/down.*

An enlargement *by scale factor* and *centre of enlargement*

A rotation *through* an *angle*, *clockwise* or *anticlockwise*, *about* a *point.*

Exercise 17.6

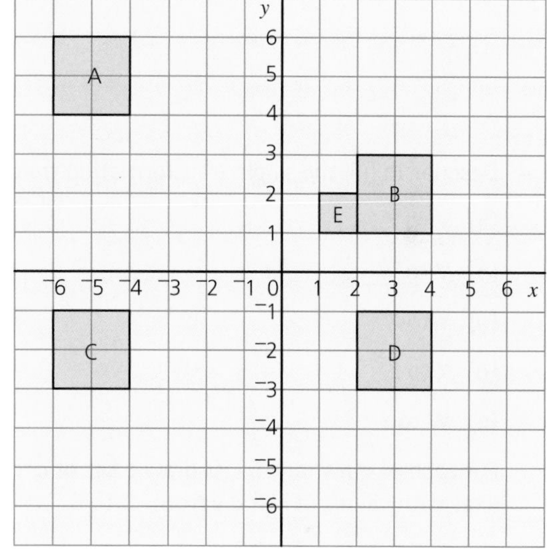

1 **(a)** Describe the reflection that maps A to C

(b) Describe the rotation that maps C to D

(c) Describe the translation that maps A to B

(d) Describe the enlargement that maps E to B

(e) Describe the enlargement that maps B to E

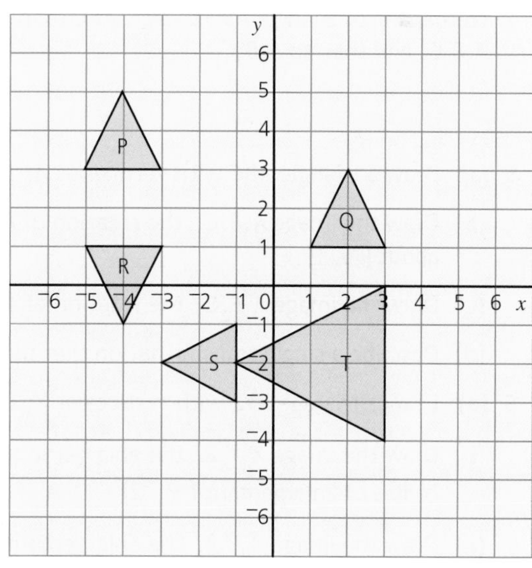

2 Describe as many single transformations as you can to map:

(a) P to R

(b) Q to P

(c) R to S

(d) S to T

(e) S to Q

3 Describe as many single transformations as you can to map:

(a) C to D

(b) B to D

(c) A to B

(d) B to A

(e) C to F

(f) D to E

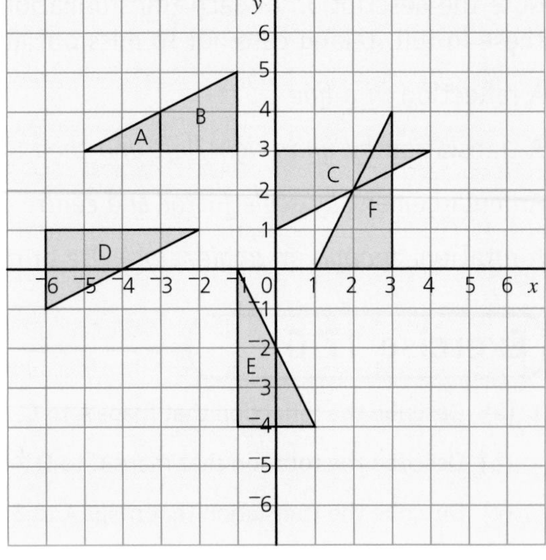

4 Describe in full the single transformation that maps:

(a) V to Y

(b) V to W

(c) Y to X

(d) Y to Z

(e) W to Y

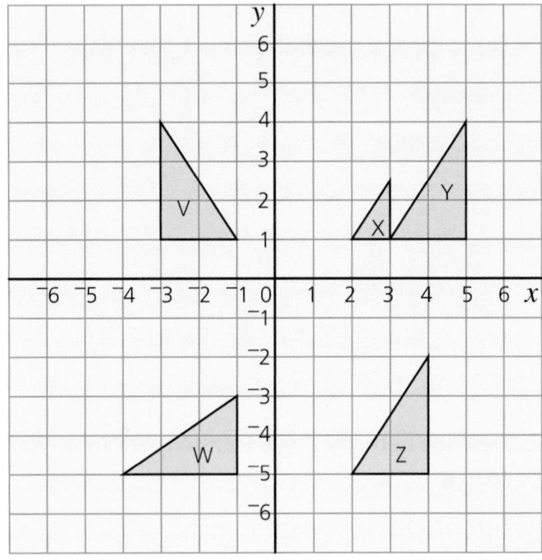

For each of questions 5–10, draw a set of coordinate axes with values of *x* and *y* from ⁻6 to 6

In these questions instead of shape A mapping on to shape B, or triangle *ABC* to *DEF*, *ABC* maps on to $A_1B_1C_1$ and then to $A_2B_2C_2$

5 (a) Draw a triangle *ABC* with vertices at *A*(⁻5, 1), *B*(⁻3, 5) and *C*(⁻1, 2)

(b) Draw the image $A_1B_1C_1$, the rotation of *ABC* through 90° clockwise about (⁻5, 1)

(c) Draw the image $A_2B_2C_2$, the rotation of $A_1B_1C_1$ through 180° about (0, 1)

(d) Describe a single transformation that maps *ABC* onto $A_2B_2C_2$

6 (a) Draw a triangle *XYZ* with vertices at *X*(⁻3, ⁻2), *Y*(⁻2, ⁻4) and *Z*(⁻4, ⁻4)

(b) Draw the image $X_1Y_1Z_1$, the enlargement of *XYZ* by scale factor 2 and centre of enlargement (⁻6, ⁻2)

(c) Draw the image $X_2Y_2Z_2$, the enlargement of *XYZ* by scale factor 2 and centre of enlargement (⁻3, ⁻5)

(d) Describe a single transformation that maps $X_1Y_1Z_1$ onto $X_2Y_2Z_2$

7 (a) Draw a rhombus *PQRS* with vertices at $P(4, 5)$, $Q(6, 2)$, $R(4, {}^{-}1)$ and $S(2, 2)$

(b) Draw the image $P_1Q_1R_1S_1$, the rotation of *PQRS* through 90° anticlockwise about (4, −3)

(c) Draw the image $P_2Q_2R_2S_2$, the reflection of $P_1Q_1R_1S_1$ in the line $y = {}^{-}x$

(d) Describe a single transformation that maps *PQRS* onto $P_2S_2R_2Q_2$

8 (a) Draw a kite *ABCD* with vertices at $A({}^{-}5, 2)$, $B({}^{-}3, 4)$, $C(1, 2)$ and $D({}^{-}3, 0)$

(b) Draw the image $A_1B_1C_1D_1$, the reflection of *ABCD* in the line $y = x$

(c) Draw the image $A_2B_2C_2D_2$, the rotation of *ABCD* through 90° clockwise about (⁻3, 0)

(d) Describe a single transformation such that $A_1B_1C_1D_1$ maps onto $A_2D_2C_2B_2$

9 (a) Draw a square *KLMN* with vertices at $K(3, 3)$, $L(4, 2)$, $M(3, 1)$ and $N(2, 2)$

(b) Draw the image $K_1L_1M_1N_1$, the enlargement of *KLMN* by scale factor 2 and centre of enlargement (1, 2)

(c) Draw the image $K_2L_2M_2N_2$, the translation of $K_1L_1M_1N_1$ by a translation of 4 units left and 2 units down.

(d) Describe a single transformation that maps $K_2L_2M_2N_2$ onto *KLMN*

10 (a) Draw a triangle *XYZ* with vertices at $X({}^{-}2, 0)$, $Y({}^{-}1, 2)$ and $Z(1, 0)$

(b) Draw the image $X_1Y_1Z_1$, the enlargement of *XYZ* by scale factor 3 and centre of enlargement (⁻1, 1)

(c) Draw the image $X_2Y_2Z_2$, the translation by 4 units down of *XYZ*

(d) Describe a single transformation that maps $X_2Y_2Z_2$, onto $X_1Y_1Z_1$

Finding a general rule for a transformation

When you were looking at translations, you probably realised that there is a simple rule to find the image of a point $P(a, b)$ after a translation by of a units right and b units up.

The image will be the point $P'(a + a, b + b) = P'(2a, 2b)$

Extension Exercise 17.7

On a set of co-ordinate axes with values of x and y from ⁻6 to 6, draw triangle A with vertices at (4, 5), (5, 1) and (1, 2)

On another set of co-ordinate axes with values of x and y from ⁻6 to 6, draw triangle B with vertices at (⁻5, 4), (⁻5, 1) and (⁻2, 2)

For each question draw the image of each triangle (A and B) after the transformation.

1 A reflection in the x-axis Label the images A_1 and B_1

2 A reflection in the y-axis Label the images A_2 and B_2

3 A reflection in the line $y = x$ Label the images A_3 and B_3

4 A reflection in the line $y = {}^{-}x$ Label the images A_4 and B_4

Copy and complete this table for your first transformation, a reflection in the x-axis, for both triangles A and B.

A	A_1	B	B_1
(4, 5)		(⁻5, 4)	
(5, 1)		(⁻5, 1)	
(1, 2)		(⁻2, 2)	
(a, b)		(a, b)	

By considering the co-ordinates of each image, you should be able to write down the co-ordinates of P' the image of any point $P(x, y)$ after a reflection in the x-axis.

Now make appropriate tables and find a rule for the transformations in questions 2, 3 and 4

Now make clean drawings of triangles A and B and try to find the rule for these.

5 A rotation through 90° clockwise about the origin

6 A rotation through 180° about the origin

7 A rotation through 270° clockwise about the origin

8 A rotation through 90° anticlockwise about the origin

9 An enlargement of scale factor 2 and centre of enlargement (0, 0)

10 Now investigate some further transformations. Try to find any other rules. Here are some you might consider.

(a) A reflection in the line $x = 3$

(b) A reflection in the line $y = 2x + 1$

(c) A rotation through 90° clockwise about (1, 1)

(d) A rotation through 180° about (2, 1)

(e) An enlargement of scale factor 2 and centre of enlargement (1, ⁻1)

Summary Exercise 17.8

1 Copy these shapes and the lines of symmetry. Construct the three reflections so that each resulting pattern has two lines of symmetry.

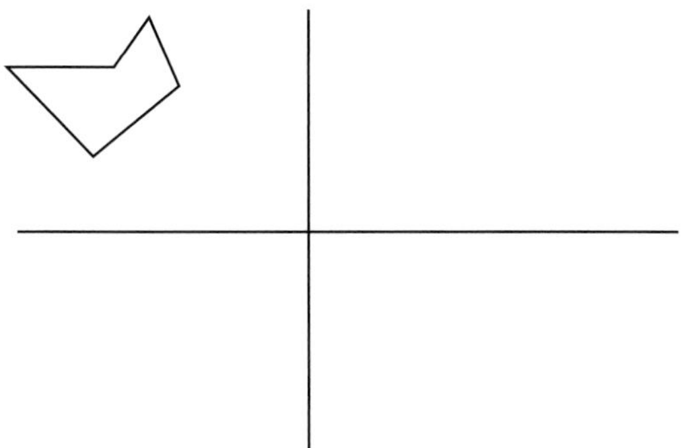

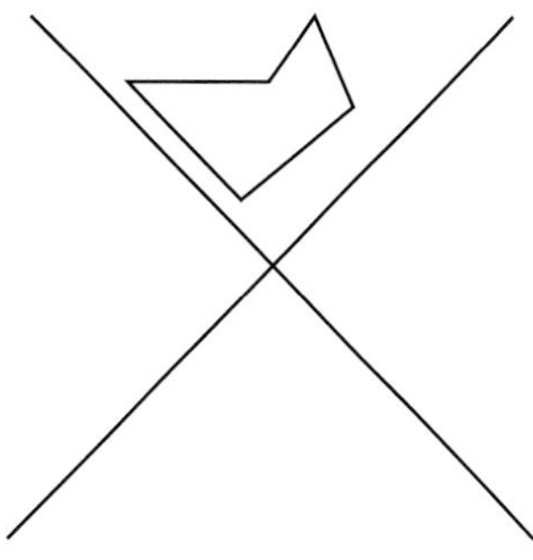

2 Copy this diagram and draw the image of the shape after:

(a) a rotation of 60° clockwise about point P

(b) a rotation of 120° clockwise about P

(c) a rotation of 60° anticlockwise about P

3 (a) Write down the order of rotational symmetry for each of these shapes.

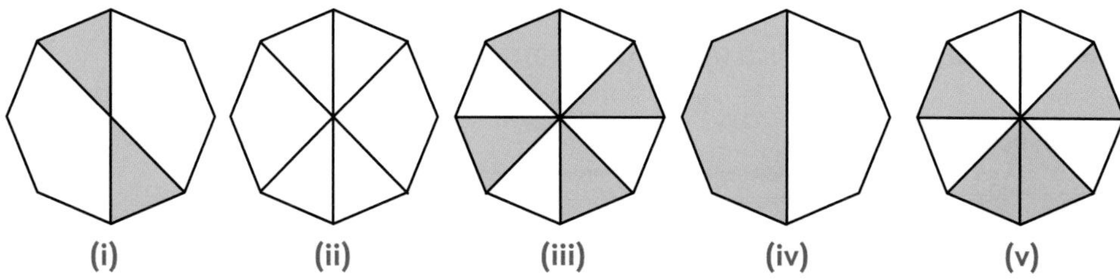

(b) Write down the number of lines of symmetry in each shape.

(c) Draw a sixth octagon with rotational symmetry of order 2 but no lines of symmetry.

4 Describe in full the transformation that maps:

(a) *ABCD* onto *EFGH*

(b) *ABCD* onto *GHEF*

(c) *ABCD* onto *GFEH*

(d) *RSPQ* onto *CDAB*

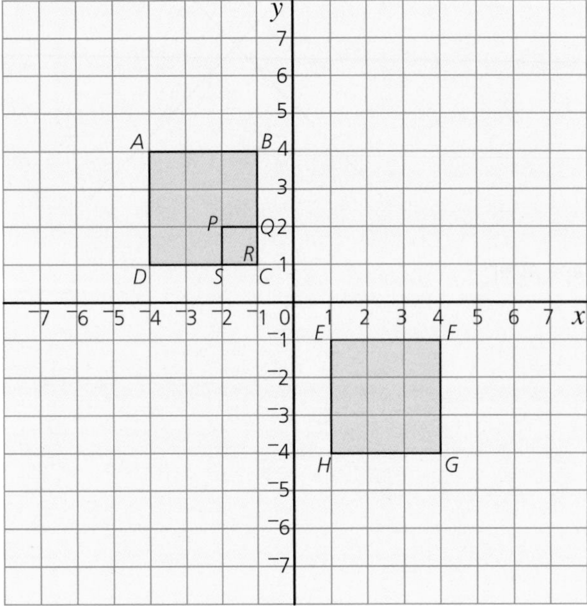

5 On a set of co-ordinate axes with values of x and y from $^-6$ to 6, draw the kite *ABCD*, which has vertices $A(1, 3)$, $B(3, 4)$, $C(4, 3)$ and $D(3, 2)$

(a) Draw the image $A_1B_1C_1D_1$, the reflection of *ABCD* in the line $y = {}^-x$

(b) Draw the image $A_2B_2C_2D_2$, the rotation of *ABCD* through 90° clockwise about the point (0, 2)

(c) Describe the single transformation such that $A_1B_1C_1D_1$ maps to $A_2D_2C_2B_2$

Activity: Hexaflexagons

A hexaflexagon is a paper hexagon made from a strip of paper. When you flex the hexaflexagon the faces change, just like magic!

This is how you make the simplest hexaflexagon.

Step 1 Construct an equilateral triangle with sides of four centimetres. Now add to it so you have a row of 10 triangles and colour them like the strip below:

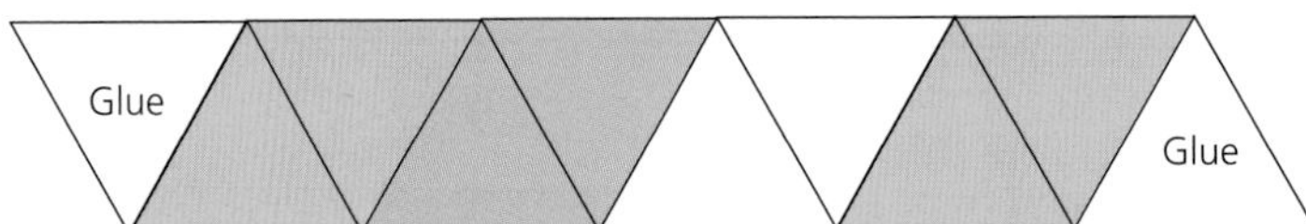

Step 2 Turn the strip over and colour the other side like this.

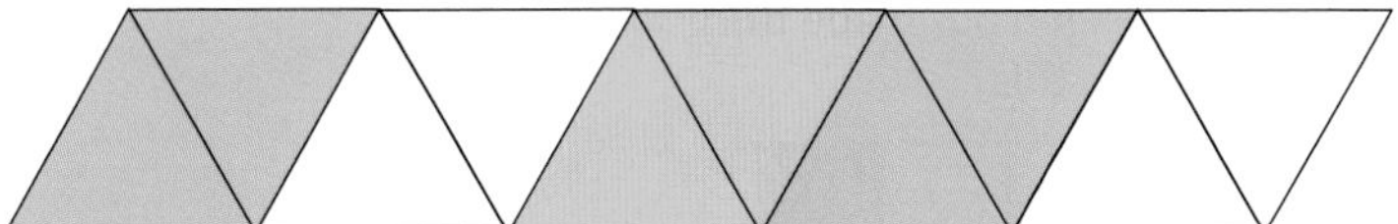

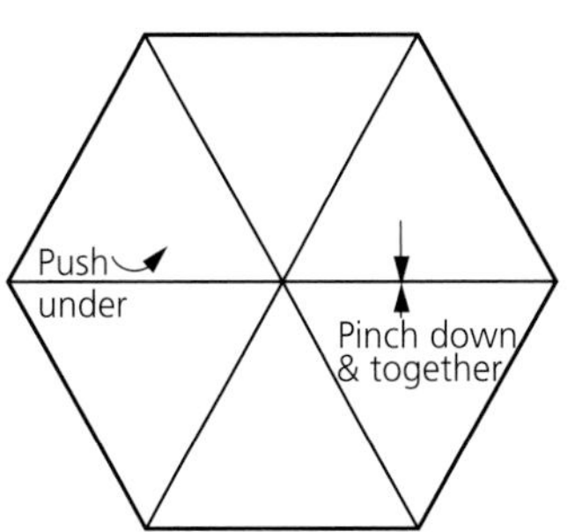

Step 3 Now fold the strip along the lines so that each pair of coloured triangles lies on top of each other. Glue together the two triangles marked Glue. You will now have a pink hexagon on one side and a white hexagon on the other.

Pinch together and down two adjacent triangular sections with a crack between them. Push the opposite corner under and down. Then, open the flexagon from the centre.

Your light green hexagon will now appear!

Now you have made your first flexagon you can go on to make a hexahexaflexagon. This is made from a row of 19 triangles. Colour it like pattern A below, then fold it as in diagrams B, C, and D below and on the next page.

A

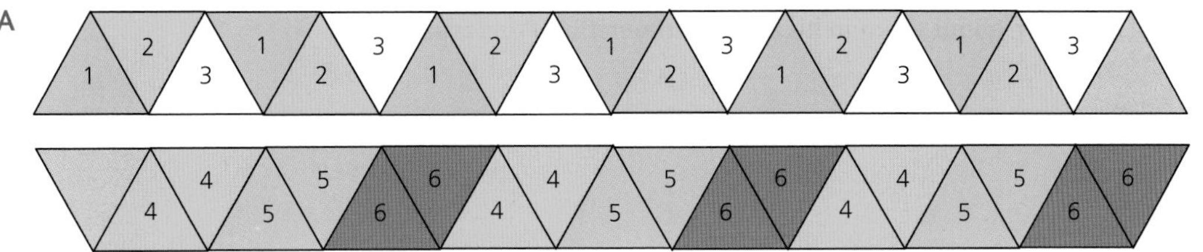

B

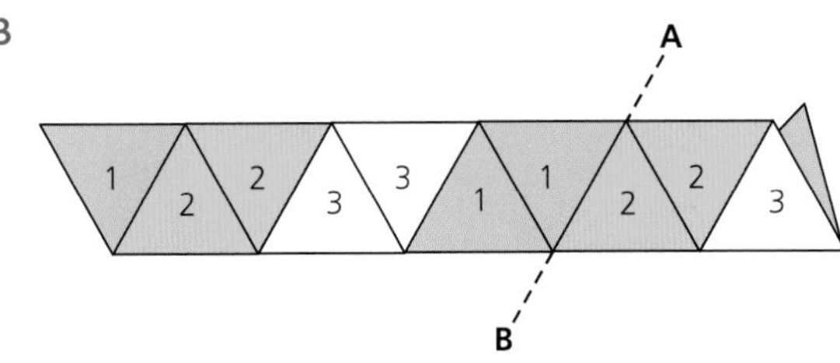

C

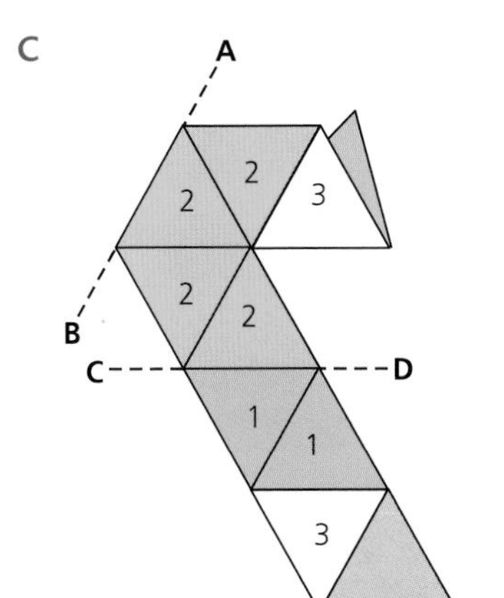

D

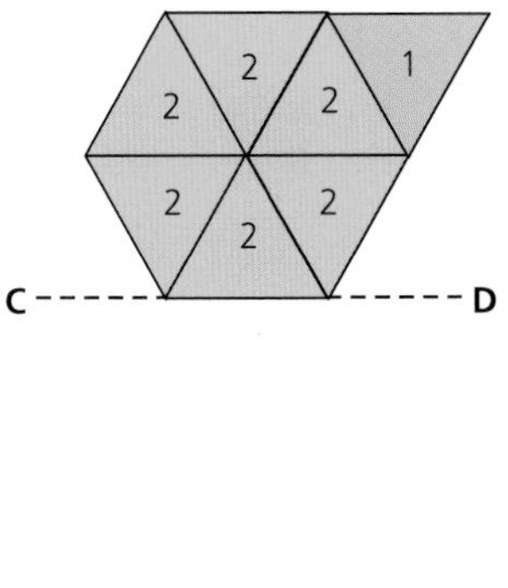

The flexagon flexes just as before. See if you can find all six coloured faces.

The tritetraflexagon

The tritetraflexagon is a variation on a hexaflexagon but made from squares. It is folded from a strip of seven squares of paper like this.

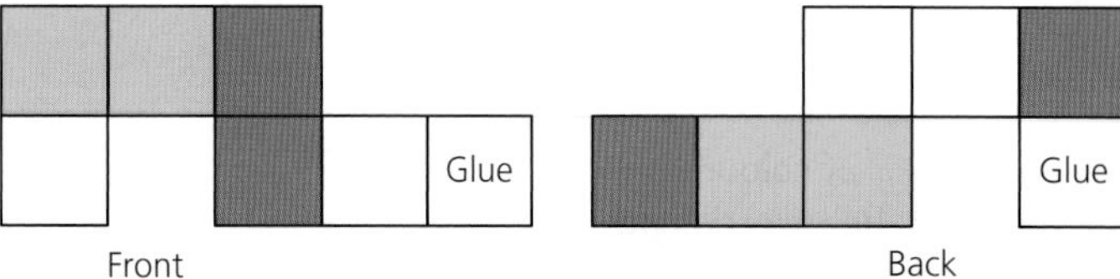

Fold this so that all the white squares are hidden. Then glue the two marked squares together. Now you have a square that is green on one side and pink on the other. To find the white square fold the green square in half on one centre line and then open it up again from the pink side.

Hexaflexagons have been used by mathematicians to send each other secret pictures or notes, or even love letters! They were invented in 1939 when an English student at Princeton University called Arthur H. Stone trimmed an inch from the sheets in his American notebook to fit his English binder. After folding the trimmed-off strips for amusement, he came upon the first hexaflexagon. Martin Gardner wrote about hexaflexagons for the magazine *Scientific American* and you can find out more about them in his book *Mathematical Puzzles and Diversions*.

Ratio and proportion

Ratio

You already know some applications of ratio. They are commonly used for mixing ingredients in recipes and when considering patterns.

Sometimes you consider only the parts of a ratio and sometimes you need to consider the total quantity.

Examples

(i) A necklace is made with red beads and white beads in the ratio 5 : 3
If 20 red beads are used, how many white beads are needed?

Ratio red : white = 5 : 3 $\qquad$ (× 4 as 5 × 4 = 20)
= 20 : 12

(ii) Another necklace used red beads and blue beads in the ratio 5 : 4
If 108 beads are used in total, how many are red and how many are blue?

Ratio red : blue : total = 5 : 4 : 9 $\qquad$ (× 12 as 9 × 12 = 108)
= 60 : 48 : 108

Ratio as a fraction

The earlier examples were solved by means of a scale factor.

You could also solve them by using fractions.

If a pattern comprises red : white in the ratio 5 : 3, then the amount of red in the pattern will be $\frac{5}{8}$ of the total and the amount of white will be $\frac{3}{8}$ of the total.

Example

A summer drink is made by mixing ginger beer and orange juice in the ration 2 : 7
How much ginger beer and orange juice will I need to fill a 3.6 litre jug of the drink?

Ginger beer $= \frac{2}{9}$ of 3.6
$= 0.8$ litres

Orange juice $= \frac{7}{9}$ of 3.6
$= 2.8$ litres

Check: $0.8 + 2.8 = 3.6$

Ratio and algebra

You are now familiar with using algebra to solve many types of problem. You can treat a missing quantity in a ratio as an unknown, form an equation and solve it. Such equations will generally use fractions.

Examples

(i) The ratio of concentrate to water in a fertiliser is 1 : 7
How much concentrate will I need to make up a total of 4 litres of fertiliser?

Let the number of litres of concentrate be x

$$\frac{1}{8} = \frac{x}{4} \qquad (\times 4)$$

$$x = \frac{4}{8}$$

$$= \frac{1}{2}$$

I will need $\frac{1}{2}$ litre of concentrate.

(ii) The ratio of boys to girls in my class is 5 : 3
If there are four more boys than girls, how many pupils are there in the class?

Let the number of pupils in the class be x

The number of boys $= \frac{5x}{8}$ and the number of girls $= \frac{3x}{8}$

$$\frac{5x}{8} - \frac{3x}{8} = 4$$

$$\frac{2x}{8} = 4 \qquad (\times 8, \div 2)$$

$$x = 16$$

Exercise 18.1

Choose the most appropriate method to solve each problem.

1 Some necklaces are made from pink and blue beads arranged in the ratio 3 : 7

(a) There are 15 pink beads in a necklace. How many blue beads are there?

(b) Another necklace uses a total of 80 beads. How many pink beads and how many blue beads are there in the necklace?

(c) My necklace has 12 more blue beads than pink beads. How many beads are there in the necklace?

2 In our school the ratio of teachers to pupils is 1 : 15

(a) There are 18 teachers. How many pupils are there?

(b) If all the pupils and all the teachers sit down to lunch together, how many chairs will they need?

3 In our school the ratio of teachers to pupils is 1 : 11
There are 150 more pupils than teachers. How many teachers are there?

4 At the end of the season the ratio of a football team's results of wins : draws : losses is 5 : 3 : 1

(a) They won 20 games. How many did they lose?

(b) How many games did they play?

5 On a school trip, the ratio of teachers to pupils must be 1 : 8 and they are travelling on a bus that has 55 seats. What is the maximum number of pupils that can go on the trip?

6 I am mixing a fruit cocktail of pineapple juice, apple juice and cranberry juice in the ratio 4 : 3 : 2

(a) How much of each ingredient will I need to fill a 4.5 litre container?

(b) If I want to serve each of my 20 guests with a 450 ml glass of the cocktail, how much will I need of each ingredient?

7 The angles of a pentagon are in the ratio 3 : 2 : 2 : 2 : 1
What is the smallest angle in the pentagon?

8 Normally the ratio of girls to boys in the class is 4 : 5 but today five boys are away at an interview and the ratio of girls to boys is 6 : 5
How many pupils are normally in the class?

9 One sheet of stars has gold, silver and bronze stars in the ratio 1 : 2 : 4

(a) There are 20 bronze stars on a sheet. How many gold stars are there?

(b) My housemaster needs to give out 60 silver stars. How many sheets must he order?

(c) The headmaster orders several sheets and finds that he has 150 more bronze stars than gold stars. How many sheets did he order?

10 In a recipe, I have to mix flour, butter and sugar in the ratio 3 : 1 : 2

(a) I need 750 g of the mixture; how much will I need of each ingredient?

(b) I find that I have exactly 200 g more of flour than sugar.

(i) How much mixture can I make?

(ii) How much butter will I need?

Proportion

In the questions above, the ratio is usually described as the relationship between the parts, for example, boys to girls.

Sometimes you have considered the relationship between one part and the whole, for example, a fertiliser might be made up of 10 ml of concentrate to each litre of mix. Then the **proportion** of concentrate to mix is 1 : 100

You can solve some problems on proportion in the same way as you solve problems with ratio. Sometimes you will use a multiplying factor, sometimes fractions and sometimes algebra, particularly when finding the original amount.

For other problems with proportion you may be comparing different units of measure.

You are familiar with the unitary method, in which you find the value of a unit quantity.

Example

A 4 litre bottle of fertiliser concentrate is sufficient for treating 10 hectares. How many litres must a farmer buy to treat 45 hectares?

4 litres for 10 hectares

(÷ 10)

$\frac{4}{10}$ litres for 1 hectare

(× 45)

$\frac{\cancel{4}^{2} \times \cancel{45}^{9}}{\cancel{10}_{\cancel{5}_{1}}}$ litres for 45 hectares

The farmer will need 18 litres.

You could have solved this by using algebra and fractions.

Example

A 4 litre bottle of fertiliser concentrate is sufficient for treating 10 hectares. How many litres must a farmer buy to treat 45 hectares?

Let the number of litres be x.

$$\frac{x}{45} = \frac{4}{10} \qquad (\times 45)$$

$$x = \frac{\not{4}^{2}}{\not{10}_{\not{5}_{1}}} \times \not{45}^{9}$$

$$= 18$$

The farmer will need 18 litres.

Some questions you will meet compare imperial quantities to metric quantities.

Example

If 1 kg is equivalent to 2.2 lb, what mass (in kilograms) is equivalent to 5 lb?

Let x be the equivalent, in kilograms, of 5 lb

$$\frac{1}{2.2} = \frac{x}{5} \qquad (\times 5)$$

$$\frac{5 \times 1}{2.2} = x$$

$$x = 2.2727\ldots$$

$$= 2.27 \text{ (to 2 d.p.)}$$

Exercise 18.2

Use the most appropriate method to solve these problems on proportion.

Use your calculator when necessary in this exercise. Where answers are not exact, round them to 1 decimal place unless specified otherwise.

1 I can buy 15 packets of crisps for £1.20

How many packets can I buy for £1.68?

2 Four of my hand spans measure 60 cm. How many hand spans will I need to measure 2 m?

3 A length of 13 feet is equivalent to 4 metres. What length (in feet) is equivalent to 7 metres?

4 I sell four dozen cakes for a total of £6.00

How much should I sell a pack of five cakes for?

5 To cook rice, you add two cups of rice to seven cups of water. How many cups of water will I need to cook five cups of rice?

6 Bob mixes 20 ml of concentrate with water to make 5 litres of fertiliser.

(a) How much concentrate will he need to make 20 litres of fertiliser?

(b) If 1 litre of fertiliser is enough to treat a 10 m^2 lawn, how much concentrate must he buy to treat 300 m^2 of lawn?

7 1 foot is 12 inches and is equivalent to 30.48 cm.

(a) How many inches are there in 5 metres?

(b) How metres are there in 5 feet?

(c) There are 3 feet in 1 yard. A cricket strip is 22 yards long and 10 feet wide.

(i) How long is a cricket pitch, in metres, to the nearest metre?

(ii) How wide is a cricket pitch, in metres, to the nearest centimetre?

8 A metal bar 5 m long has a mass of 30 kg. A 2 m length is cut off the bar. What is its mass?

9 Vincent needs 5 litres of paint to cover an area of 40 m^2.

(a) How many litres of paint will he need to cover 100 m^2?

(b) How many litres of paint will he need to paint a store room 6 m long, 4 m wide and 2.2 m high? There is only one door so you do not need to allow for this.

10 16 ounces is equivalent to 454 grams.

(a) A cricket ball has a mass of 5.5 ounces. What is this in grams?

(b) A tennis ball has a mass of 59 grams. What is this in ounces?

11 A factory makes 2400 crayons every four minutes.

(a) How many crayons does in make in one hour?

(b) How long does it take to make 500 crayons?

12 1 hectare is equivalent to 2.47 acres.

(a) The school is set in 40 acres of countryside. How many hectares is this?

(b) A 24 acre plot of land is sold at a cost of £300 per hectare. What is the sale price?

Area in enlargements

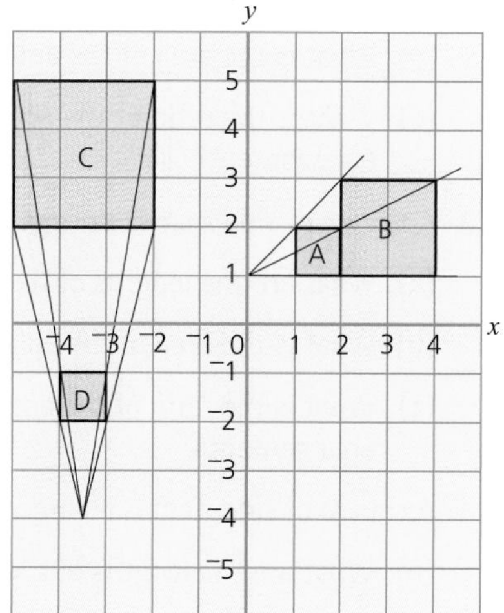

Look again at the enlargements you first saw in Chapter 17

B is the enlargement of A by a scale factor 2 with centre of enlargement (0, 1)

The area of A is 1 square unit and the area of B is 4 square units.

C is the enlargement of D by a scale factor 3 with centre of enlargement ($^-3\frac{1}{2}$, $^-4$)

The area of D is 1 square unit and the area of C is 9 square units.

The area of the image is increased by the **square of the scale factor** of the enlargement.

This is true for any enlargement.

This is a drawing of a bedroom, drawn to a scale of 1 : 100

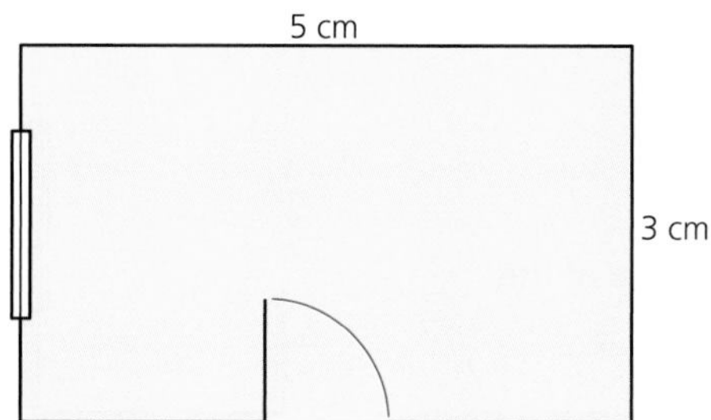

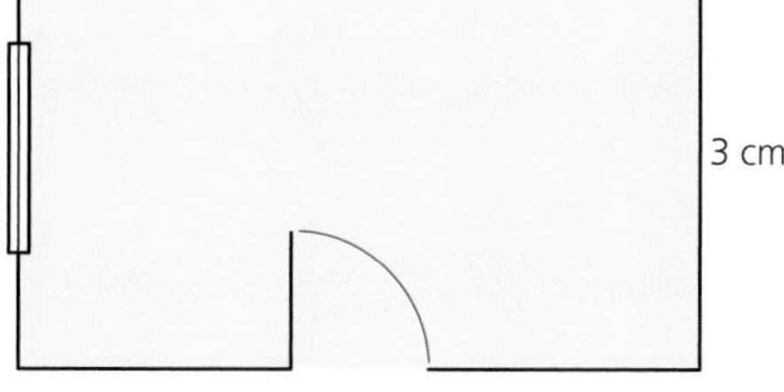

The drawing measures 5 cm by 3 cm and so has an area of 15 cm^2

The bedroom measures 5 m by 3 m (500 cm by 300 cm) and has area 15 m^2(150 000 cm^2).

The ratio of the lengths is 1 : 100

The ratio of the areas is 1 : 10 000 (100^2)

Exercise 18.3

1 A square of side 3 cm is enlarged by scale factor 2

(a) What are the lengths of the sides of the enlargement?

(b) What is the area of the enlargement?

(c) What is the ratio of the area of the original square to the area of the enlargement?

2 A square of side 4 cm is enlarged by scale factor 3

(a) What are the lengths of the sides of the enlargement?

(b) What is the area of the enlargement?

(c) What is the ratio of the area of the original square to the area of the enlargement?

3 A square of side 3 cm is enlarged by scale factor 4

(a) What are the lengths of the sides of the enlargement?

(b) What is the area of the enlargement?

(c) What is the ratio of the area of the original square to the area of the enlargement?

4 A square of side 2 cm is enlarged by scale factor of $\frac{1}{2}$

(a) What are the lengths of the sides of the enlargement?

(b) What is the area of the enlargement?

(c) What is the ratio of the area of the original square to the area of the enlargement?

5 A rectangle with sides of 3 cm and 4 cm is enlarged by scale factor 2

(a) What are the lengths of the sides of the enlarged rectangle?

(b) What is the area of the enlargement?

(c) What is the ratio of the area of the original rectangle to the area of the enlargement?

6 A rectangle with sides of 5 cm and 6 cm is enlarged by scale factor 3

(a) What are the lengths of the sides of the enlarged rectangle?

(b) What is the area of the enlargement?

(c) What is the ratio of the area of the original rectangle to the area of the enlargement?

7 A triangle of base 8 cm and height 5 cm is enlarged by scale factor 3

(a) What is the base and the height of the enlarged triangle?

(b) What is the area of the enlargement?

(c) What is the ratio of the area of the original triangle to the area of the enlargement?

8 A right-angled triangle with perpendicular sides of lengths 6 cm and 8 cm is enlarged by scale factor 4

(a) What is the length of the hypotenuse of the enlargement?

(b) What is the area of the enlargement?

(c) What is the ratio of the area of the original triangle to the area of the enlargement?

9 This kite is enlarged by scale factor 4

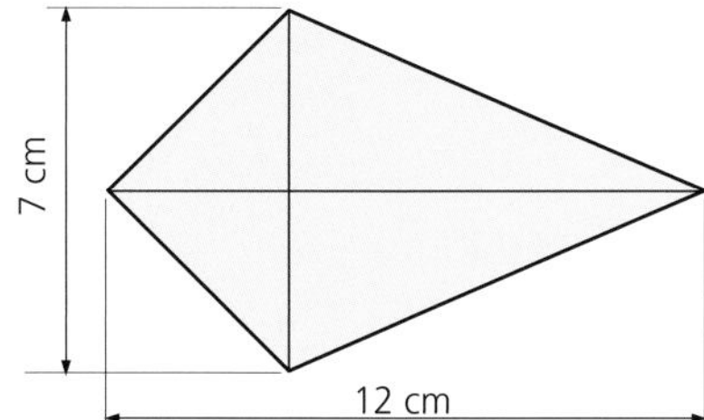

What is the area of the enlargement?

10 This trapezium is enlarged by scale factor 3

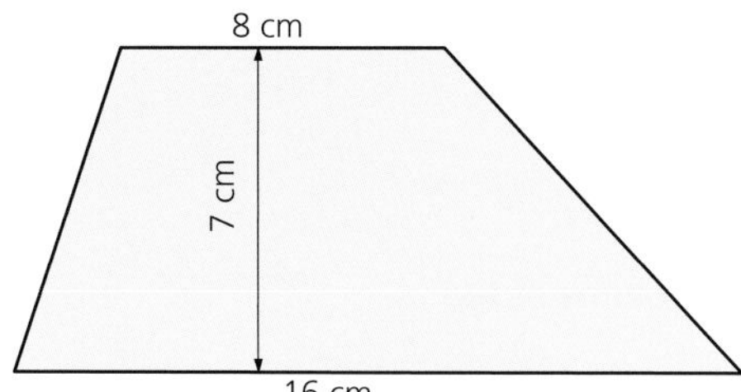

What is the area of the enlargement?

11 The ratio of the areas of two squares is 1 : 4

The smaller square has sides of length 3 cm. What are the lengths of the sides of the larger square?

12 The ratio of the areas of two squares is 1 : 9

The smaller square has sides of length 2 cm. What are the lengths of the sides of the larger square?

Volume in enlargements

Look at this cube and its enlargement by a scale factor 3

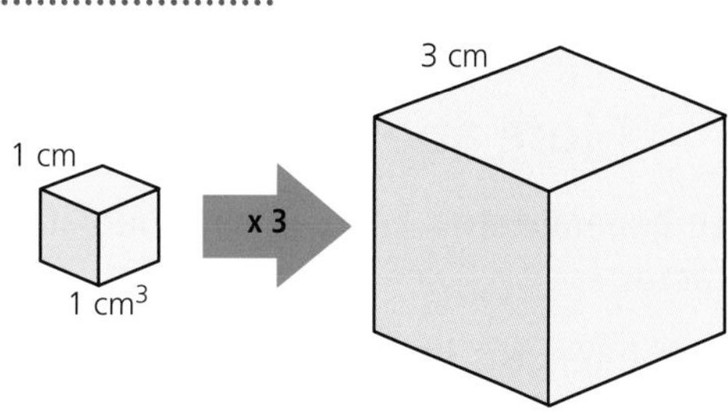

The lengths of the sides of the enlarged cube are all 3 cm

The area of each face of the enlargement is 9 cm^2

The volume of the enlargement is 27 cm^3

The ratio of the volume of the original to the volume of the enlargement is:

1 : 27 (1 : 3^3)

Exercise 18.4

1 A cube of volume 1 cm^3 is enlarged by scale factor 2

(a) What is the volume of the enlarged cube?

(b) What is the ratio of the volume of the original cube to the volume of the enlargement?

2 A cube of volume 2 cm^3 is enlarged by scale factor 2

(a) What is the volume of the enlarged cube?

(b) What is the ratio of the volume of the original cube to the volume of the enlargement?

3 A cube of edges 2 cm is enlarged by scale factor 3

(a) What is the volume of the original cube?

(b) What is the volume of the enlarged cube?

(c) What is the ratio of the volume of the original cube to the volume of the enlargement?

4 A cuboid of volume 5 cm^3 is enlarged by scale factor 3

(a) What is the volume of the enlarged cuboid?

(b) What is the ratio of the volume of the original cuboid to the volume of the enlargement?

5 A cube has been enlarged by scale factor 4

The enlarged cube has a volume of 192 cm^3. What is the volume of the original cube?

6 A cuboid has been enlarged by scale factor 2

The enlarged cuboid has a volume of 192 cm^3. What is the volume of the original cuboid?

More about area and volume

In general terms you can say that, if an object is enlarged by a scale factor k;

- the lengths in the image are enlarged by the linear scale factor k
- the area of the image is enlarged by the area scale factor k^2
- the volume of the image is enlarged by the volume scale factor k^3

Examples

(i) A square of side 4 cm is enlarged by scale factor 5. What is the area of the enlarged square?

Scale factor is $k = 5$

Area scale factor is $k^2 = 25$

$$\begin{aligned}\text{Area of image} &= 25 \times \text{area of object}\\ &= 25 \times 16\\ &= 400\end{aligned}$$

The area of the image is 400 cm^2

(ii) A model of a shed is made to a scale of $\frac{1}{20}$ of the original.

(a) If the height of the model is 12 cm, what is the height of the original?

Scale factor $k = 20$

$$\begin{aligned}\text{Height of original} &= 20 \times \text{height of model}\\ &= 20 \times 12\\ &= 240\text{ cm or }2.4\text{ m}\end{aligned}$$

The height of the original shed is 2.4 m

(b) If the volume of the original is 30 m^3, what is the volume of the model?

Volume scale factor is $k^3 = 8000$

Volume of original is $30\text{ m}^3 = 30\,000\,000\text{ cm}^3$

Volume of original is $k^3 \times$ volume of model

$$30\,000\,000 = 8000 \times \text{volume of model}$$

$$\begin{aligned}\text{Volume of model} &= \frac{30\,000\,000}{8000}\\ &= 3750\end{aligned}$$

The volume of the model is 3750 cm^3

Exercise 18.5

1 My bedroom is 3.5 m wide and 5.5 m long.

(a) Draw a plan of the bedroom to a scale of 1 : 25

(b) On your plan draw:

(i) a desk of length 1 m and width 75 cm

(ii) a bed of length 2.2 m and width 85 cm

(iii) a rug that is 1.5 m by 2 m.

2 This is a family of jugs. Each is an exact enlargement of the smallest jug.

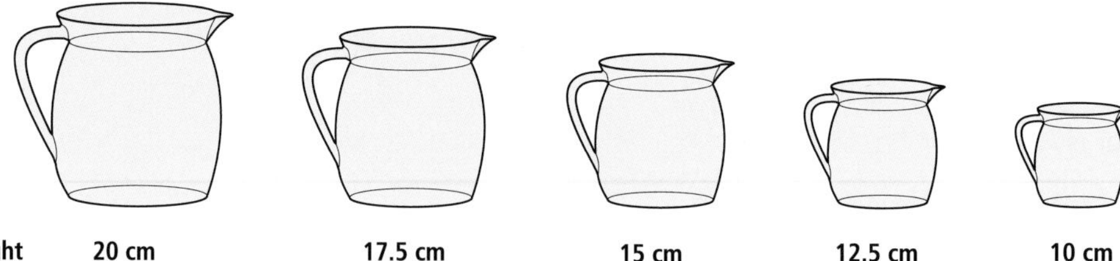

(a) The smallest jug contains 0.25 litres. What volume will each of the other jugs contain?

(b) What height of jug would have a volume of one litre?

3 I have a model of a water tower. The height of my model is exactly one hundredth of the height of the original tower.

(a) My model is 5 cm tall. How tall is the original tower?

(b) The original tower contains 250 m^3 of water. What volume of water could my model hold? Give your answer in cubic centimetres.

(c) The water tower is in the shape of a cylinder. Estimate its radius.

4 I am making a model of another water tower. The actual water tower is cylindrical and has a diameter of 10 m. It contains 200 m^3 of water. My model is being made to a scale of 1 cm to 1 m.

(a) How tall is the real water tower?

(b) How tall is my model?

(c) What will the volume of my model be?

(d) What is the curved surface area of the real water tower?

(e) What is the curved surface area of the model?

5 *Superclean* fluid comes in two sizes, a small container for domestic use and a large drum for commercial use. The large drum is an enlargement of the small drum, by a scale factor of 10

(a) The label on the large drum has an area of 45 000 cm^2. What is the area of the label on the small drum?

(b) The height of the small drum is 12 cm. What is the height of the large drum?

(c) The large drum contains 1.5 m^3. How many litres does the small drum contain?

Scale drawing

Think back to Chapter 10, where you worked on constructions and bearings. Sometimes you need to use the same ideas to draw accurate scale drawings, particularly of journeys.

Example

Two explorers set off from a base camp (*B*). Andy (*A*) goes to a point 5.5 km due east of the base camp. Charlie (*C*) goes to a point 4.5 km from the base camp on a bearing of 318°. Work out the bearing and distance of *A* from *C*.

Mark a point *B* and then, using a scale of 1 cm to 1 km, construct the relative positions of *A* and *C*.

Measure the bearing and distance of *A* from *C*.

Always start by drawing a rough sketch showing what you need to draw. Then draw a second rough sketch with the actual measurements you will draw.

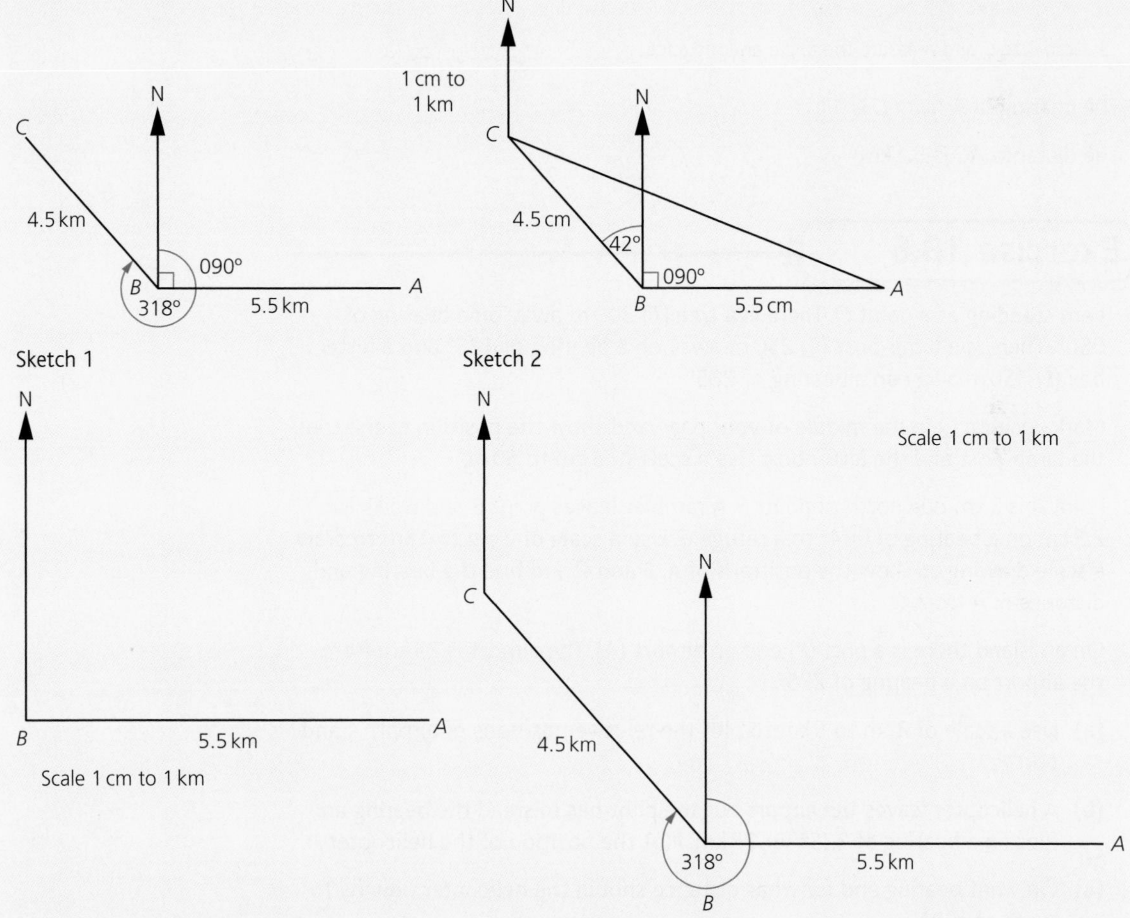

1 Mark the point *B*. Draw the north line and carefully plot the position of *A*.

2 Carefully plot the position of *C*. Label your diagram.

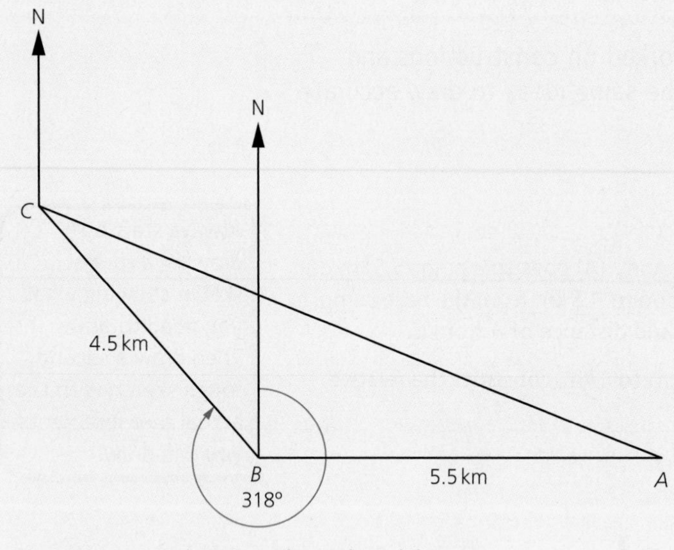

3 Join A to C and measure the angle and distance.

The bearing of A from C is 111°

The distance AC is 9.1 km

Exercise 18.6

1 I am standing at a point Q. There is a tree (T) 300 m away on a bearing of 050°. There is a lamp-post (P) 250 m away on a bearing of 125° and a letter box (L) 150 m away on a bearing of 285°

Mark position Q in the middle of your page and show the position of the tree, the lamp-post and the letter box. Use a scale of 1 cm to 50 m.

2 Point A is 3 km due north of point B. A rambler leaves point B and walks for 2.5 km on a bearing of 064° to a refuge C. Use a scale of 2 cm to 1 km to draw a scale drawing to show the positions of A, B and C and find the bearing and distance of A from C.

3 On an island there is a port (P) and an airport (A). The airport is 25 km from the airport on a bearing of 225°

(a) Use a scale of 2 cm to 5 km to plot the relative positions of airport A and port P.

(b) A helicopter leaves the airport but the pilot has misread the bearing and flies on a bearing of 325° for 25 km. Plot the position of the helicopter H.

(c) On what bearing and for what distance should the helicopter now fly to reach port P?

4 Two companies of soldiers are on patrol. A company leaves base camp *A* and marches 3500 metres on a bearing of 030° to reach the rendezvous point C.

(a) Mark point *A* to the left of your page, draw a north line and plot the position of *C*. Use a scale of 1 cm to 500 m.

B company leave camp *B*, which is 4000 m due east of camp *A*, and march for 2500 m on a bearing of 330° to a point *D*.

(b) Carefully plot the position of *B*, draw a north line and then plot the position of *D*.

(c) Measure the length on your diagram to find the bearing and distance of *D* from *C*.

5 The village of Ayton (*A*) is five miles due west of the village of Beeton (*B*). A radio mast (*R*) lies on a bearing of 046° from Ayton and a bearing of 305° from Beeton.

(a) Using a scale of 1 inch to 1 mile, plot the positions of *A*, *B* and *R*.

An engineer walks from the radio mast to the straight road joining Ayton to Beeton.

(b) By constructing a perpendicular from *R* to *AB*, show the engineer's route and measure the distance he walked.

6 A scout patrol is on an exercise. They leave their base camp *B* and walk for 1500 m on a bearing of 125°. There, they stop to eat their sandwiches. Fred says they should take the original bearing from 360° to find the way home. They work that out and walk for 1800 m before Fred decides that they are lost. Use a scale of 1 cm to 200 m to plot their positions. How far away and on what bearing is the base camp *B* from the patrol? How should Fred have worked out the correct bearing to get back to base?

7 In the grounds of mystery manor there is a stricken pine (*P*), a mausoleum (*M*) and an old statue (*S*).

The old pine is 400 m from the mausoleum on a bearing of 315°. The statue is 450 m from the mausoleum on a bearing of 043°.

(a) Plot the relative positions of *P*, *M* and *S*. Use a scale of 1 cm to 50 m.

(b) The mystery manor treasure is reported to be buried at a point equidistant from *P*, *M* and *S*. Find this point, by construction.

> You will need to find the point where the perpendicular bisectors of *PM*, *PS* and *MS* meet.

8 Blackhearted Bill's great-grandson has discovered the instructions to the pirate's buried treasure. It says that it is buried at a point that is equal in distance from the three roads on the island of Paradiso. These three roads join the villages of Lima (*L*), Mona (*M*) and Nova (*N*), with Lima lying 5 leagues to the south-south-west of Mona and Mona lying 4 leagues north-west of Nova. Using a scale of 1 cm to half a league, plot the positions of the three villages and find the place where the treasure is buried.

> You will need to construct the point where the three angle bisectors of $\angle LMN$, $\angle MNL$ and $\angle LNM$ meet.)

Extension Exercise 18.7

These questions on area and volume are not difficult, but need some thought. Use what you have learnt about proportion and ratio to solve them. Remember to set out all your working clearly.

1 Write down which of these shapes will always be in proportion, regardless of their dimensions.

(a) a pair of cones

(b) a pair of cylinders

(c) a pair of spheres

(d) a pair of square-based pyramids

(e) a pair of regular tetrahedra

2 A large metal sphere is melted down and used to make several smaller spheres. The radius of each of the smaller spheres is $\frac{1}{5}$ the radius of the original sphere. How many small spheres can be made?

3 A sphere T has a volume of V cm^3, surface area A cm^2 and radius r cm.

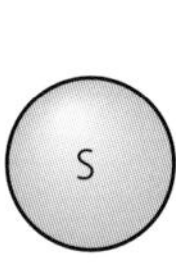

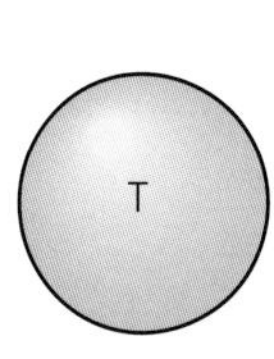

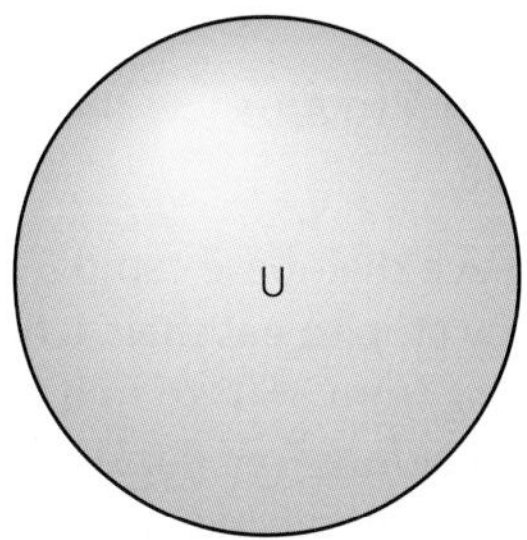

(a) What is the surface area and volume of sphere U with radius $2r$?

(b) What are the surface area and volume of sphere S with radius $\frac{2}{3}r$?

(c) **(i)** Give the ratio of the surface area of S to the surface area of U.

(ii) Give the ratio of the volume of S to the volume of U.

4 A cone is divided into three parts of equal height.

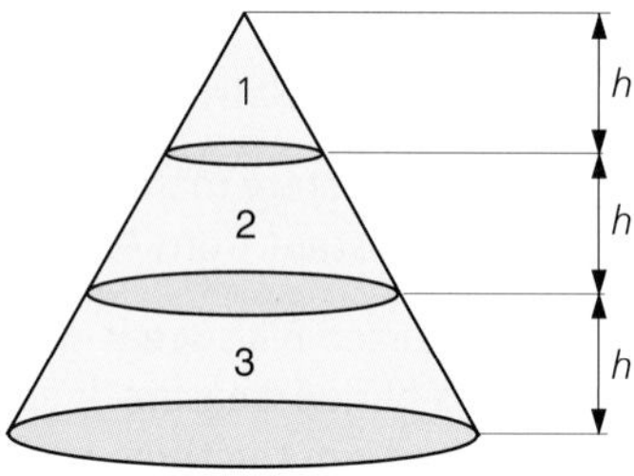

Note that the solid left behind when the top of a cone is cut off is called a **frustum**.

(a) If the area of the base of the top cone 1 is A, what is the area of the base of the whole cone?

(b) What is the ratio of the area of the base of cone 1 to the area of the base of the whole cone?

(c) Parts 1 and 2 together make a middle-sized cone.

(i) What is the area of the base of this cone?

(ii) What is the ratio of the area of base of cone 1 to the area of the base of cone 2 to the area of the base of cone 3?

(d) If the volume of the top cone 1 is V, find the volumes of the middle-sized cone and the whole cone.

(e) What is the ratio of the volume of cone 1 to the volume of cones 1 + 2 (middle-sized cone) to the volume of cones 1 + 2 + 3 (whole cone)?

(f) What is the ratio of the volume of cone 1 to the volume of cone 2 to the volume of cone 3?

5 The formula for the volume of a square-based pyramid, in which the length of the side of the base is x and the height is h is $V = \frac{1}{3}x^2h$

(a) Calculate the volume of a pyramid with a square base of side length 4 cm and height 6 cm.

(b) Write down the volume of a similar pyramid:

(i) 12 cm high

(ii) 36 cm high.

Summary Exercise 18.8

1 A square of side 2 cm is enlarged by scale factor 5

(a) What are the lengths of the sides of the enlargement?

(b) What is the area of the enlargement?

(c) What is the ratio of the area of the original square to the area of the enlargement?

2 A cube of sides 3 cm is enlarged by scale factor 2

(a) What is the volume of the original cube?

(b) What is the volume of the enlarged cube?

(c) What is the ratio of the volume of the original cube to the volume of the enlargement?

3 A cube has been enlarged by scale factor 5

The enlarged cube has a volume of 750 cm^3. What is the volume of the original cube?

4 Find the value of k and hence calculate x, y and z in this enlargement.

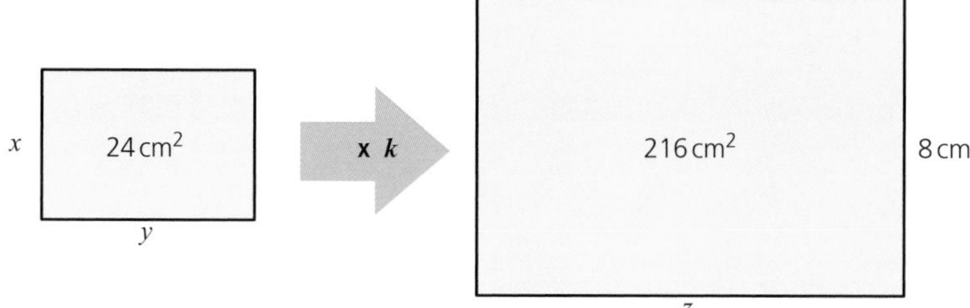

5 Suppose £10 is worth €14

(a) How many euros will I get for £25?

(b) How many pounds will I get for €40?

6 Ed the explorer walks for 3 km from the village (V) on a bearing of 058°. Then he changes direction to go round a swamp. He walks for 6 km on a bearing of 156° before camping for the night.

(a) Use a scale of 1 cm to 500 m to show Ed's journey.

Explorer Freda was waiting for Ed at a wadi (W), 5 km due east of V. In the morning she spots Ed's camp fire and goes to find him.

(b) By plotting W on your drawing, work out how far and on what bearing Freda needs to go in order to meet Ed.

7 A cone has a smaller cone cut off its tip. The small cone has height one quarter the height of the whole cone.

(a) If the smaller cone has height h cm, what is the height of the whole cone?

(b) If the small cone has a surface area of A cm^2, what is the surface area of the whole cone?

(c) Find the ratio of the volume of the small cone to volume of the original cone and hence the ratio of the volume of the small cone to the volume of the frustum.

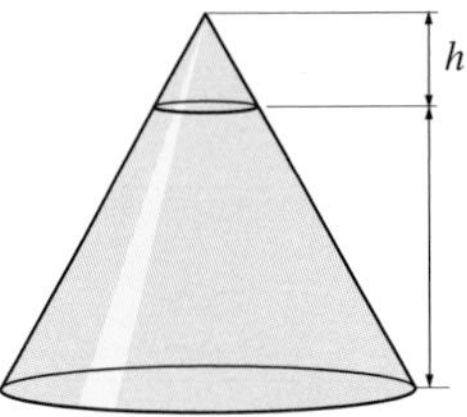

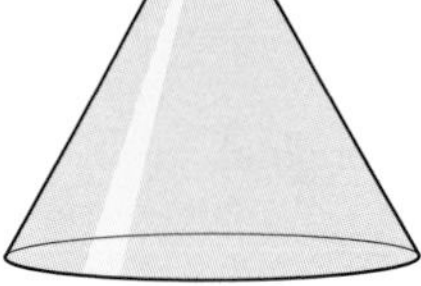

Remember that the frustum is the part that is left when you cut the top off a cone.

Activity: The golden ratio

Artists use mathematics to develop pleasing ratios for art and architecture. The most famous of these is known as the **golden ratio**. Its use by humankind dates back to at least the time of the Ancient Egyptians.

The Greeks used the golden ratio when designing and building the Parthenon. They stated the ratio as: 'The small is to the large, as the large is to the whole.'

The golden rectangle

The façade of the Parthenon is built so that the ratio of the height to the width is the same as the ratio of the width to the width plus the height – it is a **golden rectangle**.

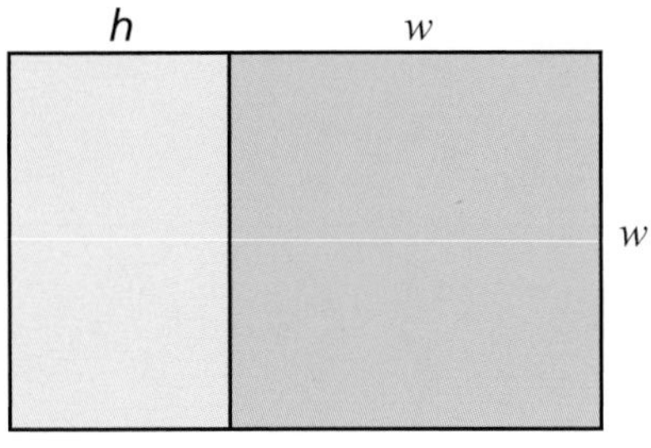

$h : w = w : w + h$

You may have noticed that photographs are usually rectangular, a little longer than they are wide.

Look at these rectangles and decide which one has the shape that you like most.

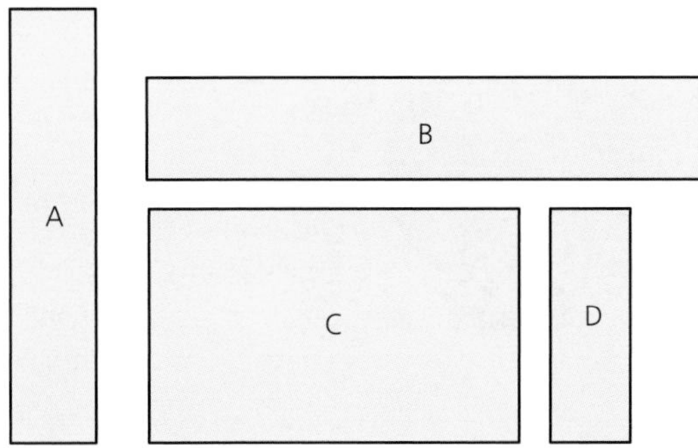

You probably chose rectangle C – it is a golden rectangle.

If the short side is 1 unit, the long side is 1.618 units, the ratio of the long side to the sum of the sides is 1.618 to 2.618 which simplifies to 1 : 1.618

The ratio of the lengths of the sides of a golden rectangle is therefore 1 : 1.618

The golden spiral

Draw a rectangle 10 cm by 16.2 cm.

Mark out a square in the rectangle, as shown. The part of the rectangle remaining will be a golden rectangle.

Now draw another line to make a square in the new rectangle. Go on doing this until you reach the stage as shown.

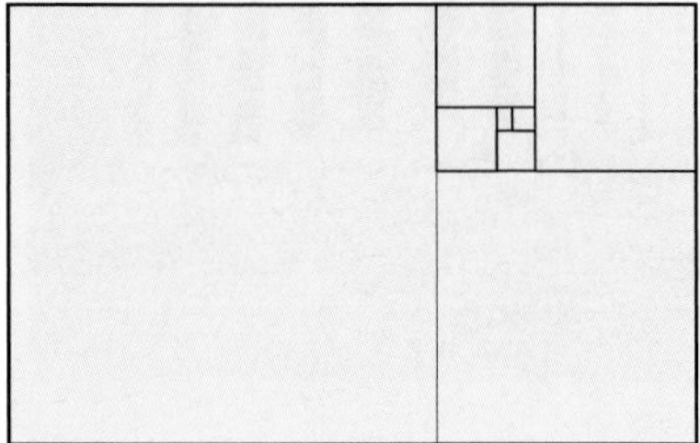

If you now draw a quarter of a circle in each square, you will get a Golden spiral.

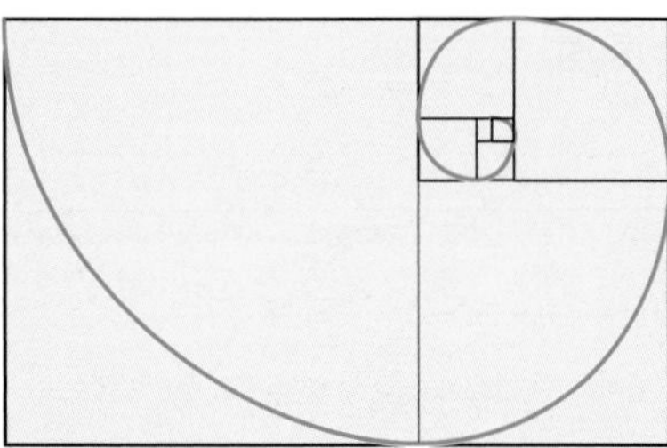

This spiral is the same as the shape of the nautilus shell.

Are you a golden child?

Measure your height.

Now measure the distance from the floor to your navel.

If the ratio: height : height of navel

is 1.618 : 1, then you are a golden child!

19 Looking at data

Data is information. It can be collected in many forms. It is not always easy to interpret data when it is in a purely numerical format. Displaying it in graphs, charts or diagrams can help you to see and interpret it more easily.

People in this country seem to be particularly concerned with the weather. You may have found yourself having to interpret charts like these in geography lessons.

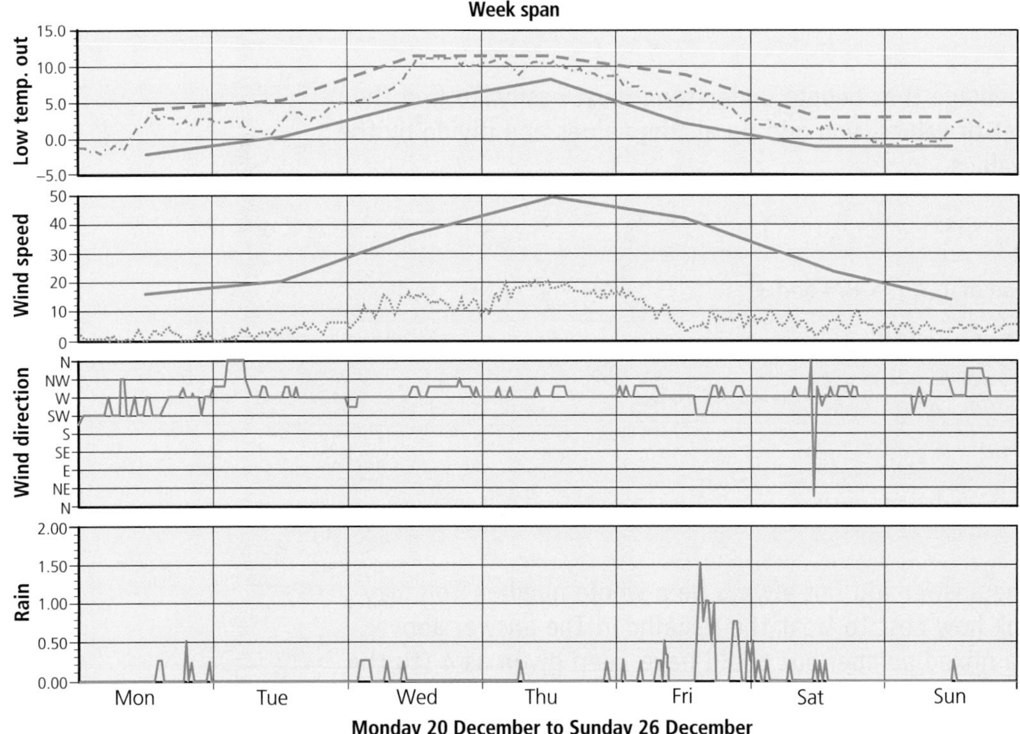

■ Weather over the last seven days

There are various ways you could interpret the data displayed on this weather chart. You will be familiar with some of these, such as finding the **mean**, **mode**, **median** and **range**.

In this chapter you will briefly review everything you should know about displaying and interpreting data and then move on to some problem solving.

Investigating a set of data

When you are studying a set of data, you should consider the numerical values included in it. You can identify the **spread** of the data, and consider some representative values.

The **range** tells you how spread out the values are.

An **average** is one measure that is taken to be typical of all the values, in some way. You should know about three averages: the **mean**, the **median** and the **mode**.

Here is a brief summary.

Range

The range can be found for a set of numerical data only. It is the difference between the largest value and the smallest value.

Mean

This is the average that people understand most easily. To find the mean of a set of values, you add up all the values and divide by the number of values.

Example

Find the mean of 1, 3, 7, 5, 8, 4 and 3

$$\text{Mean} = \frac{1+3+7+5+8+4+3}{7}$$

$$= \frac{31}{7}$$

$$= 4\frac{3}{7}$$

Note that the answer will not always be a whole number. You may have to think how best to treat the remainder. The answer above is given as a mixed number but could have been given as 4 (to the nearest whole number) or 4.4 (to 1 d.p.). Always read the question carefully to see what degree of accuracy is required, or leave it as a fraction, as in the example.

Median

The median is possibly the most misunderstood average. It is the middle value, when the data is listed in ascending numerical order.

When there is an even number of values, there are two middle values and the median is taken as the mean of these.

Examples

(i) Find the median of 3, 6, 2, 5, 7, 1, 4, 6, 8, 3, 7

Put the numbers in order. 1, 2, 3, 3, 4, 5, 6, 6, 7, 7, 8 11 numbers

The median is the sixth number (the middle number), which is 5

(ii) Find the median of 3, 9, 8, 5, 1, 5, 7, 6

Put the numbers in order. 1, 3, 5, 5, 6, 7, 8, 9 8 numbers

The median is the mean of the fourth and fifth numbers $= \frac{5+6}{2} = 5.5$

Mode

The **mode** is the value that occurs most frequently or most often. If each value occurs only once, there is no mode. In a set of grouped data, the group that contains the highest number of values is called the **modal group**. The number of times a value appears in the data set is called the **frequency**. In the two examples above the mode is 3, 6 and 7 in the first and 5 in the second.

The mode is particularly useful when analysing measurements such as shoe size, where there is no value between one size and the next (there is no size 36.2)

The mode is the only average that you can apply to a set of non-numerical data, such as makes of car or favourite colours.

Finding the total

If you know the mean of a set of data, you can calculate the total.

Example

There are 22 classes in the school, with a mean of 19.5 pupils per class. What is the total number of pupils in the school?

From the mean: $\frac{\text{total number of pupils}}{\text{number of classes}} = 19.5$

So the total number of pupils $= 19.5 \times 22$

$= 429$

Fractional averages (mean and median) such as 19.5 pupils can often look nonsensical, but in statistics this is acceptable, given the nature of the calculation.

Frequency tables and diagrams (or bar charts)

When you have collected a large amount of data it makes sense to put it into a tally chart or **frequency table** in order to analyse it. You can work out the range, mode and median directly from a frequency table but to work out the mean you need to add an extra column.

It is often easiest to read data from a diagram. You can draw a **bar chart** from the information in the **frequency table**. Always to give your frequency table a title and label the axes. Note that in a frequency diagram (a bar chart displaying frequency results), frequency is *always* on the vertical axis. A frequency diagram is a special type of bar chart showing frequency.

Example

A supermarket is selling bags of 2.5 kg of nectarines. The exact number of nectarines in each bag varies. A survey of 40 bags, counting the nectarines contained in each, gave these results.

20	18	22	19	23	18	20	21	22	19
20	23	21	20	21	21	19	22	21	21
23	22	20	21	20	21	19	21	20	22
20	21	21	18	21	19	22	21	21	20

Draw a frequency table to record this information. Use this to draw a frequency diagram to show the distribution. Calculate the range, mean, median and mode.

Number of nectarines in the bag	Tally	Frequency	Frequency × number in bag
18	III	3	54
19	卌	5	95
20	卌 IIII	9	180
21	卌 卌 IIII	14	294
22	卌 I	6	132
23	III	3	69
Total		40	824

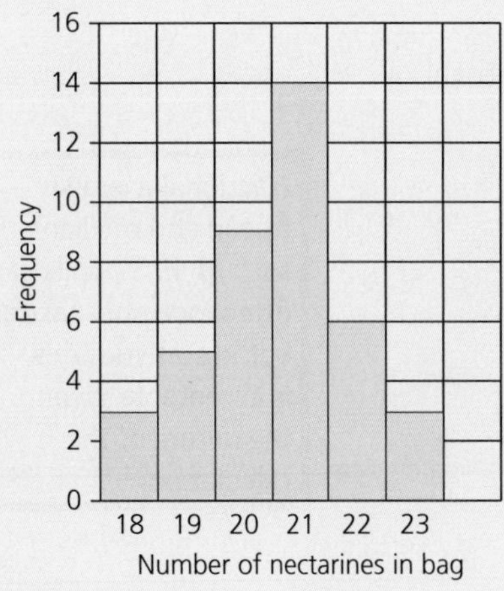

Range = 23 − 18 = 5

Mode = 21

Median = 21 when they are put in order the 20th and 21st data values both have the value 21

$$\text{Mean} = \frac{\text{total of all the data values}}{\text{number of data items}}$$

$$= \frac{824}{40}$$

$$= 20.6$$

When you check your answer you can see that the range is quite narrow and the mode and median have the same value. You should therefore expect the mean value to be very close to them, which it is.

Exercise 19.1

Round inexact answers to 1 decimal place, unless specified otherwise.

1 Work out the range, mean, mode and median of each set of data.

(a) 1, 3, 4, 5, 2, 5, 2, 6, 7, 2, 1, 2

(b) 1.3, 2.3, 1.4, 1.2, 1.5, 1.2, 2.6, 1.7, 1.5, 2.1

(c) 75, 32, 53, 25, 65, 72, 78, 91, 56, 67, 70, 62, 83, 95, 43

(d) 34, 38, 39.5, 37.5, 36, 37.5, 42, 40, 39, 40.5, 41

2 Suggest what measurements each set of data in question1 might represent.

3 A class of 20 pupils collected money for charity. The mean amount of money collected by each pupil was £7.35. How much did the class collect in total?

4 My brother is 10 years old and my sister is 21 years old. The mean of our three ages is 15 years. How old am I?

5 40 boys have a mean height of 1.48 m. 60 girls have a mean height of 1.52 m. What is the mean height of all 100 pupils?

6 In science, we planted some courgette seeds and carefully fed and watered them. At the end of term we counted the courgettes growing on each plant. The results are shown in this table.

Number of courgettes on the plant	Number of plants
3	1
4	3
5	4
6	7
7	5
8	2
Total	22

(a) What is the range of courgettes per plant?

(b) Show the results on a frequency diagram.

(c) What is the modal number of courgettes on a plant?

(d) What is the median number of courgettes on a plant?

(e) Calculate the mean number of courgettes on a plant.

7 This frequency diagram shows how many goals the hockey team have scored in their matches this term.

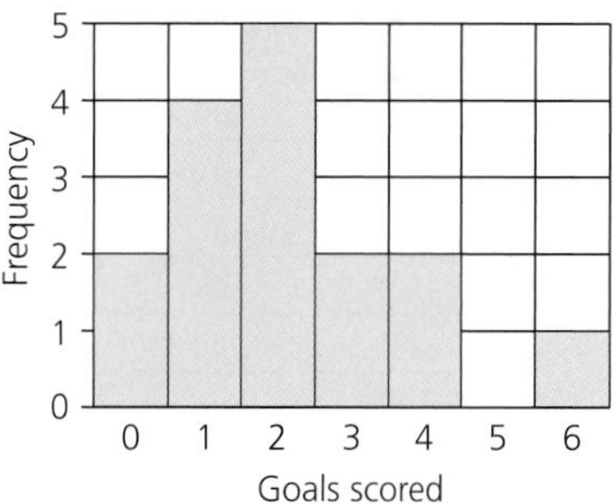

(a) How many matches did the team play?

(b) What was the modal number of goals scored?

(c) What was the median number of goals scored?

(d) Calculate the mean number of goals scored.

8 These are the marks for 30 students in a French vocabulary test.

12	15	19	11	12	9	20	15	18	16
13	14	17	15	17	18	12	15	19	17
11	14	15	17	19	16	15	17	16	15

(a) Draw up a frequency table to show the results.

(b) Calculate the range, mean, mode and median.

(c) Another group of 30 students took the same test and the total of their marks is 321. What is the mean mark for the whole group of 60 students?

(d) What can you say about the range, mode and median mark for the group of 60 students?

Grouped data

In the earlier examples data was made up of single-digit numbers but when you collect data, particularly in science or geography, you generally measure to a greater degree of accuracy. Often the data is in a narrow range with many equal values. It therefore makes sense to group the data.

Data that takes distinct and separate values or observations that can be counted, such as the number of kittens in a litter, is known as **discrete data.** Data that could take on any value, such as height, mass or temperature, is known as **continuous data.**

Example

The daily rainfall during April was recorded and the results, correct to the nearest 0.1 cm, are shown below.

1.2	0	0	0.8	2.4	1.8	0	0	0.4	0.2
0	0	1.5	1.2	2.1	2.6	3.1	1.8	0.5	0.2
0	2.1	1.8	0	1.5	0.7	2.5	2.4	0	0.7

(i) Write down the range of the values.

(ii) Group the data in appropriate bands and record it in a frequency table.

(iii) Illustrate the data in a frequency diagram.

(iv) Calculate the modal group, the median and the mean.

(i) Maximum value = 3.1 cm Minimum value = 0 Range = 3.1 cm

(ii)

Rainfall (cm)	Tally	Frequency
0.0–0.4	卌 卌 II	12
0.5–0.9	IIII	4
1.0–1.4	II	2
1.5–1.9	卌	5
2.0–2.4	IIII	4
2.5–2.9	II	2
3.0–3.4	I	1
		30

(iii)

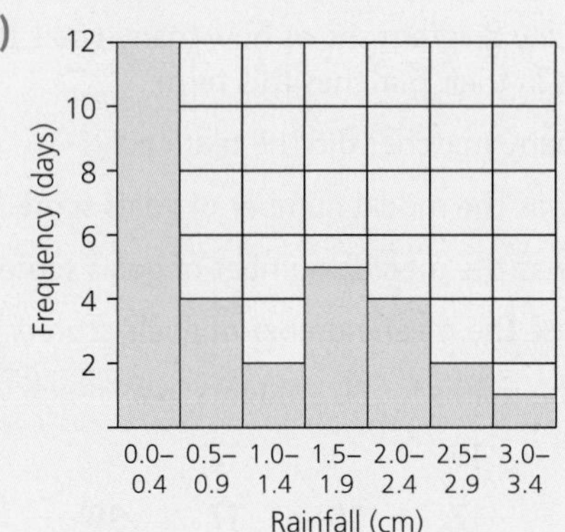

(iv) The modal group is 0.0–0.4 (to the nearest 0.1 cm)

The median is in the interval 0.5–0.9

$$\text{Mean} = (1.2 + 0.8 + 2.4 + 1.8 + 0.4 + 0.2 + 1.5 + 1.2 + 2.1 + 2.6 + 3.1 + 1.8 + 0.5 + 0.2 + 2.1 + 1.8 + 1.5 + 0.7 + 2.5 + 2.4 + 0.7) \div 30$$

$$= \frac{31.5}{30}$$

$$= 1.05...$$

The median is the mean of the 15th and 16th values when the data is rearranged in order. From the frequency table you can see both values lie in the 0.5–0.9 group.

From the results in the example you can see that April was mostly dry, with periods of no rain at all, but when it did rain it rained hard.

This example is unusual as it shows a very uneven distribution with quite different values of mean, median and mode. The fact that these are different is interesting but the distribution is not really clear until you consider the bar chart.

Note the horizontal scale on the bar chart indicates this is **continuous data**.

Exercise 19.2

1 We tested the 'battery lives' of torch batteries in the laboratory. These are our results, to the nearest hour.

24	18	22	19	30	11	23	25	29	10
17	21	27	31	14	26	25	22	18	29
22	32	17	26	31	23	27	14	24	26

(a) Calculate the range.

(b) Put these results into a frequency table, grouping the battery life in groups of five hours: 6–10, 11–15, 16–20, 21–25, 26–30, 31–35

(c) Show this information in a frequency diagram.

(d) Compare the modal group, the median and the mean.

2 The daily rainfall in September was recorded and the results, correct to the nearest 0.1 cm, are shown below.

1.2	0	1.5	0.8	2.4	1.6	1.6	1.1	0.4	2.6
1.1	1.2	1.5	1.2	2.1	2.6	3.1	1.8	2.8	0.2
1.5	2.1	1.8	0	1.5	1.7	2.5	2.4	0	0.7

(a) Write down the range of values.

(b) Group the data in appropriate bands and illustrate the distribution with a frequency diagram.

(c) Calculate the modal group, the median group and the mean.

(d) Compare the rainfall in September with the rainfall in April, in the earlier example.

3 We recorded the lengths of time 32 people spent in the park during the morning. These are our results, to the nearest minute.

5	12	25	4	2	55	17	8
12	8	46	22	9	12	50	32
6	14	8	32	45	9	3	5
26	34	16	9	5	17	12	8

Draw a frequency diagram to show the above data. You will need to group the times into sensible divisions and draw a frequency table first.

4 We recorded the lengths of time 32 people spent in the park in the early evening. These are our results, in minutes.

7	22	25	15	10	56	7	38
41	34	86	45	12	5	19	36
72	53	41	12	6	29	32	36
9	12	57	5	42	6	35	15

Draw a frequency diagram to show the above data. You will need to group the times into sensible divisions and draw a frequency table first.

5 Now compare the frequency diagrams in question 3 and question 4. What can you say about the differences and what reasons do you think would explain them?

6 These are the results of a survey of the ages of passengers taking the Eurostar train to Paris on a weekday.

Age	$0 \leqslant x < 10$	$10 \leqslant x < 20$	$20 \leqslant x < 30$	$30 \leqslant x < 40$	$40 \leqslant x < 50$	$50 \leqslant x < 60$	$60 \leqslant x < 70$	70 or over
Frequency	5	23	55	42	25	18	50	32

(a) Draw a frequency diagram to show the distribution.

(b) Why do you think there were so few young passengers on the train?

(c) Why do you think there are so many passengers aged over 60?

7 These are the results of another survey of the ages of passengers taking the Eurostar train to Paris. This one was carried out over a weekend.

Age	$0 \leqslant x < 10$	$10 \leqslant x < 20$	$20 \leqslant x < 30$	$30 \leqslant x < 40$	$40 \leqslant x < 50$	$50 \leqslant x < 60$	$60 \leqslant x < 70$	70 or over
Frequency	23	34	27	51	35	12	32	14

(a) Draw a frequency diagram to show the distribution.

(b) What difference is there between the ages of the passengers in the surveys in question 6 and 7?

Pie charts

A **pie chart** shows the proportions of various amounts that add up to a whole. Ideally, the angles will add up to 360°, but it can be difficult to make them exact.

Example

A company has a total income of £150m. This is derived from several sources.

Property: £36m   Retail: £53m   Catering: £27m   Interest: £13m

The remainder is 'miscellaneous'.

Show this information on a pie chart.

Set out a table to calculate the angles.

Income	Amount (£)	Calculation	Angle
Property	36	$\frac{36}{150} \times 360 = 86.4$	86°
Retail	53	$\frac{53}{150} \times 360 = 127.2$	127°
Catering	27	$\frac{27}{150} \times 360 = 64.8$	65°
Interest	13	$\frac{13}{150} \times 360 = 31.2$	31°
Miscellaneous	21	$\frac{21}{150} \times 360 = 50.4$	50°
Total	150		359°

Always check that the sum of the angles is 360° because you may have rounded them up or down. In this case the total is 359°

To resolve this difference you should try rounding the angles to the nearest half degree. They become:

Property 86.5°, Retail 127°, Catering 65°, Interest 31° and Miscellaneous 50.5°, which now total 360°

Now you can draw and label the pie chart.

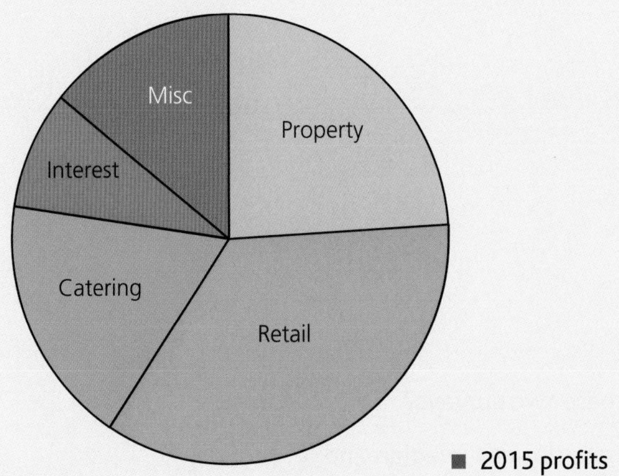

■ 2015 profits

Exercise 19.3

1 In a survey of our local park we asked 168 people to tell us their most important reason for coming to the park. 52 came for the sports facilities, 41 came for the playground, 26 came just to go running, 35 came to walk and sit and the rest did not know. Draw a pie chart to show this data.

2 In the park there is a pavilion selling refreshments. We recorded the most popular items sold during the day. 22% of sale income was from soft drinks. 46% of sale income was from snacks and sandwiches. 18% of sales were for tea of coffee and the rest was for ice cream and confectionary. Show these results on a pie chart.

3 In science we collected a number of seed pods and counted the seeds in each pod. These were our results.

2	4	6	3	5	3	5	3	4	5
3	5	6	4	7	4	4	5	3	5
5	4	2	5	3	6	4	5	4	4
4	5	5	3	6	4	5	5	5	3
6	7	3	5	4	4	6	7	5	3

(a) Draw up a frequency table for the number of seeds in each pod.

(b) This information is to be shown in a pie chart. Use the information in the frequency table to calculate each angle.

(c) Draw the pie chart.

(d) Comment on the results of this experiment.

4 This pie chart shows the results of a similar sample of seed pods, but these were gathered in a wetter environment.

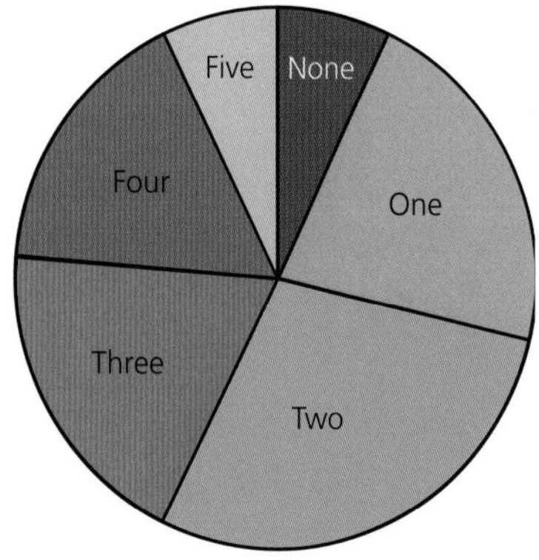

What can you say about the comparative results of these two surveys?

Compare all the information you have, including the range, mean, median and mode and the general distribution.

5 Last term we had a 'readathon'. Everyone recorded the number of books they read in two weeks. The results are shown in this pie chart.

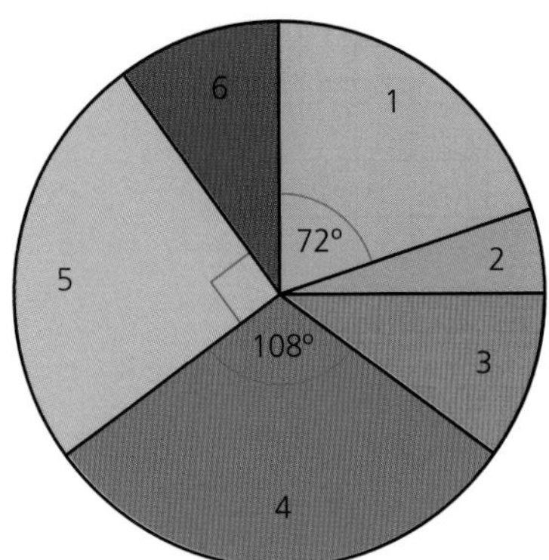

(a) Ten pupils read 5 books in the two weeks. How many pupils took part in the 'readathon'?

(b) How many pupils read 4 books in the two weeks?

(c) The same number of pupils read 6 books in the weeks as read 3 books. How many pupils read 2 books in the two weeks?

(d) What is the modal number of books read?

(e) What is the median number of books read?

(f) Calculate the mean number of books read.

(g) Another class with 16 pupils also took part in the readathon. The mean number of books they read was 3. What was the total number of books read by all the pupils?

Scatter graphs

Scatter graphs can be used to investigate whether there is a relationship between two sets of variables, such as height and shoe size. You collect the data for a number of individuals, then plot the values on a grid with suitably labelled axes. When you have plotted all the points, you can see whether there is any **correlation** between the variables. If there is, you may be able to draw a **line of best fit**.

Look at these examples, drawn after a result of a survey of the classes in year 8

8B have measured their heights and compared them to their shoe sizes. You can see that as someones height increases, so does their shoe size. **This graph has positive correlation.** You cannot draw an exact line through all the points but the points are close enough to draw **a line of best fit.**

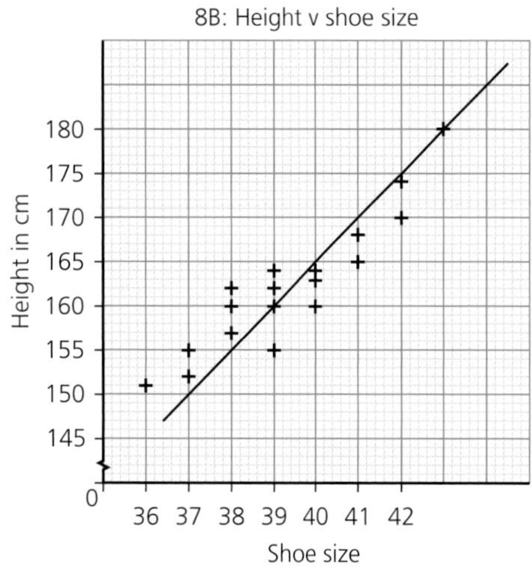

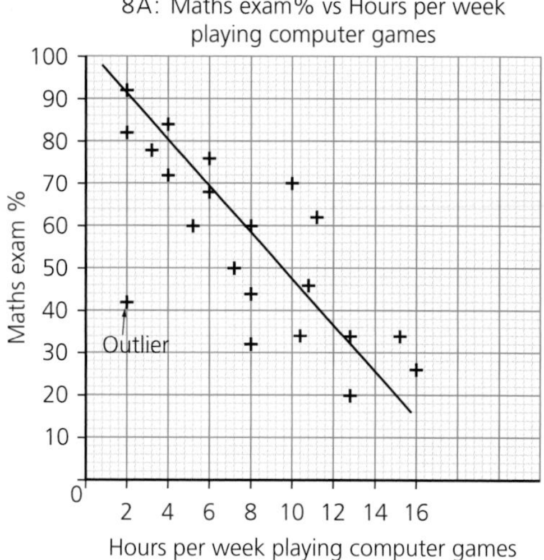

Mr Sparks has asked 8A how many hours a week they spent playing computer games and has compared that to their mathematics examination marks. You can see that the more hours spent playing games the lower the mark. The graph has **negative correlation.** Although the points are not as close together as in the first graph, you can still draw a **line of best fit.**

Note the one cross that does not fit near the line. This sometimes happens as there may be occasions when the two variables are not related. In this case, although a pupil does not spend much time on the computer, he is just is not very good at mathematics! This result is called an **outlier**.

The crosses on the first graph are very close together and they cluster roughly along a line that slopes upwards, from left to right. This means that the two variables have **strong positive correlation**. The crosses on the second graph are also in a cluster, but it is more spread out and the shape they form slopes down, from left to right. This shows **negative correlation** but it is not strong. (Perhaps to Mr Sparks' disappointment?)

Now look at 8Cs graph of their art examination results plotted against their mathematics examination results.

These marks are spread over a wide area. There is no visible **trend**, so there is no possible line of best fit. There is **no correlation**.

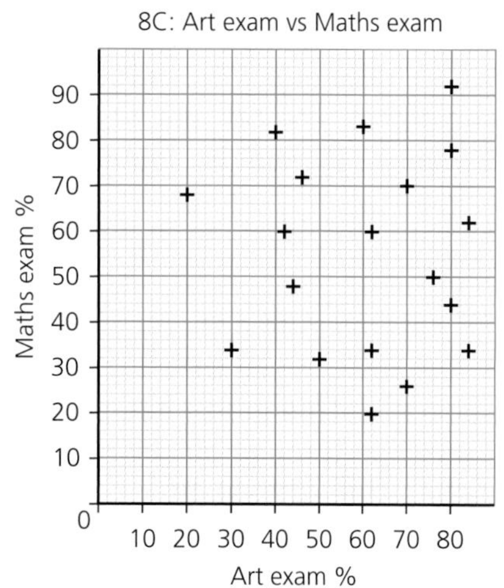

You can draw a line of best fit by inspection but it is often quite difficult to get it exactly right. Another way of drawing the line is to draw the narrowest possible rectangle that encloses all the points and then draw a line through the middle of that rectangle with the same number of points on either side of it.

When you have drawn a line of best fit, you can use it to work out other approximate data values.

Example

The graph below shows 8A's mathematics examination marks against the time they spend each week playing computer games. A new boy joins the class and tells Mr Sparks that he generally spends seven and a half hours every week playing computer games. What does Mr Sparks predict that his mathematics exam result will be?

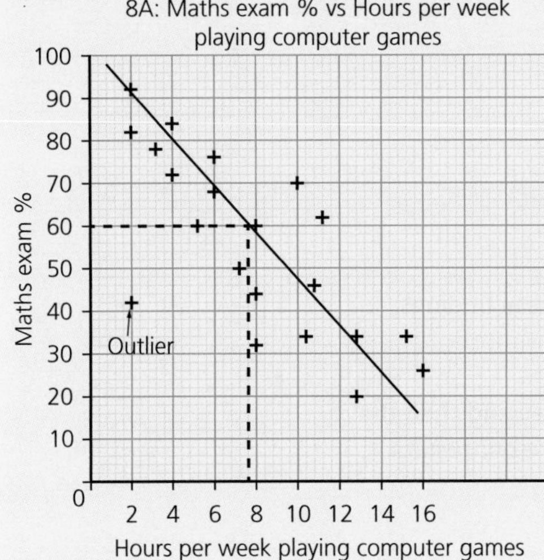

Draw the line up from the hours playing games to the line of best fit and then across to the mathematics examination mark, just as you would read from a conversion graph.

Mr Sparks predicts the new boy's mathematics examination result will be 60%.

As you can see from the example, when you read from a line of best fit you know the result will not be exactly right, unlike a conversion graph from which you can read exact values.

The process shown in the example is called **interpolation**. It is based on the known results and relies on the trend shown by the data. A similar process, in which you extend the line of best fit beyond the range of the known data, is called **extrapolation**. This is less reliable, since results obtained in this way do not relate to the known data.

Exercise 19.4

1 Look back at the scatter graph for shoe sizes against heights.

(a) What size shoes would you expect a pupil who is 168 cm tall to wear?

(b) How tall would you expect a pupil who wears size 36 shoes to be?

2 We asked people how much they would pay to go into the park, so that the money could be used to maintain the facilities and to keep out vandals. These were our results.

Maximum price	Number of people
0p	25
20p	20
50p	18
75p	15
£1	20
£1.25	12
£1.50	10
£1.75	4
£2	2
£2.50	1

(a) Show these results on a scatter graph and comment on the findings.

(b) Does your graph show positive or negative correlation?

3 Over a period of time we recorded the temperature at midday and then the number of people in the park in the early evening. These were our results.

Temperature at midday (°C)	Number of people
5	25
10	40
15	47
17	52
20	63
22	85
25	107
27	116
30	124

(a) Show these results on a scatter graph and comment on the findings.

(b) Draw a line of best fit.

(c) Does your graph show positive or negative correlation?

(d) Use the line of best fit to estimate the number of people you might expect in the park in the evening following a midday temperature of 12 °C

4 Before the January examinations we were all asked the total number of hours of revision we had done over the holidays. This information is recorded below with our final positions in the examinations.

Number of hours	18	24	13	11	10	14	20	10	18	8	10	20	24	20	19	21	9	18	21	16
Examinationposition	6	2	14	9	1	11	8	18	15	20	16	5	13	3	7	19	17	10	4	12

(a) Record this information on a scatter graph.

(b) Draw a line of best fit and state whether these results show positive or negative correlation.

(c) From your graph, estimate the possible score of a pupil who had revised for 17 hours.

(d) Some candidates have a result that does not fit the general pattern of the other results. Suggest as many reasons as you can for this.

Extension Exercise 19.5

The problems in this exercise are similar to those that you have already tackled but need a little extra care. You may even wish to use algebra.

1 **(a)** I have four numbers. Their mode is 6, their median is 7 and their mean is 7.5 What are the possible values of my numbers? Is there more than one answer?

(b) I have five numbers with a range of 10, mode of 16, median of 14 and a mean of 12. What are the possible values of my numbers? Is there more than one answer?

2 These are the results of a survey that I carried out, looking at the numbers of people living in each house in our street. Unfortunately I opened a carton of juice when I had finished and splashed some on my page. Some of the numbers and tallies have been washed away. Copy my results and fill in all the missing data.

Number in house	Tally	Frequency	Total people
2	II	[illegible]	$2 \times 2 = 4$
3	[illegible]	4	$3 \times 4 = 12$
4	[illegible]	[illegible]	[illegible]
5	~~IIII~~ II	7	$5 \times 7 = 35$
6	III	[illegible]	$6 \times 3 = 18$
7	I	1	[illegible]
	Total	[illegible]	108

Mean $= \frac{108}{[illegible]} = 4.32$

Mode $= 4$

Median = [illegible]

3 These are the results of a similar survey.

Number in house	2	3	4	5
Frequency	4	x	9	4

(a) What are the mode and median of this set of data, given that x is:

(i) 8 (ii) 9 (iii) 10?

(b) In fact, the mean, correct to two decimal places, is 3.59 what are x, the mode and the median?

4 Pupils in my school took part in a survey to find out how long their journey to school took them in the morning. The headmaster produced the results of the survey in the form of this frequency diagram.

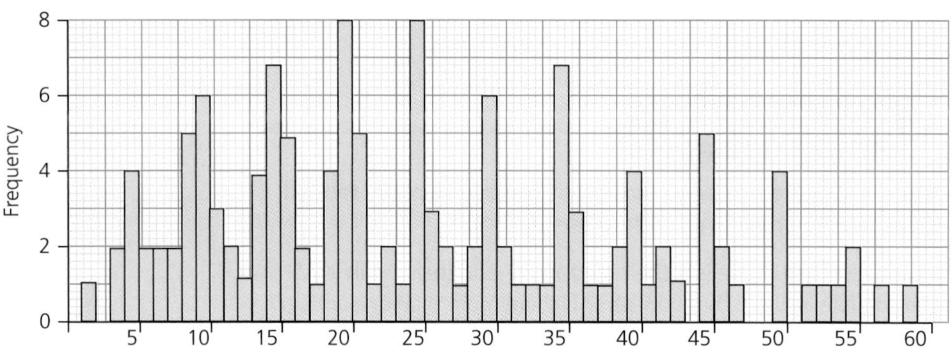

(a) What was the mode, as shown by the headmaster's frequency diagram?

(b) What was the mean length of time taken to come to school?

(c) What was the median length of time?

Mr Sparks, the maths teacher, was shown this chart. He commented that it showed that most people had rounded their journey times to the nearest 5 minutes and suggested that it should be redrawn with the times in groups of 5 minutes.

(d) Draw a frequency table with the journey times in groups 0–5, 6–10, 11–15 ...

(e) Draw the revised frequency diagram.

(f) How many pupils took part in the survey?

(g) What was the modal group in the survey?

5 As you know, teachers get quite long holidays. We asked the staff in our school how many days they spent abroad last year. Here are the results of our survey.

Number of days	0	1–7	8–14	15–21	22–28	29–40	41–100
Frequency	4	3	15	8	6	5	1

(a) Why do you think that we grouped the data in the way we did?

(b) What kind of teacher do you think might have spent between 41 and 100 days abroad last year?

(c) There is only one teacher in the last group of data. If this one teacher had spent 41 days abroad, what would you estimate the mean to be?

(d) Suppose this teacher had spent 100 days abroad. What would you estimate the mean to be in this case?

6 Last year 120 pupils in the school took part in a readathon to raise money for charity. This frequency table shows how many children raised various amounts of money:

Amount (£)	$0 \leqslant x < 10$	$10 \leqslant x < 20$	$20 \leqslant x < 30$	$30 \leqslant x < 40$	$40 \leqslant x < 50$
Frequency	8	22	47	34	9

(a) Draw a frequency diagram to show the distribution.

(b) How much money did the school raise in total? If you cannot tell exactly, how could you make an estimate?

Summary Exercise 19.6

1 Find the range and the mean, median and mode of each set of data.

(a) 1, 3, 4, 1, 2, 3, 2, 1, 4, 5

(b) 3.4, 5.1, 1.2, 4.2, 1.8, 4.2, 5.1, 3.1, 4.7, 4.2, 2.9, 5.8

(c) $2\frac{1}{2}, 3\frac{1}{4}, 1\frac{3}{4}, 2\frac{1}{4}, 3\frac{1}{2}$

2 My team is practising for the relay race on sports day. These are our times so far.

12 minutes 40 seconds, 11 minutes 55 seconds, 12 minutes 25 seconds, 11 minutes 50 seconds, 12 minutes 35 seconds and 11 minutes 47 seconds

(a) What is our mean time?

(b) On the day we did not beat our best time, but our mean time was improved by 2 seconds. In what time did we run our race?

3 My class have been growing bean plants from seeds. After a month we measured and recorded the heights of the seedlings, correct to the nearest centimetre.

48	22	34	26	0	41	25	34	37	25
37	16	23	42	0	0	35	46	24	36
27	0	20	31	37	29	19	0	33	18

(a) Draw a frequency table to record this information. Group the data in suitable bands. Use this to draw a frequency diagram to show the distribution. Calculate the mean, median and modal group of the sample.

(b) What can you say about your survey?

(c) Five plants did not grow at all. If you leave these five out of your calculations, what difference does this make to the mean, median and modal group?

(d) Do you think that these five plants should have been included in the results or not?

4 Year 8 carried out a survey of what pupils in the school thought about school lunches. They are going to show the outcome on a pie chart. This table shows their results.

Opinion	Frequency
Very satisfied	30
Satisfied	42
Neither satisfied or dissatisfied	58
Dissatisfied	24
Very dissatisfied	16
Total	

(a) Copy the table and extend it to calculate the angles of the pie chart.

(b) Draw the pie chart to show the results.

(c) What percentage of the pupils were either dissatisfied or very dissatisfied?

5 In geography, we have been recording the predicted highest temperature in the town, from the weather forecast, and the actual highest temperature measured in the school playground. These are our results,

Predicted temperature (°C)	Actual temperature (°C)
10	11
12	13
14	14.5
13	14
16	16.5

Predicted temperature (°C)	Actual temperature (°C)
15	14.5
12	13
9	11
12	13
15	16

Predicted temperature (°C)	Actual temperature (°C)
16	17
19	18
21	21
18	18.5
15	16

(a) Draw a scatter graph of these results. Is there positive or negative correlation?

(b) Draw a line of best fit.

(c) If the temperature is predicted to be 10 °C, what temperature might you expect at school?

6 In a manufacturing company, 18 employees earn £14 000 per annum, 15 employees earn £22 000 per annum, three employees earn £32 000 per annum and the chairman earns £75 000 per annum. Calculate the mean, median and modal earnings of the company. Which measure of the average would you use if:

(a) you wished to negotiate a pay rise

(b) you were the company secretary and were writing the annual report

(c) you wished to recruit more workers to the company?

Activity: Marketing the school

You have been asked to write a marketing brief for the school. Look at these statistics and write a sentence or short paragraph based on each piece of information. Remember that you are aiming to attract parents and pupils to the school!

Statistics

- There is 2% unauthorised absence.
- 4 out of 5 pupils study 2 languages.
- 48% of pupils learn an instrument.
- A small percentage of pupils have packed lunches.

What other data do you think would attract parents – and pupils – to the school?

Before your can write your marketing brief you will need to collect some data by doing some research. When planning your research remember that data can come in different forms.

1 Measured data

This is typically collected from an experiment and consists of measurements of whatever variable or physical condition is being measured. This could be, for example, temperature, height, distance or time. In terms of your marketing, this could be examination results or how many musical instruments pupils play.

2 Absolute data

This is data that is factual, for example, the number of pupils in the school.

3 Opinion

This is the hardest type of data to collect. If you are asked your opinion about something there are several variables that could affect your reply; for example, how you feel that day, what information you last heard, whether you like the person asking the question.

Here are some questions that you might ask, to find out about people's favourite subjects.

- Is mathematics your favourite subject?
- What is your favourite subject?
- What is your least favourite subject?
- Rank your subjects in order of preference with 1 being your favourite.

Which of these do you think would give you the most reliable answers?

Which do you think would give the least helpful answers?

Good luck with the research!

Glossary

2D Two-dimensional: a flat shape such as a rectangle or circle.

3D Three-dimensional: a solid object such as a cube or sphere.

Acute angle An angle that is between 0 and 90°

Alternate angles Equal angles formed when a transversal crosses parallel lines, found in an Z-shape.

Angle bisector A line that divides an angle in half.

Arc Part of the circumference of a circle.

Area The amount of space inside a 2D shape such as a rectangle or circle, measured in square units such as square centimetres (cm^2).

Asymptotes A line that a curve approaches but never meets the further you move away from zero.

Axes The plural of axis; the horizontal and vertical number lines on which a coordinate grid is based, they tell you the values of the data.

Bisect Divide a line or an angle into two equal parts.

Cancel Divide the top and bottom of a fraction by one or more common factors to reduce it to its lowest terms simplest form.

Circumference The line round the outside, or the perimeter, of a circle.

Coefficient The number multiplying an algebraic variable in a term.

Co-interior angles Angles formed when a transversal crosses parallel lines, inside a C-shape, which add up to 180°

Co-ordinates The horizontal and vertical distances from the origin (the point where the axes cross), used to plot a point on a grid; for example, the point (3, 5) is 3 units to the right and 5 units up from the origin.

Corresponding angles Equal angles formed when a transversal crosses parallel lines, found in an F-shape.

Common factors Numbers that are factors of two or more other numbers; for example, 5 is a common factor of 20 and 25

Common multiples Numbers that are multiples of two or more other numbers; for example, 100 is a common multiple of 20 and 25

Composite number A number that is not prime, but has at least three factors.

Congruent Exactly the same shape and the same size.

Conversion graph A straight-line graph that can be used to convert between standard units of measurement or currencies.

Coordinate grid The grid on which the horizontal and vertical axes and the graph are drawn.

Correlation The way in which two sets of data are related, for example, the mass of a child and its age, show positive correlation, as it grows older it becomes heavier; the price of a car and its age show negative correlation, since as it gets older its value decreases.

Cube A 3D shape with 6 faces that are all identical squares.

Cube number The result of a number multiplied by itself and itself again; for example, $3 \times 3 \times 3 = 3^3 = 27$

Cube root A number that, when multiplied by itself twice, produces another number, for example, $2 \times 2 \times 2 = 8$, 2 is the cube root of 8 and $8 = 2^3$

Cuboid A 3D shape that has 6 sides that are all rectangles, although some of the rectangles may be squares.

Cylinder A prism with circular cross-section.
Data A set or piece of information, for example, highest daily temperatures; data may refer to a group of values that can be analysed and recorded in a table or plotted on a chart or graph.
Decimal fraction A number less than one, written after a decimal point.
Decimal place The position in a number of a digit that occurs to the right of the decimal point; they include tenths, hundredths, thousandths, etc.
Decimal point The dot that separates the integer part of a decimal number from the decimal fraction.
Denominator The bottom number in a fraction, showing the number of parts into which the whole is divided.
Diagonal A line joining non-adjacent vertices in a 2D or 3D shape.
Diameter A line joining two points on the circumference of a circle and passing through the centre; the diameter is twice the radius.
Difference The result of subtracting a smaller number from a larger number; for example, the difference between 5 and 11 is $11 - 5 = 6$
Digit One of the symbols 0, 1, 2, 3, 4, 5, 6, 7, 8, 9 used to make numbers; for example, 45 is a two-digit number.
Enlargement A transformation that changes the size but not the shape of an object. It is defined in terms of a centre of enlargement and a scale factor.
Equation A mathematical sentence that includes an equals sign; equations frequently contain at least one unknown term and may be solved.
Equilateral Having all sides the same lengths.
Equivalent fractions Fractions that have the same value although their numerators and denominators are different; for example, $\frac{3}{4} = \frac{9}{12}$
Equivalent fractions, decimals and percentages Fractions, decimals and percentages that are equal; for example, $20\% = 0.2 = \frac{1}{5}$
Equivalent units The approximate comparison between metric and imperial units.
1 foot ≈ 30 cm, 1 metre ≈ 3 ft 3 in or 3.25 feet
8 kilometres ≈ 5 miles
1 lb ≈ 450 g and 1 kg ≈ 2.2 lb
1 pint ≈ 600 ml, 1 gallon ≈ 4.5 litres, 1 litre ≈ 1.7 pints
10 litres ≈ 2.2 gallons
Estimate Make an approximation, often by calculating with rounded numbers.
Expression A mathematical phrase, with no equals or inequality signs, which may can comprise numbers, unknown terms or variables (such as x) and operators. An expression could also be a fraction and may contain brackets. An expression may be simplified but cannot be solved.
Extrapolate Estimate likely values from a scatter graph, beyond the range of known values; an unreliable method.
Factor A a number that divides exactly into another number; for example, 1, 2, 3 and 6 are factors of 6 $6 = 2 \times 3 = 1 \times 6$
Factor pair Two factors that when multiplied together give the number being considered; for example, factor pairs of 6 are 1 and 6, 2 and 3
Formula A rule used to calculate a specific value, often written in letters or words; for example, the formula for the volume of a cuboid is area = length (l) × width (w) × height (h) or $A = lwh$

Fraction A number less than one, written with a numerator and a denominator, such as $\frac{3}{4}$

Hyperbola A curve where the distances of any point from a fixed point and a fixed straight line are always in the same ratio.

Hypotenuse The longest side of a right-angled triangle, opposite the right angle.

Imperial units Non-metric units in common use in Britain and America.

Mass (weight)

16 ounces (oz) = 1 pound (lb)

14 pounds (lb) = 1 stone (st) 1 ton (t) = 2240 pounds (lb)

Length

12 inches (in) = 1 foot (ft) 3 feet (ft) = 1 yard (yd)

1760 yards (yd) = 1 mile

Capacity or volume

2 pints (pt) = 1 quart (qt) 8 pints (pt) = 1 gallon (gall)

Improper fraction A fraction in which the numerator (top number) is larger than the denominator (bottom number), such as $\frac{7}{4}$

Inequality A relationship between two values that are not equal, using one of the symbols $<$ (less than), $>$ (more than), $\leqslant$ (less than or equal to) or $\geqslant$ (more than or equal to), $\neq$ not equal to.

Integer A whole number, positive or negative; for example, 4, $^{-}3$ and 17 are all integers.

Interpolate Estimate likely values from a scatter graph, within the range of known values.

Inverse An opposite calculation.; addition is the inverse of subtraction, division is the inverse of multiplication.

Isosceles triangle A triangle with two equal sides and two equal angles.

Line graph A line that represents the relationship between two variables, such as distance and time; it may be straight or curved.

Line of best fit A line drawn through the points on a scatter graph, with as many points above it as below it; it need not go through the origin, nor any of the points.

Line of symmetry The line that divides a shape into two congruent parts, one being a reflection of the other.

Linear An expression or equation in which two variables are related by a rule, and the highest power of any unknown is 1; for example $y = 3x + 2$ in a linear relationship, $y = x^2$ is not.

Long division Division by a number with two or more digits, showing each stage of the calculation and working down the page.

Long multiplication Multiplication by a number with two or more digits, showing each stage of the calculation: multiplication by first the units, then the tens, and so on, with the sum of the multiplications at the bottom.

Lowest terms A fraction or ratio in which the components (numerator and denominator) have no common factors.

Mean The average that is the sum of all the values divided by the number of values, often referred to simply as the 'average';

for example, the mean of 3, 5, 7 and 9 = $\frac{3+5+7+9}{4} = \frac{24}{4} = 6$

Median The middle value in a row of numbers arranged in numerical order; for an even number of numbers, the median is the mean of the middle two numbers.

Metric units Units of mass (weight), length and volume that are in use in Britain and in Europe as well as many other countries.

Mass

1000 milligrams (mg) = 1 gram (g) 1000 grams (g) = 1 kilogram (kg)
1000 kilograms (kg) = 1 metric tonne (t)

Length

10 millimetres (mm) = 1 centimetre (cm) 100 centimetres (cm) = 1 metre (m)
1000 millimetres (mm) = 1 metre (m) 1000 metres (m) = 1 kilometre (km)

Capacity (volume)

1000 millitres (ml) = 1 litre (l)

Mixed number A combination of a whole number and a fraction; for example, $2\frac{3}{4}$

Mode **1** The setting on a calculator that determines how it operates, for example, normal or computational.
2 The value that occurs most often in a set of data; this is the only average that may apply to non-numeric data.

Multiple A number that is a product (result of a multiplication) of a factor; for example, 6 is a multiple of 2

Negative numbers Numbers less than zero (0); for example, $^{-}4$, called 'negative 4'

Net A 2D shape that can be folded up to form a 3D shape.

Numerator The top number on a fraction; it tells you how many parts of the whole you have.

Obtuse angle An angle between 90° and 180°

Obtuse-angled triangle A triangle in which one angle is obtuse.

Order of operations The order in which a calculation should be done: brackets, index numbers or other calculation then divide, multiply add, subtract (BIDMAS).

Outlier Data that lies outside the range of most of the other data values, since it is much larger or smaller than other values.

Parabola The shape of a curved graph of the function $y = ax^2 + b$, where a and b are constants.

Parallel Lines that are the same distance apart and will never meet, however far they are extended.

Parallelogram A quadrilateral with two pairs of equal and parallel sides.

Percentage A fraction expressed as hundredths of a whole, written with a percentage sign; for example, $25\% = \frac{25}{100}$

Perfect square A number that has an integer square root.

Perimeter The line around the outside of a 2D shape.

Pie chart A chart in the shape of a circle, in which quantities are represented as proportions of the whole, according to the angle at the centre of each sector.

Polygon A 2D shape with sides that are straight lines.

3 sides – a triangle 4 sides – a quadrilateral
5 sides – a pentagon 6 sides – a hexagon
7 sides – a heptagon 8 sides – an octagon
9 sides – a nonagon 10 sides – a decagon
12 sides – a dodecagon 20 sides – an icosagon

Powers of 10 The numbers that result from multiplying 10 by itself: $10^1 = 10$, $10^2 = 100$, $10^3 = 1000$, $10^4 = 10\,000$, $10^5 = 100\,000$, $10^6 = 1\,000\,000$

Prime factor A factor that is a prime number; for example, 2 and 3 are prime factors of 6

Prime number A number that has exactly two factors, itself and 1; for example, 2, 3, 5 and 7 are prime numbers, but 1 is not.

Product The result of a multiplication; for example, the product of 3 and 4 is 12

Protractor A transparent circular or semi-circular scale used to measure angles.

Pythagoras' theorem A rule that states that the square of the hypotenuse (H) is equal to the sum of the squares of the other two sides (a and b): $H^2 = a^2 + b^2$

Pythagorean triplet A set of three numbers that satisfy the rule of Pythagoras' theorem, $a^2 + b^2 = c^2$

Quadrant **1** A quarter of a circle.

2 One of the four sections of a coordinate grid between the horizontal and vertical axes.

Quadrilateral A four sided polygon with four angles.

Quadratic equation or function An equation or function in which the highest power of the unknown is 2; for example $y = x^2$

Quotient The whole number part of the result of a division calculation; for example, for $25 \div 2 = 12$ remainder 1, 12 is the quotient.

Radius **1** The distance from the centre of a circle to the circumference.

2 A line from the centre of a circle to the circumference.

All radii are the same length in any one circle.

Ratio A relationship between the number or size of two or more parts of a group, expressed in the form 'a to b' or $a : b$

Rectangle A quadrilateral with four right angles and two pairs of equal sides.

Reciprocal The result of dividing 1 by a number; for example, the reciprocal of 2 is $\frac{1}{2}$ and the reciprocal of $\frac{3}{4}$ is $\frac{4}{3}$

Reflection A shape as seen in a mirror; the original shape is the object and the reflected shape is its image.

Reflex angle An angle between 180° and 360°

Remainder The part that is left over, in a division calculation; for example, $25 \div 2 = 12$ remainder 1

Rhombus A quadrilateral with four equal sides.

Right angle An angle that is equal to 90°

Root A number that, multiplied by itself one or more times, gives the number of which it is the root; for example, 3 is the square root of 9 ($\sqrt{9} = 3$), 2 is the cube root of 8 ($\sqrt[3]{8} = 2$). Roots may not be exact; for example, on a calculator the square root of 2 is 1.4142... but the exact value is written as $\sqrt{2}$

Rotation A turn of an object through a number of degrees, clockwise or anti-clockwise, about a centre of rotation.

Round Approximate a number to a given accuracy, such as to:

- the nearest whole number
- the nearest ten, hundred, thousand, ...
- one, two, three or more decimal places (d.p.)
- one, two, three or more significant figures (s.f.).

Scale factor The ratio of the length of an object to the length of its enlargement, or to its representation on a map or plan.
Scalene triangle A triangle in which all three sides are of different lengths.
Scatter graph A set of points that show a relationship between two sets of data.
Sector Part of a circle enclosed by an arc and two radii.
Semi-circle Half of a circle.
Sequence A succession of terms, diagrams or patterns that are connected by a rule.
Significant figures The numbers that show the magnitude of a number that has been rounded to a degree of accuracy; for example, $34\,567 \approx = 34\,600$ to 3 significant figures.
Similar Exactly the same shape but not the same size.
Simplest form *See* lowest terms
Simplify Reduce (a fraction or ratio) to its lowest terms or an expression to its simplest form.
Speed A compound unit relating distance and time, the distance travelled in unit time, usually expressed in kilometres per hour (km/h) or miles per hour (mph).
Square number A number that can be expressed as one if its factors multiplied by itself; for example, $16 = 4 \times 4 = 16$, 4 is the square root of 16 and 16 is a square number.
Standard index form A way of writing a number as a number between 1 and 10 multiplied by a power of 10; very large and very small numbers may be displayed on a calculator in standard index form; for example, 34 000 may be shown as 3.4×10^4
Sum The result of an addition; for example, the sum of 3 and 4 is 7
Surd An exact value of a root of a number, expressed in a form such as $\sqrt{2}$ or $\sqrt{43}$
Symbols Numerals or operations (+, −, ×, ÷) written as letters or simple shapes.
Transformation A change to a 2D shape, may be a translation, reflection, rotation or enlargement, that changes to position or size of a shape (the object) to form its image.
Translation A movement of an object, first parallel to the horizontal axis, then parallel to the vertical axis, to produce its image.
Variable A symbol for an unknown value, usually represented by a letter such as x.
Venn diagram A diagram that uses closed loops to demonstrate the relationship between members of sets.
Vertically opposite The angles formed when two straight lines cross. At every such point, there are two pairs of equal vertically opposite angles.

Index

2D shapes
  see also circles
  polygons 157
  quadrilaterals 156
  triangles 155–56
accuracy, degrees of 33–34
adding fractions 19, 21
algebra
  see also equations; inequalities
  alien 99
  factorising 109–10
  fractions 107
  indices in 103–08
  involving ratios 292
  multiplying out brackets 107–08
alien algebra 99
alternate angles 153
angles 153
  bearings 152–53
  bisection of 164–65
  pie charts 319
  of polygons 157–59
  sector angles 191
arcs 191
area 33
  calculation of unknown quantities 141
  of a circle 189
  in enlargements 297, 300–01
  formulae for 139–40
  of a trapezium 114
  units of 204–05
arrowheads 156
asymptotes 239
average speed 145
averages 312–13
bar charts 314
bearings 152–53
  in scale drawings 303–04
BIDMAS 12
  and calculators 42
bisecting an angle 164–65
brackets
  on calculators 42
  difference between two squares 247
  factorising 109–10
  multiplying out 107–08, 242
  multiplying two sets of 243–44
  problem solving with 249
  squared 245–46
  use with negative numbers 6
calculator maze activity 84
calculator problems 44–46
calculator puzzles and games 51–52
  Captain H2O's challenge 48
calculators 40–41
  brackets 42
  estimating answers 46–47
  fractions 43, 46
  index functions 43
  memory 44
  mode button 41
  negative numbers 41
  random number key 269
  reciprocal button 49
  remainders 52
  standard index form 64
cancelling (simplifying) 13, 16
cardinal numbers (natural numbers) 1
cards, packs of 255
certainty 254
chain letters 68
chessboard problem 46
circle problems 194
circles 189–90
  calculating the radius and diameter 193–94
  circumscribed 195
  fractions of 191
  inscribed 194
circumference 189–90
co-interior angles 153
composite numbers 7
compound interest 80–81
constructions
  bisecting an angle 164–65
  Perigal's dissection 168–69
  perpendicular bisector of a line 165
  perpendiculars 163
  reflection of a line 272
  rotations 274
continuous data 316–17
conversion graphs 229
correlation 321–23
corresponding angles 153
'Countdown' game 52
cube root trick 150–51
cube roots 59
cubes (3D shapes), volume of 139
cuboids, volume of 139
curved graphs 236
cylinders
  surface area of 202–03
  volume of 201
data 311
  averages 312–13
  frequency tables and diagrams 314
  grouped 316–17
  'marketing the school' activity 329
  pie charts 319
  range of 312
  scatter graphs 321–23
decimal fractions (decimals) 16–17, 28
  division with 29–30
  multiplying 28–29
  percentages as 71
decimal places, rounding to 34
denominators 16
  lowest common denominator 19
density 147
dependent events 258–59
diameter 189
  calculation of 193–94
difference between two squares 247
differences, largest and smallest activity 15
discounts 74
discrete data 316
distance, speed and time 142–44
division
  with decimals 29–30
  with fractions 24–25
  long 2–3
  of powers of the same base 53–54, 104
'Down to zero' game 52
dragon curve 252–53
elimination method, simultaneous equations 218–19
enlargements 280
  area in 297, 300–01
  volume in 299, 300–01
equations 85–86
  see also simultaneous equations
  with fractions 91–93
  with multiple terms 92–93

problem solving 87–88
quadratic 248–50
solving by factorising 248
with two fractions 98
what they are 211
equations in two variables 211–12
see also simultaneous equations
graphical solution 212–13
equilateral triangles 155
equivalent fractions 16
estimating answers 46–47
experimental results, graphs of 241
exterior angles of a polygon 157–58
extrapolation 323
Eye of Horus 36
factorising 109
and fractions 110
problem solving 249
solving equations by 248
squared brackets 246
factors 7
highest common factors (HCF) 10
prime 7–8, 13, 60–61
unique factorisation property 8
Fibonacci sequence 121
FOIL method, multiplying out brackets 244
formulae 135
for area and volume 139–40
calculation of unknown quantities 141
distance, speed and time 142–44
rearranging 148
substituting into 137
units of 146–47
fractals 133–34
dragon curve 252–53
fractional indices 115
fractional scale factors 280
fractions 16–17
adding and subtracting 19–20
algebraic 107
on calculators 43, 46
division with 24–25
in equations 91–93, 98
Eye of Horus 36
factorising 110
mixed addition and subtraction 21
multiplying 23–24
probabilities as 254–55
problem solving 26–27
ratios as 291–92
fractions of a circle 191
fractions of an amount 22
frequency tables and diagrams 314
functions, graphs of 234–36
golden children 310
golden ratio 309
golden spiral 310
graphs 229
of experimental results 241
of functions 234–36
points of intersection 237–38
quadratic curve 235–36
reciprocal curve 239
sales graphs 232
scatter graphs 321–23
solving equations in two variables 212–13
solving simultaneous equations 215–16
from spreadsheet data 118
travel graphs 229
'Great Uncle Ben's bequest' activity 116–18
grouped data 316–17
'Guess the number' game 51
hexaflexagon 288–90
highest common factors (HCF) 10
hyperbolas 239
hypotenuse 170
calculation of 171–72
impossibility 255
improper fractions 16
independent events 258
index numbers (indices) 8, 13, 53
on calculators 43
fractional 115
multiplying and dividing powers of the same base 53–54, 103–04
multiplying out brackets 107–08
negative 55, 104
the power 0 104
powers of 10 62
powers of powers 105
simplifying expressions 106
solving equations in x^2 57
standard index form 63
inequalities 94
with negatives 96
solving 95–96
inscribed circles 194
integers 5–6
interest
compound 80–81
simple 78–79
interior angles of a polygon 157–58
interpolation 323
intersection, points of 237–38
inverse operations 24
isosceles triangles 155–56
using Pythagoras' theorem 179
kites 156
knots (speed) 144
large numbers 61–62
light years 61–62
line graphs 229
line of reflection (mirror line) 271
linear relationships (straight line graphs) 213, 229
lines of best fit 321–23
long division 2–3
long multiplication 2
lowest common denominator 19
lowest common multiple (LCM) 10–11
lowest terms (simplest form) 16
'Marketing the school' activity 329
mean 312
median 313
memory, calculators 44
metric system 32
units of area 33
mirror line (line of reflection) 271
mixed numbers 16
division with 25
multiplying 23–24
modal group 313
mode 313
mode button, calculators 41
multiples 7
lowest common multiple (LCM) 10–11
multiplication
of decimals 28–29
of fractions 23–24
long 2
of powers of the same base 53–54, 103
multiplying factors (multipliers) 74, 75
'National Elf problem' activity 39
negative correlation 322
negative indices 55
negative numbers 5–6
and brackets 108, 242
calculators 41
in inequalities 96
*n*th term of a sequence 123
number lines 6
showing inequalities 94
numerators 16

obtuse-angled triangles 155–56
order of operations 12
  and calculators 42
order of symmetry 276
outliers 322
'Packaging the litre' activity 210
parabolas 236
parallel lines, angles of 153
parallelograms 156
  area of 139
Pascal's triangle 102, 132
percentage change 75
percentage increase and decrease 73–74
  finding the original amount 76–77
percentages 17, 69
  calculator maze activity 84
  compound interest 80–81
  conversion to decimals 71
  simple interest 78–79
percentages of an amount 69
Perigal's dissection 168–69
perpendicular bisector of a line 165
perpendiculars, construction of 163
pi (Φ) 189
pie charts 319
polygons 157
  angles of 157–59
polyhedral numbers 101–02
positive correlation 321–22
possibility space diagrams 261
powers *see* index numbers
prime factors 7–8
  finding roots 60–61
  use in calculations 13
prime numbers 7
prisms 197
  volume of 197–99
probabilities 254–55
  tables and Venn diagrams 263–64
  theoretical 257
  with two events 258–59
problem solving 4, 26–27
  by factorising and brackets 249
  mixed problems 183
  possibility space diagrams 261
  with simultaneous equations 222
  trial and improvement methods 111–12
  using algebra 87–88
  using Pythagoras' theorem 173, 177
products 7, 8
proportion 294–95
Pythagoras 170
Pythagoras' theorem 170
  calculating the hypotenuse 171–72
  finding sides other than the hypotenuse 175
  and isosceles triangles 179
  problem solving 173, 177, 183
Pythagorean triplets 180–81, 188
quadrants 191
quadratic equations 248–50
quadratic functions 235–36
quadratic sequences 124–25
quadrilaterals 156
radius 189
  calculation of 193–94
random cricket 269–70
random events 255
random number key, calculators 269
range of data 312
ratios 291
  and algebra 292
  as fractions 291–92
  golden ratio 309–10
rearrangement method, simultaneous equations 221
rearranging formulae 148
reciprocal button, calculators 49
reciprocals 25, 43
rectangles 156
  area of 139
recurring decimals 17
reflections 271–72
remainders 2–3, 4
  on calculators 52
rhombuses 156, 165
right-angled triangles 155–56
  Perigal's dissection 168–69
  Pythagoras' theorem 170–77
roots 13, 59
  calculations involving 66
  on calculators 43
  indices 115
  and prime factors 60–61
  square roots 57–59
rotational symmetry 276
rotations 274
rounding 33–34
rules of sequences 123, 129–30
sale prices 74
sales graphs 232
scale drawings 303–04
scale factor method, simultaneous equations 220
scale factors
  and area 297, 300–01
  fractional 280
  and volume 299, 300–01
scalene triangles 155–56
scatter graphs 321–23
sectors 191
semi-circles 191
sequences 119–21
  finding terms 122
  finding the rule 129–30
  problem solving 127–29
  quadratic 124–25
  working to a rule 123
Sierpinski's gasket 133
significant figures 34
similar figures 280
simple interest 78–79
simplifying
  cancelling 13, 16
  expressions with indices 106
simultaneous equations 215
  elimination method 218–19
  equations with more than two unknowns 224
  graphical solution 215–16
  problem solving 222
  rearrangement and substitution methods 221
  scale factor method 220
sketches 153
small numbers 62
speed, average 145
speed triangle 143–44
spreadsheets 117–18
square numbers, sequences based on 120
square roots 57
  calculations involving 66
  indices 115
  and prime factors 60–61
squared brackets 245
  factorising 246
squares (powers)
  quadratic sequences 124–25
  solving equations in x^2 57
squares (shapes) 156
  area of 139
squares, difference of 247
standard index form 63
  on a calculator 64
star challenge 48
straight lines
  angles on 153
  perpendicular bisector of 165

straight-line graphs (linear relationships) 213, 229
substituting into formulae 137
substitution method, simultaneous equations 221
subtracting fractions 19–21
sums 8
  largest and smallest activity 15
surds 58–59, 66
surface area of a cylinder 202–03
symmetry, rotational 276
tables 263
tetrahedral numbers 101–02
theoretical probability 257
times tables, sequences based on 120
transformations 271
  enlargements 280, 297, 299
  general rules of 285
  mixed 282–83
  reflections 271–72
  rotations 274
  translations 278
translations 278
trapeziums 156
  area of 114, 139, 140
travel graphs 229
trends 232
trial and improvement methods 111–12
triangles 155–56
  angles in 153
  area of 33, 139
  Pythagorean triplets 180–81, 188
triangular numbers, sequences based on 119, 121
'Trigon dragon patrol' activity 227–28
tritetraflexagon 290
unique factorisation property 8
unitary method 294
units of area and volume 204–05
units of formulae 146–47
variables, storage in calculators 44
VAT (value added tax) 73
Venn diagrams 263–64
vertically opposite angles 153
volume
  of a cylinder 201
  in enlargements 299, 300–01
  formulae for 139–40
  of a prism 197–99
  units of 205
volume problems 206
  'Packaging the litre' activity 210